The idea of the EU as a constitutional order has recently taken on renewed life, as the Court of Justice declared the primacy of EU law not just over national constitutions but also over the international legal order, including the UN Charter. This book explores the nature and character of EU legal and political authority, and the complex analytical and normative questions which the notion of European constitutionalism raises, in both the EU's internal and its external relations. The book culminates in a dialogical epilogue in which the authors' arguments are questioned and challenged by the editor, providing a unique and stimulating approach to the subject. By bringing together leading constitutional theorists of the European Union, this book offers a sharp, challenging and engaging discussion for students and researchers alike.

GRÁINNE DE BÚRCA is Professor at Harvard Law School.

J. H. H. WEILER is Professor at NYU School of Law and the National University of Singapore.

CONTEMPORARY EUROPEAN POLITICS

Consulting Editor
ANDREAS FØLLESDAL *University of Oslo*

Contemporary European Politics presents the latest scholarship on the most important subjects in European politics. The world's leading scholars provide accessible, state-of-the-art surveys of the major issues which face Europe now and in the future. Examining Europe as a whole, and taking a broad view of its politics, these volumes will appeal to scholars and to undergraduate and graduate students of politics and European studies.

The Worlds of European Constitutionalism

Edited by
GRÁINNE DE BÚRCA

and

J. H. H. WEILER

CAMBRIDGE
UNIVERSITY PRESS

CAMBRIDGE UNIVERSITY PRESS
Cambridge, New York, Melbourne, Madrid, Cape Town,
Singapore, São Paulo, Delhi, Tokyo, Mexico City

Cambridge University Press
The Edinburgh Building, Cambridge CB2 8RU, UK

Published in the United States of America by Cambridge University Press, New York

www.cambridge.org
Information on this title: www.cambridge.org/9780521177757

First published 2012

Printed in the United Kingdom at the University Press, Cambridge

A catalogue record for this publication is available from the British Library

Library of Congress Cataloging in Publication data
The worlds of European constitutionalism / [edited by] Gráinne de Búrca,
J. H. H. Weiler.
    p.   cm. – (Contemporary European politics)
ISBN 978-0-521-19285-9 (hardback)
1. Constitutional law – European Union countries.   I. De Búrca,
G. (Gráinne)   II. Weiler, Joseph, 1951–
KJE4445.W67   2011
342.24–dc22

                                                                                    2011013978

ISBN 978-0-521-19285-9 Hardback
ISBN 978-0-521-17775-7 Paperback

Contents

v

Contributors

GRÁINNE DE BÚRCA is Professor at Harvard Law School.

BRUNO DE WITTE is Professor of European Union Law at Maastricht University and Visiting Fellow of the Robert Schuman Centre at the European University Institute, Florence.

DANIEL HALBERSTAM is Eric Stein Collegiate Professor at the University of Michigan Law School and Professor at the College of Europe, Bruges.

NICO KRISCH is Professor of International Law at the Hertie School of Governance in Berlin.

NEIL WALKER is Regius Professor of Public Law and the Law of Nature and Nations at the University of Edinburgh.

J. H. H. WEILER is Professor at NYU School of Law and the National University of Singapore.

Introduction

GRÁINNE DE BÚRCA AND J.H.H. WEILER

The issue of constitutional authority, and more particularly the plurality of claims to legal and constitutional authority, has been a dominant theme of European Union legal scholarship in recent years. The resonance of the topic is evident in many of the major EU developments of the past decade: the momentous eastwards enlargement; the gambit of the unratified Constitutional Treaty; the growing number of national constitutional court challenges to EU authority claims; the likely EU accession to the European Convention on Human Rights; and finally the rulings of the European Court of Justice on the relationship of EU law to the international legal order.

When we were approached by John Haslam, editor at Cambridge University Press, with the suggestion that we put together a book of essays on the constitutional law of the EU, we embraced the opportunity he offered to invite a small number of the leading scholars in the field to write an in-depth essay on this compelling theme. The book is our second collaborative project, coming ten years after the publication of our first co-edited volume on the European Court of Justice.[1]

We conceived of the book as an opportunity to revisit the persistent question of contested constitutional authority in the European Union. The initial and familiar context of plural claims to final authority in the EU was the rejection by national constitutional courts of the unconditional assertion of the primacy of EU law by the European Court of Justice. The 'pluralist movement', as Julio Baquero Cruz has labelled it, came to prominence with the famous Maastricht decision of the German Bundesverfassungsgericht.[2] Its origins, however, are to be found in a range of earlier judgments of the highest courts of various

---

[1] de Búrca, G. and J. H. H. Weiler, eds., *The European Court of Justice* (Oxford University Press, 2011).

[2] Baquero Cruz, Julio, 'The Legacy of the Maastricht-Urteil and the Pluralist Movement', 14 *European Law Journal* (2008) 389–420.

1

Member States which was described over two decades ago by Joseph Weiler as the second dimension of the bi-dimensional character of the claim to supremacy of what was then EC (European Community) law.[3] And while this pluralist movement has been the subject of significant scholarly discussion since that time, the debate has gained further momentum in recent years. This is in part because of the controversial character of the ongoing European integration process, most dramatically manifested in popular contestation over the Maastricht, Nice, Constitutional and Lisbon Treaties, and in part because of the articulation of similar claims to final constitutional authority by some of the newest Member States of Central and Eastern Europe.[4]

The essays in this book reflect on this familiar dimension of the pluralism debate, but they also address another increasingly pressing aspect, namely how to think about the multiple claims of authority of other sites of governance outside and beyond the EU and its Member States. Apart from regional entities such as EFTA (European Free Trade Association), the EEA (European Economic Area), the ECHR (European Convention on Human Rights) and more generally the Council of Europe,[5] conflicting plural claims of authority have increasingly been raised by other global and international actors including the WTO (World Trade Organization), as well as the UN (United Nations) and its organs. These conflicting claims have sometimes played themselves out in the political realm, but increasingly they have come before the European Court of Justice and other international tribunals. Yet many of the fundamental questions regularly addressed by national legal systems about the proper relationship between domestic law and customary international law, as well as multilateral treaties of various kinds, and also the many novel forms of 'global administrative law' and

---

[3] Weiler, J. H. H., 'The Community System: The Dual Character of Supranationalism', 1 *Yearbook of European Law* (1981) 267–306.

[4] Sadurski, W., '"Solange, Chapter 3": Constitutional Courts in Central Europe – Democracy – European Union', 14 *Environmental Law Journal* 1 (2008) 21–35.

[5] See, e.g., the controversy in recent years over EU disconnection clauses: Smrkolj, M., 'The Use of the "Disconnection Clause" in International Treaties: What does it tell us about the EC/EU as an Actor in the Sphere of Public International Law?' (2008), available at <http://papers.ssrn.com/sol3/papers.cfm?abstract_id=1133002>; and Joris, T. and J. Vandenberghe, 'The Council of Europe and the European Union: Natural Partners or Uneasy Bedfellows?', 15 *Columbia Journal of European Law* (2008–2009) 1.

global governance are only beginning to be addressed by the European courts.

The language of constitutional pluralism is increasingly being used both to describe the existence of and the relationship between the many different kinds of normative authority – functional, regional, territorial and global – in the transnational context. It has particular traction, however, in relation to the European Union, a political and legal entity which has long defied easy categorization in the language of constitutional law or of international organizations. The essays in this book return to consider some of the original and fundamental questions about the nature and character of the EU, probing the continuities and discontinuities with international law on the one hand, and with state-based constitutionalism on the other. They examine the questions of contestation over legal and constitutional authority to which the changing transnational landscape gives rise, primarily but not only from the perspective of the European Union and its courts. While revisiting the problem of constitutional pluralism within the EU, the contributions also consider the way in which the European Union and its courts grapple with the competing authority claims of other international, regional and global sites of governance.

The collection begins with a Prologue by Joseph Weiler, in which he reacts against the ubiquity and vacuity of the term 'constitutional pluralism' as it has evolved in the EU literature since its introduction by the path-breaking work of Neil McCormick. He contrasts the idea of constitutional pluralism with his own conception of constitutional tolerance, and identifies what he considers to be the truly distinctive feature of the EU's constitutional system.

The first chapter by Bruno de Witte analyses the EU as an international legal experiment. He asks what were the characteristics of the original historical experiment that led to the establishment of the EU, and whether the EU can still be considered as an 'international organization' today. He notes the development of elements of supranationality in other legal regimes, which suggest both that EU law is not so distinctive as to be *sui generis*, and that international law can and has developed innovative features in contexts other than the EU. The upshot of his analysis is that it still makes sense to conceive of the EU as an international legal experiment and that this understanding should continue to inform our thinking about the EU. The EU is, in his words, an advanced form of international organization with some federal characteristics, but it remains an organization created and amended by international treaty with the Member States unquestionably still Masters of the Treaties.

While de Witte's chapter traces the continuities between EU and international law and rejects the usefulness of a *sui generis* character-ization, Neil Walker's chapter locates the place of the EU between the state-based and the international order, shaping its own variation on the common form of political modernity. He argues that the same three issues of political modernity that shaped the nature of the state-based system and, parasitically, of the international system, are implicated also in the EU's form: the idea of collective agency as the animating source of political community (popular sovereignty); the generative resources of political community (the balance between particularism and universalism); and political ontology (the model of the social world, the relationship between individualism and collectivism). He notes how the issue of collective agency has become more pressing in the EU as the model of elite-led integration-through-law has given way to a more expansive political project with an embryonic notion of citizenship; how in terms of generative resources the EU – being built on distinct national identities – cannot lay a strong claim to particularism, yet neither can it claim like the international order to be substantively universalistic; and finally how the relationship between individualism and collectivism within the EU remains skewed towards individual market-freedoms with a weaker social model. Although Walker does not endorse the *sui generis* concept rejected by De Witte, he describes the status of the European order – placed somewhere between an inter-governmental/international order and a national federal order – as paradigmatically 'in-between'. This in-between status, he argues, is crucial, having both a particularity that renders it capable of being exemplary, even while the thinness of its transnational model makes it of relevance to systems beyond the EU.

The next two chapters, by Gráinne de Búrca and Daniel Halberstam respectively, examine the relationship of the EU and the international legal order through the conceptual lenses of constitutionalism and pluralism. De Búrca's chapter looks anew at the case-law of the ECJ (European Court of Justice) on the relationship between EU law and the international legal order, in the light of the famous *Kadi* judgment. She suggests that the ECJ in the Kadi judgment – contrasting with the strong constitutionalist approach of the General Court below – adopted a robustly pluralist approach to this relationship, drawing a sharp line between the internal, autonomous EU constitutional order and the international order, and asserting the clear primacy of the former over the latter. When set alongside earlier rulings of the ECJ on the topic, she argues that our previous assumptions that EU law as a 'new legal order' was distinctively open to international law, both custom and treaty, may need to be revised. Drawing on Koskenniemi's reinterpretation of Kant's idea of constitutionalism as universalizability, she argues that a soft constitutional approach premised on the existence of an international community and on common principles of communication would be a better normative fit for the EU in shaping the relationship between EU and international law. The chapter concludes that even if the specific outcome of the Kadi case is commendable for its insistence on human rights review and procedural fairness requirements, the strong pluralist approach is at odds with the self-presentation of the EU as an organization with a distinctive commitment to international law, and it seems to shun the international engagement and dialogue (in this instance, judicial engagement and dialogue) that has frequently been presented as one of the EU's strengths as a global actor.

Halberstam's chapter rejects the idea of a dichotomy between global and local responses to the question of constitutionalism in an era of global governance, and presents constitutional pluralism as a third approach. While the local approach emphasizes states as the only legitimate locus of constitutional authority, and the international order as relevant only to the extent that it serves the interests of states, the global approach sees states as serving a cosmopolitan constitutional order. The third approach, however, treats the hierarchy between global and local as unsettled and accepts the fact of contested authority 'in the spirit of pluralism'. A pluralist approach, in his view, requires both the existence of a plurality of partially autonomous sites of public governance with mutually conflicting claims of authority, but also 'mutually embedded openness' regarding these competing claims. Halberstam presents constitutionalism as a tradition that grounds the legitimacy of public authority in limited, collective self-governance through law, embodying the three elements of voice (representation), rights and expertise (instrumental capacity). He suggests that the respective claims of authority of each of the plural sites of governance can be articulated in these terms. Turning to the *Kadi* case before the European courts, he argues that the global constitutionalist approach of the General Court (formerly CFI (Court of First Instance)) undermined the legitimacy of the EU in terms of voice and rights protection. Only the Advocate General attempted to promote a pluralist approach, he argues, while the ECJ rejected both global constitutionalism and pluralism, opting instead for the local constitutionalist approach. Halberstam concludes his chapter by outlining what an approach to the *Kadi* case that took constitutional pluralism seriously would look like, in particular by integrating international law more fully into its analysis. Ultimately, he posits constitutional pluralism – a horizontal accommodation among equals which avoids the consolidation of power in one institution – as a third empirically and normatively attractive alternative to either local or global constitutionalism, which could draw inspiration from the EU's experience of internal pluralism.

The final chapter by Nico Krisch stands in opposition to Halberstam's proposed model of constitutional pluralism, by reintroducing a dichotomous perspective on constitutionalist versus pluralist approaches. Krisch presents a robust idea of pluralism as the best normative fit for the sphere of global governance. While constitutionalism, on his account, draws on domestic law to formulate normative principles for the postnational order, pluralism focuses on the heterarchical ordering of authority and on the 'open political form' of the postnational order. 'Foundational constitutionalism', he argues, is presented as a justification for governmental legitimacy, combining key concepts such as the rule of law, individual rights and collective self-government. The UN and the EU draw on this narrative, and some scholars even seek to present the entire arena of global governance in constitutionalist terms. Krisch then presents a range of critiques of constitutionalist thought from scholars such as Tully, Mouffe, Hirschl and Dryzek, and argues that the capacity of constitutionalism to accommodate diversity is limited. Pluralism on the other hand, by taking difference seriously, is capable of accommodating argument and political resistance and of dealing with contestable claims of supremacy at the level of different polities. Krisch questions whether Halberstam's third possibility of constitutional pluralism is really possible, and suggests it may simply replicate or echo domestic forms of constitutionalism. Despite its risks, he argues that pluralism may be 'our best chance', in that it preserves space for contestation and experimentation, prevents domination by powerful actors and provides an effective system of checks and balances.

The volume closes with what we view as the distinctive characteristic of this volume, namely a dialogical epilogue in which the claims and arguments of the chapter authors are interrogated by Joseph Weiler, with a view to getting to the heart of each argument and exposing what is at stake in the debates.

Prologue: global and pluralist constitutionalism – some doubts

J. H. H. WEILER

Global Constitutionalism and Constitutional Pluralism: the sociological pay-off

Like an infectious virus which simply develops new resistant strains when we think we finally have it under control, so it is with <Constitutional> <kɒnstɪ'tuʃənl>. The most recent academic pandemic, particularly virulent (cerebral indigestion being one of its milder symptoms) is the result of a genetic fusion of the ubiquitous Global Constitutionalism and Constitutional Pluralism strains which dominated the 1990s and 2010s. Global Constitutionalism is already, at least in the eyes of some, a discrete academic discipline, with a soon to be published *Journal of Global Constitutionalism*, with various masters' degrees, treatises and the other usual accoutrements. Constitutional Pluralism is today the only party membership card which will guarantee a seat at the high tables of the public law professoriate. From my vantage point of editor-in-chief of the deliciously and ambiguously entitled *International Journal of Constitutional Law* (I·CON)[1] I have begun to wonder: Is there anyone out there who is not a constitutional pluralist? Who does not believe that the global space is in some form constitutionalized?

I do not recall ever using constitutional pluralism in my own writing, but like M. Jourdain, I was instructed that I too, apparently, converse in the prose of constitutional pluralism, which, paradoxically makes me (and everyone else) a comfortable *Bourgeois gentilhomme*. That, of course, is the price of success of a concept/fad: what begins as heterodoxy becomes prevailing orthodoxy, in this case when Constitutional Pluralism (the maverick constitutional pluralism strain) suddenly emerges as hopelessly politically correct.

---

[1] Our editorial policy is, Janus-like, to regard ourselves as both the 'International Journal of Constitutional Law' and the 'Journal of International Constitutional Law'. That is why I·CON can claim to be an icon.

This is a problem, since the idea is to *épater le bourgeois* or, indeed, *la bourgeoisie* as a whole, not to become one. Is that not the name of the academic game of originality, viz. power and fame? So, two new devices emerge. The first is that fusion of pluralist constitutionalism with global constitutionalism. The second is evocative of the old European states staking a claim to new territories, using the prerogative of the powerful to give names – combing the old and new as in New Amsterdam or New Caledonia, or New South Wales. In similar fashion we have a wonderfully evocative new vocabulary by the academically (truly) powerful such as Cosmopolitan Constitutionalism, Contrapuntal Constitutionalism, Multi-polar or Dialogic Constitutionalism.

Blessedly, both global constitutionalism and constitutional pluralism are remarkably underspecified concepts which allow a multiplicity of meanings without offending any received understanding. I say blessedly because it accounts for the richness which the reader will find in this book, a broad gamut of understandings of how the constitutional and the international meet and interact and how the constitutional and the constitutional meet and interact. The gamut is indeed wide: compare the approach, sensibility, definition of the problem and its solution in, say, the excellent contributions of Bruno de Witte and Nico Krisch.

But this book is not only exposé: it is also, or at least attempts to be also, a critical exposé. Let me explain the sense in which I mean this. A small 'historical' detour is necessary.

The constitutional beyond the state

Whether we go back to antiquity in, say, Aristotle's *Nicomachean Ethics* or fast forward to modernity well into the twentieth century, the notion of a constitutional legal order was typically associated with the state as distinct from any notion of an international legal order. This was even more so in relation to 'thick' or 'robust' constitutional legal orders where, in American style (a *parvenu* state, but the oldest and longest uninterrupted contemporary constitutional order[2]), the constitution meant a higher law with the apparatus of judicial review and constitutional enforcement. It is the robust version that interests us, and

---

[2] Needless to say, as someone who was educated as a lawyer in the United Kingdom, I never bought into the Dicey bluff, a droll case of intellectual penis envy – 'we too have one'.

our authors, most, since it is the interaction of such orders which gives rise in the most acute and telling way to the issues that bred the turn to constitutional pluralism. It is also the robust version, espoused with a vengeance by the European Union, which provided the siren call to so many early advocates of a (rather primitive) version of global constitutionalism.

Rereading Mauro Cappelletti's evergreen *Il Controllo Giudiziario Di Costituzionalità Delle Leggi Nel Diritto Comparato*[3] is instructive in two senses. On the one hand it is surprising to recall how exceptional the robust version was as late as the middle of the twentieth century, given its ubiquity today. On the other hand it is surprising to note how swift its spread was from that moment onwards. The first serious 'globalization' of constitutionalism was, thus, a horizontal movement: a spread, quite global in its reach, albeit still firmly situated in statal settings. When scholars such as Alfred Verdross projected a constitutional understanding and vocabulary onto the UN (United Nations) and international legal system, it was for the most part the exception that proved the rule type of exercise and one that was neither convincing at the time it was made and ideologically problematic at the same time.

It was the advent of the European Communities, and especially the well-known legal developments of the 1960s and 1970s which took the internationalization of the constitutional to a new level. Make no mistake, this experience was highly exceptional, but in its audacity and political centrality it had far-reaching conceptual and practical influence. Of course international law proper never allowed the use of domestic law as an excuse for non-performance of international legal obligations – thus displaying a supremacy principle every bit as capacious as that found in the EC (European Community) legal order. But for the most part, supreme international legal norms were imposed on states, not in states, and were result-oriented, thus insulating municipal constitutional orders from the direct commands of international law.

Even when international norms reached into the municipal legal order, long before even the great Neil MacCormick articulated the problem of incommensurate constitutional authorities, the international legal order had developed the most ingenious device to neuter the conflict – the conceptual and institutional artefact of state

---

[3] Cappelletti, M., *Il Controllo Giudiziario Di Costituzionalità Delle Leggi Nel Diritto Comparato* (Milan: Dott. A. Giuffrè, 1968, 1972).

responsibility. Failure to comply with an international law in the normal course of international law has the result of engaging the state responsibility of the offending state towards those to whom the obligation is owed, creating a secondary duty to discharge that responsibility the non-performance of which creates in turn consequences such as, say, counter-measures. What in my view has been too little understood or appreciated in the conceptual literature is the manner in which state responsibility in some ways homogenizes all violations. Critically, even in those cases where an international legal obligation were to have a 'constitutional' character, purporting to create an obligation in a state and not only on a state, and thus in principle directly affecting and effecting individuals, violation of such a norm triggers the mechanisms of state responsibility which obliterate that constitutional character.

One way to express the difference by which the European Community legal order could be thought of as 'constitutional' rather than international was not in the content of the norms (reaching in rather than imposing on) nor even their hierarchical nature (supreme). International law was capable of both and increasingly had both. The difference was that, without much discussion or perhaps even noticing, the EC system eschewed, except peripherally, the most central institution of the international legal system, its heart and lungs – state responsibility.

With the endless discussions of the juridification of the WTO (World Trade Organization) and the excitement of its system of sanctions, it remains wholly within the classical parameters of state responsibility in a way in which the EC remains, with hardly an exception, wholly outside those very same parameters.[4] This is critical. In the first place,

---

[4] I find uninteresting the debate about the self-contained nature of the European legal order and the claim that in exceptional situations, since it is treaty based and ultimately rooted in international law, if its internal legal mechanisms fail, Member States may resort, or even be forced to resort to classical international law and state responsibility. I find it uninteresting because it is too Schmittian, too concerned with conceptual purity (think of the fascination with purity implicit in the Schmittian model). I have endlessly argued that the essential characteristic of the system is defined by the quotidian and regular rather than the exceptional. Think of my wife – a confirmed vegetarian. For as long as she can remember she has not put meat in her mouth and hopefully will never do so. Schmitt would say that in the case of severe hunger she would eat meat (which she would) and thus that defines her as a carnivore. I would say that defining her as a vegetarian is for most purposes more meaningful. The fact that if, if and if, even the Member States may revert to state responsibility, does not make the European legal order any more international than the fact that if starved my wife would eat meat makes her a carnivore.

it is the removal of the mediating institution of state responsibility which gave purchase to the usage of a constitutional vocabulary as regards the European legal order.[5] And in the second place, it is the same removal which rendered the interface between the European order and that of its Member States so interesting. Without the mediation of state responsibility the encounter between a European norm claiming authority – supreme authority – *in* a Member State and a competing national constitutional norm gave rise to the notion of incommensurability which has been the source from which MacCormick (and all those who have followed him) begat constitutional pluralism.

In my own work I have been consistently sceptical about extending a constitutional vocabulary to international contexts other than the EU.[6] I have been sceptical on descriptive grounds: I do not believe that other phenomena have the hallmarks necessary for such – notably when they still fit within the normal parameters of state responsibility. My scepticism is also normative: constitutional discipline without polity and without something resembling the habits and practices of democratic legitimacy are highly problematic. They are problematic even in the EU[7] – *a fortiori* outside it. So, global constitutionalism is both descriptively and prescriptively problematic on this reading. Robert Howse and Kalypso Nicolaidis nailed that coffin true and proper in my view.[8]

I understand, too, why my work is regarded by some as being part of the constitutional pluralist discourse, even if I have eschewed the vocabulary. My own act of imperial naming, the Principle of Constitutional Tolerance, is premised on the need of the legal orders of the Member States *voluntarily* to accept the constitutional discipline demanded by the European legal order, even absent a constitutional

---

[5] Of course, this is not a holistic claim. The European order is not monolithic, and there are huge swathes where an international vocabulary is the most apt. We should not forget that we are looking at one slice of the phenomenon.

[6] Weiler, J. H. H. and J. Trachtman, 'European Constitutionalism and Its Discontents,' 17 *Northwestern Journal of International Law & Business* (1997) 354.

[7] Weiler, J. H. H., 'Europe: The Case Against the Case for Statehood', 4 *European Law Journal* (1998) 43; Mancini, F. and J. H. H. Weiler, 'Europe: The Case for Statehood ... And the Case Against: An Exchange', *Harvard Jean Monnet Working Paper 6/98*, Cambridge, Mass. (1998).

[8] Howse, Robert and Kalypso Nicolaides, 'Legitimacy and Global Governance: Why Constitutionalizing the WTO is a Step Too Far', in Roger B. Porter, Pierre Sauve, Arvind Subramanian and Americo Beviglia Zampetti, eds., *Efficiency, Equity and Legitimacy: The Multilateral Trading System at The Millennium* (Washington, DC: Brookings Institute Press, 2001).

demos. It is that voluntary acceptance – that constitutional tolerance – which is, in my eyes, at the core not only of the originality of the EU legal order but its nobility.[9] When I write:

> The Quebecois are told: In the name of the People of Canada, you are obliged to obey. The French or the Italians or the Germans are told – In the name of the peoples of Europe, you are invited to obey. In both constitutional obedience is demanded. When acceptance and subordination is voluntary, and repeatedly so, it constitutes an act of true liberty and emancipation from collective self-arrogance and constitutional fetishism – a high expression of Constitutional Tolerance.[10]

this can easily fit within the vernacular of constitutional pluralism.

I do think I have always differed in at least one pronounced way from the MacCormick paradigm – something we often discussed. His construct was rooted in legal theory which, as I understand it, stipulates that in the clash of any two constitutional orders there will be incommensurability of authority which requires the turn to constitutional pluralism. Both the problem and the solution are inherent, structural. My own construct has always been rooted in politics and political theory. There is, in my view, no structural necessity that in the contact between two constitutional orders there will be a necessary incommensurability of authority. It simply depends on the source of authority of each, a political fact (rooted in the political theory of collective authority) which is resolved in most federal states with relative simplicity: the authority of the federal demos trumps that of the authority of the constituent units' demoi – at least in the sphere of competence allocated to the federation. The reason there is incommensurability in Europe is because of the absence of a European constitutional demos. As I have preached for decades, it is precisely the combination of a demand for constitutional discipline coupled with the absence of a European constitutional demos which gave Europe its originality and nobility. That is why I implacably opposed the European Constitution project (when it was pretty unpopular to do so) because it threatened, in my view, that originality, that nobility, that uniqueness. So I am glad I have eschewed characterizing my own work with the CP imprimatur. It would disturb

---

[9]　Weiler, J. H. H., 'Federalism and Constitutionalism: Europe's Sonderweg', *Harvard Jean Monnet Working Paper 10/00*, Cambridge, Mass. (2000).
[10]　Ibid.

me to see constitutional pluralism bandied with the licence it is today if it had the result of masking that which I consider as the normative core of the European constitutional construct.

The pluralism of constitutional pluralism

But my critique goes further. There is a certain duality – adding to its underspecificity – in the term 'constitutional pluralism'. At one level it defines a certain type of constitutional order: an EU but not, say, a US or Germany. At another level it defines an approach, a school of thought. There are constitutionalists who are associated with the school of thought and others (who have become very silent, it should be said: it is certainly not chic to confess to not being a constitutional pluralist) who presumably are not. It is not always clear whether the constitutional pluralists regard this pluralism as inherent in all constitutional orders, in constitutionalism itself, or whether it is reserved for characterizing the EU and some other global constitutional orders as distinct from, for example, national constitutional orders.

On either hypothesis constitutional pluralism and constitutional pluralists are juxtaposed with something and someone: with non-pluralist constitutional orders, and/or with a non-pluralist approach to constitutionalism and/or with non-pluralist constitutionalists. It is interesting that relatively little attention is given to describe what characterizes a non-pluralist constitutional order, or a non-pluralist approach to constitutionalism or a non-pluralist constitutionalist. But presumably the non-pluralist approach is hierarchical (hierarchical constitutionalism?) and monolithic. When set up like that, beyond any explanatory power which CP may offer, there is an unmistakable normative patina to the nomenclature. Pluralist constitutionalism – good, progressive, tolerant, non-domineering; hierarchical constitutionalism – bad, regressive, intolerant, domineering. It is not surprising that constitutional pluralism is all the rage and from the other side there is a deafening silence.

It is precisely this juxtaposition – which I think is inherent in the turn to constitutional pluralism – which allows me to articulate my doubts and scepticism, at their sharpest: in my understanding, constitutional orders, whether national or transnational, inherently contain hierarchical and pluralist features. It is part of their ontology. It cannot be otherwise. What is more, there is important positive normative value in both. The hierarchical features are as important as the pluralist features.

On this view, constitutional pluralism, to the extent that I can understand it, does violence at the analytical/descriptive level as well as the normative level. Descriptively it is wrong to characterize some systems as hierarchical and others as pluralist or to describe all systems as pluralist – the two options outlined above. Normatively, it is (in my view) wrong to privilege pluralism to the detriment of hierarchy; indeed it is wrong to juxtapose them as normative opposites.

I shall now elaborate and explain this critique, though not without one caveat: it might well be that I am misunderstanding constitutional pluralism, in which case I still hope my critique will not be dismissed as irrelevant but at least as useful in mounting a challenge – which to my knowledge has not yet been mounted – the response to which will help bring clarity to the field.

Excursus: from Eve and Adam to Noah – nomos, constitution and the human condition

At the risk of boring the reader and stating some truisms, let me go back to some fundamental building blocks. I take my cue, as is my habit, from the Bible, one of the foundations of Western civilization. The division of the Hebrew Bible, and in particular the Pentateuch, into chapters is a late Christian innovation. The early Jewish custom still maintained in daily, weekly and annual worship divided the five books of Moses into 'portions' each corresponding to a central theme. The first 'portion' of the Bible takes its name from the opening line of the Bible – 'In the Beginning' – and has as its central theme the story of Eve and Adam. It is followed by Noah, which has as its central theme the deluge. This division helps draw attention to the biblical view of the most fundamental features of the human condition.

The story of Eve and Adam has its focus on the *individual* in his and her most fundamental: created, male and female, in the image of God with the concomitant ontology of unique individual dignity and equality. The full realization of this occurs when Eve, fulfilling her human destiny, reaches out and takes possession of the fruit of the Tree of Knowledge, good and evil. It is only through this gesture, as recognized by God, that the essential individual human condition is realized – the autonomous human with the ability to make moral choices and be responsible for his or her actions. It is only an individual who is able to say 'No' to God, whose 'Yes' becomes meaningful. It is only an individual who is able to discern good from evil, and has the ability to choose evil, whose choice of good becomes meaningful. It is a narrative of individual liberty at its most profound, that which defines our human condition as moral agents, each one an end in himself or herself. Pluralism finds its source here, since it springs from the recognition of, and respect for, each individual as sovereign, unique and equal in dignity.

Noah, by contrast, is a narrative of the *social*. It is not only a story about individuals who abused their liberty by not recognizing the bounds which the social condition imposes on us, but it is also a story of the responsibility we have as a society to ensure that such abuse does not take place, that justice be done, that liberty be constrained within rational social bounds. The story of the deluge is not just one of individual iniquity, the murderous act of Cain repeated endlessly. Far more important is the failure of society to exercise its authority over individuals to ensure that such iniquities do not take place.

Right there, between Eve and Adam and Noah and his generation, we have the tension between the pluralist imperative deriving from the co-existence of individuals, each one of which is a unique moral agent, a universe unto himself, and the hierarchical imperative deriving from the responsibility of the collectivity, the social as such constituting part of the human condition itself. Note, the normative importance of hierarchy, that of society over the individual, is not just based on the claim that without such the dignity and liberty of the individual could not be safeguarded but, at an even deeper level, it is an acknowledgement of self-restraint as a necessary virtue of social existence.

It is possible to narrate the evolution of Western civilization, resting both on Athens and Jerusalem, as a continuing effort to negotiate, mediate, 'balance', think through, these two pillars of the human condition. Nomos, law, has of course played a central part in this never-ending quest and, on this view, it is this quest to which modern constitutionalism, starting with the French and American Revolutions, has made a distinct contribution. The philosophical foundations of both revolutions coupled with the mechanics of the American Constitution were particularly impressive in recognizing the individual, guaranteeing his rights to various forms of liberty and placing meaningful constraints on the exercise of public power, not only that power exercised by a king but even of a democratic majority itself. Democratic constitutionalism was arguably the first modern success in redressing the balance between hierarchy and pluralism hitherto almost always hugely tilted to the detriment of the latter. But *nota bene*: the constitutional discipline is not just an affirmation of the individual, though it is that aspect, more than others, that has held us in thrall for over two centuries. It is also, simultaneously, inevitably, an assertion of the need and power to impose the will of the social over the individual to bound unchecked individual liberty. One could not offer these guarantees to the individual and to pluralism, if one did not have the authority – conceptual and practical – to ensure its observance through a distinct hierarchy of norms, where, for example, the 'constitutional' provisions guaranteeing certain profound values trumped others. This hierarchy is more than indispensable to the constitutional project: it cannot have one without the other. Within the parameters of democracy it is also a remarkable exercise in self-restraint.

The same is true when constitutionalism extends beyond the unitary state into the federal or international – where the I becomes a collectivity. And the same is true even in a polity where the state itself loses its traditional boundaries – because what is impossible to go beyond, to go past, are the primordial 'units' of the individual and the social. At the transnational level one sees a perfect manifestation of this in the regime of the ECHR (European Convention on Human Rights) – which simultaneously celebrates a form of pluralism through the doctrine of the margin of appreciation and insists on hierarchy in stipulating a binding minimal norm.

I have already polemicized against a certain profligacy in the use of the 'constitutional' in every non-unitary transnational or international legal and/or political order. I am not sure I would even want to accord such to that very ECHR. Be that as it may, I think words simply lose their meaning if one tries to describe a legal political order as constitutional when it does not have both the pluralist and hierarchical combined – though one can have endless debates on the appropriate dosages of each.

On this view, constitutional pluralism privileges one pillar and thus misconstrues the very nature of the constitutional. Moreover, by undermining the importance of the 'hierarchy' pillar, it not only undermines pluralism itself, but also the virtue of hierarchy as a check on the hubris of unbound liberty, both of the collective and the individual. Arguably, the worst assaults on the dignity and equality of the individual have resulted from such. I would even risk suggesting that in our advanced market societies, the pendulum has swung, perhaps, too much in the direction of the pluralism, to the detriment of the social and the polity.

I have already indicated that both global constitutionalism and constitutional pluralism are terribly underspecified terms, so their use in different contexts might simply be a reflection of a different understanding of what they mean. The contributions in this volume go well beyond my own circumspect and Eurocentric approach. They are brilliant, rich and interesting. But we do not let them just sit there. In the 'Dialogical epilogue' to this volume I engage with each of the authors, challenging, posing questions, expressing critical scepticism. The last word, of course, goes to the various authors. After all, that has always been the way of the world: the new push out the old.

1 The European Union as an international legal experiment

BRUNO DE WITTE[1]

1.1 Introduction

In a recent essay about legal theory and the European Union, Neil Walker wrote that theoretical inquiries about EU law as a whole – as opposed to studies of specific parts of EU law – 'cannot but draw upon an arsenal of concepts and theoretical mechanisms developed or refined in an older context in which the national and the international, with the former dominating, were the two sides and the key frames of the world order of states'.[2] This Chapter aims to replace the European Union in the 'older context' of international law, by recalling the fact that the European Communities, and the European Union, came into being as creatures of international law, as well as the fact that the many remarkable institutional features of those organisations came out of the existing toolbox of international law. Each of those single features had been experimented with before in other more limited contexts, but both the European Coal and Steel Community Treaty and the European Economic Community Treaty combined them in an unprecedented way. They were true experiments of international law, and the *first part* of the chapter will highlight some characteristics of that historical experimentation.

The more interesting question, perhaps, for today's reader is whether this 'arsenal of concepts and [...] mechanisms' drawn from the toolbox of public international law is still of decisive importance for our understanding of European Union law today. There is no disputing the fact that 'the EU has successfully expanded its substantive mandate and

---

[1] Professor of European Union law, Maastricht University and Robert Schuman Centre of the EUI, Florence. I benefited from the criticism of an earlier version by the workshop participants at New York University Law School, particularly by Joseph Weiler. Thanks also to Peter Hilpold for his comments.

[2] Walker, Neil, 'Legal Theory and the European Union: A 25th Anniversary Essay', 25 *Oxford Journal of Legal Studies* (2005) 581–601 at 587.

institutional prerogatives to a level without parallel among international organizations',[3] but there is some dispute about whether it is
still situated 'among international organizations' or has ceased to
belong to that category. In fact, the dominant strand in the EU law
literature takes the view that the European Union, whilst not a federal
state, is also no longer an international organization, but rather an ill-
defined *sui generis* legal construct. In this chapter, I will question both
the vagueness of the *sui generis* construction and the view that the EU is
no longer an international organization (and thus no longer an ongoing
international legal experiment) by wondering, in the second and third
parts of the chapter, what could have happened in the course of time,
between the 1950s and today, to make EU law cease to be part of
international law despite its international treaty pedigree. I will address
that question from two points of view. First (that is, in the *second part* of
the chapter), I will examine the practice of the states, and especially the
Member States of the EU, to explore whether they have willed, or
consented to, such a change in the legal nature of the EU. In the *third
part* of the chapter, I will turn to examine the case-law of the ECJ
(European Court of Justice) and the doctrinal interpretations of that
same question and consider two possibilities: either that *particular*
novel characteristics of EU law emerged over time which are incompatible with seeing it as an international organization; or that the *overall*
development of the EU, rather than the development of specific characteristics, justifies the view that it must no longer be considered as a living
international legal experiment, but as something altogether different.

These questions are by no means new. They have been addressed in
the literature at several moments in time, though not very often in recent
years despite the fact that the protracted process of European Treaty
reform (from 2000 to 2009) has offered some new elements for reflection on the matter. Also, this question must be addressed in the light of
the evolution of international law, characterized by the advent of other
regional organizations partly modelled on the EU, and by the development of elements of 'supranationality' in other international regimes. In
other words, the effort to sharply separate the EU from the field of

---

[3] Moravcsik, Andrew, 'The European Constitutional Settlement', in S. Meunier and
   K. McNamara, eds., *Making History. European Integration and Institutional
   Change at Fifty* (The State of the European Union, Vol. 8) (Oxford University
   Press, 2007), 23–50, at 23.

international law might be misguided for two complementary reasons: because it overestimates the novelty of EU law, and because it underestimates the capacity of international law to develop innovative features in other contexts than that of European integration.

The thesis of this chapter is, in a nutshell, that it still makes sense to view the EU as an international legal experiment, and that this should continue to inform theoretical efforts to define and explain the nature of the European Union.

1.2 The founding decade (1948–1958): an ambitious international legal experiment

Between 1948 and 1951, three European organizations were set up in quick succession: the *Organisation for European Economic Cooperation* (OEEC; later OECD) was established by a treaty signed in Paris on 16 April 1948 by sixteen European states and the three Western Commanders-in-Chief of the German occupation zones; the *Council of Europe* was established by a statute (taking the legal form of a treaty) signed in London on 5 May 1949 by ten European states; and the *European Coal and Steel Community* was established by a treaty signed in Paris on 18 April 1951 by six European states. The creation of international organizations was nothing unusual; hundreds of multilateral international organizations had been set up since the nineteenth century. However, most of them had a universal remit, or at least an extra-European one, and the focus on creating ambitious multilateral organizations which expressed the 'need of a closer unity between all like-minded countries of Europe'[4] was a new development of the postwar period. All three organizations expressed, in their own way, the aspiration towards greater European unity.

In the immediate post-war years, European federalists had hoped to create a United Europe based on a federal constitution inspired by the USA and had sought to promote the adoption of federal solutions in the context of the various political initiatives taken in that period.[5]

---

[4] Statute of the Council of Europe, Preamble, Paragraph 4.
[5] See, for detailed accounts: Vayssière, Bernard, *Vers une Europe fédérale? Les espoirs et les actions fédéralistes au sortir de la Seconde Guerre mondiale* (Bruxelles: Peter Lang, 2006); and Réveillard, Christophe, *Les premières tentatives de construction d'une Europe fédérale, des projets de la Résistance au Traité de la CED (1940–1954)* (Paris: F-X de Guibert, 2001).

The European governments chose instead not to take an openly federal route and to experiment with new forms of European cooperation whilst using the age-old instrument of the international treaty: the OEEC, the Council of Europe and the European Coal and Steel Community were all created in the form of an international organization based on a treaty subject to ratification by the parliaments of their Member States. The treaty path was also taken some years later when the European Economic Community was established by the Treaty of Rome in 1957, and was never abandoned after that. Since the 1960s, revisions of the so-called 'founding treaties' have, together with accession treaties, gradually become the main instrument for the legal deepening and widening of European integration.

The creation of a federal European state was not, despite the strong intellectual support for it, a politically credible ideal in the post-war period. It soon appeared that the real choice was between reverting to the rather ineffectual forms of international cooperation as had been repeatedly used before the war, or making creative use of the resources of international law to come up with international organizations of an unprecedented and more effective nature. The Statute of the Council of Europe was an example of the old-fashioned approach in the way its institutions and their powers were defined (the European Convention on Human Rights was a legal breakthrough, but it happened by means of a separate treaty which entered into force only much later).[6] The ECSC (European Coal and Steel Community) and EEC (European Economic Community) treaties, by contrast, were examples of the innovative approach; insightful politicians helped by fine jurists[7] devised institutions and competences which made them *different*, more functionally and politically useful, international organizations.

The drafters of the ECSC Treaty did not need to start from scratch, legally speaking, but rather could benefit from legal solutions used in

---

[6] On the extent to which the Statute of the Council of Europe, as agreed in 1949, constituted a dampener of the high hopes held by European federalists, see Zurcher, Arnold J., *The Struggle to Unite Europe 1940–1958* (New York University Press, 1958), Chapter 5.

[7] Specifically on the role of international jurists in post-war Europe, see Cohen, Antonin and Mikael Rask Madsen, 'Cold War Law: Legal Entrepreneurs and the Emergence of a European Legal Field (1945–1965)', in V. Gessner and D. Nelken, eds., *European Ways of Law. Towards a European Sociology of Law* (Oxford: Hart Publishing, 2007), 175–201.

earlier international experiments. The decision to create independent international organizations charged by their founding members with a task in their common interest was itself, when it first occurred in the mid nineteenth century, an experiment in international law.[8] Among those early organizations, the European Danube Commission was notable for its very extensive powers and for the fact that it dealt directly with the users of the Danube without the mediation of the riparian states.[9] During the inter-war period, bold experiments of supranational governance were attempted in some areas of Europe in order to defuse conflicting claims of nationalism: the Saar, Danzig and Upper Silesia were the most notable places where this international law experimentalism unfolded.[10] It has been convincingly argued that 'subsequent international legal policy proposers have implicitly relied on [...] the particular techniques that were enshrined in the international toolkit during that period'.[11]

The European Coal and Steel Community was based on an unprecedented combination of these existing techniques of international law. It was created as an international organization based on a treaty between the six original Member States signed in 1951 but, whereas this was an ordinary international agreement in formal terms, it was far from

---

[8] For a vivid description of the experimental nature of the very early international organizations, see Bederman, David J., 'The Souls of International Organizations: Legal Personality and the Lighthouse at Cape Spartel', *Virginia Journal of International Law* 36 (1995–1996) 276–377.

[9] Seidl-Hohenveldern, Ignaz, 'Danube River', in *Encyclopedia of Public International Law*, 1st edn, vol. 12 (Amsterdam: North Holland,1990) at 80–81: the Commission 'established and enforced navigation rules, collected fees, granted pilotage patents and exercised navigation police powers with the right to impose fines on individuals. The legal and judicial powers of this Commission were so far-reaching that they may well be compared to those enjoyed by supranational organizations, especially by the European Communities.' The supranational character of the Commission was tuned down in the interwar period; see Imbert, L., 'Le régime juridique actuel du Danube', *Revue générale de droit international public* (1951) at 73–76.

[10] Berman, Nathaniel, 'But the Alternative is Despair: European Nationalism and the Modernist Renewal of International Law', 106 *Harvard Law Review* (1993) 1792–1903 at 1874–1898. The term 'experiment' was much used at the time, for example in the title of the study by the Belgian jurist Kaeckenbeeck, who had been the president of the arbitral tribunal of Upper Silesia, one of the typical 'supranational' organs of the interwar period: Kaeckenbeeck, Georges, *The International Experiment of Upper Silesia* (Oxford University Press, 1942).

[11] Berman, 'But the Alternative is Despair' (1993) at 1899.

ordinary in its content. A major, and at the time startling, innovation of the 'Schuman Plan', contrasting with most pre-war and post-war co-operation projects, was that sovereign states should agree to transfer their powers to regulate the coal and steel industries to a common body, the High Authority. By signing the European Coal and Steel Treaty, as it emerged from the Schuman Plan through negotiations in 1950 and 1951, the governments of the Six agreed to relinquish national control over these two sectors of the economy and to allow the supranational High Authority to exercise autonomous 'state' powers in their stead. The term *supranational* itself only appeared once in the ECSC Treaty, and not in a very prominent place,[12] but it had been repeatedly used during the negotiations, not least by Robert Schuman himself,[13] and was rapidly adopted by political and legal commentators as the defining characteristic not only of the High Authority but also of the entire Community of which it was an organ.[14] Since then, the term *supra-national organization* has become of common usage and, today, most textbooks of the law of international organizations identify them as a separate category of IOs.[15]

[12] Article 9 para. 5 of the ECSC Treaty stated that the members of the High Authority '*exercent leurs fonctions en pleine indépendance, dans l'intérêt général de la Communauté [. . .] Ils s'abstiennent de tout acte incompatible avec le caractère supranational de leurs fonctions*'. This sentence disappeared from the ECSC Treaty in 1965, when the so-called Merger Treaty (*Traité de fusion*) merged the High Authority with the Commission of the other two European Communities.

[13] See the references to several speeches by Robert Schuman in Capotorti, Francesco, 'Supranational Organizations', 5 *Encyclopedia of Public International Law* (1983) 262–268 at 262.

[14] The leading legal commentary of the Treaty was by one of its drafters, Reuter, Paul, *La Communauté Européenne du Charbon et de l'Acier* (Paris: Librairie Générale de Droit et de Jurisprudence, 1953); see also the shorter version, by the same author, Reuter, Paul, 'Le Plan Schuman – La Communauté Européenne du Charbon et de l'Acier', in *Recueil des Cours de l'Académie de Droit International* (Hague Recueil) 1952-III. On the influential role of Professor Reuter in this period, see Cohen, Antonin, 'Le Plan Schuman de Paul Reuter: entre communauté nationale et fédération européenne', 48 *Revue française de science politique* (1998) 645–663.

[15] See, for example, Schermers, Henry and Niels Blokker, *International Institutional Law: Unity within Diversity* (4th edn, The Hague: Martinus Nijhoff, 2003), at 46–48; Klabbers, Jan, *An Introduction to International Institutional Law* (Cambridge University Press, 2002), at 27; see also, in a more detailed way, Capotorti, 'Supranational Organizations' (1983) at 262.

The supranational character of the ECSC Treaty did not spring from its substantive provisions but from what one could call, with a fashionable neologism, its operating system,[16] namely its rules on the distribution of legal authority and on decision-making by its organs. It had three institutions composed of persons who were not government representatives; its institutions (particularly the independent High Authority) had the power to adopt binding acts, often by a majority vote; some of these decisions were directly applicable to private individuals and firms; and there was binding adjudication of compliance by both the institutions and the Member States with their obligations. As Capotorti shows through examples, none of these characteristics were entirely unprecedented in international law, so that the novelty of the ECSC did not reside in one or other of those specific characteristics but rather in their cumulative presence.[17]

The term *supranational* became very prominent for a short period after the signature of the ECSC Treaty in the context of follow-up initiatives to deepen European integration. Article 1 of the Treaty establishing the European Defence Community (1952) expressly conferred 'supranational' character on that Community, and Article 1 of the draft Treaty establishing a European Political Community (1953) similarly stated: '*Il est institué par le présent Traité une Communauté Européenne de caractère supranational.*'[18] Neither of these two instruments entered into force, and the word *supranational* joined in their demise. The EEC Treaty (1957) did not contain that word at all and the EEC's 'founding father' Paul-Henri Spaak had warned against its use during the preparatory work of the Treaty so as not to raise hostility against the new organization.[19] In fact, the European Economic Community (and also the European Atomic Community created at the same time) was equipped with an 'operating system' that was as

---

[16] Diehl, Paul F., Charlotte Ku and Daniel Zamora, 'The Dynamics of International Law: The Interaction of Normative and Operating Systems', 57 *International Organization* (2003) 43–75.

[17] Capotorti, 'Supranational Organizations' (1983) at 263–264.

[18] See, on the history of these two attempts at closer European integration: Fursdon, Edward, *The European Defence Community: A History* (New York: St Martin's Press, 1980); Griffiths, Richard T., *Europe's First Constitution: The European Political Community, 1952–1954* (London: The Federal Trust, 2000).

[19] Zurcher, *Struggle* (1958), at 138–139.

supranational as that of the ECSC.[20] It is true that the Commission had a less prominent place in the decision-making system of the EEC than the High Authority had in the ECSC, but in return the power to make directly applicable rules was now extended in its scope: broadly based regulations could be adopted in a number of economic areas by the Council acting on a proposal by the Commission instead of the punctual decisions relating to the coal and steel industries which the High Authority could adopt under ECSC law. All the other supranational characteristics of the earlier Treaty were fully maintained, with the interesting addition of the preliminary reference procedure before the ECJ whose supranational potential went, however, largely unnoticed in 1958.[21] In the next two decades, the supranational character of the EEC's decision-making system became rather less pronounced than the authors of the Treaty may have thought (partly due to the Luxembourg Compromise), whereas the judicial system became rather more supranational than they might have expected.[22]

These massive international legal experiments in the 1950s did not come as a 'legal surprise' for the six Member States. The way had been paved at the national level by the unprecedented openness to international cooperation displayed by the new post-war constitutions of the three largest states participating in the ECSC project. In France, Italy and Germany, the post-war restoration of democracy had been accompanied by an express constitutional recognition of the fact that effective international cooperation was necessary in order to prevent new wars and to avoid the excesses caused by unbridled state sovereignty. Each of those three new constitutions contained a provision permitting limitations of sovereignty or transfer of sovereign powers to international

---

[20] For a discussion of the historical context in which this much disputed choice for the supranational path was made, first in 1950 and then again in 1957 (despite the intervening failures of the EDC and EPC), see Parsons, Craig, 'The Triumph of Community Europe', in D. Dinan, ed., *Origins and Evolution of the European Union* (Oxford University Press, 2006), 107–125.

[21] For a contemporary analysis of the supranational features of the EEC Treaty, as compared to the ECSC Treaty, see Jaenicke, Günther, 'Der übernationale Charakter der Europäischen Wirtschaftsgemeinschaft', 18 *Zeitschrift für ausländisches öffentliches Recht und Völkerrecht* (1958) 154–196. For a historical discussion of supranationality from the current perspective, see Barents, René, *The Autonomy of Community Law* (The Hague: Kluwer, 2004), Chapter 2.

[22] See, on this double evolution, the classic study by J. H. H. Weiler, 'The Community System: The Dual Character of Supranationalism', 1 *Yearbook of European Law* (1981) 267–306.

institutions. These provisions are still part of the constitutional law of those countries today. In *France*, Paragraph 15 of the preamble of the Constitution of the Fourth Republic adopted in 1946 states that 'subject to reciprocity, France consents to limitations of sovereignty necessary for the realisation and the defence of peace'. Article 11 of the Italian Constitution of 1948 declares in strikingly similar terms that 'Italy may consent, on equal terms with other States, to limitations of sovereignty necessary to establish an order ensuring peace and justice among nations, and it will favour international organisations which have that aim'. Article 24(1) of the German Basic Law of 1949 expresses the same intention in active, rather than passive, wording: 'The Federation may by legislation transfer sovereign powers to international institutions.'

The function of each of those provisions was to facilitate the approval and entry into force of treaties for which otherwise a prior constitutional revision would have been needed. Indeed, derogations from the constitutional allocation of state powers can normally be made only by means of a revision of the constitution; the limitation-of-sovereignty clauses were meant to allow such derogation by means of the simple signature and approval of an international treaty. Whereas Article 24(1) of the German Basic Law is quite open-ended, the French and Italian provisions contain some conditions: the question of constitutional interpretation that unavoidably arose in France and Italy was to define which international treaties were covered by these clauses, and which were not, either because their purpose was not among the ones mentioned by the constitution, or because they contained limitations going beyond what was 'necessary' for the sake of international cooperation. In the end, though, all three countries approved both the ECSC Treaty and the Treaties of Rome (EEC and EAEC (European Atomic Energy Community)) on the basis of the limitation-of-sovereignty clause, and without making amendments to the texts of their constitutions.

To conclude this first part, the European Communities were set up, in the 1950s, as ingenious experiments of international law, combining some of the innovative tools experimented with earlier on for other international organizations, but doing so in an unprecedented way and, certainly in the case of the EEC, within a broad scope of activity that was unheard of. This new development in international law, that took place in the Western half of the European continent, had been facilitated by the deliberate turn away from absolute state sovereignty in the post-war constitutional reforms of the Community's founding states. The question to be addressed in the following parts of this chapter is whether it still makes sense to speak about the European Community, as it evolved later on, and about its younger sister organization the European Union, as ongoing experiments of international law, or whether on the contrary this experimental phase has been terminated by the transformation of the EC (European Community)/EU into 'something else' which is no longer part of international law. This will be done in two separate ways. I will first (in Part Two) examine the practice of the Member States of the European Union; since they have founded the European Communities, and later created the European Union, their perception of the evolving legal nature of their creation is of prime importance. I will then (in Part Three) examine the perception of the nature of EU law by the European and national judiciary and by legal writing; that perception might be different from the one that emerges from the international practice of the Member State governments, in which case the further question would arise: Whose voice is decisive when it comes to understand the evolving nature of the European legal experiment?

1.3 The international legal nature of the European Union (I): the practice of states

Deliberate transformations of the European Communities into 'something else' have been attempted several times in the history of European integration, but none of those attempts resulted in a clear and explicit change of the legal nature of the organizations. There is, in fact, a long tradition of constitutional politics in Europe, which has involved many proposals to modify the existing European 'treaty architecture'. Already in 1975, the European Commission had adopted a now entirely forgotten Report on European Union,[23] which was its contribution to the preparation of the now almost forgotten *Tindemans Report*.[24] In its report, the Commission advocated the transformation of the European

---

[23] *Report on European Union of 26 June 1975, Bulletin of the European Communities*, Suppl. 5/75.

[24] *European Union – Report by Mr Leo Tindemans, Prime Minister of Belgium, to the European Council*, in *Bulletin of the European Communities*, Suppl. 1/1976. On the content and context of the Tindemans Report, see Burgess, Michael, *Federalism and European Union: The Building of Europe, 1950–2000* (London: Routledge, 2000) at 106–116.

Communities into a new European Union and the adoption, for that purpose, of an Act of Constitution. This Act would still have had the legal form of an international treaty but would undoubtedly have been constitutional by its aspiration, content and language. The European Council did practically nothing with these Commission proposals, or with the Tindemans Report itself, apart from approving the general idea of a gradual transformation of the European Communities into a European Union.[25] However, no concrete steps were taken, during the next decade, to start this transformation.

A conceptually similar but politically much more incisive challenge to the established Treaty regime was made by the first directly elected European Parliament through the Draft Treaty establishing the European Union which it approved on 14 February 1984.[26] The Parliament's Draft Treaty aimed primarily at a substantive deepening of the integration process and at a major reshuffling of the institutional balance (to the advantage of the European Parliament itself), within an overall perspective of constitutional transformation. In terms of Treaty architecture, the Draft Treaty aimed at bringing together, within a single treaty text, the Communities and two forms of cooperation that had been developed outside the Community structure, namely European Political Cooperation and the European Monetary System. For the European Parliament, the proposed reorganization of the treaties was inspired by a broader objective of global constitutional reform: the existing three Communities would gradually disappear and be replaced by a more integrated organization, the European Union, although the Draft did not contain any language describing the legal nature of that Union. The Member State governments, when negotiating the Single European Act shortly afterwards, did not take this route, but preferred to keep the European Communities in existence and simply tied European Political Cooperation a bit more closely to them but without fully integrating it into a common legal structure.

---

[25] European Council of The Hague, November 1976, *Bulletin of the European Communities* 11–1976, at 93–94.

[26] Official Journal of the European Communities 1984, C 77/33. For the political history of the Draft Treaty, see Corbett, Richard, *The European Parliament's Role in Closer EU Integration* (Basingstoke: Palgrave Macmillan, 1998), Chapters 6 and 7. For a legal commentary, see Capotorti, Francesco et al., *The European Union Treaty: Commentary on the Draft Adopted by the EP on 14 February 1984* (Oxford: Clarendon Press, 1986).

The European Union advocated by the Parliament in 1984 was in fact created some years later, by the Treaty of Maastricht (signed in February 1992), but its significance was contrary to the European Parliament's aspirations when it adopted its Draft Treaty on European Union; in legal terms, it diluted the existing Community law framework rather than upgrading it. The creation of the European Union can be called a legal and political paradox, in the following sense: whereas the notion of 'European Union' had been frequently used in pre-Maastricht times (and particularly in the context of the 'Spinelli' Draft Treaty of 1984) to indicate possible new arrangements for a *more integrated* Europe, the real-life European Union that was established in Maastricht was seen by many, and correctly to some extent, as a *step back* in the European integration process, since that name was used to cover two new forms of inter-state cooperation, in Common Foreign and Security Policy (CFSP) and Justice and Home Affairs (JHA), which were marked by a lesser degree of supranationality than the existing European Economic Community; so, not a jump forward towards a federal Europe, but a partial return to more traditional forms of intergovernmental cooperation – despite the fact that, in other ways, the Maastricht Treaty did indeed deepen the integration process by the creation of the Economic and Monetary Union, the invention of the co-decision procedure for EC law-making, the creation of the concept of European citizenship, etc.

With the entry into force of the Treaty of Lisbon, the question of 'Treaty architecture' has undergone another paradoxical twist. Whereas the previously existing architecture, inaugurated by the Treaty of Maastricht, consisted of two separate treaties corresponding to two separate but interconnected organizations (the EC and the EU), and whereas the Constitutional Treaty proposed a radical simplification by moving to one single organization and one single treaty, the Lisbon Treaty leaves in existence at least[27] two separate and legally equivalent treaties (the EU Treaty and the Treaty on the Functioning of the EU) but only one single organization, namely the European Union. There is, in fact, no logical explanation for the decision to keep two separate treaties, the only explanation being of a tactical-political nature: to

---

[27] That is, without counting the European Atomic Energy Community Treaty which continues its separate legal existence and is not subordinated to the TEU (Treaty on European Union) and TFEU.

make it appear that the Constitutional Treaty is effectively dead and buried, it seemed advisable to the Member State governments to artificially keep in place the existing treaties, even though one of the amendments to the 'existing' EC Treaty was to modify its name and thereby to end the long and successful life of the European Community. The European Union, on the other hand, will continue its strange career: it started as a political dream of European federalists, then became an unidentified legal object at Maastricht, then gradually was acknowledged as the overarching organization of the European integration process, and has now entirely absorbed the European Community – but without realizing the federalists' dreams, nor Altiero Spinelli's vision of the European Union as a step change towards a more integrated and federal-state-like Europe.

As for the Constitutional Treaty, signed in 2004, it is now defunct, but it is nevertheless worth remembering in the context of this chapter that the adoption of a European Constitution was seen by all the leading actors (and without much controversy) as involving, technically speaking, a *revision* in accordance with the procedure of Article 48 EU Treaty, rather than the creation *ex nihilo* of a new legal edifice: a replacement of the existing treaties that kept in existence the European Union as an organization.

Alternative views had been put forward in the early stages of the constitutional debate. Possibly the most prominent invocation of a federal future for Europe was made by the German minister of foreign affairs Joschka Fischer in his speech at the Humboldt University in Berlin on 12 May 2000. The speech was entitled (in its English translation) *From Confederacy to Federation – Thoughts on the Finality of European Integration*, a title which expressed his wish to see a change in the nature of the European Union. Two things must be noted about this speech:[28] first, Fischer saw this transformation not as an immediate objective, but as a mid-term objective to be pursued by a vanguard of states; and

---

[28] For the original German text of the Fischer speech, translations in English and French, and a series of scholarly comments, see Joerges, Christian, Yves Mény and Joseph H. H. Weiler, eds., *What Kind of Constitution for What Kind of Polity? Responses to Joschka Fischer* (Firenze: EUI Robert Schuman Center for Advanced Studies, San Domenico, 2000); also published as *Jean Monnet Working Paper* no. 7/00. See, in particular, for the point that concerns us here, the contribution by Leben, Charles, 'Fédération d'Etats-nations ou Etat fédéral?' (2000), at 85–97.

second, the choice of words in the German original version shows that Fischer did not seek to transform the European Union into a federal state, but into something unprecedented for which he proposed the novel term *Föderation* (federation) rather than *Bundesstaat* (federal state).

Whatever may have been Fischer's precise intentions in May 2000, the Convention on the Future of the Union, in which he participated, took a different route. On the one hand, the Convention was more ambitious than Fischer in deciding to adopt a Constitutional Treaty straight away (rather than keeping that term for a later stage in the European integration process as he had proposed) but, on the other hand, it did not seek to convey the view that the European Union was being transformed into a legally different entity. The Constitutional Treaty that emerged from the Convention's preparatory work did not describe the European Union as a federation nor as anything else that would denote its ceasing to be an international organization. The absence of a 'leap forward' appeared most visibly in the Constitutional Treaty's entry-into-force provision (Article 447), which confirmed that it had to be ratified by the High Contracting Parties in accordance with their respective constitutional requirements before it could enter into force. In fact, this Article 447 used the coded language typical of the law of international treaties ('ratify', 'enter into force', 'High Contracting Parties') and is perhaps the clearest formal confirmation that the Constitutional Treaty was, in the view of its drafters, a genuine international treaty. There were some other, more subtle, indications, such as the provision of Article 440 which allowed the Member States, like before, to limit the territorial application of EU law and to exclude parts of their territory from its reach: a typical international treaty clause which has no historical parallel in the constitutions of federal states.[29]

Some ambiguity on this point was created by the fact that the 2004 Treaty was said, by its title, to 'establish a Constitution for Europe'.[30] This could suggest the ambition of the governments to effect

[29] I draw this argument from Michel, Valéri and Aude Bouveresse, 'La notion de constitution', in V. Constantinesco, Y. Gautier and V. Michel, eds., *Le Traité établissant une Constitution pour l'Europe. Analyses et commentaires* (Presses Universitaires de Strasbourg, 2005) 31–60 at 47.

[30] Indeed, on the front page of the version of the Treaty printed by the Office for Official Publications of the EC, the words 'Treaty establishing a' appear in very small print, whereas the words 'Constitution for Europe' are in very large print!

a transformation similar to the one accomplished by the 1871 so-called constitutional treaties (*Verfassungsverträge*) between the German states[31] (or perhaps by the Articles of Union of 1706 creating the United Kingdom),[32] namely the creation of a new state by means of an agreement under public international law. The fact that, in 2004, no such great transformation was envisaged becomes clear when looking at the revision clause of the Constitutional Treaty which stated that all important future amendments would, again, have to be made by means of a unanimously ratified amending treaty rather than by a decision of the European Union's organs,[33] as would befit a federal state. The Treaty of Rome (2004) was indeed 'a treaty masquerading as a constitution,'[34] and the Lisbon Treaty, of course, abandons altogether the pretence to create something novel: its Article 1 states that: 'By this Treaty, the HIGH CONTRACTING PARTIES establish among themselves a EUROPEAN UNION [...] on which the Member States confer competences to attain objectives they have in common.'[35] This is a return to the very traditional language of international law.

[31] See Huber, Ernst R., *Deutsche Verfassungsgeschichte seit 1789*, vol. III (Stuttgart: Kohlhammer, 1981), at 735ff. and 788ff. Contrast with the Treaty on German Unity of 31 August 1990, which brought about the accession of one state to another state, rather than the creation of a new one.

[32] It is doubtful, though, whether the Articles of Union were an international treaty; see discussion by Wicks, Elizabeth, 'A New Constitution for a New State? The 1707 Union of England and Scotland', 117 *The Law Quarterly Review* (2001) 109–126.

[33] Both the Constitutional Treaty and the Lisbon Treaty do provide for simplified amendment procedures that allow some parts of the Treaties to be changed by a unanimous decision of the European Council rather than by an international treaty between states, but those are not the essential parts of the Treaty. In particular, no further transfers of competences to the EU can be decided on the basis of those simplified procedures; see Triantafyllou, Dimitris, 'Les procédures d'adoption et de révision du Traité constitutionnel', in G. Amato, H. Bribosia and B. de Witte, eds., *Genesis and Destiny of the European Constitution* (Brussels: Bruylant, 2007), 223–245; de Witte, Bruno, 'La procédure de révision: continuité dans le mode de changement', in C. Kaddous and A. Auer, eds., *Les principes fondamentaux de la Constitution européenne* (Helbing & Lichtenhahn: Bruylant, 2006) 147–161.

[34] Weiler, J. H. H., 'In Defence of the Status Quo: Europe's Constitutional *Sonderweg*', in J. H. H. Weiler and M. Wind, eds., *European Constitutionalism Beyond the State* (Cambridge University Press, 2003), 7–23 at 7, footnote 1.

[35] The capitalized words in the main text are printed in capitals in the version published in the *Official Journal of the European Union* (OJ 2008, C 115/16). The opening words 'by this Treaty' do not refer to the Lisbon Treaty but to the

So, all the European revision treaties so far, including the Constitutional Treaty and the Treaty of Lisbon, were instances of amendments of pre-existing multilateral treaties, the legal regime of which is set out in Articles 39 to 41 of the Vienna Convention on the Law of Treaties. Article 39 contains the very simple 'default rule' that a treaty may be amended by an agreement between (all) the parties, and that the normal rules on the conclusion of treaties apply to this amending agreement. This default rule may be set aside by the parties when concluding the original (to-be-amended) treaty.[36] The international law regime of treaty amendment is, thus, one of utmost flexibility: the contracting parties are free to arrange for the later amendment of their treaty in the way they wish.[37] Indeed, a large and increasing number of multilateral treaties contain such a special amendment procedure, which is generally aimed at facilitating adaptation to changing circumstances, often by allowing for the amendment of a treaty without the agreement of all the parties. Article 48 EU Treaty, the currently applicable amendment provision, is an example of a specific amendment clause but, contrary to most others, it does *not* provide more flexibility than the default rule of Article 39 Vienna Convention. It requires the agreement of *all* the parties (in this case, the Member States of the EU) for the valid adoption of an amendment and, *in addition*, it requires a degree of involvement of the EU institutions and (in almost all cases) the separate approval by each state according to its own constitutional requirements.[38]

> Maastricht Treaty by which the European Union was originally established in 1992. The last part of the sentence (starting with 'on which . . .') was added by the Lisbon Treaty and reinforces the international law connotations of the new opening article of the EU Treaty.
>
> [36] Article 39 is entitled *General rule regarding the amendment of treaties* and it runs as follows: 'A treaty may be amended by agreement between the parties. The rules laid down in Part II apply to such an agreement except in so far as the treaty may otherwise provide.' (Part II of the Vienna Convention sets out the rules on conclusion and entry into force of treaties.)
>
> [37] See Aust, Anthony, *Modern Treaty Law and Practice* (Cambridge University Press, 2000), at 214: 'It is wrong to think that the Vienna Convention is a rigid structure which places obstacles in the way of treaty modification: rather, it allows states to include in treaties such amendment provisions as they wish.'
>
> [38] The pre-Lisbon treaty amendment procedure was to be found in Article 48 of the then EU Treaty, whereas the new post-Lisbon treaty amendment procedure is, again and by coincidence, to be found in Article 48, despite the fact that almost all other provisions of the EU Treaty were renumbered as a consequence of the Lisbon Treaty. As mentioned before (see note 33 above), the new Article 48 contains two new so-called 'simplified procedures', but despite this, treaty revision remains very rigid also after Lisbon.

The European Union's basic rule of change is more rigid than the general international law rule also in another way, which is not visible from the text. In general international law, the contracting parties to a treaty can modify that treaty at any stage by means of a new treaty. In doing so, they are not bound to follow the same procedure as that followed when they concluded the first treaty, nor are they even bound to follow the procedure for revision set out in the first treaty if they all agree to follow a different procedure than the one provided for.[39] In EU law, by contrast, the Member States do not have this freedom of form; rather, they are bound to follow the rules for treaty revision as formulated in Article 48 EU Treaty. The ECJ affirmed this duty, a long time ago, in the *Defrenne* case, and the states' practice in the decades since *Defrenne* seems to show that they, indeed, accept the mandatory character of the treaty revision procedures.[40] The fact that the procedure of Article 48 EU Treaty must be followed by the Member States is perfectly in line with the Vienna Convention: this is indeed the amendment procedure which the Member States committed themselves to, and as long as they do not unanimously agree to disregard it (which they don't) it remains mandatory. It is also worth noting that this procedure does not in any way affect the discretion of the Member States regarding the *substance* of the amendments. There was a short-lived discussion, in the early 1990s, as to whether there were so-called 'substantive limits' to the kinds of changes which Member States could make to the existing treaties. Authors who defended the view that there was an untouchable core of Community law that the Member States were not allowed to modify[41] relied on an enigmatic statement of the ECJ in Opinion 1/91 on the European Economic Area, but in my

---

[39] See Karl, Wolfram, *Vertrag und spätere Praxis im Völkerrecht* (Berlin: Springer Verlag, 1983), at 341ff., and de Witte, Bruno, 'Rules of Change in International Law: How Special is the European Community?', 25 *Netherlands Yearbook of International Law* (1994) 299–333 at 312ff.

[40] At least, they accept that Article 48 is mandatory as a minimum requirement, but without impeding the use of additional procedural steps, such as a Convention of the type that was held in 2002–3 and which was not envisaged by Article 48 in its pre-Lisbon version.

[41] da Cruz Vilaça, José Luis and Nuno Piçarra, 'Y a-t-il des limites matérielles à la révision des traités instituant les CE?', 29 *Cahiers de droit européen* 1–2 (1993) 3–37; Bieber, Roland, 'Les limites matérielles et formelles à la révision des traités établissant la Communauté européenne', *Revue du Marché commun et de l'Union européenne* (1993) 343–350.

opinion there is no evidence that the Member States ever accepted any such substantive limits to their treaty-amending power. They act, to use a famous German expression, as the *Herren der Verträge*, bound by nothing else than their respective national constitutional rules and by the rules of international treaty law; they act as 'independent and sovereign states having freely decided [...] to exercise in common some of their competences'.[42] The existing principles of the *acquis communautaire* are, however, effectively protected by the common accord rule, which implies that all states must agree before they can turn back some of the integrative steps made on earlier treaty-making occasions. The fact that the Member State governments act as 'Masters of the Treaty text' does not mean that they also control what happens with the treaties once they enter into force. The dynamic evolution of EU law in between treaty revisions partly escapes from their control and they can correct unwanted evolutions only on the occasion of a further treaty revision and on the unlikely condition that they find a consensus to correct, say, a particular interpretation of the treaty text adopted by the Court of Justice.

European Union treaty revisions are thus firmly situated within the scope of the international law of treaties. This would seem to lead to the logical conclusion that the European Community, first, and the European Union, now, remain creatures of international law, and therefore continue to belong to the legal category of international organizations. The European Treaties do not use express language confirming this, but it might be noted that the EU Member States have accepted this qualification in the broader international arena. Indeed, there are many multilateral treaty provisions that use the terms 'international organization' or 'regional international economic organization' (REIO) where it is clear from the context that the (only) organization that is intended by that term is the European Community.[43] The EU Member

---

[42] This phrase was used by the Member State governments in the introductory part of the Decision on Denmark, adopted at the Edinburgh summit of 12 December 1992, but it referred back to their earlier adoption of the Treaty on European Union (Treaty of Maastricht).

[43] See, among many other examples, the Energy Charter Treaty (1991), Article 1(2) and 1(3); the Convention on Biological Diversity (1992), Article 35; the UN Framework Convention on Climate Change (1992), Article 20; the UNESCO Convention on the protection and promotion of the diversity of cultural expressions (2005), Article 27. See, on the practice of these 'REIO' references, Paasivirta, Esa and Piet Jan Kuijper, 'Does One Size Fit All? The European

States participate in drawing up those multilateral international conventions and could therefore object to the qualification of the EC or the
EU as international organizations, but they do not.

1.4 The international legal nature of the European Union (II): judicial and doctrinal interpretations

Although the view that the European Union is, and remains, a creature
of international law may seem logical in view of the preceding pages, it
is in fact heavily contested. This contestation has been encouraged by
some rulings of the European Court of Justice and developed by a large
part of legal writing. It is today a commonly held view in the EU law
literature that 'even if the EEC did conform to the status of international
organization in its early days (which is unlikely) it has now moved well
beyond that'.[44] The European Community proved to be so peculiar that
many Community lawyers started to argue, from a very early stage, that
it was not an international organization at all, but 'something else', a *sui
generis* legal order that does not fit in the traditional dichotomy between
(federal) states and international organizations, and that to continue to
refer to it as an international organization is 'to try to push the tooth-
paste back in the tube'.[45] However, this view was not shared by all EU
legal writers, and it was contested or ignored by public international
lawyers who continued to include the European Community, and *a
fortiori* the European Union, within the category of international organization. They take the view that 'no matter how *sui generis* the
European Community might be, it is often considered as the most highly
developed specimen of the species, and as a model for other international organizations to emulate'.[46] The contrast between these two

Community and the Responsibility of International Organizations', 36
Netherlands Yearbook of International Law (2005) 169–226 at 206ff.

[44] Douglas-Scott, Sionaidh, *Constitutional Law of the European Union* (London:
Longman, 2002), at 260. Many similar quotations could be added to this one.

[45] Weiler, J. H. H. and Ulrich R. Haltern, 'Constitutional or International? The
Foundations of the Community Legal Order and the Question of Judicial
Kompetenz-Kompetenz', in Anne-Marie Slaughter, Alec Stone Sweet and Joseph
H. H. Weiler, eds., *The European Courts and National Courts – Doctrine and
Jurisprudence* (Oxford: Hart Publishing, 1998) 331–364, at 342.

[46] Klabbers, Jan, 'The Changing Image of International Organizations', in J. M.
Coicaud and V. Heiskanen, eds., *The Legitimacy of International Organizations*
(Tokyo: United Nations University Press, 2001), 221–255 at 224. Again, many
similar quotations from international legal writing could be added.

scholarly accounts (that of EU law and that of international law) on the question of legal qualification is quite remarkable, and it is even more remarkable that very few authors, on either side, have much time for trying to explain and justify their positions. In fact, the most elaborate arguments are those presented by some public international law academics who contest the separation of EU law from international law.[47] On the other side of the barrier, EU law scholarship affirming the non-international legal nature of EC law (or EU law) has mainly relied on the authority of the European Court of Justice. So, let us start by looking at what the ECJ has held on this question; not that much, in matter of fact.

1.4.1 *Judicial interpretations*

Somewhat surprisingly, perhaps, it appears that the European Court of Justice has never formulated a strong objection against viewing the EC or the EU as international organizations. It is true that the ECJ has repeatedly stated that 'the EEC Treaty has created its own legal system',[48] or similar language, but it did *not* add that this legal system was situated outside the scope of international law. In its famous early judgments *Van Gend & Loos* and *Costa*, the European Court sought to differentiate the EEC Treaty from 'other' or 'ordinary' international treaties, but that otherness was not expressly held to mean that the EEC Treaty had created something else than an international organization.[49] Much has been made of the fact that the ECJ held, in its *Van Gend en*

---

[47] A very elaborate (and quite compelling) argument in favour of the international law thesis was presented by Pellet, Alain, 'Les fondements juridiques internationaux du droit communautaire', in *Collected Courses of the Academy of European Law*, vol. 5, book 2 (The Hague: Kluwer 1994), 193–271; and also, more briefly, by Dupuy, Pierre-Marie, 'L'unité de l'ordre juridique international' 297 *Hague Recueil* (2003), 438–450. See also Marschik, Axel, *Subsysteme im Völkerrecht. Ist die Europäische Union ein 'Self-Contained Regime'?* (Berlin: Duncker & Humblot, 1997), at 193–305.

[48] For example, in ECJ, Cases C-6/90 and C-9/90, *Francovich and Others* v. *Italian State*, (1991) ECR I-5357, para. 31.

[49] See however the Opinion of Advocate General Poiares Maduro in the recent *Kadi* case who states that the ECJ, in *Van Gend en Loos*, had considered the EEC Treaty to form a new legal order which was 'beholden to, but distinct from the existing legal order of public international law' (Opinion of 23 January 2008 in Joined Cases C-402/05 P and C-415/05 P, *Kadi and Al Barakaat* v. *Council*, para. 21). The ECJ, in fact, did not quite use those words in its 1963 judgment nor later, and, as I argue in this chapter, had good reasons to not do so.

Loos judgment of 1963, that the EEC Treaty had created 'a new legal order of international law', whereas it dropped the last three words one year later in *Costa* v. *ENEL* when it simply spoke of 'a new legal order'. This has been interpreted as a deliberate tearing of EC law from its international legal moorings. Yet, as we know, the way in which the Court described the peculiar nature of the EEC Treaty was very similar in both these early judgments, so it would be very odd if that description had led, in 1963, to the conclusion that this was a special legal order still of international law, and only one year later to the opposite conclusion that it was a special legal order no longer of international law.

It is striking that, in the many intervening years since *Costa*, the European Court of Justice never felt inclined to develop a sustained doctrine upholding the specific *and* non-international nature of the European Community. The Court has often emphasized the autonomous nature of the Community legal order, but never stated with so many words that this autonomous legal order had ceased to be part of international law. In fact, there was no need for the Court to adopt the premise that the Community was 'something other' than an international organization in order to affirm the peculiar characteristics of EC law. A famous example of this peculiarity is the Court's early affirmation that the general international rule allowing states to retaliate in the event of non-compliance by other parties to the same treaty (*inadimplenti non est adimplendum*) did not apply in the context of EC law. This innovative characteristic was deduced by the Court from a specific feature of the EEC Treaty itself, namely the power of the independent Commission to bring infringement actions against non-complying states.[50] There is, thus, a specific system of state responsibility in EC

---

[50] ECJ, Joined Cases 90/63 and 91/63, *Commission* v. *Luxembourg and Belgium*, (1964) ECR – special English edition, 625: 'the (EEC) Treaty is not limited to creating reciprocal obligations between the different natural and legal persons to whom it is applicable, but establishes a new legal order which governs the powers, rights and obligations of the said persons, *as well as the necessary procedures for taking cognizance of and penalizing any breach of it*. Therefore [...] *the basic concept of the Treaty requires that the Member States shall not take the law in their own hands*' (emphasis added). The significance of the last sentence is perhaps clearer in the original French version of the judgment: '*l'économie du traité comporte interdiction pour les Etats membres de se faire justice eux-mêmes.*' The same principle was repeated by the Court many times after 1964; for a recent example: ECJ, Case C-111/03, *Commission* v. *Sweden*, judgment of 20 October 2005, para. 66. See Dero, Delphine, *La réciprocité et le droit des Communautés et de l'Union européennes* (Brussels: Bruylant, 2006), at 23ff.

law which does not allow states to adopt counter-measures for violation of EC obligations by the other parties, which logically follows from choices made by the states themselves when they created the EEC and in particular from their decision to vest the Commission with an independent power to take incompliant Member States to court. There is some dispute in the literature, though, on whether this system is entirely self-contained or whether recourse to the general international rules of state responsibility could be permissible if the EU judicial system were totally ineffective in a given situation.[51]

In its recent *Kadi* judgment, the ECJ once again insisted heavily on the autonomy of the Community legal system,[52] but again without stating its extraneousness to international law; it discussed what it called 'the relationship between the international legal order under the United Nations and the Community legal order',[53] and although this formula might suggest that the Community legal order is not one of international law, it does not actually say this, and the outcome of the case did not depend on the legal qualification of the EC.[54] There may, in fact, be a very good reason for the ECJ to be cautious in this matter of legal qualification: it was not only the guardian of the integrity of the *Community* legal order, but also, though in a much more limited way, of the integrity of the European *Union* legal order and of the links between the Community and Union legal orders. Most of the arguments

---

[51] Defending a residual role in EC law for the general rules of state responsibility: Simma, Bruno and Dirk Pulkowski, 'Of Planets and the Universe: Self-Contained Regimes in International Law', 17 *European Journal of International Law* 3 (2006) 483–529 at 516–519. For a detailed argument that even if one assumes that the EC enforcement system is entirely self-sufficient, this is still compatible with the general rules of international responsibility, see Gradoni, Lorenzo and Attila Tanzi, 'Diritto comunitario: una *lex specialis* molto speciale', in L. S. Rossi and G. Di Federico, eds., *L'incidenza del diritto dell'Unione europea sullo studio delle discipline giuridiche* (Napoli: Editoriale Scientifica, 2008) 37–70.

[52] Holding that 'an international agreement cannot affect the allocation of powers fixed by the Treaties or, consequently, the autonomy of the Community legal system' (ECJ, Judgment of 3 September 2008 in Joined Cases C-402/05 P and C-415/05 P, *Kadi and Al Barakaat* v. *Council*, para. 282). Similar language is used in para. 316.

[53] Ibid., para. 290.

[54] See Griller, Stefan, 'International Law, Human Rights and the European Community's Autonomous Legal Order: Notes on the European Court of Justice Decision in *Kadi*', 4 *European Constitutional Law Review* (2008) 528–553 at 550.

that might be used for demonstrating that the Community legal order has ceased to be international law would not apply to EU law in the second and third pillar, so that the European Union would end up with one of its legal systems inside, and another one outside, the bounds of international law, despite the fact that those two legal systems were very closely connected through the common and final provisions of the EU Treaty. It was much safer then not to make any strong statements about the legal nature of the European Community.

The wisely agnostic attitude of the ECJ on the question of the nature of EU law also protects it from entering into a doctrinal controversy with national constitutional courts on this matter. The qualification of the EU (or previously the EC) as international organizations is, indeed, upheld in the constitutional law of most Member States. Today, some countries have specific clauses in their constitutions to deal with the transfer of powers to the European Union (which were either introduced by 'old' members at the time of the Maastricht Treaty or by 'new' members at the time they acceded to the EU), but many countries continue to adopt a generic approach of allowing for transfers of powers, or limitations of sovereignty, for the benefit of *international organizations* or *international institutions* generally speaking.[55] So, even today, after more than fifty years of European integration, there is only a limited amount of specificity of the European Union in national constitutional texts, and it is quite clear that, from the point of view of national constitutions, generic references to international organizations include the EU. The new Member States of Central Europe have been as conservative (or cautious) in adapting their constitutions to EU membership as the old Member States.[56] Therefore, the prevalent view, from the perspective of national constitutional law, seems to be that the EU is indeed a creature of international law and therefore an international organization, and that state sovereignty has not been

---

[55] See Claes, Monica, 'Constitutionalising Europe at its Source: The "European Clauses" in the National Constitutions: Evolution and Typology', 24 *Yearbook of European Law* (2005) 81; Louis, Jean-Victor and Thierry Ronse, *L'ordre juridique de l'Union européenne* (Paris: LGDJ, 2005), 334–346.

[56] For example: Article 3a of the Constitution of Slovenia, Article 68 of the Constitution of Latvia. For a comparative analysis of the new Member States, see Albi, Anneli, *EU Enlargement and the Constitutions of Central and Eastern Europe* (Cambridge University Press, 2005).

abandoned or transferred but rather is being 'exercised in common' within the framework of the EU.[57]

A contrasting view was put forward rather recently by the French *Conseil constitutionnel*. In a number of decisions starting in 2004 (including its decision dealing with the Constitutional Treaty), it stated that the French Constitution recognizes '*l'existence d'un ordre juridique communautaire intégré à l'ordre juridique interne et distinct de l'ordre juridique international*'.[58] Thus, for the French Constitutional Court, Community law was no longer part of international law, but, in its usual laconic fashion, it did not give any arguments for this view which contrasts with earlier views of the highest French courts and, indeed, with the *Conseil's* own characterization of the Constitutional Treaty as (just) an international treaty.[59] Moreover, the statement referred to the 'Community legal order' and it is not clear where that left the non-Community elements of the European Union legal order.

1.4.2 *Doctrinal interpretations*

If we now turn to *legal writing*, what are the main arguments used to affirm the *sui generis* nature of EU law apart from the simple reference to ECJ statements which, as we have seen, do not actually deny the international law nature of EU law? We have briefly discussed, above, the argument taken from the self-contained nature of the EU's system of dispute settlement and compliance; this is an important feature of the *autonomy* of the EU legal order but does not put it in *contrast* with the general rules of international law. The other main specific argument, to be discussed below, is taken from the principles of direct effect and

---

[57] The idea that European integration is nothing but the common exercise of sovereign powers of the nations is clearly expressed in Article 88-1 of the French Constitution and Article 34 of the Belgian Constitution. Despite its old-fashioned and artificial flavour, it continues to command widespread support among constitutional authors in many countries, not least those of the new Member States. See also the passage from the Decision on Denmark cited in the text at note 42 above.

[58] *Conseil constitutionnel*, Décision no. 2004–505 DC of 19 November 2004, *Traité établissant une Constitution pour l'Europe*, para. 11.

[59] The Constitutional Treaty '*conserve le caractère d'un traité international souscrit par les Etats signataires du traité instituant la Communauté européenne et du traité sur l'Union européenne.*' (ibid., para. 9).

primacy of EC law that were affirmed in the early 1960s and further developed by the ECJ later on.

Primacy is inherent in international law, though not in the sense given to the concept in *Costa* and subsequent judgments of the ECJ. Already in 1930, the Permanent Court of International Justice held that it was 'a generally accepted principle of international law that in the relations between powers who are contracting parties to a treaty, the provisions of municipal law cannot prevail over those of the treaty'.[60] This statement is, in fact, limited to the 'relations between powers' on the international plane; it does not apply to the *internal* workings of the national legal systems, in respect of which international law does not seem to claim a priority of treaty norms over conflicting national norms. Indeed, the received view among international law scholars is the following:

From the standpoint of international law states are generally free as to the manner in which, domestically, they put themselves in the position to meet their international obligations; the choice between the direct reception and application of international law, or its transformation into national law by way of statute, is a matter of indifference [. . .]. These are matters for each state to determine for itself according to its own constitutional practice.[61]

One finds this view repeated, without much discussion, in all international law textbooks. The European Court of Justice also mentioned this view in a judgment from 1999, but added an interesting qualification to it:

according to the general rules of international law there must be *bona fide* performance of every agreement. Although each contracting party is responsible for executing fully the commitments which it has undertaken it is nevertheless free to determine the legal means appropriate for attaining that end in its legal system, unless the agreement, interpreted in the light of its subject-matter and purpose, itself specifies those means.[62]

The EC Treaty was an agreement of the kind referred to in the sentence above. Its *wording* did not specify the means by which the Member

---

[60] Permanent Court of International Justice, *Greek and Bulgarian Communities*, PCIJ, Series B, No.17, p. 32.
[61] Jennings, Robert Y. and Arthur Watts, eds., *Oppenheim's International Law*, vol. I (9th edn, London: Longman, 1992) at 82–83.
[62] ECJ, Case C-149/96, *Portugal* v. *Council*, judgment of 23 November 1999, para. 35. Of course, the agreement to which the ECJ refers in this extract is not the EC Treaty or EU Treaty but an external agreement concluded by the EC.

States must comply with their commitments (except for the fact, recorded in what is now Article 267 TFEU (Treaty on the Functioning of the EU), that they must allow their courts to refer preliminary questions to the ECJ on the interpretation of EC law), but, interpreting the Treaty in the light of its *subject-matter* and *purpose*, the ECJ came to the conclusion that some of its provisions should have direct effect in the domestic legal system (*Van Gend en Loos* and its progeny) and that all those norms that have direct effect should also have primacy over conflicting national law (*Costa* and its progeny).

The principle that Community law prevails, or should prevail, over national law even in front of national courts was reminiscent of the supremacy of federal law over national law, which is entrenched in the constitutions of prominent federal states such as the USA and Germany. It is not surprising, therefore, to find many and also early examples, in the EC law literature, of a federal reading of the primacy of Community law. Very shortly after the foundational judgments *Van Gend en Loos* and *Costa*, in which the European Court of Justice formulated the doctrines of direct effect and primacy, Peter Hay devoted a chapter of his work on *Federalism and Supranational Organizations* (1966) to what he termed the 'Federal Relation of Community Law to National Law'. In 1986, Jacobs and Karst wrote, in their contribution to the Florence project *Integration through Law*, that 'although the Community judicial structure departs from the federal model, the result in terms of primacy is the federal result: *Bundesrecht bricht Landesrecht*'.[63] In 1991, Joseph Weiler wrote, in his 'Transformation of Europe', that the doctrines of direct effect and primacy rendered the relationship between Community law and national law 'indistinguishable from analogous relationships in constitutions of federal states'.[64] A few years later, Jo Shaw wrote, in her European law textbook, that 'the organisation of the relationship between EC law and national law [...]

[63] Hay, Peter, *Federalism and Supranational Organizations: Patterns for New Legal Structures* (University of Illinois Press, 1966); Jacobs, Francis and Kenneth Karst, 'The "Federal" Legal Order: The U.S.A. and Europe Compared – A Juridical Perspective', in M. Cappelletti, M. Seccombe and J. Weiler, eds., *Integration Through Law – Europe and the American Federal Experience*, vol. 1, book 1 (The Hague: de Gruyter, 1986), 169–243 at 234.

[64] Weiler, J. H. H., 'The Transformation of Europe', 100 *Yale Law Journal* (1991) 2403–2484 at 2413.

demonstrates the hallmarks of a federal system'.[65] These are just a few examples, at different points in time, from the English-language literature. Many more examples could be given of writers finding a close analogy between the way in which Community law is judicially enforceable within its Member States, and the way in which federal states guarantee the supremacy of federal over Member State law.

On a closer look, though, the primacy of EU law is quite different from federal supremacy as we know it in the USA and Germany. In both those countries, as well as in other federal states such as Canada or Switzerland, the supremacy of federal law is effectively guaranteed by the fact that its enforcement is largely in the hands of federal courts. In Germany, there are both federal and Member State courts, but they all apply federal and *Länder* law interchangeably. The courts of final instance, in all subject areas, are federal courts, which can therefore impose the supremacy rule where needed. Similarly, in Canada, the Supreme Court is the court of last instance for all cases decided by both federal and provincial courts, and can therefore correct any failure of provincial courts to recognize the 'paramountcy principle', the Canadian version of supremacy. In the United States, judgments of state courts which fail to enforce federal law when necessary are subject to appellate review by the Supreme Court. The scope of this principle has, however, been narrowed by the Supreme Court judgments recognizing the sovereign right of states to exclude the judicial enforcement of federal law against themselves.[66]

In the EU legal order, the inconsistency of a national norm with a Community norm can be directly examined by the European Court of Justice only in the framework of an infringement action brought by the Commission under Article 258 EC, where the European Court can make Union law prevail as a matter of course, just like any international court will give precedence to international law over the domestic laws of the states parties to a dispute. Usually, however, inconsistencies between national law and EU law will come to light through litigation before Member State courts and will have to be solved by them, possibly, but

[65] Shaw, Jo, *Law of the European Union* (2nd edn, Basingstoke: Palgrave, 1996), at 76.

[66] On the latter point see, from a comparative law perspective: Halberstam, Daniel, 'Comparative Federalism and the Issue of Commandeering', in Kalypso Nicolaidis and Robert Howse, eds., *The Federal Vision: Legitimacy and Levels of Governance in the US and the EU* (Oxford University Press, 2001) 213–251.

only possibly, with the preliminary guidance of the Court of Justice. In contrast with all federal states, there is no right of appeal to the Court of Justice against judgments of national courts which fail to recognize the primacy of European law. Therefore, it is crucially important that the national courts should faithfully absorb and apply the primacy doctrine laid down by the Court of Justice, a fact that explains the insistence of that court, and of legal commentators, on the 'essential' character of primacy. Promoting the acceptance of the primacy *doctrine* is essential, because its effective *application* is left in the hands of the Member State courts.

This institutional factor has important substantive consequences. The national courts conceive of themselves as organs of their state, and try to fit their 'European mandate' within the framework of the powers attributed to them by their national legal system. For those courts and, indeed, for most constitutional law scholars throughout Europe, the authority of EU law is rooted in their constitution, and subject to restrictions that may be imposed by the constitution.[67] If the constitution is seen as the basis for recognizing the primacy of Union law, then absolute primacy of the type postulated by the European Court is only possible by way of a 'self-limitation' clause in the constitution. There are, in fact, only a few of the Member States of the EU that have taken that step, the vast majority having firmly put their constitution at the apex of the legal pyramid. Even in those few countries, such as the Netherlands and Estonia, the possibility remains that the constitution could, in the future, be amended so as to undo the recognition of the absolute supremacy of EU law. This situation is in stark contrast with the position prevailing in federal states. All federal systems are predicated on the primacy of the federal constitution. The binding nature of the constitutional division of competences between the federal and Member State government rests on the judicially uncontested authority of the federal constitution.[68] Indeed, Belgium can dispense altogether

---

[67] For the evidence backing this statement, see the various 'national reports' in Slaughter, Anne-Marie, Alec Stone Sweet and Joseph H. H. Weiler, eds., *The European Courts and National Courts – Doctrine and Jurisprudence* (Oxford: Hart Publishing, 1998); and the comparative analysis in Claes, Monica, *The National Courts' Mandate in the European Constitution* (Oxford: Hart Publishing, 2006).

[68] This is not to deny that there may be serious *political* contestation of the authority of the federal constitution in some parts of the country, as is the case in Canada and Belgium.

with a 'technical' supremacy rule only because the authority of the federal constitution, and of the Constitutional Court that is its supreme interpreter, is accepted by the political authorities and the judiciary. In Canada, Germany and the United States, the supremacy rule plays a much less prominent role in legal debates precisely because the hierarchical primacy of the constitution is firmly established. In the EU legal order, on the contrary, the hierarchical relationship between EU law and national law needs to be more heavily emphasized by the European Court and its supporters because the ultimate hierarchy of norms is not settled in favour of EU law.

A final element that contributed to set the question of EC law primacy apart from the experience of federal states was that the European Community, and its law, could no longer be considered in isolation from the broader structure in which they were incorporated by the Treaty of Maastricht. The Treaty of Maastricht, and more clearly still the Treaty of Amsterdam, conveyed the idea of one overarching organization, the European Union, which had a single institutional framework and formed a single political reality, within which the European Community was incorporated.[69] The primacy of Community law had, therefore, become a typical characteristic of one part (albeit the most important part) of the EU edifice, and the light federal colour that primacy gave to the EC legal order was diluted by the incorporation of the EC into this wider, and more traditionally intergovernmental, organization. In the *Costa* v. *ENEL* judgment, it may be recalled, the European Court had heavily insisted on the special characteristics of the EEC Treaty in order to conclude on its necessary primacy within the national legal orders. The second and third pillar parts of the EU Treaty did not share many of these special supranational characteristics of the EC Treaty, so that one could doubt whether its primacy over national law should be recognized to the same extent. With the entry into force of the Lisbon Treaty, EC law became entirely absorbed by EU law, but there is still the special area of CFSP law (the former second pillar), where the Court of Justice will not be able to give preliminary rulings, and will therefore hardly be able to pronounce itself on questions of direct effect and supremacy. The Declaration on Primacy, which is

---

[69] Curtin, Deirdre and Ige Dekker, 'The EU as a "Layered" International Organization: Institutional Unity in Disguise', in P. Craig and G. de Búrca, eds., *The Evolution of EU Law* (Oxford University Press, 1999), 83–136.

attached to the Lisbon Treaty, does not clarify this point either, since it just refers to the existing case-law of the ECJ.[70]

On the basis of the preceding reflections, I doubt whether primacy is really a feature of EU law that tears it away from international law. The doctrine of primacy, as presently formulated by the ECJ and accepted by the Member State courts, has, no doubt, a distinct federal flavour but it can also, and perhaps more realistically, be described as a creative development of international law. The central rule of international treaty law is *pacta sunt servanda*. States are bound by their treaty obligations, and whenever a conflict between a treaty obligation and a norm of national law is brought before the International Court of Justice, or any other international court, the answer is clear: the treaty rule will prevail. The originality of the EEC Treaty was to grant to the newly established Court, the ECJ, a jurisdictional competence which was unique in the panorama of international law, namely that of guiding the activity of national courts while they are applying EC law, by means of the preliminary rulings procedure. The ECJ has cleverly used this procedural mechanism, which was meant to be used for the interpretation of the *substantive meaning* of EC law norms, to clarify also the *formal status* of EC law within the national legal system, through its doctrines of primacy and direct effect. This combination of a jurisdictional innovation at the time the Treaty of Rome was drafted, and a creative and courageous attitude of the European Court judges in the early 1960s, allowed for the emergence of the doctrine of primacy which, though unprecedented, was not, and is not, incompatible with the nature of international law.[71] Seen from this angle, the primacy doctrine does not so much signal a shift away from international law; it rather illustrates the dynamic potential of international law. The fact that, as a general rule, international law leaves to states a choice among various methods of domestic enforcement of international obligations

---

[70] Declaration (nr 17) concerning primacy, attached to the Final Act of the Treaty of Lisbon, *OJ 2008, C 115/344*:

The Conference recalls that, in accordance with well settled case law of the Court of Justice of the European Union, the Treaties and the law adopted by the Union on the basis of the Treaties have primacy over the law of Member States, under the conditions laid down by the said case law [. . .].

[71] The importance of the preliminary rulings procedure in allowing for the emergence of the primacy doctrine was emphasized by Wyatt, Derrick, 'New Legal Order, or Old?', 7 *European Law Review* (1982) 147–166.

does not prevent specific treaties or international decisions from imposing specific requirements in this respect. The EC Treaty was such a
treaty. Due to its substantive content, but also, and above all, to the
preliminary rulings mechanism, the affirmation of the domestic primacy
of EC law was logically inscribed in the Treaty, although it took some
resolve from the ECJ to spell it out in *Costa* v. *ENEL*.

The EU Treaty may no longer be the only treaty of its kind. Given
appropriate circumstances, primacy within the domestic legal orders
may be inscribed in other international treaties as well. For example, the
European Court of Justice has held that national courts must give
priority, in the case of a conflict with national law, to the Brussels
Convention on the recognition and enforcement of judgments,[72]
which was, formally speaking, a separate agreement from the EC
Treaty, although it was concluded among the same states. It can,
furthermore, be argued that the Agreement on the European
Economic Area should also be considered as a treaty requiring primacy
in the domestic legal systems of its contracting parties.[73] The potential
domestic impact of international law can, finally, also be illustrated
by an entirely different, but quite radical, claim of supremacy. The
UN (United Nations) Interim Administration in Kosovo (UNMIK)
which was set up by Security Council Resolution 1244, was given the
power to adopt laws and regulations vested with direct effect and
primacy over conflicting local (Serbian) laws. Thus, the separation
between the international and municipal legal order entirely collapsed
in Kosovo, in a manner far more radical than anything experienced by
EU Member States under Community law.[74]

---

[72] ECJ, Case 288/82, *Duijnstee*, [1983] ECR 3663, para. 14. The Convention has
since then been replaced by an EC Regulation, so that the question of the
Convention's primacy over national law is now moot.

[73] Sevón, Leif and M. Johansson, 'The Protection of the Rights of Individuals under
the EEA Agreement', *European Law Review* 4 (1999) 373–386: The EEA
(European Economic Area) Agreement (like the EC Treaty) does not expressly
require the states parties to adopt the supremacy rule, but the elements on which
the ECJ based its supremacy doctrine in *Costa* v. *ENEL* would seem to be equally
present in the EEA Agreement (at p. 382).

[74] See, among others, Knoll, Bernhard, *The Legal Status of Territories Subject to
Administration by International Organisations* (Cambridge University Press,
2008), who refers to the 'unmediated import of international law' (at p. 329) and
the 'collapse of dualism' (at p. 335).

After this lengthy discussion of the implications of the ECJ's primacy doctrine for the understanding of the legal nature of the European Union, let us now move to what is probably the most convincing argument for the view that the EU has ceased to be an international organization, That argument is not based on *particular* characteristics of the EU (such as primacy or the self-contained compliance mechanism) but rather on the combination of a number of peculiarities: the broad and flexible nature of EU competences which extend into all areas of law-making; the existence of a (partially) common currency and a common (though derivative) citizenship; the fact that the Member States have accepted the need to abandon their power to conclude treaties in the areas that are now within the EU's exclusive competence;[75] the decision-making regime, marked by the involvement of institutions not controlled by the Member State governments and by recourse to majority voting in the state-controlled Council of Ministers; the relatively effective mechanism of state compliance; the habit of obedience by national courts to their duty to apply EU law. None of these characteristics is an inconceivable development of the law of international organizations. But their combination is indeed unique and makes it seem somewhat odd or artificial[76] to discuss the European Union as an example of an international organization.

Whilst accepting this view, I would argue that the way in which one should address the oddity of the EU is not by denying its international legal character, but by trying to find a more specific concept that describes an organization such as the EU in positive terms (beyond the lame *sui generis* description). The term *supranational organization* served that purpose for many years, but it has now fallen into disuse, partly because of its now unfashionable hierarchical overtones, and partly because it failed to reflect the mode of integration that prevailed in the second and third pillars of the EU. The term *confederation* is

---

[75] This is perhaps the characteristic that is most unusual from the point of view of general international law; see discussion in de Witte, Bruno, 'The Emergence of a European System of Public International Law: The EU and its Member States as Strange Subjects', in J. Wouters, A. Nollkaemper and E. de Wet, eds., *The Europeanisation of International Law* (The Hague: TMC Asser Press, 2008) 39–54.

[76] Weiler and Haltern, 'Constitutional or International?' (1998), for whom 'it has [...] become increasingly artificial to describe the legal structures and processes of the Community with the vocabulary of international law'.

occasionally proposed, but it bears the stigma of weakness and instability which derives from the historical examples of confederations, and
is therefore definitely unpopular as a denomination for the European
Union.[77]

Alternative terminology should, in order to be attractive *and* true to
reality, encapsulate both the international legal nature of the EU and its
uniquely massive pooling of Member State powers and constitutional
mode of operation. No such alternative terminology has obtained
Europe-wide currency so far, but influential descriptions in this vein
have been proposed in Germany (the *Staatenverbund*) and in France
(the *fédération d'Etats-nations*). The latter is a rather paradoxical
denomination which is particularly popular among French authors.[78]
It translates badly in many other languages, if only because the definition of the EU Member States as 'nation-states' is contested in the
domestic arena of countries such as Spain, Belgium or the UK. If one
simplifies the concept to 'federation of states' (leaving aside the
'nation'), one comes close to the German *Staatenverbund*. This term
was coined by Paul Kirchhof,[79] and adopted in the Constitutional
Court judgment (the *Maastricht Urteil*) which he drafted in 1993, as a

---

[77] On the 'stigma of confederation', see Burgess, *Federalism* (2000) at 259–260.
Nevertheless, Burgess proposes to rehabilitate and revitalize the old concept as an
adequate description of the EU (at pp. 265–269).

[78] Among the French authors who have discussed or promoted the use of this
concept in connection with the EU are: Zoller, Elizabeth, 'Aspects
internationaux du droit constitutionnel. Contribution à la théorie de la
fédération d'Etats', 294 *Hague Recueil* (2002) 39–166; Leben, 'Fédération',
(2000); Constantinesco, Vlad, 'Europe fédérale ou fédération d'Etats-nations',
in R. Dehousse, ed., *Une constitution pour l'Europe*? (Paris: Presses de Sciences
Po, 2002) 115–149; Jacqué, Jean-Paul, 'Le projet de traité établissant une
constitution pour l'Europe – Constitutionnalisation ou révision des traités', in
P. Demaret, I. Govaere and D. Hanf, eds., *European Legal Dynamics* (Brussels:
Peter Lang, 2007) 41–52 at 51: 'une fédération à caractère non-étatique'.
Jean-Claude Piris proposes the expression 'partially federal Union': Piris,
Jean-Claude, 'The European Union: Towards a New Form of Federalism?', in
J. Fedtke and B. S. Markesinis, eds., *Patterns of Regionalism and Federalism:
Lessons for the UK* (Oxford: Hart Publishing, 2006), 69–87. For an elaborate
legal historical study arguing that the federation has existed for a long time as a
'third model', in between the (federal) state and the international organization,
see Beaud, Olivier, *Théorie de la Fédération* (Paris: Presses Universitaires de
France, 2007).

[79] Kirchhof, Paul, 'Der deutsche Staat im Prozeß der europäischen Integration', in
J. Isensee, and P. Kirchhof, eds., *Handbuch des Staatsrechts*, VII (Heidelberg:
CF Müller, 1993), 855–886 at 879–881. Kirchhof presented an updated but

deliberate alternative to either *Bundesstaat* (federal state) or *Staatenbund* (confederation of states). According to Everling, this term 'stresses, *albeit in a fashion that is almost impossible to convey in other languages*, that the Member States are bound more tightly in the Union than in the traditional confederation of states'.[80] Accordingly, the author proposes 'compound of states' or 'union of states' as possible closest equivalents in English. In direct reaction to the *Staatenverbund* terminology, Ingolf Pernice coined the more Europe-friendly term *Verfassungsverbund*, although, on a closer look, that term refers to the conjunction of the European Union and the Member States' legal orders (forming together a 'multilevel constitution'),[81] rather than to the European Union legal order on its own.[82] The term 'constitutional' was picked up around the same time, in English-language writing, by Alan Dashwood, who defined the European Union as a 'constitutional order of states'.[83] This last expression remains, also today, an elegant way of blending a sober assessment of the organizational nature of the EU with an appreciation of the substantive value system that now informs its operation.

very similar version of his views, in English, in 'The Legal Structure of the European Union as a Union of States', in A. von Bogdandy and J. Bast, eds., *Principles of European Constitutional Law* (Oxford: Hart Publishing, 2005) 765–802.

[80] Everling, Ulrich, 'The European Union Between Community and National Policies and Legal Orders', in A. von Bogdandy and J. Bast, eds., *Principles of European Constitutional Law* (Oxford: Hart Publishing, 2005) 677–725 at 719 (emphasis added).

[81] This multilevel constitution is defined, in an English-language rendering of Pernice's views, as 'a constitution made up of the constitutions of the Member States bound together by a complementary constitutional body consisting of the European treaties (*Verfassungsverbund*)': Pernice, Ingolf, 'Multilevel Constitutionalism and the Treaty of Amsterdam: European Constitution-Making Revisited?', 36 *Common Market Law Review* (1999) 703–750 at 707.

[82] For a more recent restatement (in German) of Pernice's views, see Pernice, Ingolf, 'Theorie und Praxis des Europäischen Verfassungsverbundes', in C. Calliess, *Verfassungswandel im europäischen Staaten- und Verfassungsverbund* (Mohr Siebeck: Tübingen, 2007), 61–92. This volume contains a number of critical reflections on both of the rival concepts, *Staatenverbund* and *Verfassungsverbund*. Curiously, the term *Föderation*, proposed by Joschka Fischer in his Humboldt speech of May 2000 (see text at note 28 above) does not seem to have any currency in the German academic debate.

[83] Dashwood, Alan, 'States in the European Union', 23 *European Law Review* (1998) 201–216.

1.5 Conclusion: the continuing experiment

As may have become clear in the preceding pages, my view of the former legal nature of the European Community and the former and current legal nature of the European Union is that they constitute, as Wyatt and Dashwood put it, 'a developed form of international organization which displays characteristics of an embryonic federation'.[84] The content of the Lisbon Treaty, and the way in which it was adopted, do not signal a change in this respect. They show that the Member State governments were not willing to contemplate a fundamental change of the EU's legal nature; on the contrary, they have actively experimented, in the Lisbon Treaty, with the toolkit of international treaty law, with generous use of protocols, declarations, transition clauses, derogations, opt-outs, etc. As was mentioned before, most EU law authors disagree with this qualification of the EC and EU as international organizations. Does it really matter which view is taken? Does it matter whether the object which Don Quixote puts on his head is called a barber's plate or a helmet; and if one needs to decide this question, shouldn't one simply follow the view preferred by the majority without further discussion?[85]

Apart from the fact that, in this matter, there is no overall majority, but rather contrasting majority opinions of international and EU law jurists, it would still seem rather important to get the overall qualification of the European Union right, for a variety of reasons.

Practical consequences may derive from which qualification is adopted. They may not be very important for the *activity of the European*

---

[84] Wyatt, D., M. Dougan, B. Rodger, A. Dashwood and E. Spaventa, *Wyatt and Dashwood's European Union Law* (5th edn, London: Sweet & Maxwell, 2006) at 132.

[85] Kundera, Milan, *Le rideau* (Paris: Edition Gallimard, 2005), at 141: '*Un pauvre gentilhomme de village, Alonso Quijada, a décidé d'être un chevalier errant et s'est donné pour nom Don Quichotte de la Manche. Comment définir son identité? Il est celui qu'il n'est pas. Il dérobe à un barbier son plat à barbe en cuivre qu'il prend pour un casque. Plus tard, par hasard, le barbier arrive dans la taverne où don Quichotte se trouve en compagnie; il voit son plat à barbe et veut le reprendre. Mais Don Quichotte, fier, refuse de tenir le casque pour un plat à barbe. Du coup un objet apparemment si simple devient question. Comment prouver d'ailleurs qu'un plat à barbe posé sur une tête n'est pas un casque? L'espiègle compagnie, amusée, trouve le seul moyen objectif de démontrer la vérité: le vote secret. Tous les gens présents y participent et le résultat est sans équivoque: l'objet est reconnu comme un casque.*'

Court of Justice itself. As was repeatedly mentioned above, the ECJ did not feel the need to construct an elaborate theory about the nature of the EC or EU because the flexibility inherent in international treaty law allowed it to freely construct the autonomy and specificity of EU law without being hindered by mandatory rules of general international law. Therefore, whether EU law is qualified as part of international law or not should not be of much practical consequence for the case-law of the ECJ. In particular, qualifying EU law as international law does not imply that the treaties should be understood and interpreted from an intergovernmental perspective and that limitations of sovereignty should be narrowly construed. The European Court has convincingly shown, since *Van Gend en Loos*, why the EC Treaty was a treaty that should be construed in a broader and purpose-oriented way, and other international courts have followed the same jurisprudential line in interpreting 'their' treaty. Still, the recognition that EU law is an advanced species of the genus international law explains more easily some crucial characteristics of the EU legal order without hindering its autonomous development.[86]

Practical consequences may, however, be more visible in *domestic law*. When, for instance, national courts are faced with a conflict between a norm of EU law and a norm contained in another international treaty, they will tend to prioritize the former if they consider EU law to be different from international law, and they will tend to apply the usual *lex posterior* or *lex specialis* conflict rules if they consider that EU law is part of international law. In my view, there is no good reason why EU law should *systematically* have priority over other, conflicting, international obligations before a national court. Think, for example, of the hypothetical case in which an EU act, as interpreted by the Court of Justice, appears to be in conflict with a human right, as interpreted by the European Court of Human Rights. Should a national court give unquestioned priority to the EU law norm over a norm of the European Convention on Human Rights?

There are other, more abstract benefits in recognizing the European Union as an ongoing international law experiment. *Internally* (within

---

[86] For arguments in the same sense, see Hartley, Trevor C., 'International Law and the Law of the European Union – A Reassessment', *British Year Book of International Law* (2001) 1–35.

EU legal studies), it would bring a more sober perspective to a theo-retical field which has been 'overheated', recently, by the European constitutional reform adventure. One lesson emerging from a frenetic decade of attempted treaty reform is that the Member State govern-ments still act as 'Masters of the Treaties' who determine the long-term future of the European Union and use the full range of international legal techniques to reach a provisional consensus on that future; on the other hand, the very international law-based consensus rule for treaty revision also implies that, in practice, the clock cannot be turned back, and indeed the gradual constitutionalization of the EU legal order has continued during the past decade, and it will and should continue in the future, even without a Constitutional Treaty.[87] *Externally* (within the field of international law and relations), reaffirming the nature of European integration as an international legal experiment would restore EU law to its position of being a special branch of international law, and make the 'European way of law'[88] a more amenable source of inspiration for other states, in other parts of the world, when they devise their own forms of international cooperation. Advanced inter-national organizations are being created year after year, and display some or many of the features of the European Union. There are many examples of international organizations with what used to be called supranational features; they have been given the power to adopt operational decisions that are binding on states, and are often adopted

---

[87] On the latter point there is a solid consensus in the EU law literature; see, among others: de Búrca, Gráinne, 'Reflections on the EU's Path from the Constitutional Treaty to the Lisbon Treaty', *Jean Monnet Working Paper* 03/08 (2008); Walker, Neil, 'European Constitutionalism in the State Constitutional Tradition', 59 *Current Legal Problems* (2006) 51–89; Peters, Anne, 'The Constitutionalisation of the European Union – Without the Constitutional Treaty', in S. Puntscher and Riekmann and W. Wessels, eds., *The Making of a European Constitution – Dynamics and Limits of the Convention Experience* (Wiesbaden: Verlag für Sozialwissenschaften, 2006), 35–67; Griller, Stefan, 'Is this a Constitution? Remarks on a Contested Concept', in Stefan Griller and J. Ziller, eds., *The Lisbon Treaty – EU Constitutionalisation without a Constitutional Treaty?* (Wien, New York: Springer, 2008), 21–56; Lenaerts, Koen, 'De Rome à Lisbonne, la Constitution européenne en marche?', 44 *Cahiers de droit européen* 3–4 (2008) 229–253.

[88] Slaughter, Anne-Marie and William Burke-White, 'The Future of International Law is Domestic (or, the European Way of Law)', 47 *Harvard Journal of International Law* (2006) 327–352.

by a majority vote.[89] A regional organization like the Andean Community was consciously modelled on the institutional regime of the European Communities, including the creation of an Andean Tribunal of Justice which is engaged in an active dialogue with (some) national courts through a preliminary reference mechanism.[90] Both the quality of international law scholarship and the progressive development of international law are weakened if the conceptual links with European Union law are cut off. Conversely, the institutional devices developed throughout the history of the EU can serve as a useful toolbox for those who create or reform other international organizations; and the constitutional principles of the EU legal order can serve as a model for the 'framing and taming' of other forms of international public authority.[91]

---

[89] For a general view, see Bernstorff, Jochen von, 'Procedures of Decision-Making and the Role of Law in International Organizations', 9 *German Law Journal* (2008) 1939–1964.

[90] For an analysis of the actual functioning of the Andean preliminary reference system, which is successful but only in a specific area of the law and in relation to some national courts, see Helfer, Laurence R. and Karen J. Alter, 'Building Judicial Supranationalism in the Andes: Understanding Preliminary Reference Patterns in the Andean Community', 41 *New York University Journal of International Law and Politics* (2009) 872–928.

[91] See Bogdandy, Armin von, 'General Principles of International Public Authority: Sketching a Research Field', 9 *German Law Journal* (2008) 1908–1938 at 1926.

2 | The place of European law

NEIL WALKER

2.1 The EU and political modernity

Studies of the EU across different disciplines tend to divide between those that start from an assumption of continuity and those that start from an assumption of discontinuity.[1] The point of departure for analysing the EU's legal, political, social or economic character is either a familiar and historical-grounded set of accomplishments, aspirations, practices and concepts; or it is a *tabula rasa*, with no guarantee how or indeed whether any part of our existing heritage of achievements and ideas will be drawn into the new picture. The present study is emphatically located in the former category. It assumes, and seeks to substantiate the assumption that rather than signalling a break with the paradigm of political modernity centred upon the modern state and its legal and constitutional edifice, the EU reflects and contributes to a variation in the form of political modernity. More specifically, it claims that the deep issues that define, shape and challenge late political modernity in the era of the emergence of polities beyond the state such as the EU remain substantially the same deep issues as defined, shaped and challenged high political modernity in the age of the 'state system'[2]. The central aim in what follows is to demonstrate how three such defining – and overlapping – issues, and the oppositions and tensions that they generated in politics and in law in the phase of high modernity, continue to frame our understanding of late modernity, so providing important insights into the conflicted role of the EU polity within the constellation of late modernity. In particular, they tell us something significant about the nature and extent of the EU's historical reliance

[1] See, e.g., Friese, H. and P. Wagner, 'Survey Article: The Nascent Political Philosophy of the European Polity', 10 *The Journal of Political Philosophy* (2002) 342; Walker, Neil, 'Legal Theory and the European Union: A 25th Anniversary Essay', 25 *Oxford Journal of Legal Studies* (2005) 581–601.
[2] Falk, R., *The Study of Future Worlds* (New York: The Free Press, 1975).

upon law as a medium of integration, about the dangers and limitations of such reliance, and also, finally, about whether and to what extent such dangers and limitations might be overcome *within* law itself.

The first and most basic issue that shapes our understanding of political modernity is the development of the very idea of *collective agency* as the animating source and subject of political community. Indeed, the articulation and operationalization of an expansive notion of collective agency, it is argued, supplies *the* indispensable threshold condition of political modernity. The canonical modern form assumed by this core idea of collective agency has been 'the people'[3] – or popular sovereign – conceived of as a discrete state-centred and state-centring 'unity of a manifold'.[4] But the arrival of the idea of the people as sovereign leaves open and often contested a range of questions concerning both its internal limits and its external accompaniment. Internally, what kinds of difference and what divisions are consistent with the conception of the people as a single collective agency? Externally, what other political forms, and what, if any, other kinds of political community may emerge and subsist alongside the state conceived of under the sign of popular sovereignty?

The second defining issue of political modernity addresses not the sources but the *generative resources* of political community. The category of generative resources covers both the kinds of arguments and the kinds of affects – the reasons and the passions – that create and maintain the bonds of political community. In identifying and locating these, a fundamental question concerns the balance or trade-off between resources of universal provenance and resources of particular provenance, and so between polity-generic and polity-specific factors in the making and sustenance of a polity.[5] To what extent does the appeal to political community draw on reasons for collective action and other mobilizing cues that are peculiar to that political community, and to what extent does it draw upon grounds and affects that speak in a universal or at least more general register? How and to what extent can these two reservoirs of resources and the forms of appeal associated

---

[3] See, e.g., Canovan, M., *The People* (Cambridge: Polity Press, 2005).

[4] Lindahl, Hans, 'Sovereignty and the Institutionalization of Normative Order', 21 *Oxford Journal of Legal Studies* (2001) 165–180 at 175.

[5] On the relationship between universalism and particularism in political thought, see Vincent, A., *Nationalism and Particularity* (Cambridge University Press, 2002), esp. 1–13.

with them be reconciled? And does the emphasis or balance between universalism and particularism alter depending upon the answer to the first question, namely the kind of collective agency, if any, that holds or aspires to the title to political community?

The third issue that shapes political modernity is what we may call the question of '*political ontology*.'[6] We are here concerned neither with the general subject – or agency – of political community nor with the distinctiveness or otherwise of the generative resources available to a political community. Rather, what is addressed is the basic model of the social world in the pursuit or fulfilment of which we might justify the design of *any* political community – whatever form its title takes and wherever it draws the energy to mobilize and sustain itself – or indeed any constellation of political communities. In particular, we are concerned with what kinds of entities can be said to exist or to possess basic value in society, and in what kind of hierarchy or other relationship *inter se*; and with how this ontological picture justifies this or that normative range and emphasis on the part of a political community or a combination of political communities. The basic tension or antinomy here is between what one writer calls 'singularism' and 'solidarism';[7] but which we may, with all due acknowledgment of the history of diverse and overuse of these terms, relabel collectivism and individualism. On the one hand, the social collectivity may be seen as the sole or primary unit of value within political life. On the other hand, the individual may be seen as the sole or primary unit of value within political life. The question of 'where' to balance and 'how' to reconcile these two possibilities supplies the third key tension of political modernity.

As we shall see in Section 2.2 below, these three core issues – the form of collective agency, the nature of its generative resources and the type of basic ontology it endorses – and the contrasts they draw, the questions they raise and the dilemmas they pose (popular sovereignty versus other forms of political title, particularism versus universalism and collectivism versus individualism) assume a particular pattern in the state-centred world of high modernity. In this Westphalian universe, the only major political form that accompanies the state is the inter-state

---

[6] Pettit, Philip, 'Rawls's Political Ontology', 4 *Politics, Philosophy and Economics* (2005) 157–174.
[7] Ibid. 157–158.

or international form, itself largely derivative of and parasitic upon the state. The fundamental distinctions of that world, then, tend to be binary ones, based on a mutually exclusive 'inside/outside'[8] sovereignty-coded understanding and representation of legal and political space. There is the domain of internal state sovereignty – of relations *within* the self-contained totality of the sovereign polity. And there is the domain of external state sovereignty – of relations *between* sovereigns. In turn the three basic defining tensions of modernity, themselves binary in nature, can be mapped in a reasonably simple (if highly stylized) way onto that basic binary and mutually exclusive configuration.

As explained in Section 2.3, however, once we shift to the late modern world of increasingly transnationalized legal, political, economic and cultural relations and to the key position of the EU within that movement, we are faced with a more complex picture. The defining issues and the key tensions these issues harbour remain the same, but they are written onto a configuration of legal and political space that is no longer organized either in binary terms or in terms of a relationship of mutual exclusivity. The EU occupies a very distinctive place within this new tableau of authority. As a political and legal entity, it does not replicate nor does it replace either the state or the international. Rather, it stands between them, incorporates strains of each and interlocks with them both. To grasp the EU's situation in the political and juridical world of late modernity, therefore, requires that we map the defining issues of high modernity and their attendant tensions onto the more complex, deeply interpenetrated and ever-shifting authority configuration of which the EU itself constitutes but one, if key, component.

In so doing, we can begin to appreciate how and why the EU's interconnected capacities to address, either in its own terms or in combination with the other sites of political authority, the three defining predicaments of modernity – the proper source of collective agency, the provenance of the resources of political community and the balance between individualist and collectivist ontologies – is becoming ever more precarious as it enters its second half century. Historically, the EU's long-standing emphasis upon individualism aligned to a historically contingent form of collectivism in response to the ontological question has both helped compensate for and (re)contributed to the

---

[8] Walker, R. B. J., *Inside/Outside: International Relations as Political Theory* (Cambridge University Press, 1993).

difficulties it has encountered in the face of each of the other two questions; that is to say, its structural weakness in response to the resources question and its self-reinforcing reluctance and precarious-ness of common cause before the collective agency question. What is more, this cluster of responses helps to explain the distinctive and diverse emphasis upon law within the EU. As the EU's emphasis upon individualism becomes less sustainable with the gradual expansion of its remit, reputation and self-understanding, it follows that the deficiencies in the EU's capacity to address the resources and agency questions become all the more evident and the need to treat them ever more urgent. In turn, this manifests itself as a profound challenge to the place of law within the EU. We conclude by offering some thoughts on how the EU, and in particular the EU in its legal register, may respond to that predicament.

2.2 Shaping political modernity

Let us begin our substantive discussion by asking how the three defining issues of political modernity shaped both the state and the international realm, so placing the situation of the EU in some kind of historical context and comparative relief.

2.2.1 The domain of the state

Above it was suggested that the very idea of the encompassing collective agency of a 'people' or popular sovereign is crucial to the emergence of political modernity. Indeed, one might go as far as to say that the idea of politics and of the political realm with which we are familiar today only dates from the modern age and 'the invention of the people'[9] as an active collective subject. Prior to the age of political modernity, whose first full constitutional flowering took place in France and North America at the end of the eighteenth century, there were various incip-ient notions of peoplehood descended from the Greek *demos* and the *populus Romanus*. But these lacked the mature characteristics of the later form in which the people assume a prior and constituent

---

[9] Morgan, E. S., *Inventing the People: The Rise of Popular Sovereignty in England and America* (New York: Norton, 1988).

power over the polity and its governmental arrangements.[10] More specifically, only with the arrival of the form of peoplehood associated with popular sovereignty do we find fully developed the notions of the abstractness, autonomy, comprehensiveness and self-constraint of authority that together provide the conditions of possibility of the modern political realm.

The idea of secular authority as located neither in a particular imperial or monarchical office nor in a concrete and highly exclusionary active constituency (such as the citizenry of the classical city-state) but in an abstract transgenerational collective entity, is a gradual accomplishment of political modernity. So, too, is the detachment of title to rule from the sense of an inherent and inherited 'order of things' that such a process of abstraction achieves. Indeed, it is not until the writing of Jean-Jacques Rousseau that this development finds its first full theoretical expression.[11] Abstraction of such a thoroughgoing order also implies autonomy. For the first time the domain of politics, now framed by this abstract collective agency, is not in thrall either to an immanent or transcendental design or to some conception of propriety right and status relations reified by tradition. Rather, the content and operation of the political domain is self-determined and worldly, flowing from the general or popular will – even if at one remove the content and direction of that will continues to be influenced by the religious – and so otherworldly – belief systems of many of those who contribute to its formation.[12]

In turn, this removal of prior metaphysical or social constraint underlines the comprehensiveness of the political realm. There stands no external limit to what can be done in the name of the sovereign order of the political, either in terms of its substance or of the mechanisms necessary to its implementation and enforcement, other than the

---

[10] Bernard Yack makes a helpful double distinction between the modern notion of the people as popular sovereign, or *pouvoir constituant*, and the older ideas of the people either as select co-participants in a republican form of rule – as 'governmental sovereign' (p. 30), or simply as the plebs or multitude of ordinary folks in any community: 'Nationalism, Popular Sovereignty and the Liberal Democratic State', in T. V. Paul, G. J. Ikenberry and J. A. Hall, eds., *The Nation-State in Question* (Princeton University Press, 2003), 29–50.

[11] Rousseau, J. J., *The Social Contract*, trans. M. Cranston (Harmondsworth: Penguin, 1968[1762]).

[12] See, e.g., Taylor, Charles, *Modern Social Imaginaries* (Durham, NC: Duke University Press, 2004), Chapter 4.

constraint imposed by the operation of other sovereign orders and apparent in the form of the boundaries set to the reach of the particular people, territory and system of government. Finally, however, there is a crucial dimension of auto-limitation, one with both procedural and substantive elements. Procedurally, what counts as an expression of an abstraction and artifice such as the popular will – just because it *is* an abstraction – depends upon certain institutionalized devices for the representation of the popular will, even if consistent with the absence of external authority these devices must themselves be deemed to rest on nothing other than the popular will.[13] Substantively, certain implicit or explicit checks flow from the expectation to act consistently with the very ethos underpinning the new idea of an autonomous and collectively self-authorized political domain; one that signals and reinforces the passing of an older 'social imaginary'[14] that placed the idea of harmony and conformity with some external or natural order at the centre of collective existence. In a nutshell, this new ethos can be summed up in the twin notions of freedom and equality. The deep justification for the emerging order of collective agency lies in the novel ontological emphasis upon the equal worth of each individual and the respect consequentially due both to his or her freedom to choose and pursue a particular life-plan and to his or her contribution to the determination of the collective good. In turn, this leads to forms of collective self-conditioning that correspond to the two mutually supportive sides of Benjamin Constant's modern liberty;[15] on the one hand, the protection alongside the new comprehensive sphere of the political of a sphere of private autonomy through a bill of rights or other safeguard of civil liberties; on the other hand, the development of those forms of political freedom and voice that would eventually lead to a fully enfranchised system of representative democracy.[16]

---

[13] This is one of the so-called paradoxes of constituent power. For extended discussion. see the essays collected in Martin Loughlin and Neil Walker, eds., *The Paradox of Constitutionalism: Constituent Power and Constitutional Form* (Oxford University Press, 2007).

[14] Taylor, *Modern Social Imaginaries* (2004).

[15] Constant, B., 'The Liberty of the Ancients Compared with that of the Moderns' in B. Constant, *Political Writings* (Cambridge University Press, 1988), 307–328.

[16] On the symbiosis of private and political autonomy, see, e.g., Habermas, Jürgen, 'Constitutional Democracy: A Paradoxical Union of Contradictory Principles?', 29 *Political Theory* (2001) 766–81.

What is the relationship between the universal and the particular in the development of this new form of collective agency? In the American and French revolutionary contexts the universal dimension undoubtedly provided a founding inspiration. In the settlement of the first French republic, the 'rights of (universal) man' precede the rights of Frenchmen.[17] Similarly, the 'self-evident' equality of the independent Americans of the 1776 Declaration of Independence is reduced to the unstated minor premise of a syllogism whose major premise holds that 'all men are created equal'.[18] If we recall the humanist premises of the new popular sovereignty, the universalist strain is hardly surprising. If the idea of equal freedom is derived from the human condition itself, then entitlement to the relevant political benefits should not depend on accidents of geography.

Yet the idea of popular sovereignty is clearly a double-edged sword. It may be the vehicle for a universal ethics. But inevitably, and even more sharply, its situational logic demands that it speaks to and for a particular collectivity. Precisely because it is concerned with the conditions of political *agency*, the kind of collective identity that the idea of popular sovereignty invokes is an active and so reflexive or self-regarding one.[19] It follows that unless those who are deemed to be represented in and by that popular sovereignty perceive themselves as being included within that agency, they will experience any government supposedly in their name as illegitimate. It becomes clear, then, why popular sovereignty has inspired not only these many visions of the modern civic republic in which the virtue of political community is an abstract, universal and infinitely replicable good, but also various modern forms of nationalism in which the people are deemed to have an antecedent and unique unity of culture, history and language and a dedicated community of attachment. Historically, the Romantic nationalist movement of the first half of the nineteenth century, with

---

[17] As famously celebrated by Tom Paine in his pamphlet, *Rights of Man; Common Sense; and Other Political Writings*, ed. with an introduction by Mark Philp (Oxford University Press, 1995 [1791].

[18] For background and texts, and a particularly acute reading of its intended and actual symbolic impact on the world beyond the emerging American polity, see Armitage, D., *The Declaration of Independence: A Global History* (Cambridge, Mass.: Harvard University Press, 2007).

[19] See, e.g., Taylor, Charles, 'Religion and European Integration', in K. Michalski, ed., *Religion in the New Europe* (Budapest, New York: CEU Press, 2006), 1–22.

its 'Springtime of Peoples'[20] and its illusion that there could be an independent state for every nation, can be seen as the early product of the more particularistic appeal to popular sovereignty and as a reaction against the more universalist strain.[21] And while the extremes of national particularism have left an indelible dark mark on the twentieth-century history of the state,[22] no inventory of the modern state could fail to note the resilient rootedness of constitutional self-identification in particular reasons of state and particular themes and symbols of belonging and common commitment.[23]

It is just as important, however, to note the symbiotic relationship between universal and particular appeals to community at the state level as it is to acknowledge the dominance of the particularist strain. For in practice, the two types of generative resource inevitably co-exist, and indeed 'often lie undistinguished in the rhetoric and imaginary of democratic societies'.[24] As the contemporary debate over 'constitutional patriotism' indicates, even the most avowedly universalist framework of self-government must draw from and reinvest in its own particular experience.[25] Conversely, the humanist gene in the idea of popular sovereignty means that even the most introverted, culturally monolithic and exclusionary national ideology will develop certain universalist themes. What is more, the two strains tend to be consciously mixed up in certain types of nation-building projects, with quite distinctive patterns of results. A particular nationalism is often claimed to have been forged from universal roots, as in the French commitment to *laïcité* and the American culture of liberty. However, as the history of empire – both classical and 'lite'[26] – demonstrates, this kind of thinking and ideological projection often blurs into and justifies its opposite. For

---

[20] Calhoun, C., *Nations Matter; Culture, History, and the Cosmopolitan Dream* (Minneapolis: University of Minnesota Press, 2007), at 16.

[21] Yack, 'Nationalism' (2003), at 34–47.

[22] See, e.g., Hobsbawm, E., *The Age of Extremes: The Short Twentieth Century, 1914–1991* (London: Michael Joseph, 1994).

[23] Kahn, P. W., *Putting Liberalism in its Place* (Princeton University Press, 2005).

[24] Taylor, 'Religion' (2006), at 7.

[25] On the importance of the universalistic strain in the ideas of constitutional patriotism promoted by Jürgen Habermas and others, and on the unavoidable tensions between this strain and more particularistic dimensions of attachment to a place and its law, see Mueller, Jan-Werner, 'A General Theory of Constitutional Patriotism', 6 *International Journal of Constitutional Law* (2008) 72–95.

[26] Ignatieff, Michael, *Empire Lite: Nation-Building in Bosnia, Kosovo and Afghanistan* (London: Vintage, 2003).

the development of imperial influence and control has often been fuelled by self-conscious efforts to sponsor one way of political life *as if* it were the only legitimate way – to universalize the particular, so to speak – so in effect offering the world the benefits, and demanding that it meet the requirements, of a particular national experience and character.[27]

At the level of political ontology, too, states tend to rely upon a combination of the two approaches – of both individualist and collectivist commitments. On the one hand, we have already remarked upon the deep and direct ethical connection between the rise of popular sovereignty and the advent, as a universal good, of modern individualism. Indeed, the fact that liberalism, with its core idea of constructing a political architecture in which individuals can act without interference in ways that reflect their understanding of what gives meaning and value to their lives, is often portrayed as *the* 'dominant ideology'[28] of Western political modernity testifies to the extensive and resilient power of the individualist stream. On the other hand, collectivism speaks to an older tradition of thinking in which the polity of the Greek city-state is seen as prior to the individual and as providing the deep purpose and end of individual action.[29] Yet it is a tradition that did not find the new conditions of political modernity inhospitable. For in as much as popular sovereignty, with its clear demarcation of political space into 'us' and 'them', demands a measure of recognition of the particularity of political community, acknowledgement of and reflexive engagement with that particularity is apt to retrieve or to generate some sense of a self-standing and non-disaggregable collective good of the community.

This collective dimension of the good life will typically (although, as the examples of universalizing the particular indicate, by no means exclusively) be understood as a value-set particular to the community in question. That is to say, the goods that it speaks to will first and foremost be goods that are distinctive to that community. Beyond this, such collective goods will fall into different categories. To begin with, there will be those goods which, although not necessarily public goods of self-evident worth in the narrow and classical economic sense of

---

[27] See, e.g., Calhoun, *Nations Matter* (2007), Chapter 6.
[28] Freeden, M., *Ideologies and Political Theory: A Conceptual Approach* (Oxford: Clarendon Press, 1996), at 139.
[29] See, e.g., Aristotle, *Politics*, Book I, trans. with a commentary by Trevor J. Saunders (Oxford University Press, 1995), at 1253a.

providing something of added value to the community as whole under conditions of non-rivalness and non-excludability,[30] we can nevertheless label *manifest collective goods*. What we are referring to here are those collective goods, such as peace or a sustainable environment, whose value is entirely or largely undisputed either because they are indispensable to the continued existence of the community in a form valued by members of that community or its mutually implicated parts, or because they speak to an objective which has a clear and considerable positive-sum quality and from which, therefore, all may expect or at least hope to benefit. Alongside these manifest collective goods, there are other collective goods whose quality as such is bound up with the fact that they are constructed and achieved *in common*. These common goods in turn can be both implicit and explicit in nature. *Implicit common goods* refer to those benefits inherent in the very idea of living together in a stable community. These include the value of national (or other collective) solidarity – of an accomplished framework of mutual concern and support – and the sense of social, economic and spiritual or 'ontological security'[31] such solidarity brings to those who share in it. They also include a more general value associated with the development and preservation of a national (or other collective) culture, as well as the sense of belonging, of dignity, of posterity and of distinctiveness or 'originality'[32] such a culture brings to those who share it. Moreover, in addition to such implicit common goods, and, indeed, building on the platform of capacities for common action provided by such implicit goods, communities may also determine and pursue certain other *explicit common goods*, such as economic egalitarianism (through redistribution), or an educated society, or a healthy society.

The ability to decide and realize such explicit common goods, which as we have already noted is itself the public expression of individualism, also requires the development of common government institutions, including the institutions of representative democracy we find in most

[30] See, e.g., Olsen, M., *The Logic of Collective Action* (Cambridge, Mass.: Harvard University Press, 1971). Paradigm examples of public goods under the standard economic definition include clean air and street lighting.

[31] Giddens, A., *The Constitution of Society* (Cambridge: Polity, 1984), at 375.

[32] Weiler, J. H. H., ed., *The Constitution of Europe: 'Do the New Clothes Have an Emperor' and Other Essays on European Integration* (Cambridge University Press, 1999), at 338. See also Smith, A. H., *National Identity* (Harmondsworth: Penguin, 1991), Chapter 1.

contemporary states. On the one hand, decision-making and executive institutions are procedurally and epistemically indispensable to the transformation of the *volonté de tous* into the explicit common goods identified as comprising the *volonté générale*, as well as to the effective pursuit of both these explicit common goods and the manifest collective goods. On the other hand, and from a sociological perspective, common institutions of government, especially common representative institutions of government, can also be important in a boot-strapping sense for the nurturing of just that sense of shared public life – or public sphere – necessary to supply the platform of implicit common goods on which rests the very legitimacy and effective capacity of these same common institutions of government and the explicit common goods that emanate from these.[33]

While the pursuit of a collectivist ontology clearly, then, involves a mutually supportive relationship between the various species of collective goods and inclusive institutions of government, the relationship between collectivism and individualism is also far from being merely antagonistic. Although the balance between individualism and collectivism will differ, and indeed the twentieth century saw both deep ideological conflicts and sharp oscillations between the two poles, no modern state will entirely sacrifice either to the benefit of the other. No state has a public philosophy which reduces the good of community entirely to the aggregation of individual goods, just as no state has a public philosophy which attributes no value to the individual other than as an indivisible part of the collective and its common good. Rather, the ontological commitments of the modern state are always a blend of the two in ways that show the inextricability of the libertarian and communitarian impulses in the idea of popular sovereignty. Indeed, at least at some minimal level of provision; each may be understood as the precondition of the other – individual autonomy and well-being required to encourage the pursuit of collective goods and a solid basis of common interest required to guarantee the protection of personal freedom.[34]

In summary then, we can see how the achievement of popular sovereignty at the state level pushes in two directions simultaneously.

---

[33] See, e.g., Mason, A., *Community, Solidarity and Belonging: Levels of Community and Their Normative Significance* (Cambridge University Press, 2000), esp. Chapters 4 and 5.

[34] See, e.g., Habermas, 'Constitutional Democracy' (2001).

It pushes towards a universalist mode of justification and mobilization, and through that towards an individualist political ontology. At the same time, it pushes towards a particularist mode of justification and mobilization, and through that towards a collectivist political ontology. What is more, both of these oppositions – between universalism and particularism and between individualism and collectivism – conceal a symbiotic relationship. The idea of collective agency that lies at the heart of the modern state requires both the universalist–individualist and the particularist–collectivist strands in order to survive and prosper.

2.2.2 The domain of the international

The idea of popular sovereignty may have been unlike anything that preceded it, but its comprehensive scope also served to deter contemporary rivals. In creating the space for modern political relations as we conceive them, it proceeded to occupy that space jealously. As is apparent from the early history of the United States, even an idea as strongly co-implicated in the development of political modernity as federalism, with its conception of a clear divide between different spheres of governmental authority, could only with much difficulty and after great conflict be reconciled with the singularity of the legal and political order required of the model of popular sovereignty.[35] As we shall see, the terms of trade between compound arrangements such as those in the federal tradition on the one hand and the idea of sovereignty on the other have remained conflicted, and indeed have vividly resurfaced as an unresolved issue in the context of the EU.[36]

The only dimension of political authority that the idea of popular sovereignty did not seek to contain or absorb was that which *by its own terms* lay beyond it, as its remainder; namely the inter-state or international relations between sovereigns. However, just because of the

[35] See e.g Deudney, D.,'The Philadelphian State System: Sovereignty, Arms Control and Balance of Power in the American State System', 49 *International Organization* (1995) 191–229.

[36] With reference to the American/European comparison, see, e.g., Goldstein, L., *Constituting Federal Sovereignty: The European Union in Comparative Context* (Baltimore, London: Johns Hopkins University Press, 2001); Fabbrini, S., *Compound Democracies: Why the United States and Europe are Becoming Similar* (Oxford University Press, 2007); Glencross, A., *What Makes the EU Viable? European Integration in the Light of the US Antebellum Experience* (Basingstoke: Palgrave Macmillan, 2009).

state-centredness of this political imaginary, in so far as the international realm was at all viewed as a political realm – a domain of collective agency over common affairs – it was so largely in state-derivative terms. And while the international sphere nevertheless came to possess its own version of the quality of abstraction enjoyed by the state of popular sovereignty, in its classic early modern phase internationalism palpably lacked the autonomy, the comprehensiveness of remit and implementation capacity and the self-limitation of the sovereign state.

As regards the quality of abstraction, through the sponsorship of the very notion of an international order or system of states, with international law as its distinctive regulatory currency, understandings of the international domain moved beyond a purely realist template.[37] The basic idea of an international order as elaborated in the classic foundational texts of modern internationalism, that is to say, already posited a detachment from the concrete holders and *de facto* balance of power at any time.[38] But in each of the other respects relevant to the construction of political community the international order was thinly conceived and state-parasitic. Crucially, the very units that made up the international domain – that constituted its relevant collective agency – were states rather than individuals, Unlike the state, therefore, the international domain was not an original and primary community, but a community

---

[37] On how international law thinking has generally defined itself *against* realism, see Slaughter, Anne-Marie, 'International Law in a World of Liberal States', 6 *European Journal of International Law* (1995) 1–39.

[38] This would be true, for example, of such key foundational figures in the discipline of international law as Grotius, Pufendorf and Vattel. See Grotius, Hugo, *The Law of War and of Peace* [*De jure belli ac pacis*], trans. Louise R. Loomis, with an introduction by P. E. Corbett (Roslyn, NY: W. J. Black, 1949 [1625]); von Pufendorf, Samuel, *Of the Law of Nature and Nations* [*De Iure Naturae e Gentium*]. [eight books / written in Latin by the Baron Pufendorf; translated into English, from the best edition, with a short introduction] (Oxford: L. Lichfield, 1703 [(1672)]); de Vattel, E., *The Law of Nations, or Principles of the Law of Nature applied to the Conduct and Affairs of Nations and Sovereigns*. [from the French of Monsieur de Vattel; from the new edition by Joseph Chitty; with additional notes and references by Edward D. Ingraham] (Philadelphia: T. & J. W. Johnson, 1883 [1758]). In a broader non-legal register, it is also of course true of the work of Kant and his development of the idea of cosmopolitan order. See Kant, Immanuel, *Toward Perpetual Peace and Other Writings on Politics, Peace, and History*, ed. and with an introduction by Pauline Kleingeld, trans. David L. Colclasure, with essays by Jeremy Waldron, Michael W. Doyle and Allen W. Wood (New Haven: Yale University Press, 2006 [1795]).

made up of pre-existing political communities, and so of a secondary and heteronomous quality. Its remit was not comprehensive, but within the gift of the constituent states even within the realm of external and so putatively 'inter-national' affairs, while these states retained for themselves exclusive control over internal affairs.[39] In terms of implementation capacity, too, international authority was far from comprehensively self-contained, since the settlement of disputes and the enforcement of remedies in the international realm – and so the sharper edge of legal discipline, remained within the control of the states themselves. And while the gradual elaboration of general principles of international law spoke to some measure of self-limitation, this paled into insignificance alongside the cumulative effect of these various forms of external constraint.

The last century has witnessed some attempts to reimagine the international domain as a thicker and more autonomous form of political community. The use of the rhetoric of 'international community', as pioneered in the work of Alfred Verdross and his followers,[40] is indicative of fledgling efforts to reconceive of the international order as a primary and no longer exclusively state-centred order. The budding contemporary language of international constitutionalism in self-conscious succession to the community approach amplifies this new way of understanding the authoritative foundations of international law.[41] In keeping with this new strand of discourse there has been some rudimentary filling out of both the normative and operating systems of international law. Through the development of obligations *erga omnes*, of peremptory norms or *ius cogens*, and of world order treaties such as the UN (United Nations) Charter, the notion of international law as a distinct and self-evolving system, and also in some

---

[39] On the loose coupling of internal and external dimensions of sovereignty in the history of international relations, see Krasner, S., *Sovereignty: Organized Hypocrisy* (Princeton University Press, 1999).

[40] See Verdross, A., *Die Verfassung der Völkerrechtsgemeinschaft* (Berlin: Springer, 1926); Simma, Bruno, 'The Contribution of Alfred Verdross to the Theory of International Law', 6 *European Journal of International Law* (1995) 33.

[41] The literature is huge. For an overview, see Fassbender, Bardo, '"We the Peoples of the United Nations": Constituent Power and Constitutional Form in International Law', in Martin Loughlin and Neil Walker, eds., *The Paradox of Constitutionalism: Constituent Power and Constitutional Form* (Oxford University Press, 2007), 270–290.

measure a self-constraining system, has gained more support.[42] The exponential growth in the range of international law-making (and law-makers) both in the primary legislative form of treaties and in rule-making arrangements set up under or outside the authority of treaties speaks to the development of a more comprehensive remit,[43] to which breadth must be added the unprecedented depth reached by human rights and other regimes that pierce the veil of the state and claim direct applicability to its citizens and subjects. And the development by many of these regimes of their own adjudicatory, monitoring and enforcement mechanisms, from the International Court of Justice at the Hague to the extensive WTO (World Trade Organization) dispute resolution proce-dures and the new International Criminal Court, adds significant imple-mentation capacity in certain functional domains.

Yet while these various developments modify the state dependence of the international domain and of international law, they certainly do not remove it. Still less do they endow the international domain with a model of political agency remotely comparable in thickness to the model perfected by the state. Transnational law may have increased significantly in its density in the latest and ongoing age of globalization of the factors of production and communication, but this, as the recur-rent tone of contemporary debates suggests,[44] is as likely to lead to the fragmentation as to the intensification of any idea of international or global agency. As a form of political community based on collective authority, the international level remains, in terms of social identity and

---

[42] See, e.g., de Wet, Erika, 'The International Constitutional Order', 55 *International and Comparative Law Quarterly* (2006) 51–76; Peters, Anne, 'Compensatory Constitutionalism: The Function and Potential of Fundamental International Norms and Structures', 19 *Leiden Journal of International Law* 3 (2006) 579–605.

[43] See generally, Boyle, A. and C. Chinkin, *The Making of International Law* (Oxford University Press, 2007), Chapter 1. Global Administrative Law scholars have been particularly active in charting non-Treaty forms of law-making; for an early manifesto, anticipating what is by now a vast literature, see Kingsbury, B., N. Krisch and R. Stewart, 'The Emergence of Global Administrative Law', 68 *Law and Contemporary Problems* (2005) 15–61.

[44] See, e.g., Koskenniemi, Martti, 'The Fate of International Law: Between Technique and Politics', 70 *Modern Law Review* (2007) 1–30; Teubner, G. and A. Fischer-Lescano, 'Regime-Collisions: The Vain Search for Legal Unity in the Fragmentation of Global Law', 25 *Michigan Journal of International Law* (2004) 999; Dupuy, Pierre-Marie, 'L'unité de l'ordre juridique international', 297 *Hague Recueil* (2003) 438–450.

of systemic range, coherence and capacity, a quite different and much lesser creature than the state original.

Just as the situational logic of the state in terms of the resources of political community is predominantly particularistic, that of the international domain is universalistic. International law seeks to transcend the particularity of the state and the particular differences between states, and in so doing has developed two different registers of universalism.[45] In the early, classical age of modern international law, and indeed in many subsequent phases,[46] formal universalism was to the fore, whereas in the last sixty years there has been an explicit turn to a more substantive notion of unity.[47] In formal terms, the international rule of law of the classical period invoked the promise of a society of states bound together by a 'thin' ethic of universal respect and recognition. Just like the classical international idea of collective agency, this was a highly state-derivative notion. The premise of the 'sovereignty' of the individual in the design of collective arrangements which came to be so influential at the state level was mirrored at the international level through the idea of the sovereignty of states with quite different interests whose commitment to the rule of law *inter se* was predicated upon liberal forbearance towards and support for their different collective self-interests. The point of international law in this formalist vision was one of co-existence and cooperation between political entities with different dominant values, objectives and conceptions of their common political goods. In contrast, the 'turn to ethics'[48] in the post-war period – both the initial wave centred around the birth of the UN and the process of decolonization and the second post-Cold War wave from the 1990s – has signalled a new agenda of substantive common ground. The shape of this has already been indicated in our discussion of the cumulative moves towards a more communitarian and constitutional approach. Whether in the early development of new doctrinal foundations and institutional architecture for human rights promotion and protection at the UN and regional levels and the concomitant positing of the

---

[45] For an excellent overview, see Jouannet, E., 'Universalism and Imperialism: The True–False Paradox of International Law?' 18 *European Journal of International Law* (2007) 379–407.

[46] For example, in the inter-war years.

[47] See, e.g., Jouannet, 'Universalism and Imperialism' (2007), at 382–86.

[48] Koskenniemi, Martti, '"The Lady Doth Protest Too Much": Kosovo and the Turn to Ethics in International Law', 65 *Modern Law Review* (2002) 159.

individual as an additional (to states) subject of international law, or in the contemporary development of new common substantive principles and application machinery in the context of criminal, humanitarian or environmental law, the ambitions of international law have moved beyond formal cooperation and co-existence.

The emphasis on universalism is both a strength and weakness of international law. Moreover, the tension and oscillation between the formal and substantive streams of universalism both respond to and reinforce its mixed virtue. The strength of an international law based upon formal universalism lies in its modesty – in its prudently limited ambition. It accepts difference between states as deep-rooted and substantively unbridgeable and claims that it is just because of such difference that we need to find and can find common resort to legal form and method. The strength of an international law based upon substantive universalism, in contrast, lies in its *lack* of modesty – in the audacity of its ambition. It claims that just because its morality is universal and so applies to common humanity, it must subsume and so prevail over (whether through incorporation or rejection) any more particular morality. Yet as the flipside of their contrasting strengths, formal universalism and substantive universalism in international law also reveal weaknesses that encourage, but cannot be fully cured by, resort to the other. Each is frequently charged both with promising too much and with delivering too little.

The charge that international law in either of its universalist variants promises too much has deep roots. These lie in the history of Western imperialism, and relatedly in the development, shadowing the Romantic nationalism of the early nineteenth century, of a more particularist strain in international law that began to stress the cultural specificity and superiority of certain (typically European) regional sources and forms.[49] The shadow of imperialism and expansionism, on this view, has not retreated even in the post-colonial era, but continues to reflect and reinforce the domination of the North over the South.[50] The point is more apparent as regards substantive universalism. The values of the

---

[49] See, e.g., Jouannet, 'Universalism and Imperialism' (2007), at 380–382.
[50] See, e.g., Tully, James, 'The Imperialism of Modern Constitutional Democracy', in Martin Loughlin and Neil Walker, eds., *The Paradox of Constitutionalism: Constituent Power and Constitutional Form* (Oxford University Press, 2007), 315–338.

international legal order, or at least the dominant interpretation of the values of the international legal order, are often criticized as being in fact interest-bound and culture-bound, based on the prevailing mores of powerful Western societies who are overrepresented historically, institutionally and reputationally, as well as through underlying economic and military power, in the global theatre of international law. What is more, the argument against a robustly substantive approach, whether this takes the form of stretching the definition of humanitarian or self-defensive intervention or increasing the powers of the Security Council to take emergency measures against the supposedly common security threat of international terrorism,[51] is reinforced by the claim that, both through encroaching on the sovereign autonomy and 'liberal freedom' of the states and by doing so in accordance with a less general, visible and stable body of rules, it also serves to undermine the virtues of formal universalism.[52]

But the argument that in its universal ambition international law promises too much is also heard not infrequently at the formal level. Ideas of pluralism, tolerance and cosmopolitanism, together with a conviction of the importance of a stable framework of rules for facilitating international peace and the international circulation of goods, persons, services and communications, underwrite the case for formal universalism. And once again these ideas, whether by reason of their source (Western liberal orthodoxy) or their effect (the lubrication of the existing framework of international relations with its prevailing asymmetries of power), may be criticized for being skewed in favour of a dominant configuration of states. In summary, both substantive universalism, and – perhaps even more insidiously on account of its modest façade – formal universalism, may be challenged finally, as bearing false witness – as highly particular views of the world masquerading as universal to hegemonic effect.

The flip side of this criticism is the charge that international law's emphasis on universalism means that it achieves too little. Here, the argument is that if and to the extent that universalism is not simply a

---

[51] See e.g Scheppele, K. L., 'The Migration of Anti-Constitutional Ideas; The Post 9/11 Globalization of Public Law and the International State of Emergency', in Sujit Choudhry, ed., *The Migration of Constitutional Ideas* (Cambridge University Press, 2006), 347–373 at 350.
[52] See Jouannet, 'Universalism and Imperialism' (2007), at 386–392.

cover for an illegitimate selectivity of approach, then because of its state-derivative quality it is simply insufficiently robust to prosecute its own ambition. However benevolently intended, substantive universalism at the global level is vulnerable to the charge of hubris, of nurturing an ambition that underestimates the limits imposed by the resilient power and deep-rooted differences of state sovereigns. And if formal universalism, as we have seen, seeks to cut a more modest figure in the face of this deep sovereigntist structure, its hold also remains tenuous. It remains fragile both before the moralism of substantive universalism and before the arguments of legal exceptionalism and *realpolitik* that often emerge in the actual discourse and practice of international relations between uneven and unstably aligned powers.[53]

In either case – too thick and promising too much or too thin and delivering too little – what threatens to undermine universalism in international law is the shadow of particularism. Either international law stands accused of a closet particularism of its own, or it is frustrated by other more powerful particularist forces at the national or regional levels. International law's universalist emphasis, then, is both inescapable and indispensable but also inherently vulnerable, and like the secondary quality of its claim to collective agency and political community, this fragile standing is ultimately a function of its state-dependence.

If we turn, finally, to the question of political ontology, again the historical state-dependence of international law has coloured and limited what can be done in its name. As in the case of the state, we find a combination of collectivism and individualism, but in both cases the purchase of international law is relatively weak. On the one hand, the fact that the key units of international law are themselves collective subjects who bring their internally generated common goods to the international table means that the producers of international law each already articulates a collectivist ontology. But precisely because of the power of these collective producers, it is less likely that the *product* itself will constitute an independent collective good. Rather, to recall the message of liberal internationalism,[54] international agreements tend to

---

[53] On this fragility, see, e.g., Koskenniemi, Martti, 'International Law in Europe: Between Tradition and Renewal', 16 *European Journal of International Law* (2005) 113–124.

[54] See, e.g., Doyle, M. W., *Ways of War and Peace* (Princeton University Press, 1997).

be concerned with finding the optimal *ad hoc* balance amongst the enlightened self-interests of the various autonomously conceived collective units. This does not mean that certain global concerns such as peace, environmental security and democracy are incapable of being recognized and settled upon as manifest collective goods rather than subject to continuous negotiation as merely concurrent or aggregative interests. However, any such development typically struggles against a strong state-centred gravitational force. What is more, as is attested to by the unevenness of voice, the existence of powerful veto rights, the marginalization of non-state constituencies and the low public visibility and interest associated even with the United Nations, despite its achievement as most powerful global institutional complex in the history of international relations, the state-centred bias is self-reinforcing to the extent that it militates against the development of just the kind of governance structures through which, by analogy with the internal governance structures of states, new implicit and explicit common goods at the global level might be nurtured.

In the case of individualism, the limits of international law were until recently even more palpable. Because states and not individuals were the recognized subjects of international law there was little scope for international law to generate individual legal entitlements and obligations, still less to require their direct application. Led by the development of global frameworks for the protection of human rights, this has changed somewhat since the second half of the twentieth century. Yet it remains the case that individuals are very much the secondary and residual subjects of international law and the individualist dimension of its political ontology remains relatively underdeveloped.

In summary, therefore, the international domain displays its state-parasitic quality across all three key issues of political modernity. The international community is at best a secondary political community whose constituent units are states. Its generative resources are restricted to the universal domain, and within that domain there has been a historical preponderance of formalism over substantivism in accordance with a situational logic in which only the state has legitimate access to more particular reasons and emotions. And, to complete the picture of historical subservience, the scope of both collectivist and individualist elements of its political ontology remains circumscribed by the dominant position of the state.

2.3 Situating the European Union

There is certainly nothing novel in the suggestion that, as a development of late political modernity, the EU lies somewhere 'in between'[55] the national and the international domains. But if this in-between placement is broadly acknowledged, it is quite diversely characterized. De Tocqueville once said that is easier to invent something new than to find a new word to describe it, and in that spirit many have been prepared to adopt and adapt the old languages either of statehood[56] or of internationalism[57] to account for the EU. A third group prefers to underline the EU's novelty, to stress the *sui generic* character[58] of its 'unidentified political object'.[59] This unidentified object may approximate to a compound democracy,[60] a transnational consociation,[61] a commonwealth,[62] a post-Hobbesian non-state,[63] a *Bund*,[64] or a *federation d-états-nations*,[65] to name but a few of the candidate neologisms.

It is never clear, however, what or how much such definitional claims seek to accomplish, nor, it follows, precisely what is at stake in disputes

[55] On the resilience of this idea, see Wind, M., 'The European Union as a Polycentric Polity: Returning to a Neo-medieval Europe?' in J. H. H. Weiler and M. Wind, eds., *European Constitutionalism Beyond the State* (Cambridge University Press, 2003), 103–131.

[56] See, e.g., Mancini, F., 'Europe: The Case for Statehood', 4 *European Law Journal* (1998) 29–42.

[57] For an excellent overview of the resilience of internationalist language in the European supranational context, see De Witte, B., 'The European Union as an International Legal Experiment', Chapter 1 in the current volume.

[58] See, e.g., MacCormick, Neil, *Who's Afraid of the European Constitution?* (London: Imprint Academic, 1995).

[59] As described by Jacques Delors in 1985. For discussion, see Drake, H., *Jacques Delors: Perspectives on a European Leader* (London: Routledge, 2000), at 5.

[60] See Fabbrini, *Compound Democracies* (2007).

[61] See e.g. Dehousse, R., 'European Institutional Architecture After Amsterdam: Parliamentary System or Regulatory Structure?', 35 *Common Market Law Review* (1998) 595.

[62] See, e.g., MacCormick, Neil, *Questioning Sovereignty: Law, State and Nation in the European Commonwealth* (Oxford University Press, 1999).

[63] Schmitter, P., 'If the Nation-State Were to Wither away in Europe, What Might Replace It?', in S. Gustavsson and L. Lewin, eds., *The Future of the Nation State* (Stockholm: Nerenius & Santérus, 1996).

[64] Avbelj, M., *Theory of the European Bund* (PhD thesis, European University Institute, 2009).

[65] See Beaud, Olivier, *Théorie de la Fédération* (Paris: Presses Universitaires de France, 2007).

between them. Either the labels are merely suggestive of certain important features of the supranational body politic but not intended to be exhaustive or mutually exclusive, in which case there is not much of moment in the choice and little to fight over. Or the labels are intended as strong descriptions and are meant to be mutually exclusive. But in that case the labels claim too much, for the proof of distinctiveness demands greater detail and complexity of understanding than any mere label is capable of evoking. A purely nominal approach to the specificity of the EU, then, tends towards opposite errors; either towards the easy indulgence of conceptual window-shopping or towards gratuitous and ultimately sterile disagreement.

If, instead, we ask how the EU fares in terms of each of the three broad and closely interconnected key issues of political modernity – political agency, generative resources and political ontology – we move beyond the idea of a singular, terminologically reductive answer while keeping very much in the foreground the comparative example of these mainstays of political modernity – the state and the international. By so doing, we can come to appreciate how, considered singly and in combination, the answers the EU has provided to these questions – each of which is decidedly law-centred – has come under increasing strain as supranational Europe has completed its first half century.

If we start once again with the question of collective agency, it is indisputable that the EU is not and never has been an exclusively individual-centred political community – and so cannot be a primary political community in the pure sense of the state. Equally, it is rarely claimed that it is an international organization *simpliciter*, that it is merely the creature of its Member States without any special adornments. Rather, if we remind ourselves of the four measures of collective agency within a polity – abstraction, autonomy, comprehensiveness and self-constraint – the EU scores at intermediate points on the continuum between the poles of statehood and international organization classically conceived.

The process of abstraction by which supranational Europe acquired an identity as a distinct political community has been a highly uneven and complex one. In the telling of this story, it is often, and with considerable substance, suggested that the EU is a project driven much more by structural hardware than cultural software – by laws, institutions, political projects and administrative processes rather than by a

strong community of attachment or sympathy.[66] Yet in structural terms
the EU has displayed neither unity nor continuity. Its staggered origins
between 1951 and 1957 were as three separate international organizations, and even when a Merger Treaty was agreed in 1965 this supplied
common institutions rather than a single legal entity. The creation of
the European Union in 1992 under the Treaty of Maastricht introduced
a new complexity, as it merely supplemented the existing European
Communities. Indeed, only with the implementation of the Treaty of
Lisbon in 2009 have all predecessor organizations been replaced and
succeeded by the European Union, though even with the accomplishment of institutional unity the Treaty regime will remain a plural one.
More generally, the 'semi-permanent Treaty revision process'[67] in place
since the passage of the Single European Act of 1987 and embracing
major reforms at Maastricht, Amsterdam, Nice and now Lisbon, has
meant that the EU has been far more structurally unsettled in the second
quarter century of its life than in the first. And if we add to the mix the
four waves of Enlargement that have transformed the original Western
European club of six members to today's sprawling association of
twenty-seven, with the latest Central and Eastern Enlargement of the
early years of the new century by far the largest and geographically most
dispersed to date, we find a discontinuity in territorial focus to match
that of institutional design.[68] What is more, internal non-fixity has from
the outset been combined with external blurring. Supranational Europe
has had to share a crowded institutional space with and has been
required to negotiate close and complex relations with other regionally
specific or regionally concentrated organizational innovations, most
notably the North Atlantic Treaty Organisation and the Council of
Europe.[69]

---

[66] See, e.g., Shaw, J. and A. Wiener, 'The Paradox of the "European Polity"', in
   M. Green Cowles and M. Smith, eds., *The State of the European Union*, vol. 5
   (Oxford University Press, 2000), 64–89.

[67] de Witte, Bruno, 'The Closest Thing to a Constitutional Conversation in Europe:
   The Semi-Permanent Treaty Revision Process', in P. Beaumont, C. Lyons and
   N. Walker, eds., *Convergence and Divergence in European Public Law* (Oxford:
   Hart Publishing, 2002), 39–57.

[68] For extended analysis, see Cremona, M., ed., *The Enlargement of the European
   Union* (Oxford University Press, 2003).

[69] See, e.g., Laffan, B., *Integration and Co-operation in Europe* (London:
   Routledge, 1992).

Yet for all the lack of clarity of the structural picture, it is undeniable that supranational Europe has nevertheless acquired some measure of collective identity, some abstract sense of itself as distinct from its shifting and variegated legal and institutional machinery, from its Member States and indeed from other regimes sharing the same regional space. For much of the EU's history, however, it has been quite possible to account for this in ways that downplay the political dimension of that collective identity, and that suggest only a moderate return in terms of the other agency criteria of autonomy, comprehensiveness and self-constraint. Such an approach to the limitations of the EU as an original political form would typically stress two features.

In the first place, it would stress the importance of the institutional bureaucracy of the EU. It would emphasize the way in which a significant concentration of personnel across the various supranational institutions – in particular the Commission as official keepers of the generic EU interest, but also the Council, Parliament and Courts – had created an unparalleled intensity of transnational administrative self-consciousness.[70] In this way there has emerged a truly European cadre of officials whose primary allegiance is to the European project and whose basic sense of political community lies with one another. On this view, collective European agency has a tangible but narrow cultural base. It is something that, in common understanding, takes place 'at' Brussels, Luxembourg, etc., rather than 'in' Europe in a deeper, territorial sense – the choice of preposition betraying a two- rather than a three-dimensional understanding of political community.[71]

In the second place, however, this sense of collective agency becomes extended and amplified through the robust legal persona of the EU. Writing in the early 1980s, before the Single European Act and the gradual development of qualified majority voting as the supranational norm, Joseph Weiler drew attention to the 'the dual character of

---

[70] There is an extensive political science and sociological literature on this. For a recent overview, see Cini, M., *European Union Politics* (2nd edn, Oxford University Press, 2007), Part Three, 'Institutions and Actors'.

[71] This continues to be how the EU is typically viewed from the mass-mediated outside. In American newspapers, for example, events take place 'at' the EU, in the form of the Commission headquarters in Brussels, much as events take place 'at' the United Nations, in the form of its headquarters in New York. See further, Walker, Neil, 'Europe at 50: A Midlife Crisis? Democratic Deficit and Sovereignty Surplus', 15 *Irish Journal of European Law* (2008) 23–34.

supranationalism'[72] as the defining frame of supranational Europe's early evolution. At that stage, the highly developed character of legal or normative supranationalism in the core area of the internal market stood in stark contrast to a modestly conceived decisional or political supranationalism, but the two were closely related. Indeed, the early prominence of legal supranationalism, and the intrepid contribution of the European Court of Justice to this, was possible and explicable precisely *because* decisional or political supranationalism remained largely undeveloped, with the Member States retaining a *de jure* or *de facto* veto power in many areas of European policy-making. The key to the attractiveness of law as the vehicle of supranational agency, then, had to do with its *instrumental* potential. It lay in its regulatory capacity to steer, consolidate and guarantee positive-sum intergovernmental bargains across wide-ranging aspects of economic integration and some more limited aspects of market-correcting regulation, without threatening key national political prerogatives.

At the heart of this instrumentally grounded legal supranationalism was a strong assertion of the autonomy of the supranational legal order. In its early establishment of the doctrines of primacy and direct effect, the Court elaborated a view of the juridical universe in which the supranational legal order was treated as independent of those of the states and as taking priority over state law in areas of overlap.[73] What is more, as guardian of the supranational legal order the Court understood itself to have competence over the limits of its own and the Community's jurisdiction. This has reinforced a sense of its autonomy, even if, unlike states for whom the two attributes automatically went together, the EU has claimed 'autonomy *without* [...] exclusivity',[74] and so without comprehensiveness of jurisdiction over its territory and subject population. Yet the Court has conceived of its jurisdictional frontiers in highly open-ended terms, curtailed neither by express restrictions in the treaties nor by any recognition of the superior normative authority of any other legal site but only by the shifting

---

[72] Weiler, J. H. H., 'The Community System: The Dual Character of Supranationalism', 1 *Yearbook of European Law* (1981) 267–306.

[73] See in particular *Van Gend en Loos* v. *Nederlandse Administratie der Belastingen* [1963] ECR; *Costa* v. *ENEL* [1964] ECR 585.

[74] Walker, Neil, 'Late Sovereignty in the European Union', in Neil Walker, ed., *Sovereignty in Transition* (Oxford University Press, 2003), 3–32 at 23.

boundaries of an increasingly 'holistic'[75] conception of market integration. And as a further measure of legal self-assertion, the Court in various landmark decisions has sought to assume, in a manner that preempts or repels external interference, a more general role in policing its own boundaries. In its claim, against the danger of encroachment of state constitutional law, that respect for fundamental rights also forms an integral part of the general principles of Community law,[76] just as in its cultivation and stewardship of a small 'c' constitutional identity in which all EU institutions would be subject to internal judicial supervision[77] and upon which other transnational courts could not transgress,[78] the Court has sought to seal off its legal order from intrusive forms of external influence.

The assertion of such a robust legal persona has been the key to the capacity of the EU, operating from its narrow stronghold of institutional power, to exercise continental regulatory authority. It has made for a form of collective agency of unprecedented transnational reach and strength, yet without directly encroaching on the fuller political agency of the states themselves. Such an approach resonated very closely with many of the earliest economic justifications of the EU. In their very different ways, for instance, two of the most political influential of the early grand theories of integration, the German ordoliberal tradition[79] and Hans Ipsen's idea of the EU as a special purpose association,[80] were supported by legal-instrumentalist premises. For the ordoliberals, the Treaty of Rome supplied Europe with its own economic constitution, a supranational market-enhancing system of rights whose legitimacy depended on the absence of democratically responsive

---

[75] On 'market holism' see Somek, A., *Individualism: An Essay on the Authority of the European Union* (Oxford University Press, 2008).

[76] *Nold* v. *Commission* [1974] ECR 491.

[77] *Parti Ecologiste ('Les Verts')* v. *European Parliament* [1986] ECR 1339; [1987] 2 CMLR 343.

[78] Opinion 1/91 (Draft Opinion on the EEA) [1991] ECR I-6079.

[79] See, e.g., Mestmacker, E.-J., 'On the Legitimacy of European Law', 58 *RabelsZ* (1994) 615; see also Chalmers, D., 'The Single Market: From Prima Donna to Journeyman', in Jo Shaw and G. More, eds, *New Legal Dynamics of European Union* (Oxford: Clarendon Press, 1996), 55–72. On the continuities between the legal and political thought of the Weimar Republic and post-war thinking about supranationalism more generally, see Joerges, Christian and N. S. Ghaleigh, eds., *Darker Legacies of Law in Europe* (Oxford: Hart Publishing, 2003).

[80] Ipsen, H-P., 'Europäische Verfassung – Nationale Verfassung', 22 *Europarecht* (1987) 195–213.

will formation and consequential pressure towards market-interfering socio-economic legislation at the supranational level, a matter which should instead be left to the Member States – and even there only in so far as compatible with the bedrock economic constitution. Ordoliberal theory, then, provides a classic case in which the rule of law, through generating and ring-fencing a framework of economic exchange centred on the four freedoms, provides a platform for the efficient operation of a capitalist economic logic. Ipsen's theory, to which Giandomenico Majone's contemporary work on the idea of a European 'regulatory state'[81] is a notable successor, shares with ordoliberalism the idea that supranationalism should transcend partisan politics. Here, however, the instrumentality of law is extended so that the invisible hand of the market is supplemented by the expert hand of the technocrat. The scope of European law is not restricted to negative integration – to the market-making removal of obstacles to wealth-enhancing free trade – but also extends to certain positive measures of an administrative nature. In Majone's elaborately developed model – one that has continued to capture the sensibility of a significant part of the Brussels elite – these regulatory measures are concerned not with macro-politically sensitive questions of distribution, but with risk-regulation in matters such as product and environmental standards, where expert knowledge is deemed paramount, and where accountability, it is argued, is best served by administrative law measures aimed at transparency and enhanced participation in decision-making by interested and knowledgeable parties rather than the volatile preferences of broad representative institutions.

However, the delicate balance achieved by centring the EU's collective agency within a narrow institutional framework aided by a strong legal instrumentalism could not hold indefinitely. As is well known, the pursuit of the narrow economic objectives of the Union have increasingly spilled over into politically contentious areas of traditionally national jurisdiction such as working conditions, social discrimination, social security, health, education and internal security. This has

---

[81] Majone, G., 'The Rise of the Regulatory State in Europe', 17 *West European Politics* (1994) 77–104; on the connections between Ipsen and Majone, see Joerges, Christian, '"Good Governance" in the European Internal Market: An Essay in Honour of Claus-Dieter Ehlermann', *European University Institute Working Paper RSC No. 2001/29* (2001).

occurred both negatively, through the expansion of the scope of application of EU economic law to include questions of the relationship between market objectives and wider market-correcting public policy considerations; and positively, through the incremental spread of EU competence into some of these areas, aided and abetted by the gradual increase in majority voting from the Single European Act onwards. As a result of this expansion, both the ordoliberal approach and the regulatory state approach have become increasingly vulnerable to the charge of drawing an artificial distinction between technical questions of market-making and standard-setting and deeply contested questions of value preference and transnational resource and risk allocation.[82]

Such a tension was in truth present from the very outset of the supranational project, but becomes all the more evident as the EU, either through its negative or its positive jurisdiction, makes more and more interventions that involve politically salient choices and reduce the capacity of states themselves to make these choices or to pursue them effectively. If the strong and centrally guaranteed commitment to the juridical protection and perfection of the single market that lay at the heart of legal instrumentalism flourished in a context where market-making measures impinged only lightly on other social policy objectives, or at least where states retained the procedural means to veto politically controversial collective commitments in pursuit of these other social policy objectives – and therefore were slow to make such collective commitments in situations where there were obvious winners and losers – so the expansion of the scope of negative integration and the concomitant growth of 'political supranationalism', with its shift towards a majoritarian logic, decisively changed the dynamic of integration. Inevitably, more and more controversial value choices began to be reflected onto the legal domain – thereby removing some of the objective, efficiency-maximizing veneer from legal supranationalism.[83]

---

[82] See, e.g., Follesdal, A. and S. Hix, 'Why there is a Democratic Deficit in the EU: A Reply to Majone and Moravcsik', 44 *Journal of Common Market Studies* (2006) 533–562.

[83] Weiler, J. H. H., 'The Transformation of Europe', in J. H. H. Weiler, ed., *The Constitution of Europe: 'Do the New Clothes Have an Emperor?' and Other Essays on European Integration* (Cambridge University Press, 1999), 10–101.

The danger, then, was that the very strength of the legal instrument in supplying 'both the object and agent of integration'[84] – in providing the primary measure of the integration settlement as well as the means of arriving at that settlement – would become a liability. The threat was that the legal proofing of particular agreements against political reappraisal and the prevention of new supranational initiatives except through still highly consensual and only moderately democratically inclusive procedures, would become more a way of avoiding or excluding the legitimate expression of political choice and less a means of protection against free-riding or against ideologically inspired resistance to or fickleness towards positive-sum collective commitments. In response to this, as we shall see in due course, the question of collective agency has come to be revised through more expansive discourses of citizenship and constitutional democracy in a process which has further complicated the role of law. But for now let us simply record that in the early rise and long consolidation of supranational authority, the prominence of the institutional and legal-instrumental dimension offered both a vital channel and a limiting condition of its collective agency.

Let us turn now to the generative resources of the EU, and in particular to the question of whence it draws its reasons and its bonds of political community. Put simply, European law has traditionally been both (even) less well situated than broader sites of international law to draw upon one aspect of universalism – namely substantive universalism – and less well situated than national constitutional sites to draw upon particularist themes. Globally situated and directed forms of international law may, as we have seen, be highly vulnerable to the charge of imperialism – to the domination of Western interests under the label of universalism. But because they claim to draw no determinate boundaries over population or territory these global sites can at least in principle make a direct claim to represent universal interests and values. In contrast, any such invocation of universalism by the EU cannot (any more than its invocation by states can) deny that its geographical boundaries and populations are not coterminous with the fullest jurisdiction of law considered as a substantive universal. Unlike the national constitutional level, moreover, the EU, as by far the most integrated and politically powerful of the regional free trade associations, cannot even

---

[84] Dehousse, R. and J. Weiler, 'The Legal Dimension', in W. Wallace, ed., *The Dynamics of European Integration* (London: Pinter, 1990), 242–260 at 243.

draw upon a common and regularly reinforced supranational tradition as an intimation of incipient universalism.

Accordingly, the EU's attempts to bridge the gap between its boundaries and the frontiers of universalism have tended instead either towards assertiveness or towards deference – either a 'levelling up' *from* the European experience or a 'levelling down' *to* the European experience. Assertively, in pursuit of the levelling-up approach, it may be proposed that the EU contribution to universal values is somehow *seminal*, often incorporating the quite literal claim that in Europe lies the historical seed of the very idea of universalism. This is seen, perhaps most famously in recent times, in the preamble to the Constitutional Treaty (and substantially retained in the successor Lisbon Treaty), where the 'special area of human hope' that is asserted to be Europe is also claimed as the seat of the 'cultural, religious and humanist inheritance' from which, it is further claimed, have developed 'the universal values of the inviolable and inalienable rights of the human person, freedom, democracy, equality and the rule of law'.[85] And if the assertive claim risks too much and raises the spectre of the incorrigible imperialism of the old world, the deferential claim may instead demand too little. When the EU treats itself as a mere local *reverberation* of a substantive principle that sounds universally – where, for example, it has been inclined to treat certain international treaty norms as automatically incorporated into the EU legal order just because the broader international order seems more suited to the universal title – its own regional claim to authority can sound duly muffled.[86]

---

[85] Treaty Establishing a Constitution for Europe, Article I-6, 16 December 2004, 2004 O.J. (C 310/1).

[86] See, for example, from the earlier jurisprudence of the ECJ, *Haegeman* v. *Belgium* (*Haegeman II*) [1974] ECR 449; *Bresciani* [1976] ECR 129; *Hauptzollamt Mainz* v. *C. A. Kupferberg* [1982] ECR 3641. Arguably, the ECJ has become much more assertive in recent years against the universal claims of the international order, and this assertiveness has typically taken the form not of a regional particularism unconcerned with matters of universal significance, but (in an approach that is at least implicitly *seminal*) of the claim to a privileged perspective of its own from which to interpret presumptively universal norms. The much-discussed recent *Kadi* jurisprudence may be seen as a clear example of this tendency. See Cases C-402/05P and C-415/05P, *Kadi and Al Barakaat* v. *Commission and Council*, judgment of the Court (Grand Chamber) of 3 September 2008. For extended discussion, see de Burca, Gráinne, 'The ECJ and the International Legal Order: A Re-evaluation', Chapter 3 in the current volume.

Equally, if we look in the other direction towards particularism, just because the EU already is a composite of national particulars, any claims of its own to particular identity and to a legitimacy derived from that particular identity have tended to suffer in comparison to these national particulars. Historically, there have been at least four routes to particularism sought by supranational Europe, each engaged in its own artifice, and each encountering the limitations, obstacles or pitfalls associated with that artifice. A first is *aggregative particularism*. Following the logic of composition, the particularity of the EU may be defined in lowest common denominator terms, as the floor of things-held-in-common by the national units – as, for example, in the long-standing invocation of the language of 'common constitutional traditions' in the ECJ's human rights jurisprudence.[87] A second is what we might call *negative particularism*, where what Europe has in common is defined in terms of what *it is not* rather than what it affirmatively is. This is a theme which, for example, in the simultaneous moment of European constitutional drafting and global controversy over the legality of war with Iraq in 2001–3 threatened to harden into a rhetorical orthodoxy of anti-Americanism. It is also a theme which one finds in the dark side of European migration or security politics, as a reason not to welcome or not to trust those of a particular ethnicity, or territorial origin, or faith.[88] A third is what we might call *self-denying particularism*, a sense in which what is legally peculiar to the EU is itself a rejection of particularism – as summed up in the recently adopted EU motto, 'united in diversity'. A fourth is what we might call *cosmetic particularism*. This is the thin specificity of those attempts to create the bonds of a common Europe through ideological surfaces rather than the depths of common practice, to be found in any number of Commission-inspired slogans and campaigns over the years. Most recently we find this in the litany of EU-specific flags, mottos, anthems and special anniversaries, all specifically mentioned in the aborted Constitution,[89] though now no longer accorded the dignity of treaty recognition in the successor Lisbon Treaty. On one view, indeed, even the very idea of a documentary Constitution is itself just one more artefact of cosmetic particularism.

[87] Subsequently consolidated in Article 6(2) TEU (Treaty on European Union).
[88] See, e.g., European Union Agency for Fundamental Rights, *Annual Report 2009*.
[89] Article I-8 CT.

The point is not to be unduly critical of these approaches to the question of what is politically, and potentially juridically, particular to the EU. They all contain a kernel of insight, and are not necessarily without generative capacity in norm-making or symbolic terms. Yet they clearly lack the solid and familiar situational grounding of their national counterparts

If neither substantive universalism nor a narrow particularism has been a promising source of generative resource for the EU, different considerations apply to formal universalism. From the outset, the EU has sought to make a special virtue out of its adherence to the form of law, and to the ideas of universalism associated with this formalism. Here, the EU holds an advantage over classic international law in that the benefits of formalism can be seen to arise at two distinct levels. Not only is the traditional doctrine of *pacta sunt servanda* important in ensuring universal commitment amongst Member States, but the reach of EU law into national systems and their subjects and citizens entails that formal universalism also has an application at the level of the individual legal actor. The specific contribution of formal universalism lies in its commitment to an ethic of formal equality both amongst states as otherwise unevenly powerful collective political and economic players and amongst their individuals as participants and 'factors of production' in the transnational market-place. Formal universalism, then, speaks directly to those values of certainty, calculability and reciprocity that are closely aligned to the market-making and market-enhancing aims of the EU. Again the legal dimension is vital, as it is precisely the basic technology of law and of legal reasoning, with its commitment to and guarantee of universalizability, that generates the idea of formal equality and the reciprocal commitments necessary to make the implementation of a regime of formal equality credible.

Legal *universalism*, then, with its emphasis on formal equality of legal status and protection, speaks to a set of values that are different from but complementary to legal *instrumentalism*, which is concerned with the capacity to articulate and ensure the overall design capacity of supranationalism. What the prominence of legal universalist argument has also done is to reinforce the overall centrality of law to the situational ethics of the EU. Yet, as with instrumentalism and for reasons that spring from the same source, formal universalism has become an increasingly precarious virtue. Where the EU becomes more involved in compensatory social legislation, or in areas such as internal security and defence with a more distant link to the market-place, and where the emphasis moves from judicially led negative integration to legislation-centred positive integration, the shape of the appropriate legal tools changes and formal universalism becomes less suited to the regulatory tasks at hand.[90] The emphasis, then, begins to shift away from formal universalism towards a more substantively committed attitude, whether universalist or particularist, and the question of how an 'in-between' entity such as the EU can legitimately draw upon either approach arises more sharply than ever.

If we turn, finally, to the question of political ontology, here we find a very distinctive balance between individualism and collectivism in the historical development of the EU. On the one side, there is a red line connecting formal universalism (at the inter-subjective rather than the inter-state level) to individualism. If the formal universalism of the treaty framework, in a continental extension of Constant's 'Freedom of the Moderns',[91] fashions a legally guaranteed system of negative freedom for all within the internal market area from state-sponsored barriers to economic activity, then this already places the individual and the pursuit of individual ends, whether as an expression of self-interest or as a vindication of moral autonomy and rationality,[92] in a privileged position. The ECJ (European Court of Justice), moreover, has from the outset underscored the individualist emphasis of the general scheme by adopting an explicitly *rights-centred* approach. It has construed the Treaty obligation to establish an internal market and the four freedoms 'not as a programmatic goal to be realized through political legislation but as a set of directly enforceable individual rights'.[93] In similar vein, the principle of non-discrimination on grounds of nationality and the

---

[90] This is a theme, for example, of much of the literature on comitology (see, e.g., Joerges, Christian and E. Vos, eds., *EU Committees: Social Regulation, Law and Politics* (Oxford: Hart Publishing, 1999)) and on new methods of governance (see, e.g., Walker, Neil and Gráinne de Búrca, 'Reconceiving Law and New Governance', 13 *Columbia Journal of European Law* (2007) 519.

[91] On the relevance of Constant's writings to the EU, see, e.g., Bellamy, R., 'The Liberty of the Post-Moderns? Market and Civic Freedom in the EU', LSE 'Europe in Question' Discussion Paper Series 01/2009 (2009).

[92] For discussion of the different Hobbesian and Kantian strands of individualism in the context of the EU, see Scharpf, Fritz, 'Legitimacy in the Multilevel European Polity', in P. Dobner and M. Loughlin, eds., *The Twilight of Constitutionalism* (Oxford University Press, 2010).

[93] Ibid.

economic aspects of the new post-Maastricht citizenship provisions have been transformed into a further set of rights to access the social benefits and public services of all Member States.[94]

Such a rights-centred approach, therefore, adds to the existing emphases on legal instrumentalism and legal universalism to provide further reinforcement of the Union's legocentric posture. In so doing, it completes one historically dominant and, in its own terms, consistent orientation of the EU towards the key questions of political modernity. A narrowly conceived and largely depoliticized form of collective agency is joined to an emphasis upon formal universalism and philosophical individualism in pursuit of a vision of an expanded economic area in which the greater specialization and economies of scale thereby encouraged promotes a broader range of goods and services, lower per capita costs of public goods, higher productivity and increased employment and overall wealth.

This individualist emphasis, however, sits in increasingly uncomfortable balance with the more collectivist traditions and imperatives of the EU. As Joseph Weiler has long insisted, to concentrate only on the individualist dimension of the EU in its historical evolution and with reference to its record of accomplishment is to obscure the way in which this has developed in symbiosis with certain broader collective ideals.[95] In particular, the collective goods of peace and general prosperity have figured large in the narrative of the EU. Certainly, both were closely connected to the emphasis on individual economic well-being. Post-war peace was a precondition of the social stability and economic confidence that brought a rise in individual standards of living, just as enhanced economic well-being, and the forms of economic cooperation[96] and exchange necessary to foster that well-being, rapidly reduced the prospects of any recurrence of hostilities across Western Europe. Even more

[94] See, e.g., *Martinez Sala* v. *Freistaat Bayern* [1998] ECR I-2691; *Baumbast* v. *Secretary of State for the Home Department* [2002] ECR I-7091. See also Menendez, A. J., 'European Union Citizenship after *Martinez Sala* and *Baumbast*. Has European Law Become More Human But Less Social?', *RECON Working Papers 2009/5* (2009).

[95] See Weiler, 'The Transformation of Europe' (1999); see also his 'Europe – Nous coalisons des Etats, nouse n'unissons pas des hommes', unpublished paper (2009).

[96] E.g. the making of common economic cause over the traditional war-making industries in the original European Coal and Steel Community, established by the Treaty of Paris in 1951.

obviously, an increase in the material well-being of individuals was necessary to collective prosperity. But there was also more to peace than the servicing of individual well-being, just as there was more to prosperity than the aggregation of such well-being. Peace also spoke, minimally, to the very survival of a community of national communities in a continental environment unprecedented in its geographical concentration and historical resilience of conflict. And maximally, it spoke to the overcoming of old hatreds in a spirit of mutual forgiveness and of the forging of a common commitment to a more harmonious way of negotiating differences. As for collective prosperity, this spoke to a shared recognition and celebration of the overcoming of poverty and its causes, consequences and attendant indignity, and also to the material and psychological benefits and solidaristic dividend that accrued from a common sense of economic wealth and security being commonly enjoyed.

Yet for all their significance to the European project, these collective goods suffer from two important limitations. One, again noted by Weiler, concerns their declining relevance over time, and the sense that here the EU has been the victim of its own early success. As the memory of war and the fear of its recurrence receded, peace ceased to offer such a tangible, mind-concentrating collective virtue. And as the era of post-war economic reconstruction, with its strong welfarist undertow, came to an end, the relentlessness of the drive to prosperity provided a platform for the development in the 1980s and 1990s of a more narrowly acquisitive strain of materialism. The dilution of the initial impact and transformation of the initial meaning of these two foundational collective goods does not, of course, mean that they are irrelevant today. It does mean, however, that their place as mobilizing and defining values is less central, that they inevitably contribute less to the collectivist side of the balance sheet in the construction of supranational political community.

A second limitation of peace and prosperity concerns the distinctiveness of their character as collective goods and the uniqueness of their fit with the broader circumstances of supranational Europe. Both peace and prosperity meet the criteria of what we earlier named manifest collective goods. That is to say, their value as collective goods is palpable and uncontested, in one case because the very survival of the supranational community and its constituent parts is dependent upon its achievement and maintenance, and in the other because the realization of the good can be seen as something which in principle offers benefits to all. What is more, the pursuit of both of these goods clearly operates in symbiosis with the individualist pursuit of economic freedom. This is not to deny that peace and prosperity were genuinely endorsed as collective goods, nor that in the manner described above this endorsement produced certain self-reinforcing communitarian sentiments. Rather, it is to caution that as the attraction of these foundational goods has waned, we cannot assume that the other candidate collective goods which may be required to take their place will be so readily mobilized or so clearly compatible with the individualist core of the community.

In particular, as the power of the two foundational collective goods has faded, the collective dimension of community life will inevitably depend less on manifest value and prior or foundational purpose and more on the constructed goods of community. Yet we cannot assume that the EU is well placed to generate collective goods within the two sub-categories of such constructed goods, neither implicit nor explicit common goods. As regards the implicit common goods – those, such as a general sense of mutual trust or solidarity or the possession of a common culture, that are part and parcel of the very value of living together in a common community – any suggestion that these may provide transnational benefits entirely begs the question of their plausibility at that level. As the problems encountered by the EU whenever and however it seeks to develop its own sense of particular justification demonstrate, to what extent the EU possesses the sociological wherewithal to generate implicit common goods is highly doubtful.

In turn, this doubt is intimately linked to the question of the viability of explicit common goods. The development of explicit common goods, to recall, requires institutions of government able and willing to take decisions that track all relevant interests as well as other institutions capable of implementing these decisions effectively. However, the generation of such institutional capacity itself depends upon the existence of a suitably strong motivation to put things in common, which in turn depends upon (and, in a circular process, reinforces) a prior platform of implicit public goods. What is more, in the EU not only, as we have argued, is the robustness of that prior platform of 'common sense' in doubt, but the bar is set particularly high in terms of what constitutes a suitably strong motivation to generate the requisite institutional capacity. This is so because such a motivation has to be sufficiently broadly and deeply held to overcome those formidable legal and political impediments to capacity-building that arise from pressures to protect the collective prerogatives of other and prior (national) political communities and, relatedly, to preserve the predominance of an individualist ontology within the EU.

An assessment of this high bar of legal and political impediments brings us back to the basic difficulties persistently faced by the EU as it tries to move beyond its market-making core. Legally, as already noted, the scope of application of EU law for the purposes of ensuring negative integration against other national public policy considerations, and the common goods associated with these, is greater than its capacity to achieve positive integration at the supranational level in those same areas of public policy and common goods. This discrepancy is in some measure an unavoidable consequence of transnational economic freedom providing the jurisdictional core of the Union. But it is exacerbated by the asymmetric way in which the Court has traditionally treated and today continues to treat the relationship between those economic freedoms and competing public policy goals.[97] Economic liberties, and the rights in which they are encased, are typically accorded full value, while some competing national public goods and the institutional solutions associated with the promotion of these goods are subject to strict proportionality requirements,[98] and yet other national concerns of significant importance, typically budgetary concerns over the access to domestic welfare and social service resources by non-nationals, are disregarded completely.[99] And even when the discrepancy can in legal principle be overcome and it is possible for the EU to re-regulate for common market-correcting public goods at the European level, the

---

[97] See Scharpf, 'Legitimacy' (2010); Menendez, 'European Union Citizenship', (2009); Somek, *Individualism* (2008); Azoulai, L., 'The Court of Justice and the Social Market Economy: The Emergence of an Ideal and the Conditions for its Realization', 45 *Common Market Law Review* (2008) 1335–1356.

[98] See, e.g., the importance accorded to free movement of capital in the Golden Shares litigation (*Commission* v. *Portugal (Golden Shares)* [2002] ECR I-4731; the expansion of the scope of Article 95 as a market-making competence in the tobacco litigation (*Germany* v. *Parliament and Council (Tobacco Advertising)* [2000] ECR I-8419); and the elevation of freedom of establishment over collective socio-economic claims in recent labour law case-law (*Viking* C-438/05 11.12.2007; *Laval* C 341–05 18.12.2007).

[99] As in economic citizenship cases such as *Martinez Sala* and *Baumbast*, note 94; see also Scharpf, 'Legitimacy' (2010); Menendez, 'European Union Citizenship' (2009).

highly consensual and multistage legislative requirements through Commission, Parliament and Council and the difficulty of generating in such a diffuse institutional framework the concerted political commitment required to develop ambitious and state-encroaching forms of transnational social regulation, means that this will often not take place.

In a nutshell, the early symbiosis of individualism and a certain type of manifest collective good has given way to a situation in which the structural ascendancy of individualism increasingly demands to be countered by just the kinds of collectivism that individualism itself resists and that are in any case difficult to generate in substitution for national common goods in the transnational arena. What we are left with, then, is a lop-sided structure in which law plays a central role for its instrumental, formal and rights-promoting attributes. In this way, a truncated form of collective agency enables a combination of universalism and individualism, which matches one side of the nation-state narrative of political modernity. But despite a growing need for a counterbalance, the conditions remain underdeveloped for providing a complementary narrative line based upon the particularity of the transnational and the generation of common goods associated with that particularity.

2.4 The place of law in the supranational future: problem or solution?

If law has always been central to the success of the European supranational project, in the ways set out above it has also set limits to that success. Its combination of instrumentalism, formal universalism and rights assertiveness has proved crucial to the establishment of a single economic area. But as this has threatened to become too singular and too narrow a goal, is not this same combination of law-centred mechanisms, in its very conduciveness to that narrow goal, not in danger of becoming part of the problem rather than part of the solution?

Any easy conclusion to that effect would be to reckon without the polyvalence of law and the basic flexibility of its medium. Ironically, just as supranational law's star may have lost some of its internal energy, its external appeal has become more prominent.[100] The initial

---

[100] See further, Walker, Neil, 'The EU and the Rule of Law: Necessity's Mixed Virtue', in G. Palombella and N. Walker, eds., *Relocating the Rule of Law* (Oxford: Hart Publishing, 2008), 119–138.

1993 Copenhagen criteria governing the Central and Eastern European
wave of Enlargement included a stipulation that applicant states should
respect the rule of law, anticipating its formal specification as a condition of membership in the 1997 Treaty of Amsterdam.[101] A similar
approach is taken today to the EU's 'new' near-neighbours under the
Stabilization and Association Process in the Western Balkans and the
broader European Neighbourhood Policy (ENP).[102] In these various
processes the building of the institutional guarantees of legal rationality
in the form of a well-functioning court system and legally regulated and
respectful state bureaucracy are seen not only as direct contributions to
the 'civilization' of the state, but also, in a strong echo of the formal and
instrumental reasoning discussed above, as a further indirect contribution thereto by providing both the universalist ethic and the design
framework of a successful (and effectively civilizing) market economy.

And it is with the promotion of the virtues of a juridically grounded
formal rationality and instrumentalism that we approach the nub of
the increasingly influential idea of Europe as a uniquely 'normative
power'[103] or civilian power, relying upon a combination of example
and civil persuasion rather than the military might or threat offered by
other regional actors. Increasingly, too, the modelling or exemplary
aspect of this is treated more insistently and more holistically. It is not
just that the European way offers lessons in polity-building, but, that,
increasingly, it offers *itself* as paradigmatic. As Kleinfeld and Nicolaidis
put it, '(m)any in the EU believe that the Union's unique contribution to
the world is its own process of "enmeshment," which is purported to
have brought peace and prosperity to the continent. The EU's main
model of change is its own integration process, whereby economic

---

[101] Article 49 TEU.

[102] See *European Neighbourhood Policy*, European Commission 2004, 273. See
  also the European Security Strategy of the same period: 'European Security
  Strategy: A Secure Europe in a Better World', 2003, available online at http://
  consilium.europa.eu/uedocs/cmsUpload/78367.pdf. See more generally,
  Cremona, M., 'The European Neighbourhood Policy: Partnership, Security and
  the Rule of law', in A. Mayhew and N. Copsey, eds., *European Neighbourhood
  Policy and Ukraine* (Falmer: University of Sussex, Sussex European Institute,
  2005) 25–54.

[103] See, e.g., Manners, I., 'Normative Power Europe: A Contradiction in Terms?',
  40 *Journal of Common Market Studies* (2002) 235–258; Johansson-Nogues, E.,
  'The (Non) Normative Power EU and the European Neighbourhood Policy: An
  Exceptional Policy for an Exceptional Actor', 7 *European Journal of Political
  Economy* (2007) 181–194.

integration through trade liberalization is pursued on a reciprocal basis and underpinned by converging standards, harmonization and mutual recognition.'[104] Here, then, the very 'in-between' situational logic which means that Europe cannot make the kinds of justificatory claims appropriate to the polar points of international law and state law works in its favour. On the one hand, its 'particular' experience as a self-contained polity or transnational regime means that, unlike international law, its persuasive authority can include an important exemplary component for other polities or transnational regimes. On the other hand, the thinness of its transnational model means that, compared to the national case, its 'transfer value' is not undermined – or at least not so obviously undermined – by the cultural rootedness of that particular experience.

Be that as it may – and allowing that soft power of this sort is certainly not immune from charges of imperial overreach[105] – we must also acknowledge that the generally higher profile and impressive sheen of European law's external façade cannot cure its internal defects. The increased salience of external legal authority can ensure that the 'law brand' is not diminished overall in the supranational theatre – that there is no *general* ideological impediment to law's chances of success – but it cannot alter the *specific* structural conditions that make law, in the functional mix we have set out, progressively less adequate to the conditions of the European project. So can law, then, taking account of its resilient symbolic strength, be *remixed* in such a way that it promises to become part of the European supranational solution again rather than stuck as part of the problem? This question brings us, in our concluding discussion, back to the foundational issue of political modernity – to the question of collective agency – and to the puzzle of how and whether law may contribute differently than it has to date in the treatment and resolution of the question of collective agency in the supranational context.

We may recall that the original settlement of the agency question in the EU context involved a very particular compromise. Put bluntly,

---

[104] See Kleinfeld, R. and K. Nicolaidis, 'Can a Post-Colonial Power Export the Rule of Law? Elements of a General Framework', in G. Palombella and N. Walker, eds., *Relocating the Rule of Law* (Oxford: Hart Publishing, 2008), 139–169 at 163. See also Kalypso Nicolaidis, 'Trusting the Poles? Constructing Europe through mutual recognition', 14 *Journal of European Public Policy* (2007) 682–698.

[105] Ibid.

political agency was retained by the states while legal agency was given to the EU, to be serviced by a powerful but numerically modest central cadre. Such a settlement rests on an implicit belief in the soundness of some combination of the two principles of delegation and demarcation.[106] Politically, the EU remains a secondary and derivative political community, much like any regime of international law, with original authority continuing to vest in and be delegated from the states. Legally, however, the scope and terms of the delegation are extensive and entrenched, and this is justified by the need to demarcate an area free from political horse-trading and the intrusion of inappropriate ideological considerations into formal and technical questions of market-making, market-perfecting and even market-correcting. However, as the management of Europe's economic area gradually and inexorably impinges upon broader public policy considerations, questions of political choice become unavoidable. And in response to this, alongside the intergovernmental Council, the directly elected Parliament has begun to take on many of the more familiar characteristics of a politically representative national chamber, while the Commission and the Court have also inevitably become more frequently and more deeply involved in political value judgements over competing individual and collective goods.

Politics, then, becomes more prominent within the governing discourses and institutional logics of the EU but, importantly, this happens *after the fact*, in response to growing pressures upon a system not built with this kind of broader political debate in mind and lacking a conception of constituent power and of title – of ultimate collective agency – that is adequate to that politicization. Instead, the question of title remains both obscure and controversial. Obscure, because, beyond the false neatness of a combination of the opposites – of legal autonomy and political dependence – it is not clear what the collective agency of an 'in-between' entity of the unprecedented character of the EU might entail. Controversial, because whatever it might entail it is bound to highlight differences and engender friction between those who are jealous of the political prerogatives of the states and those who would prefer a more expansive conception of supranational political community. Yet, arguably, unless the question of title is readdressed and treated in candid recognition of the evolving circumstance of supranationalism,

---

[106] For extended discussion, see Walker, 'Europe at 50' (2008).

this combination of obscurity and controversy will continue to feed through into the quotidian dynamics of the Union. First-order debates over the proper balance of goods and interests within the EU or over the particular content of the EU's own sponsored collective goods will continue to be overshadowed by – and so confused with or disabled by – second-order debates over whether and to what extent the EU *in principle* possesses independent political title to balance different deep political values and to develop robust collective goods of its own.

The beginning of attempts to face this problem and to grapple with what political agency might mean beyond a purely state-derivative conception can be seen in a number of recent initiatives in which law is allowed a more constitutive role in supranational affairs alongside its tried and tested triumvirate of instrumentalism, formal universalism and rights-recognition. To some extent, for example, this is true of the citizenship initiative at Maastricht, with its new understanding of membership of the supranational community. But a far more broadly receptive context for such a development was the documentary constitutional debate leading to the Constitutional Treaty of 2004. The subsequent failure of the Treaty, of course, renders any discussion of its merits hypothetical, but arguably the Treaty went some way towards addressing issues key to our concerns.

Typically, Constitutions serve four types of functions, and political pressure in favour of a constitutional initiative only mounts whenever the performance of one, or usually more, of these inter-related functions becomes attractive or urgent to a suitable coalition of important constituencies within a polity. These functions have to do with matters of form, content, process and, of direct relevance to us, authorship. The adoption of the documentary constitutional form tends to have a highly symbolic value, involving a claim that the use of the big 'C' word is appropriate to the scale of the transformation or the nature of the polity-setting in question. Content-based considerations concern the capacity of the constitutional instrument to deal with a range of fundamental questions about the institutions of government and the values and ends of the polity, and to do so in a holistic manner. Process-based considerations have to do with the way in which a typically wide-ranging constitution-making procedure can have both epistemic and motivational benefits – bringing a greater number of relevant considerations to the debate and helping to legitimate outcomes. Authorship-based considerations concern the choice or confirmation of who has basic title to political community – in whose name resides the agreement called the Constitution and the whole system of law and institutional framework recognized and vindicated by that Constitution.

The arrival of Europe's constitutional moment was a tale of highly mixed motives, one in which we can see all four functional imperatives at work.[107] The formal and symbolic dimension was important on either side of the debate, with supporters claiming the Constitution as a sign of the polity's maturity – of the ripeness for settlement of its *finalité politique* – and opponents claiming that the constitutional label, steeped as it was in the history of the modern state, presumed too much. Content-wise, the Constitution offered an opportunity for wide-ranging treaty reform, and did so against a backdrop where recent attempts at amendment by treaty had increasingly appeared to lack the gravitas necessary for them to succeed against sceptical state parties.[108] The Convention process, too, was intended as a way of smoothing the passage of the instrument, as well as bringing a broader range of national political and civil society voices to the table.[109]

For all its importance, indeed partly *because* of its importance, the question of authorship was addressed much more obliquely. Partly, this was a practical matter. The initiation of the constitutional process depended on the states as the existing Masters of the Treaties, and so it would have taken a more febrile political atmosphere than we saw in 2003 for them not to assume their familiar role as authors, and indeed in so doing to legislate for their own continuing authority over any subsequent amendment to the Constitutional Treaty.[110] Partly, too, it was a conceptual matter. As we have seen, the very idea of a form of title that in the political last analysis does not rest either (for states) with 'the people' or (for the international domain) with the states themselves is unknown in modern politics, and the question of how to imagine something beyond pure intergovernmentalism without falling into the

---

[107] See, e.g., Walker, Neil, 'Europe's Constitutional Momentum and the Search for Polity Legitimacy', 3 *International Journal of Constitutional Law* (2005) 211–238.

[108] See, e.g., Weiler, J. H. H., 'On the Power of the Word: Europe's Constitutional Iconography', 3 *International Journal of Constitutional Law* (2005) 173–190.

[109] See, e.g., Karlsson, Christen, 'Deliberation at the European Convention: The Final Verdict', 14 *European Law Journal* (2008) 604–619.

[110] CT Article IV-443; Article IV-447.

opposite error of contriving a single and irreducible people and popular sovereign of a new European superstate remains a vexed one.[111]

Yet we can at least begin to think of what a third way might look like. If, against the sceptic, it can be claimed that European constituent power is not merely derivative of national constituent power, we nevertheless must still acknowledge the national legacy of its foundations and, alongside the newer supranational dimension of authority, the resilience of the original national constituent powers. The collective 'people' of second-order supranational understanding, therefore, cannot simply replace the various first-order collective 'peoples', and so can never be just like the otherwise politically unencumbered and unmediated 'people' of our first-order state imaginary. The second-order people must instead describe a compound structure, incorporating but also augmenting the aggregate of first-order collective peoples.

If we are prepared to look, there is at last some intimation of these possibilities in the Constitutional Treaty debates, not least in the two-tier drafting process itself, with the new pan-European Convention preceding the familiar Intergovernmental Conference. Various formulations in and after the aborted Constitutional Treaty also hint at third way openings. In the Preamble and Article 1 'the citizens [singular] and States' were referred to as the ultimate authors, but elsewhere in the Preamble the 'peoples [plural] of Europe' are also invoked. And in subsequent official communications concerning the Constitution and the question of democratic renewal more generally, especially from the European Commission,[112] we often find the 'people' reduced to the singular alongside 'the States'. So what emerges is a vague sense of a dual constituent power, and indeed regular references in political discourse to 'dual legitimacy',[113] even if there is uncertainty as to the identity of its components, and an incomplete sense of the relationship between the two.

---

[111] See Walker, 'Europe's Constitutional Momentum' (2005).

[112] See, as just one of many examples, the frequent slippage between plural and singular in *A Constitution for Europe: Presentation to Citizens*, an information document produced by the Commission in the wake of the signing of the CT in 2003: available at http://europa.eu.int/futurum.

[113] Not least by the President of the Constitutional Convention: see, e.g., Giscard d'Estaing, Valéry, 'The Convention and the Future of Europe: Issues and Goals', 1 *International Journal of Constitutional Law* (2003) 346.

Of course, today the Constitution is yesterday's news, with the pro-
moters of the successor Lisbon process working assiduously to eradicate
all elements of the Constitutional Treaty's indulgence of constitutional
form, process and authorship while retaining most of its content.[114]
What, then, if anything, can be gained from resurrecting the half-
formed ideas of an unsuccessful initiative? Does constitutional failure,
and the hesitant nature of the initiative taken by the failed project over
the question of collective agency, not suggest that this kind of approach
is impractical, or undesirable, or both?

We need not draw such a negative conclusion. Perhaps the most
telling fact about the constitutional initiative, even if this has been
obscured by its failure and, indeed, by those so embarrassed by its
failure that they have sought to eradicate the whole experience from
common memory,[115] is not that it ran aground but that it was floated at
all. That a set of issues suggesting the possible transformation of the
basic form, constituent process, institutional content and authoritative
source of the Union achieved the necessary salience to be the subject of a
first constitutional initiative in a fifty-year-old polity is a tribute both to
the objective importance and urgency of what was at stake and to the
existence of sufficient commitment to put things in common, at least to
place them on the agenda for constitutional resolution. And even if, in
the wake of constitutional failure, support for a self-styled constitutional solution has eroded, nothing has happened either to render the
underlying issues in question less pressing nor, crucially, to suggest that
any better method of addressing them has been found than the constitutional way. Indeed, as the protracted birth pains of even the more
modestly conceived Lisbon Treaty have shown, reversion to the normal
treaty process has done nothing to alleviate the problems that helped
persuade Europe's leaders to seek a constitutional alternative in the
first place.

---

[114] See, e.g., Walker, Neil, 'Not the European Constitution', 15 *Maastricht Journal of European and Comparative Law* (2008) 135–141.

[115] See in particular the declaration of the June 2007 European Council that the 'constitutional concept' that it had endorsed so enthusiastically only four years previously, on the occasion of receiving a draft of the Constitutional Treaty from the Convention on the Future of Europe, was to be summarily 'abandoned'. Presidency Conclusions, Brussels European Council (21–22 June 2007).11177/ 1/07 Rev 1 Conc 2.

In these circumstances, unlikely as its immediate prospects may be, a revival of the constitutional project cannot be ruled out, and with it a second and perhaps more considered opportunity to look at the key question of collective agency. Of course, even if this does happen, and even if some version of dual legitimacy is pursued as a new compound approach to supranational title, that will provide no magic solution to the problems of the unbalanced polity. As has frequently been pointed out, the constitutional crucible offers no copper-bottomed guarantee of more inclusive participation, no deliberative panacea and no promise of increased support by its citizens even to the extent that any such participatory and deliberative dividends may be forthcoming.[116] Instead, the specification of a distinctive collective authorship and political agency that the constitutional self-attribution of title announces has a more limited purpose. Yet it is also a prior purpose. This is so because it speaks to a state of collective affairs in whose absence it is difficult to see how *any* attempts to pursue deeper political reforms and strengthen the institutional coherence, decision-making efficacy and common political culture of the EU – *regardless* of where and how these attempts strike the balance between expertise and voice, representation and participation, or majority will and minority veto – can be securely grounded. For the constitutional arena – and perhaps *only* the constitutional arena – offers the possibility that, as we bring down the curtain on an era of 'permissive consensus'[117] that allowed first-order decision-making to proceed and its benefits to accrue substantially unaffected by second-order considerations of what and who the EU stood for other than a legally demarcated set of interests delegated by the constituent states, we might begin the process of overcoming increasingly disabling second-order differences over the basic character of the EU polity in and through the very act of recognizing and addressing such differences as *our* common predicament. More specifically, a documentary constitutional commitment to overcome that predicament may, in a self-reinforcing fashion, supply the platform for the generation of a reflexive

---

[116] Perhaps most effectively, and most trenchantly, by Andrew Moravcsik, see, e.g., his 'What Can We Learn from the Collapse of the European Constitutional Project?', 47 *Politische Vierteljahresschrift* (2006) 2; Ladeur, K. H., '"We, the European People . . ." – Relâche?', 14 *European Law Journal* 2 (2008) 147–67.

[117] See, e.g., Hooghe, L. and G. Marks, 'A Postfunctionalist Theory of European Integration: From Permissive Consensus to Constraining Dissensus', 39 *British Journal of Political Science* (2008) 1–23.

awareness of such a common sense of authorship over time and for the gradual accumulation of a constitutional tradition that deepens and consolidates that common sense.[118]

And while it would, indeed, be an error to see this as any more than one modest element in the remaking of the European polity along lines which command general adherence, we should not fall into the opposite error of underestimating its importance. As we have sought to demonstrate, a Constitution is always both trace and catalyst, and this applies as much to the earlier foundations of state constitutionalism, and also to the many contemporary proposals for the constitutional refounding or revamping of national polities, as it does to the new supranational polity. The written constitution is an important trace in that its very promulgation, or even its threshold consideration, is already a sign, however modest, of the commitment and common understanding it seeks to encode. And the written constitution is also a catalyst in so far as it provides a means by which and a context in which to stimulate the deepening of that commitment and common understanding. Indeed, it is precisely this Janus-faced quality – the backward-looking recollection of common resources and gathering of existing potential just in order to solve forward-looking collective action problems – that has given documentary constitutionalism its uniquely modern hue. For in its assumption that nothing is more apt than our own joint commitments to shape our common world, constitutionalism invokes a social technology that was unknown to pre-modern cultures.

I suggested at the beginning of this chapter that the EU is best understood as a continuation of political modernity by other means rather than a clean break from the modern era. If that is indeed the case, then it may not announce a failure of our common imagination, but simply a reinvestment in it, to turn again to the legal techniques of documentary constitutionalism for new answers to old questions.

---

[118] See, e.g., Habermas, Jürgen, 'On Law and Disagreement: Some Comments on 'Interpretative Pluralism,' 16 *Ratio Juris* (2003) 187–199.

3 | *The ECJ and the international legal order: a re-evaluation*

GRÁINNE DE BÚRCA *

3.1 Introduction

The central role of the European Court of Justice in the process of 'constitutionalizing' EU law, whereby the Court has deemed certain provisions of EU law to be an integral and directly enforceable part of the law of the Member States, has long generated animated debate amongst EU law scholars. One part of this story which has not always attracted the same degree of attention is the way in which the Court of Justice extended aspects of its constitutionalization strategy to international legal norms. The relative paucity of EU Treaty provisions governing the status and effect of international law in the new European Communities at the time left considerable room for the Court to shape the answer to these questions. In some of its early case-law, the ECJ (European Court of Justice) adopted what has been called an 'automatic incorporation' approach to international agreements,[1] deeming them to be part of the EU legal order and their provisions to be enforceable in domestic and EU courts at the suit of individuals. In this way one of the most important sources of international law – international treaties – were from a relatively early stage treated by

* An earlier and longer article based on this chapter was presented as a paper at workshops at Fordham, NYU, Harvard and Yale Law Schools, and the Weatherhead Center for International Affairs at Harvard in 2008, and is published in the *Harvard International Law Journal*, 51 (2010). Thanks for helpful advice and comments on the longer versions are due to José Alvarez, George Bermann, Nehal Bhuta, Gabriella Blum, Iris Canor, Bruno de Witte, Martin Flaherty, Oliver Gerstenberg, Ryan Goodman, Andrew Kent, Benedict Kingsbury, Vladyslav Lanovoy, Katerina Linos, Jens Meierhenrich, Gerry Neuman, Alec Stone Sweet, Joel Trachtmann, Mark Tushnet, Neil Walker, Joseph Weiler, Antje Wiener and to all of the participants at the various workshops. Thanks for diligent research assistance are due to Joanna Geneve and Jasper Pauw.
[1] Mendez, Mario, *The Legal Effect of Community Agreements: Lessons from the Court* (PhD thesis, European University Institute, 2009).

the Court as a presumptively integral part of the new European legal order.[2] Even if the dimension of this case-law which generated the most extensive commentary was that which subsequently departed from the basic automatic-incorporation approach, namely the Court's decision to rule out the direct judicial enforceability of the GATT (General Agreement on Tariffs and Trade) and WTO (World Trade Organization) agreements,[3] the general approach of the ECJ to international treaties was to treat them as fully part of the EU legal order and judicially enforceable at the suit of litigants. Further, this embrace of treaties as a central part of the EU legal order was accompanied by what seemed to be a fairly open approach to customary international law as part of EU law.[4] By developing and using a range of doctrinal devices such as the principle of consistent interpretation and the treatment of international legal principles as part of the general principles of EU law, the ECJ exhibited an attitude of notable openness towards international law. In all, its approach to international legal obligations appeared to be one of engagement and loyalty, with the Court positioned as an agent to ensure compliance on the part of the EU and its Member States with the EU's international obligations. This picture of the ECJ as a faithful enforcer of international legal obligations meshed well with the more general self-image promoted by the EU of an organization devoted to the international rule of law, whose international profile was defined in significant part by this distinctive commitment to international law and institutions.

Placed against this background picture of the Court as an agent of integration of the EU and the international legal orders, the landmark

---

[2] See cases 181/73 *Haegeman* v. *Belgium* (*Haegeman II*) [1974] ECR 449, 87/75 *Bresciani* [1976] ECR 129, and 104/81 *Hauptzollamt Mainz* v. *C. A. Kupferberg* [1982] ECR 3641.

[3] See in particular cases 21–24/72 *International Fruit Co.* v. *Produktschap voor Groenten en Fruit* [1972] ECR 1219 and C-149/96 *Portugal* v. *Council* [1999] ECR I-8395.

[4] See cases C-286/90 *Anklagemyndigheden* v. *Poulsen and Diva Navigation* [1992] ECR I-6019, para. 9 and C-162/96 *Racke GmbH & Co.* v. *Hauptzollamt Mainz* [1998] ECR I-3655 para. 46. For a detailed treatment of the ECJ's approach to customary international law, see Eeckhout, P. and W. Wouters, 'Giving Effect to Customary International Law Through EC Law', in J. Prinssen and A. Schrauwen, eds., *Direct Effect: Rethinking a Classic of EC Legal Doctrine* (Groningen: Europa Law Publishing, 2002), 183.

judgment of the ECJ in the *Kadi I/Al Barakaat* case in 2008,[5] in which the Court expressed a cautious and even sceptical attitude towards fundamental parts of the international legal order and underscored the constitutional autonomy of the EU from international law, came as something of a surprise. The tone and reasoning of the judgment – which was a judgment of the Grand Chamber in a highly anticipated and closely observed case – seemed very much at odds with the picture described above of an open judicial embrace of international law as an integral part of the EU legal order.[6]

This chapter takes the occasion of the judgment in *Kadi I* and its progeny[7] as a moment for re-evaluating the Court's approach to the place of international law in the EU legal order, and to the place of the Union within the international legal order. While the Court's GATT/WTO case-law previously appeared to stand out as the exception to an otherwise welcome judicial incorporation of international legal obligations,[8] a rereading in the light of the *Kadi I* ruling and recent developments in other areas of case-law[9] suggests the development of a more

[5] Cases C-402/05P and C-415/05P, *Kadi and Al Barakaat* v. *Commission and Council*, judgment of the Court (Grand Chamber) [2008] ECR I-6351.

[6] Indeed, even the General Court in its follow-up ruling in *Kadi 2* expressed reservations about the ECJ's approach, and appeared to follow and apply the reasoning of the ECJ with some reluctance: T-85/09, *Kadi* v. *Commission*, judgment of 30 September 2010.

[7] For some of the concurrent and subsequent line of related case-law see T-256/07 *People's Mojahedin Organization of Iran* v. *Council* (PMOI 1) [2008] ECR II-3019, T-284/08 *People's Mojahedin Organization of Iran* v. *Council* (PMOI 2) [2008] ECR II-3487, T-318/01, *Othman* v. *Council and Commission*, judgment of 11 June 2009, C-399/06 P and C-403/06 P, *Hassan and Ayadi* v. *Council and Commission*, judgment of 3 December 2009 and T-135/06–138/06, *Al-Faqih et al.* v. *Council*, judgment of 29 September 2010.

[8] For a recent notable WTO-related judgment, see C-120–121/06P, *Fiamm* v. *Council and Commission*, [2008] ECR I-6513, and the commentary of Dani, M., 'Remedying European Legal Pluralism: The FIAMM and Fedon Litigation and the Judicial Protection of International Trade Bystanders', 21 *European Journal of International Law* (2010) 303.

[9] See, e.g., Case C-308/06, *International Association of Independent TankerOwners (Intertanko) and others* v. *Secretary of State for Transport* [2008] ECR concerning international maritime law, in which the ECJ revived a technique it had abandoned in other cases involving the invocability of international agreements – namely by insisting that an agreement must 'confer individual rights' before it can be invoked as a standard to review Community legislation. The ECJ seemed to use this formalist technique to avoid discussing the relationship between the international standard on liability for maritime pollution and the EU Directive on ship-source pollution, and to avoid considering the nature and extent of the EU's obligations

selective and instrumental judicial approach over time. What stands out as a dominant theme in the case-law is the importance placed by the Court on the autonomy of EU law, and the way in which this concern for autonomy has come to take precedence over the Court's interest in the enforcement of EU compliance with international law. From a normative perspective, to be sure, the question of how and to what extent the EU should give effect to international law is a complicated one, as is the question of the extent to which the Court of Justice should act as the enforcement arm of the EU's international obligations. International obligations vary considerably in their content, nature and scope, and the international law-making process is a complex, flawed and differentiated one. Nevertheless, the tension between the EU's publicly avowed commitment to international law as a core feature of its international identity and the increasingly rather *ad hoc* and instrumentalist approach of the ECJ to international obligations, with its growing emphasis on the autonomy of the EU vis-à-vis the international legal order, is notable. First, the contrast between an international identity which is built on the idea of a distinctive commitment to international law and a selective and seemingly self-serving judicial practice risks the charge of hypocrisy. More practically, it suggests that the EU's attitude to international law and international obligations is considerably more complex, ambivalent and unreflective than the conventional presentation suggests. The EU – as evidenced by the uneven case-law of the ECJ on the subject – currently lacks a coherent constitutional stance on the relationship of international law to EU law, and this lack of a clear constitutional stance undermines the attempts of the EU to develop and strengthen its global role, not least by weakening the reliance which other international actors can place on the commitments undertaken by the EU.

A significant part of the chapter's analysis is focused on implications for the EU legal order of the *Kadi I* judgment, in view of the high political and symbolic importance of the case, and its explicit and

---

under the UN Convention on the Law of the Sea. For discussion, see Mendez, Mario, 'The Legal Effect of Community Agreements: Maximalist Treaty Enforcement and Judicial Avoidance Techniques', 21 *European Journal of International Law* (2010) 83, and van Rossem, J. W., 'Interaction Between EU Law and International Law in the Light of *Intertanko* and *Kadi*', 40 *Netherlands Yearbook of International Law* (2009) 183.

relatively developed judicial reasoning on the relationship between EU law and the international legal order. However, the analysis and critique of the Court's approach developed here is intended to provide a framework against which to reconsider the evolving approach of the Court to the international obligations of the EU more generally. A great deal has been written on the stance of the ECJ towards international law, and this chapter does not revisit the ground covered by that extensive and informative scholarship.[10] Instead, the aim is twofold. The first is to highlight the tension described above between the cultivated image of the EU as a virtuous international citizen and what seems to be the increasingly instrumentalist approach of the Court to the international legal obligations of the EU. The second is to suggest that the EU needs to develop a more coherent constitutional approach to international law if it aims to avoid charges of hypocrisy, and to have a credible voice on the global stage. Developing a coherent constitutional approach does not imply the need to choose either the subordination of the EU legal order to the international legal order on the one hand or the insistence on the autonomy and primacy of the EU legal order over the international order on the other. In analysing the approaches of the General Court and the ECJ in the *Kadi I* case, which lean towards the monist–subordination and the pluralist–autonomy ends of the spectrum respectively, the chapter proposes an alternative, Kantian-inspired, soft constitutionalist approach which would maintain the openness of the EU to the international legal order without implying the automatic and hierarchical subordination of all EU norms to international norms.

[10] For some of the core works on the subject, see Kronenberger, V., ed., *The European Union and the International Legal Order: Discord or Harmony?* (The Hague: Martinus Nijhoff, 2001); Koskenniemi, Martti, ed., *International Law Aspects of the European Union* (The Hague, London: Kluwer Law International, 1998); Peters, Anne, 'The Position of International Law within the European Community Law Legal Order', 40 *German Yearbook of International Law* (1997) 9; Eeckhout, P. and W. Wouters, 'Giving Effect to Customary International Law Through EC Law', in J. Prinssen and A. Schrauwen, eds., *Direct Effect: Rethinking a Classic of EC Legal Doctrine* (Groningen: Europa Law Publishing, 2002), 183; and Klabbers, Jan, *Treaty Conflict and the European Union* (Cambridge University Press, 2009).

3.2 The Kadi I and Al Barakaat cases[11]

3.2.1 Facts and background

In the case of Kadi I,[12] a Saudi Arabian national with substantial assets in the EU brought an action for the annulment of an EU Regulation in so

---

[11] The academic literature on this case is enormous and growing. See, for example, D'Aspremont, J. and F. Dopagne, 'Kadi: The ECJ's Reminder of the Elementary Divide between Legal Orders', 5 International Organizations Law Review (2008) 365; P. Eeckhout on EJIL Talk!, at www.ejiltalk.org/kadi-and-al-barakaat-luxembourg-is-not-texas-or-washington-dc/ and for his analysis of the Court of First Instance's reasoning: 'Community Terrorism Listings, Fundamental Rights, and UN Security Council Resolutions: In Search of the Right Fit', 3 European Constitutional Law Review (2007) 183–206; Tridimas, Takis, 'EU Law, International Law, and Economic Sanctions Against Terrorism: The Judiciary in Distress', 32 Fordham International Law Journal (2009) 660; see Halberstam, D. and E. Stein, 'The United Nations, the European Union, and the King of Sweden: Economic Sanctions and Individual Rights in a Plural World Order', 46 The Common Market Law Review (2009) 13; Griller, Stefan, 'International Law, Human Rights and the European Community's Autonomous Legal Order: Notes on the European Court of Justice Decision in Kadi', 4 European Constitutional Law Review (2008) 528–553; Wessel, R., 'The Kadi Case: Towards a More Substantive Hierarchy in International Law', 5 International Organizations Law Review (2008) 323–327; Craig Barker, J., Paul James Cardwell, Duncan French and Nigel White, 'Kadi and Al Barakaat', 58 The International and Comparative Law Quarterly (2009) 241; De Sena, P. and M. C. Vitucci, 'The European Courts and the Security Council: Between Dédoublement Fonctionnel and Balancing of Values', 20 European Journal of International Law (2009) 193–228; Harpaz, G., 'Judicial Review by the European Court of Justice of UN "Smart Sanctions" Against Terror in the Kadi Dispute', 14 European Foreign Affairs Review (2009) 65; Eckes, C., 'Judicial Review of European Anti-Terrorism Measures – The Yusuf and Kadi Judgments of the Court of First Instance', 14 Environmental Law Journal (2008) 74; Godhino, J., 'When Worlds Collide: Enforcing United Nations Security Council Asset Freezes in the EU Legal Order', 16 Environmental Law Journal (2010) 67; Isiksel, N. T., 'Fundamental Rights in the EU after Kadi and Al Barakaat', 16 Environmental Law Journal (2010) 551; and for a survey of the commentary on these cases see Poli, S. and M. Tzanou, 'The Kadi Rulings: A Survey of the Literature', 28 Yearbook of European Law (2009) 533–558; also Cremona, M. , F. Francioni and S. Poli, eds., 'Challenging the EU Counter-Terrorism Measures through the Courts', European University Institute Working Paper LAW No. 2009/10 (2009).

[12] I discuss here only the facts of the Kadi case, although it was subsequently joined together with the Al Barakaat case on appeal to the ECJ, since the legal analysis was essentially identical. C-402/05 P and C-415/05 P, Yassin Abdullah Kadi v. Council of the EU and Commission of the EC, and Al Barakaat International Foundation v. Council of the EU and Commission of the EC [2008] ECR I-6351. The judgments of the Court of First Instance in the two cases, T-315/01, Kadi and

far as it affected him. Kadi had been listed in the annex to EU Regulation 467/2001 as a person suspected of supporting terrorism. The effect of this Regulation, which had direct legal effect in the national legal systems of all EU Member States, was that all his funds and financial assets in the EU would be frozen. The 2001 Regulation was replaced a year later by Council Regulation 881/2002, and Kadi's name was again included in the annex to that measure. The EU Regulation was adopted to implement EU Common Position 2002/402, which in turn was adopted to implement a series of UN (United Nations) Security Council (UNSC) Resolutions concerning the suppression of international terrorism and adopted under Chapter VII of the UN Charter.[13] The UNSC Resolutions required all states to take measures to freeze the funds and other financial assets of individuals and entities which were associated with Osama bin Laden, the Al-Qaeda network and the Taliban, as designated by the Sanctions Committee of the Security Council. The list, which was prepared by the Sanctions Committee in March 2001 and subsequently amended many times, contained the names of the persons and entities whose funds were to be frozen. Kadi's name was added to the list in October 2001. A later UNSC Resolution allowed for states to permit certain humanitarian exceptions to the freezing of funds imposed by the three earlier Resolutions, subject to the notification and consent of the Sanctions Committee.[14] The EU in turn modified the Common Position and the Regulation to provide for the permitted humanitarian exceptions in relation to food, medical expenses and reasonable legal fees.[15]

Kadi argued that he was the victim of a serious miscarriage of justice and that he had never been involved in terrorism or in any form of financial support for such activity.[16] He argued to the General Court that the European Community (as it then was) had lacked legal

---

T-306/01, *Yusuf and Al Barakaat* were given on 21 September 2005, and the opinion of Advocate General Maduro was given on 16 January 2008.

[13] The relevant UN SC Resolutions were 1267(1999), 1333(2000) and 1390(2002).

[14] UN SC Resolution 1452(2002). The Security Council also adopted Resolution 1455(2003) in January 2003 to improve the implementation of the measures for the freezing of funds.

[15] Common Position 2003/140/CFSP and Council Regulation 561/2003.

[16] For an account of the weakness of the cases against several of the applicants who brought the applications before the ECJ, but in particular Al Barakaat, see the conclusions of the 9/11 Commission in its Monograph on Terrorist Financing appended to its final report, and especially Chapter 5. See www.9-11commission. gov/staff_statements/911_TerrFin_Monograph.pdf. See also William Vlcek,

competence under the EU treaties to adopt the Regulation, and also that the Regulation violated his fundamental rights to property, to a fair hearing and to judicial redress. Both the General Court, and subsequently also the ECJ, although on different grounds involving rather complicated legal reasoning, rejected the argument that the EU lacked the power to adopt the Regulation, and held that the treaties provided a sufficient legal basis for the measure. The more important argument for current purposes, however, was the claim that the measure unjustifiably interfered with Kadi's fundamental rights. The applicant made this argument on the basis of the European Court of Justice's well-established case-law to the effect that 'fundamental rights recognised and guaranteed by the constitutions of the Member States, especially those enshrined in the European Convention on Human Rights, form an integral part of the Community legal order'.[17] In particular he pleaded infringement of the right to property in Article 1 of Protocol 1 to the ECHR (European Convention on Human Rights), the right to a fair hearing in accordance with earlier case-law of the ECJ, and the right to judicial process under Article 6 ECHR and ECJ case-law.

Kadi argued that there had been no failure on his own part to exhaust any available remedies, since he had already sought to make use of whatever means existed to have his assets un-frozen and his name removed from the list. He had approached the Sanctions Committee directly and had been told that representations made by individuals would not be accepted and that complaints concerning sanctions imposed at the national level must be addressed to the competent courts. He had then sought the assistance of the Saudi Arabian Ministry of Foreign Affairs in asserting his rights before the Sanctions Committee, and had also taken steps in the USA to make representations to the Office of Foreign Assets Control, all apparently without redress.

In response, the EU Council and Commission relied on the UN Charter[18] and argued that the EU, just like the EU Member States, was itself bound by international law to give effect, within its spheres of power and competence, to Resolutions of the Security Council, especially those adopted under Chapter VII of the UN Charter of the

---

'Hitting the Right Target: EU and Security Council Pursuit of Terrorist Financing', available at www.unc.edu/euce/eusa2007/papers/vlcek-w-09h.pdf.

[17] CFI *Kadi* judgment, para 138, citing Case 4/73 *Nold* v. *Commission* [1974] ECR 491, Paragraph 13.

[18] In particular Articles 24(1), 25, 41, 48(2) and 103 of the UN Charter.

United Nations. The Council argued that any claim of jurisdiction on the part of the Court 'which would be tantamount to indirect and selective judicial review of the mandatory measures decided upon by the Security Council in carrying out its function of maintaining international peace and security, would cause serious disruption to the international relations of the Community'.[19] In other words the Council's argument consisted not only of the instrumental claim that any indirect review by the General Court of the UN measures would disrupt the functioning of the UN system, but also of the separate claim that it would also seriously disrupt the functioning of the international relations of the EU.[20]

3.2.2 The General Court's (formerly CFI's) analysis

The General Court took the view that in order to consider the applicant's substantive claim of violation of fundamental rights by the application of the Regulation, it would have to first respond to the various arguments concerning the relationship between the international legal order under the UN and the 'domestic or Community legal order', and concerning the extent to which the EC (European Community) was bound by Security Council Resolutions under Chapter VII.[21]

The Court went on to rule that, in accordance with customary international law and with Article 103 of the UN Charter, the obligations of EU Member States under the Charter prevailed over every other obligation of domestic or international law, including those under the European Convention on Human Rights and under the EU Treaties. UN Charter obligations included obligations arising under binding decisions of the Security Council.[22] The General Court stated that the EU Treaty

---

[19] General Court *Kadi* judgment, para 162.
[20] See at para 174 'the Council submits that where the Community acts without exercising any discretion, on the basis of a decision adopted by the body on which the international community has conferred sweeping powers for the sake of preserving international peace and security, full judicial review would run the risk of undermining the United Nations system as established in 1945, might seriously damage the international relations of the Community and its Member States and would fall foul of the Community's duty to observe international law'.
[21] Para 178.   [22] Para 184.

recognized such overriding obligations on its Member States,[23] and that even though the EU itself is not directly bound by the UN Charter and is not a party to the Charter, it is indirectly bound by those obligations in the same way as its Member States are, by virtue of the provisions of the EU Treaty.[24] Ultimately, the Court concluded that not only may the EU not infringe the obligations imposed on its Member States by the UNC or impede their performance, but the EU is actually *bound*, within the exercise of its powers, by the very Treaty by which it was established, to adopt all the measures necessary to enable its Member States to fulfil those obligations.[25] This obligation explained the EU's adoption of the Common Position and the EU's adoption of the Regulation freezing Kadi's assets.

To this extent, the General Court expressly rejected the dualist argument advanced by Kadi to the effect that 'the Community legal order is a legal order independent of the United Nations, governed by its own rules of law',[26] and held instead that it was bound – albeit by virtue of the EU treaties rather than directly under the UNC itself – by the obligations imposed by the Charter on Member States. At this point, it might seem that the applicant's case could go no further. The General Court had accepted the subordination of EU law to binding Resolutions of the Security Council, which would suggest that the General Court could hardly then proceed to review the Resolution in question for conformity with principles of EU law, even principles

---

[23] Paras 185–191. The General Court cited Articles 307 and 297 of the EC Treaty at the time in support of this argument. The relevant parts of Article 307 (now Article 351TFEU) provide 'The rights and obligations arising from agreements concluded before 1 January 1958 or, for acceding States, before the date of their accession, between one or more Member States on the one hand, and one or more third countries on the other, shall not be affected by the provisions of this Treaty. To the extent that such agreements are not compatible with this Treaty, the Member State or States concerned shall take all appropriate steps to eliminate the incompatibilities established. Member States shall, where necessary, assist each other to this end and shall, where appropriate, adopt a common attitude.' The relevant parts of Article 297 (now Article 347 TFEU) provide that 'Member States shall consult each other with a view to taking together the steps needed to prevent the functioning of the common market being affected by measures which a Member State may be called upon to take in the event of serious internal disturbances affecting the maintenance of law and order, in the event of war, serious international tension constituting a threat of war, or in order to carry out obligations it has accepted for the purpose of maintaining peace and international security'.

[24] Paras 192–204.   [25] Para 204.   [26] See para 208.

concerning protection for fundamental human rights. And indeed the Court expressly confirmed this point, ruling in a detailed series of steps that it would be unjustified under international law or under EU law for the Court to assert jurisdiction to review a binding decision of the Security Council according to the standards of human rights protection recognized by the EU legal order.[27] The General Court concluded this section of its judgment with the emphatic ruling that: 'the resolutions of the Security Council at issue fall, in principle, outside the ambit of the Court's judicial review and that the Court has no authority to call in question, even indirectly, their lawfulness in the light of Community law.'

At this stage, however, the judgment made a surprising leap, in the light of what had gone before. Suddenly, and without explanation as to the source of its jurisdiction in this regard, in particular by comparison with the elaborate reasoning which preceded the earlier conclusions in the judgment, the General Court declared: 'None the less, the Court is empowered to check, indirectly, the lawfulness of the resolutions of the Security Council in question with regard to *jus cogens*, understood as a body of higher rules of public international law binding on all subjects of international law, including the bodies of the United Nations, and from which no derogation is possible.'[28] Given the cautious approach in its earlier analysis, this bold move was unexpected. While the assertion that the Security Council must be bound by *ius cogens* norms finds support in arguments and assumptions made by many others,[29] and the General Court devoted several paragraphs of its judgment to making this argument,[30] the Court's assertion of its own jurisdiction to review Security Council action for conformity with *ius cogens* norms was less

---

[27] Paras 218–225.   [28] Para 226.

[29] See, e.g., Bianchi, Andrea, 'Assessing the Effectiveness of the UN Security Council's Anti-Terrorism Measures: The Quest for Legitimacy and Cohesion', 19 *European Journal of International Law* (2008) 881–919 at fn. 27 and part 5. See also Hoffman, Florian and Frédric Mégret, 'The UN as a Human Rights Violator: Some Reflections on The United Nations Changing Human Rights Responsibilities', 25 *Human Rights Quarterly* (2003) 314; and Reinisch, August, 'Developing Human Rights and Humanitarian Law Accountability of the Security Council for the Imposition of Economic Sanctions', 95 *American Journal of International Law* (2001) 851–872. Compare Oosthuizen, Gabriël, 'Playing the Devil's Advocate: The UN Security Council is Unbound by Law', 12 *Leiden Journal of International Law* (1999) 549–563.

[30] Paras 227–230 of the judgment.

predictable, given the lively scholarly debate over whether the actions of the Security Council are subject to judicial review and if so by whom.[31] The Court simply deduced from the argument that Security Council Resolutions must comply with the peremptory norms of international law that the General Court is empowered 'highly exceptionally' to review such Resolutions for compatibility with *ius cogens*.[32]

Having engaged in this unexpected and circumlocutory chain of reasoning to reach the conclusion that it could exercise such exceptional judicial review, the remainder of the judgment in which the Court actually considered the claims that the applicant's rights to property, to a fair hearing and to judicial process had been violated is rather more predictable, apart from the Court's surprising assumption that the right to property was part of *ius cogens*.[33] On the right to property, the General Court followed the trend of earlier ECJ rulings including that of *Bosphorus*.[34] The ECJ in *Bosphorus* had upheld the confiscation, pursuant to a Security Council Resolution implemented by the EU, of an aircraft leased by an innocent third party from the Yugoslav government before the Balkans war broke out.[35] The ECJ in that case had also

---

[31] Much of the debate has focused on the question of the possible jurisdiction of the International Court of Justice to review Security Council action. For an excellent overview see Alvarez, José, 'Judging the Security Council', 90 *American Journal of International Law* (1996) 1–39; also Caflisch, L. , 'Is the International Court Entitled to Review Security Council Resolutions Adopted under Chapter VII of the United Nations Charter?', in N. Al-Nauimi and R. Meese, eds., *International Legal Issues Arising under the United Nations Decade of International Law* (The Hague: Kluwer Law International, 1995), 633–662; Akande, D., 'The ICJ and the Security Council: Is There Room for Judicial Control of the Decisions of the Political Organs of the UN?' 46 *International and Comparative Law Quarterly* (1997) 309–343; de Wet, Erika, 'Judicial Review as an Emerging General Principle of Law and Its Implications for the International Court of Justice', 47 *Netherlands International Law Review* (2000) 181–210. In any case, since individuals have no standing before the ICJ it seems an unlikely forum for significant adjudication concerning the Security Council on the question of targeted sanctions.

[32] General Court, Kadi, para 231.

[33] For criticism of the novel and rather creative approach of the General Court to the content of these *ius cogens* norms, see Tomuschat, Christian, 'Note on Kadi', 43 *Common Market Law Review* (2005) 537–551, and Eeckhout, Piet, 'Community Terrorism Listings, Fundamental Rights, and UN Security Council Resolutions: In Search of the Right Fit', 3 *European Constitutional Law Review* (2007) 183–206.

[34] Case C–84/95 *Bosphorus* v. *Minister for Transport* [1996] ECR I–3953.

[35] Ibid., paras 242–252.

concluded that, despite the absence of compensation for the seizure of the aircraft, the deprivation of property was not arbitrary. The General Court in *Kadi I* ruled that, since the measures impugned were adopted as part of the international campaign against terrorism, and given the humanitarian exceptions, the provisional nature of the measure and the possibility for state appeal to the Sanctions Committee, the freezing of Kadi's assets did not violate *ius cogens* norms.[36] Only arbitrary deprivation of property would violate *ius cogens*, according to the Court.

In similar vein the General Court ruled that neither the right to a fair hearing nor the right to judicial process – in so far as these are protected as part of *ius cogens* – had been violated. The Court emphasized the possibility of the applicant petitioning his government to approach the Sanctions Committee with a view to requesting his de-listing,[37] and concluded that even though he had no opportunity to make his views known on the correctness and relevance of any of the facts (which were classified as secret and never made known to him) on the basis of which his funds were frozen, this would not violate any right to a fair hearing once the Security Council considered there were international security grounds which militate against granting such.[38] On access to a judicial remedy, the General Court ruled that limits on the principle of access to court, for example in times of public emergency or in the context of state immunity, were clearly compatible with *ius cogens*,[39] and in any case that the procedure set up by the Sanctions Committee – in the absence of any international judicial process – to allow for a petitioned government to apply to it to re-examine a case was a reasonable method of protecting the applicant's rights.[40]

This unusual judgment by the General Court attracted a good deal of attention, much of it critical. Some critics focused on the quality of the reasoning on the competence of the EU to adopt the Regulation, others on the complex argument about the relationship between the EU and the Security Council,[41] others on the bold claim of jurisdiction to review the Security Council, while virtually all commentators were critical of

---

[36] General Court *Kadi* judgment, para 242. [37] Ibid., paras 261–268.
[38] Ibid., para 274. [39] Paras 285–289. [40] Para 290.
[41] Almquist, J., 'A Human Rights Critique of European Judicial Review: Counter-Terrorism Sanctions', 57 *International & Comparative Law Quarterly* (2008) 303–331 at 318–319.

the curious reasoning of the Court on the content of *ius cogens*,[42] which is a famously amorphous yet narrow and contested category of international law. What is striking for present purposes, however, is the following. First, the General Court rejected a dualist conception of the place of the EU in the international legal order, and clearly subordinated EU action to that of the Security Council (and obligations imposed by the UN more generally) in so far as the scope of their powers overlap. Second, and despite this subordination, the General Court claimed jurisdiction to review Resolutions of the Security Council for compatibility not with human rights protected under EU law, but with peremptory norms of international law. In the end, while none of its complicated reasoning provided any relief to Kadi, the judgment presents a provocative picture of a regional organization at once faithful and subordinate to, yet simultaneously constituting itself as an independent check upon, the powers exercised in the name of the international community under the UN Charter.

3.2.3 The ECJ judgment

The judgment of the Court of Justice, in reversing that of the General Court, was evidently strongly influenced by the Opinion of Advocate General (AG) Maduro, although it differed from the Advocate General's opinion in certain key respects.[43] But the Court followed the advice of the Advocate General in annulling the EU Regulations in so far as they imposed sanctions on *Kadi* (and in the *Al Barakaat* case, which by now had been joined[44]), finding that they constituted an unjustified restriction of his right to be heard, the right to an effective legal remedy and the right to property.

---

[42] See note 33 above.

[43] While the Advocate General's approach is fundamentally dualist in tone, specifying in Paragraph 24 that 'international law can permeate that legal order only under the conditions set by the constitutional principles of the Community', notable differences between his opinion and the judgment of the Court include his suggestion of the possibility of adopting something akin to a *Solange/Bosphorus*-type approach to Security Council measures in Paragraphs 38 and 54 of his opinion, and the suggestion in Paragraph 32 that those EU Member States which are members of the Security Council may be individually responsible for ensuring that they act in conformity with EU obligations.

[44] See note 12 above.

The Court's reasoning was robustly dualist, emphasizing repeatedly the separateness and autonomy of the EU from other legal systems and from the international legal order more generally, and the priority to be given to the EU's own fundamental rules. A related and significant feature was the lack of direct engagement by the Court with the nature and significance of the international rules at issue in the case, or with other relevant sources of international law. The judgment is striking for its treatment of the UN Charter, at least in so far as its relationship to EU law was concerned, as no more than any other international treaty, and for the perfunctory nature of its nod to the traditional idea of the EU's openness to international law. The Court denied that its review of the EU regulation implementing the UN Resolution would amount to any kind of review of the Resolution itself,[45] or of the Charter,[46] and suggested that its annulment of the EU instrument implementing the Resolution would not necessarily call into question the primacy of the Resolution in international law. Given the legal significance of binding Security Council Resolutions under Chapter VII of the Charter, and given the language of Article 103 of the Charter,[47] the Court's depiction of international law as a separate and parallel order whose normative demands do not penetrate the domestic (EU) legal order is all the more striking.

Without specifically mentioning the UN Charter, the Court declared that 'an international agreement cannot affect the allocation of powers fixed by the Treaties or [...] the autonomy of the Community legal system';[48] that 'the obligations imposed by an international agreement cannot have the effect of prejudicing the constitutional principles of the EC Treaty';[49] and that the EU is an 'internal'[50] and 'autonomous legal system which is not to be prejudiced by an international agreement'.[51]

---

[45] Compare the case in which the ECJ annulled the EU's implementation of the Framework Agreement on Bananas in the WTO context, without thereby affecting the WTO agreements themselves: C-122/95, *Germany* v. *Council* [1998] ECR I-973.

[46] Judgment of 3 September 2008, paras 286–288.

[47] Article 103 of the UN Charter provides that 'In the event of a conflict between the obligations of the Members of the United Nations under the present Charter and their obligations under any other international agreement, their obligations under the present Charter shall prevail'.

[48] ECJ judgment in Kadi, para 282.   [49] Ibid., para 285.   [50] Ibid., para 317.

[51] Ibid., para 316.

On the relationship of the EU to international law more generally, the Court repeated earlier judgments which had declared that the EU 'must respect international law in the exercise of its powers'[52] and that relevant EU measures should be interpreted in the light of relevant international law rules, and in the light of undertakings given by the EU in the context of international organizations such as the UN.[53] In one of the few sentences in its judgment which acknowledges anything distinctive about the international norms at issue in the case, the Court emphasized that particular importance should be attached by the EU to the adoption of Chapter VII Resolutions by the UN, and that the reasons for and objectives of such Resolutions should be taken into account in interpreting any EU measures implementing them.[54] The bottom line of the judgment, however, was that the UN Charter and UN SC Resolutions, just like any other international law, exist on a separate plane and cannot call into question or affect the nature, meaning or primacy of fundamental principles of EU law. In an interesting legal counterfactual, the Court asserted that even if the obligations imposed by the UN Charter *were* to be classified as part of the 'hierarchy of norms within the Community legal order' they would rank higher than legislation but lower than the EU Treaties and lower than the 'general principles' of EU law which have been held to include 'fundamental rights'.[55] It should be noted here that the category of 'general principles' of EU law, including fundamental human rights, is not a small one, but is an extensive and growing body of legal principles whose content – although 'inspired' by national constitutional traditions, international human rights agreements and especially by the European Convention on Human Rights – is determined almost entirely by the ECJ.[56] Even after the incorporation of the Charter of Fundamental Rights into the EU Treaties by the Lisbon Treaty, and even after the likely accession by the EU to the ECHR, Article 6(3) TEU (Treaty on European Union) still preserves the general principles of EU law – and consequently the role of the ECJ in

---

[52] Ibid., para 291, citing C-286/90 *Poulsen and Diva Navigation* [1992] ECR I-6019.

[53] Ibid., paras 291–294.   [54] Para 294.   [55] Paras 305–308.

[56] For discussion of the category of general principles see Tridimas, Takis, *The General Principles of EC Law* (Oxford University Press, 1999); Bernitz, Ulf, Joakim Nergelius and Cecelia Gardener, *The General Principles of EC Law in a Process of Development* (2nd edn, The Hague: Kluwer Law International, 2008).

formulating them – on an equal constitutional footing with these other sources.[57] In *Kadi I*, the ECJ did not expressly distinguish between certain core principles of EU law which take precedence over international law including the UN Charter, but appeared to treat all EU-recognized 'fundamental rights' as belonging to the normatively superior category.[58]

The ECJ dismissed the relevance of the *Behrami* judgment of the European Court of Human Rights which had been decided a year earlier,[59] and the immunity from ECtHR (European Court of Human Rights) review granted in that case to acts which were attributed to the UN Security Council), for reasons similar to those given by AG Maduro in his opinion.[60] Further, unlike AG Maduro, the Court did not give a direct answer to the question whether an EU regulation implementing a UNSC Resolution might be given immunity from EU judicial review if the sanctions system set up by the Resolution offered sufficient guarantees of judicial protection.[61] However, the language of Paragraph 321 appears to suggest that general immunity from jurisdiction for Security Council measures would be inappropriate, since it declared that 'the existence, within that United Nations system, of the re-examination procedure before the Sanctions Committee, even having

---

[57] Article 6(3) TEU as amended by the Lisbon Treaty provides 'Fundamental rights, as guaranteed by the European Convention for the Protection of Human Rights and Fundamental Freedoms and as they result from the constitutional traditions common to the Member States, shall constitute general principles of the Union's law'.

[58] See paras 303–304 of the judgment.

[59] Apps no. 71412/01&. 78166/01 *Behrami* v. *France*, and *Saramati* v. *France, Germany and Norway*, admissibility decision of the European Court of Human Rights, 2 May 2007 (Grand Chamber) concerning NATO action in Kosovo, in which the Court of Human Rights declined to review acts of the UN authority in Kosovo (UNMIK) and acts of NATO forces (KFOR) carried out in pursuance of a UN Security Council Resolution, in part because the UN is 'an organisation of universal jurisdiction fulfilling its imperative collective security objective'.

[60] AG Maduro sought to confine the significance of the *Behrami* ruling to the specific circumstances of the case and to what might be called the 'ratio decidendi' of the judgment: i.e. that the ECtHR declined jurisdiction on the basis that the acts in question were attributable only to the UN and not to the participating states, and that the acts took place outside the territorial application of the ECHR. This, in AG Maduro's view, meant that the case was not a relevant precedent for the ECJ in *Kadi* where the act being challenged was adopted by the EU rather than by the UN Security Council.

[61] ECJ judgment in *Kadi*, paras 321–326.

regard to the amendments recently made to it, cannot give rise to generalised immunity from jurisdiction', before going on in the next paragraph to say that such immunity would anyhow be unjustified in the instance case because the Sanctions Committee procedure lacked sufficient guarantees of judicial protection. It is difficult to know whether the Court intended by these paragraphs to hint that certain Security Council Resolutions might enjoy immunity from review if they did provide sufficient guarantees of protection, because the Court chose not to address the question with any clarity.[62] This would in fact have been one obvious route for the ECJ to take in *Kadi I*, i.e. to borrow from the *Bosphorus* approach of the European Court of Human Rights,[63] and to confer provisional immunity from review on UNSC measures where the levels of due process and basic rights protection provided by the Security Council could be considered sufficient. But the ECJ evidently decided not to adopt such an approach, and also chose not to engage in a more direct dialogue with the UN Security Council along the lines of the famous '*Solange*' jurisprudence of the German constitutional court.[64] Ultimately, the ECJ disposed of the case entirely in accordance with the internal legal priorities and values of the EU. It concluded by annulling the relevant EU regulations, albeit keeping them in effect for three months with a view to giving the EU institutions a period of time during which to remedy the due process breaches. This, the EU institutions duly purported to do. Following the publication and communication to the applicants of summary reasons provided by the UN Sanctions Committee, and having allowed them a brief opportunity to respond to the allegations, the Commission in November 2008 adopted a Regulation maintaining the sanctions against Kadi, who promptly brought a further action for annulment before the General Court.[65] In *Kadi 2* the General Court, while clearly disapproving of the reasoning of the ECJ in *Kadi I* concerning the relationship of EU law to

---

[62] For discussion of this question see Halberstam, D. and E. Stein, 'The United Nations, the European Union, and the King of Sweden: Economic Sanctions and Individual Rights in a Plural World Order', 46 *The Common Market Law Review* (2009) 13.

[63] See *Bosphoros* v. *Ireland*, Application no. 45036/98, Judgment of the European Court of Human Rights of 30 June 2005.

[64] For discussion of the *Solange* approach, see below notes 121–127 and text.

[65] Commission Regulation 1190/2008, amending the earlier Regulation 881/2002 to maintain Kadi's name in the relevant Annex. OJ L322/25, 2008.

international law and to the UN Charter and UN Security Council Resolutions in particular, nonetheless followed the approach outlined by the ECJ in *Kadi 1*.[66] The General Court robustly reviewed the adequacy of the evidence offered to justify the continued sanctions, and the Commission's purported guarantees of the rights of the defence, and rejected these as being superficial and inadequate.[67] Consequently, the General Court annulled the Regulation, without this time maintaining it in force to allow any further attempt to cure the continuing breaches of procedural rights.[68]

3.3 Varying judicial conceptions of the international legal order

The different reactions of the General Court and the ECJ to the question of the relationship between EU law and international law, in particular the UN Charter and UN Security Council Resolutions, are premised on very different views about the authority of international law and institutions, and on a different conception of the proper role of that court within the international 'disorder of orders'.[69] The General Court initially took the view that although the EU was indirectly bound by Security Council Resolutions, and although the General Court had no direct jurisdiction to review the Security Council, it should nevertheless indirectly review the Security Council's action for possible violation of minimum international standards of *ius cogens*. The ECJ, while referring in general terms to the respect owed by the EU to international treaties including the UN Charter and to Security Council Resolutions, emphasized that *no* international treaty could affect the autonomy of the EU legal system, and that even if the UN Charter were to be ranked as part of EU law it would be ranked below the normative level of the EU treaties themselves, and lower than the general principles of EU law.

The General Court concluded that EU Member States were, both as a matter of international law and as a matter of EU law, bound by the overriding obligations established under the UN Charter, including

---

[66] T-85/09, *Kadi v. Commission*, judgment of 30 September 2010, paras 112–126 in particular.

[67] Ibid., paras 171–188 and 193–194.

[68] At the time of writing, the case of T-85/09, *Kadi II* is on appeal to the ECJ.

[69] Walker, Neil, 'Beyond Boundary Disputes and Basic Grids: Mapping the Global Disorder of Normative Orders', 6 *International Journal of Constitutional Law* (2008) 373–396.

those imposed by SC Resolutions. It ruled that that the EU itself was indirectly bound via its Member States' obligations under the UN Charter, albeit (given that the EU is neither a member of the UN nor an addressee of Security Council Resolutions) as a matter of EU treaty law rather than under 'general international law'. The General Court took the view that customary international law and treaty law determine that the international obligations created under the UN Charter are binding on the EU and that they override other conflicting obligations. However, the General Court reached its conclusion on the overriding binding force of the UNC through a process of reasoning based on the text of the Vienna Convention on the Law on Treaties, the provisions of the UN Charter, of customary international law and the provisions of the EU Treaty. Unlike the approach of the ECtHR in the *Behrami* case, mentioned above,[70] which deferred to the authority of the UN Security Council and refused to review its decisions, the General Court did not bring the substantive purposes and goals of the UN into the picture, and did not place them on a higher level than the purposes and goals of the EU. The General Court's reasoning was largely formal and jurisdiction-based, following the legal hierarchy which it took to be established by an array of international and regional treaties of which the EU Treaty forms a part. More significantly, the General Court asserted its own power or even its duty where *ius cogens* is concerned, despite the overriding binding force of the Security Council Resolutions, to exercise a substantively minimal and residual judicial review over the UNSC. Thus even though its judgment presents the EU legal order as formally subordinate to that established by the UN Charter, there was no institutional reticence on the part of the General Court – unlike the ECtHR in *Behrami* – about taking on the job of reviewing the UN Security Council.

The ECJ adopted a very different approach. While the Advocate General had treated the question of the obligations of the EU under international law, and the status of international law within the EU legal order as marginal to the case, the ECJ addressed this question directly. The Court made clear that had it been inclined to adopt a unitary, integrated approach – which of course it did not, ruling instead that the EU legal order is an entirely separate and internal order from that of international law – it would rank international treaties, including the

---

[70] See note 59 above.

UN Charter and UNSC Resolutions, below the level of the EU Treaties. Both the Court and the Advocate General took the view that the ECJ's primary obligation is to protect the values of the EU's 'municipal' constitutional legal order, including European human rights values, regardless of whether this entails an indirect rejection of the Security Council's actions. Given their premises, they attributed no particular relevance to the possible applicability of Article 103 of the Charter. The ECJ ruled that annulment of the EU Regulation implementing the UN Resolution for violation of EU legal principles 'would not entail any challenge to the primacy of that Resolution in international law'.[71] The ECJ should take its cue from EU constitutional law, not from public international law, even if this meant that the EU or the Member States would be held responsible as a matter of international law for breaching UN Charter obligations. Both the Advocate General and the ECJ posited two quite distinct and separate sources of law – 'municipal' EU law on the one hand, and international law on the other – and for the purposes of Kadi's challenge to the EU Regulation implementing the UNSC Resolution, it was the former which was of interest to the Court. In other words, the ECJ judgment in *Kadi I* was premised on the view that there are different and distinct sources of legal authority, and that regardless of whether the EU could face international sanctions for non-compliance with a UN Security Council Resolution, this would not affect the Court's duty to review the implementation of the Security Council's decision by reference to European standards of fundamental rights.

Neither the ECJ nor the General Court can plausibly claim formal jurisdiction to review the conduct of the UN Security Council. Yet when confronted with one of the novel challenges of international governance – in this case the exercise of increasingly law-like powers by the Security Council – the two courts adopted quite different approaches to the dilemma. The General Court's approach was one of deferential engagement, in the sense of being unwilling to subject the Security Council to review for compliance with the full expanse of EU standards, but insisting nonetheless on considering the legality of its action under minimum norms of non-derogable international law. These *ius cogens* norms are at best a very small and somewhat contested category, which are not open to the kind of fluid development of other categories of

---

[71] ECJ judgment in *Kadi*, para. 288.

international law such as 'general principles' or even customary international law. The General Court's vision of the international legal space in the case was a vertical, integrated one in which the EU ranks below the UN, but in which even lower courts like the General Court are nonetheless empowered or even required by international law to apply peremptory norms of international law to the organs of the UN. The ECJ on the other hand did not purport to engage directly with the Security Council or with UN governance at all, other than by referring to the general 'respect' owed by the EC to 'the relevant rules of international law', and it insisted that the Court's jurisdiction to review the implementation of UN Resolutions by reference to EU-defined standards of protection did not imply any review of the Resolution itself.[72] The vision of the international legal space presented by the ECJ in *Kadi I* was a horizontal and segregated one, with the EU existing alongside other constitutional systems as an independent and separate municipal legal order, and with no role envisaged for the ECJ in articulating the relationship or in developing principles of communication between international norms (such as UNSC Resolutions) and EU legal norms. The conception of the judicial role underpinning the ECJ judgment was one in which the primary role and responsibility of the Court is to safeguard the autonomy of EU law and to uphold the values of the European legal order. This certainly suggests a different conception of the judicial role in EU foreign relations than that depicted in the opening part of the chapter, in which the ECJ tended to present itself as playing a central role in the enforcement of international law and the mutual articulation of the EU and international legal orders.

3.4 Pluralist vs. constitutionalist approaches to the international legal order

In this section it will be argued that the different responses of the General Court and the ECJ in *Kadi I* can best be understood in the context of an ongoing debate between scholars who advocate a *constitutionalist* reading of the international order and those who advocate a *pluralist* reading. More specifically, the different visions underpinning the approaches of the General Court and the European Court of Justice reflect these two prevalent and broadly contrasting intellectual

---

[72] Ibid., paras 286–287.

approaches to the problem of the multiplication, overlap and conflict of normative orders in the global realm. The ECJ, following the opinion of AG Maduro, adopted a robustly pluralist approach to the relationship between the EU and the international order, while the General Court adopted a strongly constitutionalist approach. Pluralist approaches share with dualism the emphasis on separate and distinct legal orders, but while pluralism emphasizes the plurality of diverse normative systems, the traditional focus of dualist thought has been on the relationship between national and international law. Similarly, strong constitutionalist approaches to the international order overlap significantly with monist approaches in their assumption of a single integrated legal system, but the category of constitutional approaches to the international legal order is very wide and includes some which do not necessarily assume such systemic integration and which cannot comfortably be described in the traditional language of monism. The main difference between constitutionalist and pluralist approaches is not that one is normatively oriented and the other descriptively oriented, although many proponents of a pluralist approach have the advantage of greater descriptive plausibility of their accounts, and some variants of the constitutionalist approach may seem both unrealistic and unattractive in view of the deep diversity of the international realm. Nonetheless, contemporary constitutionalist and pluralist approaches to the international legal order alike make both descriptive and normative claims which will be discussed further in the following sections.

3.4.1 Pluralist approaches to international law and governance

There is a growing body of literature which describes and advocates a pluralist approach to international law and governance.[73] Although

---

[73] Schiff Berman, Paul, 'Global Legal Pluralism', 80 *Southern California Law Review* (2007) 1155–1237, and 'A Pluralist Approach to International Law', 32 *Yale Journal of International Law* (2007) 301; Burke-White, William, 'International Legal Pluralism', 25 *Michigan International Law Journal* (2004) 963; Krish, Nico, 'The Pluralism of Global Adminstrative Law', 17 *European Journal of International Law* (2006) 247–278; Walker, Neil, 'The Idea of Constitutional Pluralism', 65 *Modern Law Review* (2002) 317–359; Halberstam, Daniel, 'Constitutionalism and Pluralism in Marbury and Van Gend', in M. Maduro and L. Azoulay, *The Past and Future of EU Law* (Oxford: Hart Publishing, 2008). For a more sceptical account see Baquero Cruz, Julio, 'The Legacy of the Maastricht-Urteil and the Pluralist Movement', 14 *European Law*

some of the earlier literature on legal pluralism was more sociological than normative in nature,[74] the recent scholarship on international and global legal pluralism in particular is notable for its advocacy of the merits of legal pluralism. It emphasizes the value of diversity and difference amongst and between different national and international normative systems and levels of governance, and the undesirability and implausibility of constitutional approaches which seek coherence between these. There are, however, different strands of argument within the growing body of contemporary scholarship on global legal pluralism, some of which advocate what I call strong pluralism, while others favour a softer variant.

Amongst the strong pluralists is Nico Krisch, who has written previously – and in this volume (see Chapter 5) – about the problem of accountability at the level of global governance. Krisch has argued that the pragmatic accommodations of pluralism are normatively preferable to constitutionalist approaches premised on ideals of coherence and unity.[75] He suggests that pluralist approaches, by comparison with constitutionalist approaches, could lead to stronger transnational

---

Journal (2008) 389–420. See also the related discussions in Avbelj, M. and J. Komarek, eds., 'Four Visions of Constitutional Pluralism', *European University Institute Working Paper LAW No. 2008/21* (2008). More generally, de Sousa Santos, Boaventura, *Toward a New Legal Common Sense* (2nd edn, London: Butterworths, 2002) identified a 'third phase' of legal pluralism focusing in particular on the global context: 'Whereas before the debate was on local, infrastate legal orders coexisting within the same national time-space, now it is on suprastate, global legal orders coexisting in the world system with both state and infrastate legal orders.' See also Tamanaha, Brian, 'Understanding Legal Pluralism: Past to Present, Local to Global', 30 *Sydney Law Review* (2008) 375–411; Teubner, Günther, 'Global Bukowina: Legal Pluralism in the World Society', in Teubner, ed., *Global Law Without a State* (Aldershot: Dartmouth, 1997), 3–28.

[74] E.g. Griffiths, John, 'What is Legal Pluralism?', 24 *Journal of Legal Pluralism* (1986) 1–55; Merry, Sally Engle, 'Legal Pluralism', 22 *Law and Society Review* (1988) 869; Galanter, Marc, 'Justice in Many Rooms: Courts, Private Ordering and Indigenous Law', 19 *Journal of Legal Pluralism* 1 (1981) 1–47.

[75] Krish, Nico, 'The Pluralism of Global Administrative Law', 17 *European Journal of International Law* (2006) 247–278. The version of pluralism Krisch advocates in the regional context (i.e. within Europe, within the EU and the ECHR, and in the interaction between these two) is a softer form of pluralism than that which he advocates in the global context. In the European context he points to the importance of mutual persuasion, even while emphasizing the autonomy and authority of each unit. See Krisch, Nico, 'The Open Architecture of European Human Rights Law', 71 *Modern Law Review* (2008) 183–216. See also Krisch's Chapter 5 in this volume 'The Case for Pluralism in Postnational Law' and his

accountability. He defends the 'disorderly' and disconnected landscape of global administrative accountability, arguing that it allows for mutual influence and gradual approximation, while preventing any one level or site of governance from exercising control over the others.[76] Pluralist approaches, on his account, are contrasted favourably with constitutionalist approaches which 'adopt unity as a regulative ideal' and force the political order into a coherent unified framework by downplaying the extent of legitimate diversity in the global polity. Understanding the international order in pluralist terms presents the relationships between different systems as being governed by politics rather than by law, with different actors and rules competing for authority through politics rather than legal argument.[77] Pluralism's *ad hoc* mutual accommodation between different legal regimes is preferred over the imposition of what are viewed as sovereigntist or universal-harmonization schemes.[78]

Pluralist approaches to the international legal order claim to preserve space for contestation, resistance and innovation, and to encourage tolerance and mutual accommodation.[79] Thus David Kennedy argues for 'a more vigorous but fragmented public capacity, for a normative order that embraces legal pluralism', and challenges the idea that there is such a thing as an 'international community'.[80] Even within the growing body of scholarship on *constitutional* pluralism, which presents the global order as a plurality not just of legal but of national and transnational constitutional sites, the emphasis is on the proliferation of separate systems which engage primarily through 'agonistic processes of negotiation'.[81] And despite the normative emphasis on

---

recent book, Krisch, Nico, *Beyond Constitutionalism: The Pluralist Structure of Postnational Law* (Oxford University Press, 2010).

[76] See Krisch's Chapter 5 in this volume 'The Case for Pluralism in Postnational Law'.

[77] Krisch, 'Open Architecture' (2008).

[78] See Schiff Berman, 'Global Legal Pluralism' (2007), at 1163 and 2007.

[79] Ibid., at 1237. See also Cohen, Jean, 'A Global State of Emergency or the Further Constitutionalization of International Law: A Pluralist Approach', 15 *Constellations* (2008) 456–484.

[80] Kennedy, D., 'One, Two, Three, Many Legal Orders: Legal Pluralism and the Cosmopolitan Dream', 31 *New York University Review of Law and Social Change* (2007) 641, and Kennedy, D., 'The Mystery of Global Governance', 34 *Ohio Northern University Law Review* (2008) 827–860.

[81] Walker, Neil, 'The Idea of Constitutional Pluralism', 65 *Modern Law Review* (2002) 317–359; also Avbelj and J. Komarek, 'Four Visions' (2008).

tolerance, accommodation and the possibility of mutual learning, there is an acknowledgement that the proliferation of separate and self-contained constitutional systems seeking to establish their own authority may well 'exacerbate conflict and pathologize communication', or 'encourage a strident fundamentalism, a refusal of dialogue with other sites and processes'.[82]

In sum, what unites pluralist approaches to the international legal order is their emphasis on, and their interpretation of the significance of, the existence of a multiplicity of distinct and diverse normative systems, and the likelihood of clashes of authority claims and competition for primacy in specific contexts. From the perspective of its advocates, the multiple pressure points of global legal pluralism, and the constant risk of mutual rejection of the authority claims of different functional or territorial sites, provide a more promising model for promoting responsible and responsive global governance than constitutional or cosmopolitan approaches which emphasize coherence or unity. Robust pluralist approaches deny the possibility of a shared, universally oriented system of values and question the meaningfulness of the idea of an international community. They do not seek the development of a shared communicative framework for addressing the different authority-claims of different polities or legal orders. Rather than advocating coordination between legal systems, they promote agonistic, *ad hoc*, pragmatic and political processes of interaction. Pluralist approaches applaud this diversity, competition and lack of coordination as being more likely to lead to a healthy degree of global accountability. And for the most part, pluralist approaches to the international realm have been consciously advocated as a corrective to or in opposition to constitutional 'monist' or 'sovereign' approaches, which are presented as being naively, misleadingly and even dangerously focused on unity, universalism and consensus.[83] Constitutional approaches are presented in the pluralist literature as misconceived or even dangerous attempts to transpose the model of domestic government, the solutions designed for domestic political constituencies, and the political imaginary of domestic constitutionalism onto the transnational stage.

---

[82] Walker, 'Idea of Constitutional Pluralism' (2002).
[83] E.g. Krisch's Chapter 5 in this volume 'The Case for Pluralism in Postnational Law'; Schiff Berman, 'Global Legal Pluralism' (2007); Kennedy, 'One, Two, Three' (2007); and Cohen, 'Global State of Emergency' (2008).

3.4.2 Constitutionalist approaches to international law and governance

Unlike the literature on international legal pluralism, which, although growing, is relatively recent in origin, there is a genuinely enormous literature on constitutionalist approaches to international law.[84] An influential part of this is to be found in German legal scholarship

---

[84] The literature is too large to cite comprehensively or even representatively, but below are a few of the canonical texts, as well as some of the recent collections of essays dedicated to the subject. Simma, Bruno, 'From Bilateralism to Community Interest in International Law', 250 *Hague Academy Course* 6 (1994), 217–384; Tomuschat, Christian, 'Obligations Arising for States Without or Against their Will', 241 *Recueil des Cours* IV (1993) 195; Fassbender, Bardo, 'The United Nations Charter as Constitution of the International Community', 36 *Columbia Journal of Transnational Law* (1998) 529–619; de Wet, Erika, 'The International Constitutional Order', 55 *International and Comparative Law Quarterly* (2006), 51–76; Peters, Anne, 'Compensatory Constitutionalism: The Function and Potential of Fundamental International Norms and Structures', 19 *Leiden Journal of International Law* 3 (2006) 579–610; Bogdandy, Armin von, 'Constitutionalism in International Law: Comment on a Proposal from Germany', 47 *Harvard Journal of International Law* (2006) 223–242, provides a useful review of the extensive German literature on the subject.

  In the field of international trade law there is a wide 'constitutionalist' literature, see in particular the work of Ernst-Ulrich Petersmann: Petersmann, Ernst-Ulrich, 'Constitutionalism and the Regulation of International Markets: How to Define the "Development Objectives" of the World Trading System?', *European University Institute Working Paper LAW No. 2007/23* (2007), available at <http://ssrn.com/abstract=1024105>; 'Why Rational Choice Theory Requires a Multilevel Constitutional Approach to International Economic Law – The Case for Reforming the WTO's Enforcement Mechanism', *University of Illinois Law Review* (2008), 359, available at <http://ssrn.com/abstract=1001166>; 'Justice in International Economic Law? From the "International Law among States" to "International Integration law" and "Constitutional Law"', *European University Institute Working Paper LAW No. 2006/46* (2006), available at <http://ssrn.com/abstract=964165>; 'State Sovereignty, Popular Sovereignty and Individual Sovereignty: From Constitutional Nationalism to Multilevel Constitutionalism in International Economic Law?', *European University Institute Working Paper LAW No. 2006/45* (2006/), available at SSRN: <www.ssrn.com/abstract=964147.>; also Cass, Deborah, *The Constitutionalization of the World Trade Organization* (Oxford University Press, 2005); and Krajewski, Marcus, 'Democratic Legitimacy and Constitutional Perspectives of WTO Law', *Journal of World Trade* (2001).

  Some of the recent collections of essays include Macdonald, Ronald St. J. and Douglas M. Johnston, eds., *Towards World Constitutionalism* (Leiden: Martinus Nijhoff, 2005); Joerges, Christian and Ernst-Ulrich Petersmann, *Constitutionalism, Multilevel Trade Governance And Social Regulation* (Oxford:

throughout the twentieth century,[85] and its intellectual roots are often traced to Kant's cosmopolitanism.[86] And as might be expected from such an extensive literature on a rich and elusive concept like constitutionalism, there are a great many different kinds of argument and approach to be found.

One obvious risk with a concept like constitutionalism is that it is eroded through overuse and overextension, such that it becomes no longer meaningful to describe a particular approach to international law and governance as constitutionalist.[87] Fassbender in this vein has criticized the inflationary use of the word 'constitution' by equating it with an increase in regulation, or with the evolution of a hierarchical system of rules.[88] Nonetheless there are a great many varieties of international constitutionalist approaches which can properly be so called.[89] These include the influential German school represented by

---

Hart, 2006); Dunoff, Jeffrey L. and Joel P. Trachtman, eds., *Constitutionalism, International Law and Global Government* (Cambridge University Press, 2009). See also more generally the *Leiden Journal of International Law*, volume 19, Symposium Issue (2006).

[85] For an account of three distinct strands of this constitutionalist literature on international law, see Fassbender, Bardo, 'The United Nations Charter as Constitution of the International Community', 36 *Columbia Journal of Transnational Law* (1998).

[86] In particular Kant, Immanuel, 'Idea for a Universal History with a Cosmopolitan Intent', trans. Ted Humphrey, in Kant, *Perpetual Peace and Other Essays* (1883), and 'Perpetual Peace: A Philosophical Essay', trans. Mary Campbell Smith, in Kant, *Perpetual Peace and Other Essays* (1795, 1903). Kant's second definitive article of *Perpetual Peace* was that the law of nations 'shall be founded on a federation of free states'.

[87] Neil Walker, in 'Making a World of Difference: Habermas, Cosmopolitanism and the Constitutionalization of International Law', *European University Institute Working Paper LAW No. 2005/17* (2005), available at <http://ssrn.com/abstract=891036>, draws attention to the risks of the rhetorical, bootstrapping use of constitutionalism which the application of the term to the international legal order entails, and argues that the prospects of a cosmopolitan-inspired constitutionalization of international law depend on how these risks are approached.

[88] Fassbender, Bardo, 'The Meaning of International Constitutional Law', in Ronald St. J. Macdonald and Douglas M. Johnston, eds., *Towards World Constitutionalism* (Leiden: Martinus Nijhoff, 2005), 837–851. Elsewhere he has made his own strong constitutionalist claim, arguing the UN Charter should be considered as the constitution of the international legal order: Fassbender, 'The United Nations Charter' (1998).

[89] For an unusual adaptation of international constitutionalist thought, see the systems-theoretic argument for 'societal constitutionalism' made by Teubner,

Verdross,[90] Simma[91] and Tomuschat,[92] which emphasizes the idea of an international legal system premised on an 'international community' and international solidarity as opposed to one premised on the separate interests of individual nation-states.[93] Another is the Hayek-inspired, political power-limiting version of international constitutionalism which posits the need for an internationally judicially enforceable and directly effective 'global integration law' protecting economic freedoms and rights.[94] A further important branch of international constitution-alist thought is the 'law of law-making'[95] approach which posits the need for a law 'through which transnational decision-making can be structured in a way which ensures its legitimacy and the rule of law'.[96] The concern animating such approaches is that forms of transnational governance which would otherwise escape domestic constitutional con-trol should be confined by law. More specifically, such approaches argue for an appropriate translation, to the transnational context, of a set of constitutional principles analogous to those developed in the

Günther, 'Societal Constitutionalism: Alternatives to State-Centred Constitutional Theory' in Christian Joerges, I. J. Sand and G. Teubner, eds., *Transnational Governance and Constitutionalism* (Oxford: Hart Publishing, 2004) 3–28. See also Teubner, G. and A. Fischer-Lescano, 'Regime-Collisions: The Vain Search for Legal Unity in the Fragmentation of Global Law', 25 *Michigan Journal of International Law* (2004) 999.

[90] His classic text is Verdross, A., *Die Verfassung der Völkerrechtsgemeinschaft* (Berlin: Springer, 1926).

[91] Simma, 'From Bilateralism to Community Interest' (1994).

[92] Tomuschat, Christian, 'International Law: Ensuring the Survival of Mankind on the Eve of A New Century. General Course on Public International Law', 281 *Recueil des Cours* (1999) 9–438; also 'Obligations Arising' (1993).

[93] Bryde, Brun-Otto, 'International Democratic Constitutionalism', in Ronald St. J. Macdonald and Douglas M. Johnston, eds., *Towards World Constitutionalism* (Leiden: Martinus Nijhoff, 2005) 103–125 at 115. See also A. Von Bogdandy's discussion of the German school, 'Constitutionalism in International Law' (2006).

[94] Ernst-Ulrich Petersmann is the leading exponent of this view. For some of his most recent writings on the topic see 'Constitutionalism and the Regulation of International Markets (2007); 'Why Rational Choice Theory' (2008); 'Justice in International Economic Law?' (2006); 'State Sovereignty, Popular Sovereignty and Individual Sovereignty' (2006).

[95] This approach is inspired by Frank Michelman's work on domestic constitutionalism. See in particular *Brennan and Democracy* (Princeton University Press, 2005), Chapter 1.

[96] Joerges, Christian, 'Constitutionalism in Postnational Constellations: Contrasting Social Regulation in the EU and the WTO', in Christian Joerges and Ernst-Ulrich Petersmann, *Constitutionalism, Multilevel Trade Governance And Social Regulation* (Oxford: Hart, 2006), 491–527.

national constitutional context such as rule of law, checks and balances, human rights protection and democracy.[97] Many advocates of an international constitutionalist understanding have drawn on the development of the European Union with its unusually dense legal order in support of an argument that a constitutionalist approach beyond the state is possible and plausible.[98]

What strong constitutionalist approaches to the international order have in common is their advocacy of some kind of systemic unity, with an agreed set of basic principles and rules to govern the global realm. The strongest versions of constitutionalism propose an agreed hierarchy amongst such rules to resolve conflicts of authority between levels and sites. Constitutionalist approaches to the international regime have, however, generated their fair share of criticism even from within the community of international lawyers.[99] Von Bogdandy, writing of the German school, has argued that, as a legal project 'international constitutionalism might simply be overly ambitious and might lead to normative over-extension'.[100] Other objections include those of 'legal realists [...] who fear that an excess of constitutionalist ideology in international law will raise the level of textualism within the professional community', 'ethical concerns about the unrepresentative status of international judges who would be called upon to adjudicate disputes over the interpretation of constitutional text' and 'local communities seen to be vulnerable to the exploitative or insensitive practices of [centralized] authority and large-scale corporate power'.[101] To the extent that the EU is positively cited as a prototype, there are obvious problems in extrapolating from this example to the

---

[97] See, e.g., Peters, Anne, 'Compensatory Constitutionalism: The Function and Potential of Fundamental International Norms and Structures', 19 *Leiden Journal of International Law* 3 (2006) 579–610.

[98] See, for example, de Wet, Erika, 'International Constitutional Order' (2006).

[99] See, e.g., Schilling, T., 'Constitutionalization of General International Law – An Answer to Globalization?: Some Structural Aspects', *Jean Monnet Working Paper No. 6/2005* (2005), available at <www.jeanmonnetprogram.org/papers/05/050601.html>; Dunoff, Jeffrey L., 'Constitutional Conceits: The WTO's "Constitution" and the Discipline of International Law', 17 *European Journal of International Law* (2006) 647–675.

[100] Bogdandy, 'Constitutionalism in International Law' (2006).

[101] Johnston, D., 'World Constitutionalism in the Theory of International Law', in Ronald St. J. Macdonald and Douglas M. Johnston, eds., *Towards World Constitutionalism* (Leiden: Martinus Nijhoff, 2005, 3–29 at 19.

broader transnational domain, and even the meaningfulness of the idea of constitutionalism in the EU context has been called into question.[102]

Yet despite the range and variety of critique, some formerly sceptical voices have recently joined the advocates of a constitutionalist approach.[103] Most notably, Jürgen Habermas and Martii Koskenniemi, drawing in different ways on Kant's writings, have expounded the merits of a cosmopolitan constitutionalist approach to international law. For Habermas, the crucial underpinning of Kant's cosmopolitan project is the 'cognitive procedure of universalization and mutual perspective-taking' which Kant associates with practical reason.[104] Habermas opens the final chapter of his recent book by asking 'Does the constitutionalization of international law still have a chance?' when confronted with the traditional objections of realists who affirm 'the quasi-ontological primacy of brute power over law'.[105] Habermas seeks to reclaim and re-present Kant's cosmopolitanism as the basis for the international legal order. While drawing on Kant's peace-making and freedom-securing goals of constitutionalism, he rejects the idea of a 'world republic'[106] and argues for a different path to the constitutionalization of international law. Describing the constitutionalization process in the development of modern nation-states as 'the reversal of the initial situation in which law serves as an instrument of power',[107] he argues that major powers are more likely to fulfil expectations of fairness and cooperation the more they have learned to view themselves at the supranational level as members of a global community, and 'are

---

[102] Grimm, Dieter, 'The Constitution in the Process of Denationalization', 12 *Constellations* (2005) 447–463 at 458–9. See also his Grimm, Dieter, 'Integration by Constitution', 3 *International Journal of Constitutional Law* (2005) 193–208.

[103] Compare Koskenniemi, Martti, 'Global Legal Pluralism: Multiple Legal Regimes and Multiple Modes of Thought' (2005), available at <www.helsinki.fi/eci/Publications/MKPluralism-Harvard-05d%5B1%5D.pdf>.

[104] Commenting on Habermas's turn to constitutionalism, Neil Walker suggests that for Habermas 'the constitutionalism of international law seems to inhere partly in the substantive quality of the norms generated, partly in their institutional efficacy, and partly in their universalizability – as a matter of both process and outcomes'; see Walker, 'Making a World of Difference (2005).

[105] Habermas, Jürgen, *The Divided West*, trans. Ciaran Cronin (Cambridge: Polity Press, 2006), Chapter 8 at 116.

[106] Ibid., at 123.   [107] Ibid., at 142.

so perceived by their own national constituencies from which they must derive their legitimation'.[108]

Koskenniemi, drawing similarly on a renewed reading of Kant, has also recently defended the 'constitutionalist mindset' in relation to the international legal order.[109] While criticizing the resort by international lawyers to a 'vocabulary of institutional hierarchies' he argues that Kant's constitutionalism was less an institutional or architectural project, and more 'a programme of moral and political regeneration'. Koskenniemi argues that Kant sought to institutionalize a constitutional mindset 'from which to judge the world in a manner that aims for universality, impartiality, with all the virtues of [Fuller's] inner morality of law'. And he concludes that since constitutional vocabularies not only frame the internal world of moral politicians, but also inform political struggles, such vocabularies as self-determination, fundamental rights, division of power, and accountability are 'historically thick and contest the structural biases of present institutions'.[110]

These Kantian rereadings of cosmopolitan constitutionalism, in my view, offer the ECJ a potentially attractive alternative – a *soft constitutionalist* alternative – to strong constitutional approaches and to strong pluralist approaches alike. The crucial components of such a soft constitutionalist approach would be the following: first, the assumption of an international community of some kind; second, an emphasis on universalizability (the Kantian idea of decision-making which seeks validity beyond the preferences of the decision-maker); and third, an emphasis on common principles of communication for addressing conflict. These three features distinguish the soft constitutionalist approach clearly from pluralist approaches, since the latter assume the existence of a plurality of distinct and separate entities without any overall community, they emphasize the autonomous, authoritative decision-making processes and values of each, and they envisage communication and conflict-resolution through agonistic political processes, *ad hoc* negotiation and pragmatic adjustment. Soft constitutionalist approaches are also distinct from strong constitutionalist approaches

---

[108] Ibid.
[109] Koskenniemi, Martti, 'Constitutionalism as Mindset: Reflections on Kantian Themes About International Law and Globalization', 8 *Theoretical Inquiries in Law* (2007), 9.
[110] Ibid.

in that they do not insist on a clear hierarchy of rules, but on commonly negotiated and shared principles for addressing conflict.

Some variations on what I have called the soft constitutionalist approach can be found in the literature, often proposed by scholars who seek to distinguish their ideas from the strongly monist or hierarchical elements of international constitutionalist thought, but who identify with both the descriptive plurality and the comity-oriented strands of international pluralist thought.[111] Examples are in the work of von Bogdandy, who uses the notion of judicial 'coupling' to suggest how the different legal systems might interact with one another in a way that is informed by the values and principles of domestic constitutional law,[112] Burke-White, whose approach blends the descriptive component of pluralism with the constitutional aspirations of universalist standards, positive comity and commitment to a common enterprise of international law,[113] Kumm,[114] Halberstam[115] and Cohen,[116] amongst others.

The General Court in its judgment in *Kadi 1* adopted a strong constitutionalist approach which was premised on the systemic unity of the international legal order and the EU order, and on a hierarchy of legal authority within this integrated system. The ECJ on the other hand rejected this strong constitutionalist approach, opting instead for a strong pluralist approach. The ECJ presented the European Union as a separate and self-contained system which determines its relationship

---

[111] Elements of a soft constitutional approach are to be found in Neil Walker's work on constitutional pluralism, where he writes of 'the increasing significance of the relational dimension within the post-Westphalian configuration [. . .] the units are no longer isolated, self-sufficient monads, [. . .] their very identity and raison d'etre as polities or putative polities rests at least in some measure on their orientation towards other sites.' See Walker, 'Idea of Constitutional Pluralism' (2002).

[112] Bogdandy, Armin von, 'Pluralism, Direct Effect, and the Ultimate Say: On the Relationship between International and Domestic Constitutional Law', 6 *International Journal of Constitutional Law* (2008) 397.

[113] Burke-White, William, 'International Legal Pluralism', 25 *Michigan International Law Journal* (2003–2004) 963.

[114] Kumm, Mattias, 'Why Europeans Will Not Embrace Constitutional Patriotism', 6 *International Journal of Constitutional Law* (2006) 117.

[115] Halberstam, Daniel, 'Constitutionalism and Pluralism in Marbury and Van Gend', in M. Maduro and L. Azoulay, *The Past and Future of EU Law* (Oxford: Hart Publishing, 2008), and also his Chapter 4 in this volume.

[116] Cohen, 'Global State of Emergency (2008).

to the international order in accordance with its own internal values and priorities rather than in accordance with any mutually negotiated principles or norms. For reasons which are set out in the next section, I argue that a soft constitutionalist approach to the international legal order would provide a better framework for EU international relations than either the strong constitutionalist approach of the General Court in *Kadi 1*, or the strong pluralist approach of the ECJ. A soft constitutional approach would fit better with the aspirations of the EU as a global actor and with its declared identity as a 'good international citizen',[117] but would not abandon the concerns with rights-protection which may have animated the ECJ's ruling. Had the Court of Justice, as the judicial branch of this major regional organization, invoked international law norms rather than insisting on the primacy and relevance only of internally determined EU standards when refusing to implement the Security Council Resolution without due process guarantees, it would not only have provided a better example for other states and organizations contemplating the implementation of the UN sanctions regime, but it would also have strengthened the claim that the EU is an actor which maintains a strong commitment to international law and institutions.

3.5 The case for a soft constitutional approach to the relationship between the international and the EU legal orders

The ruling given by the ECJ in *Kadi I* seems at first glance to be a vindication for advocates of a pluralist conception of the international legal order. Not only did the Court adopt a pluralist approach to the question of the relationship between EU law and international law, but more significantly, the Court in so doing – and by comparison with the approach of the General Court – annulled the EU Regulation implementing the Security Council Resolutions because of their non-compliance with individual due process rights. Regardless of how it fits with the EU's international identity, the claim that a robustly pluralist approach is more likely to strengthen international accountability seems to be supported by the judgment and its outcome.[118] The Court

---

[117] Dunne, Tim, 'Good Citizen Europe', 80 *International Affairs* 1 (2008) 13–28.
[118] Indeed the Security Council in Resolution 1822 (2008) of 30 June 2008 took certain steps, even if still small ones, in response to the kind of challenges brought

of Justice effectively ignored the Security Council Resolution for the purposes of its judgment, treating the aims of the Resolution and its purposes as a matter mainly for the EU's political branches when implementing it. Instead the Court focused judicial attention only on the question whether the EC implementing measure could be said to violate principles of the EU's internal constitutional order, without reference to principles of international law and without reference to the UN.

Yet while the specific outcome of the *Kadi I* case may be commendable from the short-term perspective of its insistence on minimum

by litigants such as Kadi against UN sanctions, by deciding that at least some parts of the 'statements of case' which Member States now provide to the Sanctions Committee when seeking the listing of an individual should be made public and placed on a SC website, or made available for qualified release on request by states. The Resolution also called on the Sanctions Committee to make such brief 'statements of case' available in respect of past listings and to keep listings under review to make sure they are still warranted. It also required Member States who had been notified (i.e. when one of their citizens or an individual who is located in that state has been listed) to inform individuals who have been listed (or de-listed) of this fact and of whatever reasons have been made public. Nevertheless, in its 2008 Report, the Analytic Support and Sanctions Monitoring Team of the Sanctions Committee established by the Security Council, while evidently concerned by the possibility that the ECJ might follow the Opinion of AG Maduro, seemed unwilling to contemplate the establishment of any kind of review panel which would be competent to review the Security Council's decisions or processes. See S/2008/324, paras 39–41. A proposal by Qatar to make the focal point process into more of an independent review panel was not taken up by the Security Council: see

For further information on the pressure to reform the Security Council sanctions system see the 'Targeting Terrorist Financing' project of the Watson Institute for International Studies at Brown University <www.watsoninstitute.org/ project_detail.cfm?id=51>, which also describes the various reform efforts of the so-called 'Interlaken', 'Bonn-Berlin' and 'Stockholm' processes spearheaded by different states; see also the report by Bardo Fassbender commissioned by the UN Secretary General's Office for Legal Advice, 'Targeted Sanctions and Due Process' <www.un.org/law/counsel/Fassbender_study.pdf>. The Austrian government also sponsored an initiative on the UNSC and the Rule of Law, whose final report is entitled 'The Role of the Security Council in Strengthening a Rules-based International System: Final Report and Recommendations from the Austrian Initiative, 2004–2008' and published by both the Federal Ministry for European and International Affairs, and the Institute for International Law and Justice at NYU; see <www.bmeia.gv.at/fileadmin/user_upload/bmeia/media/ Vertretungsbehoerden/New_York/Kandidatur_SR/FINAL_Report_-_The_UN_ Security_Council_and_the_Rule_of_Law.pdf>.

procedural-fairness requirements for those whose assets are to be indefinitely frozen pursuant to the implementation of a UNSC Resolution, the strong pluralist approach which underpins the judgment of the Court is at odds with the self-presentation of the EU as an organization which maintains particular fidelity to international law and institutions, and it is an approach which carries certain costs for the EU. The judicial strategy adopted by the Court of Justice in *Kadi I* was an inward-looking one which eschewed the kind of international engagement and dialogue that has frequently been presented as one of the EU's strengths as a global actor.

Other judicial strategies were undoubtedly available to the Court.[119] In particular the ECJ itself pointed towards a 'soft constitutionalist' pathway but nevertheless chose not to take it. In Paragraph 298 of its judgment in *Kadi I*, the Court noted that the UN Charter leaves it to Member States to decide how to transpose UNSC Resolutions into their legal order. This provided a potential doctrinal route by which the Court could have reached the same substantive result, even while drawing directly on principles of international law rather than emphasizing the particularism of the EU's fundamental rights. In other words, the ECJ could have insisted on respect for basic principles of due process and human rights protection under international law, even where these were neglected within the existing UNSC listing and de-listing processes.[120] By failing to do so, the Court lost an important opportunity

---

[119] For an argument that there was no such other route for the ECJ to take, and that the only effective solution to the problems of targeted UN sanctions against individuals is the installation of an independent administrative mechanism to review the listing and de-listing decisions made by the Security Council, rather than 'decentralized' review by states and organizations like the EU which would jeopardize the authority of the SC and risk fragmenting the system of sanctions, see Reich, J., 'Due Process and Sanctions Targeted Against Individuals Pursuant to Resolution 1267 (1999)', 33 *Yale Journal of International Law* (2008) 505. See also Bothe, M., 'Security Council's Targeted Sanctions against Presumed Terrorists', 6 *Journal of International Criminal Justice* (2008) 541–555.

[120] For a similar suggestion see Bianchi, 'Assessing the Effectiveness', (2008), who argues that interpretative techniques should be perfectly adequate to ensure the conformity of Security Council resolutions with human rights guarantees which could then be provided by states. See also Halberstam, and Stein, 'The United Nations' (2009). For an argument that the UN sanctions regime itself could be made compatible with international and European human rights standards see Cameron, Iain, 'UN Targeted Sanctions, Legal Safeguards and the European Convention on Human Rights', 72 *Nordic Journal of International Law* 2 (2003) 159–214.

to engage in dialogue about due process as part of customary international law, a dialogue which is relevant to international community as a whole and not just the European Union. Argument could have been advanced not only about customary international law as a basis for due process protection, but also about references to the protection of human rights in the UN Charter itself, as well as the general principles of international law and *ius cogens* principles which were invoked by the General Court. In doctrinal terms, the ECJ could have decided that the Resolutions could not be implemented as they stood, without the interposition by the EU, within its freedom of transposition, of a layer of due process such as to protect the interests of affected individuals. This would have involved treating the EU's implementation of the SC Resolution as an opportunity to address that deficiency. By focusing only on the EU's municipal guarantees of fundamental rights protection and ignoring international law, the ECJ not only failed to influence an important international debate on an issue which currently affects every member of the UN, but it also rejected an opportunity to develop channels of mutual influence between the EU and the UN legal orders. The fact that the ECJ instead chose the pluralist language and the reasoning which it did sent out a clear message to other players in the international system about the autonomy of the European legal order, and the priority which it gives to its internally and autonomously determined values. If courts outside the European Union are inclined towards judicial borrowing, then the ECJ's ruling in *Kadi I* seems to offer encouragement to them to assert their local understandings of human rights and their particular constitutional priorities over international norms, and in particular over Chapter VII Resolutions of the Security Council.

Another available strategy for addressing the conflict exposed by the facts of the *Kadi I* case was the approach taken by the German Constitutional Court in its famous '*Solange*' judgments.[121] However, the ECJ eschewed the dialogic approach pioneered by the German Constitutional Court. Instead the Court in *Kadi 1* opted for an internally oriented approach and a form of legal reasoning which emphasized the particular requirements of the EU's general principles of law and the importance of the autonomous authority of the EU legal order. If we

---

[121] See in particular *Solange I*, BVerfGE 37, 271 (1974), [1974] 2 CMLR 540 and *Solange II*, BVerfGE 73, 339 2 BvR 197/83 (1986), [1987] 3 CMLR 225.

look back to the *Solange* jurisprudence of the German Constitutional Court, which has been considered by many observers to provide a persuasive model for addressing the kind of conflict at issue in *Kadi*, we see that the German Court's decision – especially but not only in *Solange II* – is expressed in more directly dialogic and outward-looking terms which reflect the core elements of a soft constitutionalist approach.[122] The conflict at issue in the German case was between a provision of the German Basic Law and an EU regulation, but in that sense also a conflict between the internal constitutional norms of one political entity and the legal requirements imposed by an international or supranational system of which the former entity is a part. In its *Solange I* judgment the *Bundesverfassungsgericht* (Federal Constitutional Court) declared that each of the two organs in question – which in that case were the Constitutional Court and the ECJ respectively – had a duty 'to concern themselves in their decisions with the concordance of the two systems of law'.[123] The relationship between the EU and Germany was not presented by the German Constitutional Court in hierarchical terms, but neither was it described in strongly pluralist or confrontational terms. Instead the judgment emphasized the mutually disciplining relationship between the two legal systems.[124]

Underscoring the dynamic nature of this mutual relationship, the Constitutional Court went on to articulate expressly what it considered to be deficient on the EU level with respect to the protection of fundamental rights, and it also declared that its review of the implementation of EU measures and their compatibility with fundamental rights for this purpose was not just in the interests of the German Court but 'also in the interests of the Community and of Community law'.[125] Subsequently in its second *Solange* ruling in 1986, the *Bundesverfassungsgericht* adopted a less confrontational approach (which may have inspired the

---

[122] *Solange II*, BVerfGE 73, 339 2 BvR 197/83 (1986), [1987] 3 CMLR 225.
[123] *Solange I*, BVerfGE 37, 271 (1974), [1974] 2 CMLR 540.
[124] Ibid.: 'The binding of the Federal Republic of Germany (and of all Member States) by the Treaty is not, according to the meaning and spirit of the Treaties, one-sided, but also binds the Community which they establish to carry out its part in order to resolve the conflict here assumed, that is, to seek a system which is compatible with an entrenched precept of the constitutional law of the Federal Republic of Germany. Invoking such a conflict is, therefore, not in itself a violation of the Treaty, but sets in motion inside the European organs the Treaty mechanism which resolves the conflict on a political level.'
[125] Ibid.

European Court of Human Rights' later judgment in *Bosphorus* v. *Ireland*[126]) in ruling that, given the improvements in the EU human rights regime since the first *Solange* judgment, the German Constitutional Court would no longer examine the compatibility of EU legislation with German fundamental rights as long as the ECJ continued to protect fundamental rights adequately.[127]

The choice of the ECJ in *Kadi I* not to borrow from the *Solange* approach, but to reject any judicial role in the process of the shaping of the relationship between the different legal systems, and to eschew discussion of the possible international law norms which the Security Council may be required to observe, seems to have been carefully chosen. More specifically, it seems to have been deliberately calculated by the Court as an opportunity instead to emphasize the autonomy, authority and separateness of the European Union from the international legal order. Rather than being a decision which can be understood only on its particular facts and in the context of the Security Council's growing anti-terrorist powers, the *Kadi I* judgment seems to have been chosen by the ECJ as the moment in which to emphasize the external dimension of the European constitutionalism which it had first declared in the famous *Van Gend en Loos* case over forty years before. It is this which is the most striking feature of the *Kadi I* case, and it is one which may well surprise those who have assumed that the difference between US and EU approaches to international law lay in the greater receptiveness and openness on the part of the EU – including its judiciary – to international law and institutions.

In the USA, as is well known, an active debate continues not only over the status of customary international law and the duty of domestic courts to apply it,[128] but also, and in spite of the language of the supremacy clause of the Constitution, about the status of international

---

[126] See note 63 above.

[127] *Solange II*, BVerfGE 73, 339 2 BvR 197/83 (1986), [1987] 3 CMLR 225. This stance was subsequently confirmed and even strengthened in the *Solange III* judgment of the Federal Constitutional Court, BVerfGE 2 BvL 1/97 of 7 June 2000.

[128] See the 'revisionist' school of foreign relations law spearheaded by Curtis Bradley and Jack Goldsmith, reflected most recently in debate over the meaning of the Supreme Court's ruling in *Sosa* v. *Alvarez-Machain* 542 U.S. 692 (2004): see Bradley, Curtis, Jack Goldsmith and David Moore, 'Sosa, Customary International Law, and the Continuing Relevance of Erie', 120 *Harvard Law Review* (2007) 869; also Goldsmith, Jack and Eric Posner, *The Limits of*

treaties in domestic law.[129] The changing nature of the scholarly debate in the USA in recent years on these fundamental doctrinal questions of the authority and status of international law to some extent mirrors changing approaches within the US political system towards international law and engagement. This approach – under Democrat as well as Republican administrations, even if more aggressively so in the context of the latter – has regularly been depicted as an attitude of exceptionalism, the pursuit of unilateralism, and a general distrust of international law and institutions.[130] The power of the USA in the international realm, together with the conviction of many Americans about the merits of the form of government and the functioning of democracy in the USA, explains in part the cautious or sceptical approach towards international law and institutions, for the reason that the latter are perceived to be undemocratic and that they may restrain or thwart US interests. In contrast, as indicated above, Europe in general and the European Union in particular have long been associated with an attitude of respect for, and fidelity to, international law and institutions.[131] This has indeed become an explicit part of the EU's self-image[132] and a cultivated aspect

    International Law (Oxford University Press, 2005). More recently, for a proposal that states should be able to withdraw from customary law, see Bradley, C. and G. Mitu Gulati, 'Withdrawing from International Custom', 120 *Yale Law Journal* (2010) 202.

[129] Vazquez, Carlos, 'Treaties as the Law of the Land: The Supremacy Clause and Presumption of Self-execution', 121 *Harvard Law Review* (2008) 600–694.

[130] For a small sample from a vast literature see Koh, Harold, 'On American Exceptionalism', 55 *Stanford Law Review* (2003) 1479–1529; Spiro, Peter J., 'The New Sovereigntists: American Exceptionalism and its False Prophets', 79 *Foreign Affairs* 6 (2000) 9–15; see also the European Journal of International Law symposium issue on 'Unilateralism in International Law: A US-European Symposium' volume 11, numbers 1 and 2 (2000), and the collection of essays edited by Ignatieff, Michael, *American Exceptionalism and Human Rights* (Princeton University Press, 2005).

[131] For a critical analysis of this tendency to contrast Europe favourably see Safrin, Sabrina, 'The UN-Exceptionalism of US Exceptionalism', 41 *Vanderbilt Journal of Transnational Law* (2008) 1307. For a more nuanced account of Europe's version of exceptionalism, see Licková, Magdalena, 'European Exceptionalism in International Law', 19 *European Journal of International Law* (2008) 463–490.

[132] For some recent examples see the 2003 European Security Strategy; also the speech by Javier Solana at the Stockholm Conference on preventing genocide, Brussels, 28 January 2004 on the EU's commitment to 'effective multilateralism': 'International law is the guiding spirit and lifeblood of our multilateral system. That system is made strong through our commitment to upholding and developing international law. The establishment of the International Criminal

of its international identity.[133] Following the Lisbon Treaty amendments, a strong statement of this public commitment has now been enshrined in the provisions of one of the EU's basic 'constitutional' documents, the Treaty on European Union. Article 3(5) TEU reads:

In its relations with the wider world, the Union shall uphold and promote its values and interests and contribute to the protection of its citizens. It shall contribute to peace, security, the sustainable development of the Earth, solidarity and mutual respect among peoples, free and fair trade, eradication of poverty and the protection of human rights, in particular the rights of the child, as well as to *the strict observance and the development of international law, including respect for the principles of the United Nations Charter.* (emphasis added)

Apart from such high-level constitutional and political commitments and declarations, the ECJ, as argued at the outset of this chapter, had for several decades professed respect for international law, at least in the relatively small number of significant foreign relations cases which it decided. The Court had supplemented Article 216(2) TFEU (Treaty on the Functioning of the EU) (formerly Article 300(7) EC)[134] by ruling consistently that once an international treaty concluded by the EU

Court has shown that the multilateral system can be adapted and strengthened to meet new challenges. We have a responsibility now to ensure that it can do its job. We have a responsibility also to ensure that the UN can do its job; that it is made effective and equipped to fulfil its responsibilities. The United Nations cannot function unless we are prepared to act to uphold its rules when they are broken'; available online at <www.europa-eu-un.org/articles/en/article_3176_en.htm>.

    Another example is the recent speech of the EU Presidency on 'The Rule of Law at National and International Levels' at the meeting of the 6th Committee of the UN at the 62nd General Assembly of the UN in NY on 25 October 2007: 'The European Union is deeply committed to upholding and developing an international order based on international law, including human rights law and the rule of law with the United Nations at its core. We believe that international law and the rule of law are the foundations of the international system. Thus, the rule of law is among the core principles on which the EU builds its international relations and its efforts to promote peace, security and prosperity worldwide'; available online at <www.europa-eu-un.org/articles/en/article_7569_en.htm>.

[133] See also Manners, Ian and R. Whitman, 'The Difference Engine: Constructing and Representing the International Identity of the European Union', 10 *Journal of European Public* 3 (2003) 380–404.

[134] Article 216(2) TFEU provides that agreements concluded by the EU 'are binding upon the institutions of the Union and on its Member States'.

entered into force, its provisions formed an integral part of EU law.[135] As far as the effect of such international agreements which are an 'integral part' of the EU legal order is concerned, the Court had almost always declared, with the notable exception of the GATT and World Trade Organization Agreements,[136] that international agreements entered by the EU were directly enforceable before domestic courts.[137] In relation to international agreements to which the EU is not party but to which all Member States are party, the ECJ took the view in relation to the GATT 1947 that the EU (at the time, the Community) had succeeded to the obligations of the states and was bound by its provisions by virtue of the powers the EU had acquired in the sphere of the common commercial policy.[138] Like the GATT 1947, the EU is not a party to the UN Charter, but the General Court in *Kadi 1* had followed a similar (if controversial) approach to that taken in the GATT cases by ruling that the EU was nonetheless bound by its provisions.[139] As far as customary international law rather than treaties is concerned, the ECJ on a number of occasions explicitly ruled that the EU must respect the rules of customary international law in the exercise of its powers, that such rules bind the EU and form part of its internal legal order.[140] And in previous cases in which the reviewability of EU measures implementing Security Council Resolutions arose, the ECJ, while not in any way questioning its own jurisdiction to review those implementing measures, nevertheless expressed itself in very different terms from those of the ECJ in *Kadi I*. Thus in the *Bosphorus* and *Ebony Maritime* cases, the tone of the Court's judgment was considerably more internationalist than in *Kadi I*, expressing concern about the 'purposes of the

---

[135] Case 181/73 *Haegeman* [1974] ECR 449, para. 5; *Opinion 1/91 (EEA Agreement I)* [1991] ECR 6079, para. 37.

[136] The ECJ's treatment of the multilateral trade agreements, and the decision to treat them as 'non-self-executing' by comparison with many other international treaties, has generated a vast literature. For a recent collection of essays on the subject see Zonnekeyn, Geert A., *Direct Effect of WTO Law* (London: Cameron May, 2008), available at <http://works.bepress.com/geert_zonnekeyn/1>.

[137] Mendez, *Legal Effect of Community Agreements* (2009).

[138] Cases 21–24/72 *International Fruit Company NV* v. *Produktschap voor Groenten en Fruit* [1972] ECR 1219.

[139] See n. 24 above and text.

[140] Cases C-286/90 *Anklagemyndigheden* v. *Poulsen and Diva Navigation* [1992] ECR I-6019, para. 9 and C-162/96 *Racke GmbH & Co.* v. *Hauptzollamt Mainz* [1998] ECR I-3655, para. 46.

international community' and its fundamental interests, rather than about the separate and autonomous nature of the EU legal order.[141]

The general perception, fed by such constitutional and judicial pronouncements, of the EU as an organization which maintains a distinctive fidelity to international law has been bolstered by academic and popular commentary. Some of this commentary has focused on the phenomenon of Europe as a 'soft power'[142] which, lacking the military might of the USA, considers that it can best wield a different form of influence through persuasion, negotiation, conciliation and incentives, and by demonstrating its bona fides as a cooperative international actor under international law.[143] Others have expressly drawn attention to the comparison between the EU and the USA in this respect, praising the European approach precisely for offering an alternative, in international relations, to the exceptionalist and unilateral approach of the US.[144] The professed commitment within Europe and by the European

---

[141] C-84/95: *Bosphorus Hava Yollari Turizm ve Ticaret AS* v. *Minister for Transport, Energy and Communications, Ireland and others*, judgment of 30 July 1996, para 26 and C-177/95: *Ebony Maritime SA and Loten Navigation Co. Ltd* v. *Prefetto della Provincia di Brindisi*, judgment of 27 February 1997, para 38: 'As compared with an objective of general interest so fundamental for the international community, which consists in putting an end to the state of war in the region and to the massive violations of human rights and humanitarian international law in the Republic of Bosnia-Herzegovina, the impounding of the aircraft in question, which is owned by an undertaking based in or operating from the Federal Republic of Yugoslavia, cannot be regarded as inappropriate or disproportionate.'

[142] Nye, J., *Soft Power, The Means to Success in World Politics* (New York: Public Affairs, 2004).

[143] For some of the extensive literature on Europe's aspirations as a so-called normative power see the recent special issue of the journal *International Affairs* (volume 80, issue 1, 2008) on 'Ethical Power Europe', in particular the introduction by Lisbeth Aggestam (2008) 1–11, and the essay on 'good international citizenship' by Tim Dunne, 'Good Citizen Europe' (2008), 13–28. For earlier contributions see Manners, I., 'Normative Power Europe: A Contradiction in Terms?', 40 *Journal of Common Market Studies* (2002) 235–258; Howse, Robert and Kalypso Nicolaides, 'This is my EUtopia: Narrative as Power', 40 *Journal of Common Market Studies* (2002) 767–792; also Krastev, Ivan and Mark Leonard, *New World Order: The Balance of Soft Power and the Rise of Herbivorous Powers* (London: European Council on Foreign Relations, 2007); Bretherton, Charlotte and John Vogler, *The European Union as a Global Actor* (London: Routledge, 1999); Sjursen, H., 'The EU as "Normative" Power: How can this be?', 13 *Journal of European Public Policy* 2 (2006) 235–251; Garton Ash, T., 'Europe's True Stories', *Prospect* 131 (February 2007).

[144] Habermas, *Divided West*, (2006).

Union to international law and international institutions has been the subject of more cynical commentary by US commentators,[145] but notably they tend to share the perception that the EU and European powers in general differ from the USA in the extent to which they are prepared to trust in and to follow international law and institutions.[146]

3.6 Conclusion

I have argued in this chapter that the ECJ's new-found – or at least its more overtly and strongly expressed – judicial pluralism in *Kadi 1* has significant implications for the image the EU has cultivated of itself as an actor committed to 'effective multilateralism',[147] which professes a distinctive allegiance to international law and institutions, and which seeks to carve out a global role for itself as a normative power. Even as Europe's political institutions assert the EU's distinctive role as a global actor committed to multilateralism under international law, and even as the Lisbon Treaty's amendment to the EU Treaties has enshrined the EU's 'strict' commitment to international law, the European Court chose to use the much-anticipated *Kadi I* ruling as the occasion to proclaim the internal and external autonomy and separateness of the EU's legal order from the international domain, and the primacy of its internal constitutional values over the norms of international law. When placed alongside other judicial developments such as its long-standing and recent case-law on the GATT/WTO agreements[148] and more recent cases dealing with international maritime law such as *Intertanko*,[149] the approach of the ECJ to the international legal order begins to resemble the kind of *ad hoc*, instrumentalist engagement with

---

[145] E.g. Kagan, Robert, *Of Paradise and Power: America and Europe in the New World Order* (New York: Knopf, 2003); Rubenfeld, Jed, 'Unilateralism and Constitutionalism', 79 *New York University Law Review* (2004) 1971–2028.

[146] For arguments which challenge the assertion that the European and American approaches to international law are so different from one another, see Delahunty, R., 'The Battle of Mars and Venus: Why do American and European Attitudes to International Law Differ?', *St Thomas Law School Working Paper Series No 1744* (2006), available at <http://law.bepress.com/cgi/viewcontent.cgi?article=8181&context=expresso>, and the op-ed published by Jack Goldsmith and Eric Posner, 'Does Europe Believe in International Law?', *Washington Post* (25 November 2008).

[147] See the 'European Security Strategy: A Secure Europe in a Better World' (2003), available online at <http://consilium.europa.eu/uedocs/cmsUpload/78367.pdf>.

[148] See the FIAMM case, note 8 above.   [149] Case C-308/06, see note 9 above.

international law of which the USA is often accused, and which the EU had long professed to set itself against. This chapter has argued that the EU in general and the ECJ in particular need to develop a more coherent constitutional framework for EU international relations, and that this framework should be inspired by a soft constitutionalist approach rather than by either the strong pluralism or the strong constitutionalism reflected in the judgments of the ECJ and the General Court respectively in the landmark *Kadi 1* case.

4 | Local, global and plural constitutionalism: Europe meets the world

DANIEL HALBERSTAM*

4.1 Introduction

The idea that constitutionalism is central to the legitimate exercise of public power has dominated the modern liberal imagination since the Enlightenment. The ideal of limited collective self-governance has spawned a rich and highly diverse tradition of hard-fought national constitutions from the time of the Glorious Revolution into the present. Today, however, constitutionalism faces its greatest challenge yet: the question of its continued relevance to modern governance. With the explosion of governance beyond the state, many wonder whether constitutionalism as we know it is being marginalized or altogether undermined.

   The dilemma of constitutionalism in the age of global governance has elicited two principal responses – one local and one global. On the one hand, there are those who, alarmed by the threat of global intrusion, have sounded the retreat into local constitutionalism as the only source of legitimate public power. Local constitutionalists (or 'new sovereignt-ists', as they are sometimes called)[1] deny the normative pull of international, transnational and global governance by anchoring all legal authority in local (i.e. national) constitutions.[2] The realm beyond the

* Eric Stein Collegiate Professor of Law and Director, European Legal Studies Program, University of Michigan Law School. I would like to thank the editors and the contributors to the current volume, as well as José Alvarez, Catherine Barnard, George Bermann, Francesca Bignami, Scott Hershovitz, Don Herzog, Ellen Katz, Kalypso Nicolaidis and Eric Stein for comments and discussions, and Sean Powers for steadfast research assistance.
1   See Spiro, Peter J., 'The New Sovereigntists: American Exceptionalism and its False Prophets', 79 *Foreign Affairs* 6 (2000) 9–15.
2   See, e.g., Posner, E. and J. Goldsmith, *The Limits of International Law* (Oxford University Press, 2005); Yoo, John, *The Powers of War and Peace: The Constitution and Foreign Affairs After 9/11* (University of Chicago Press, 2005); Bradley, Curtis, 'International Delegations, the Structural Constitution, and

state is, on this view, pure power politics with resort to legalism as a simple tool of self-interest alone. On the other hand, there are those who view global governance optimistically as overcoming the inherent limitations of local constitutionalism.[3] The strong version of this second response seeks nothing less than to redefine constitutionalism itself by placing the local in the service of the global.[4] These global constitutionalists view the state simply as playing one particular role within a rational design for a comprehensive system of multi-layered governance that spans all issues and all people around the globe.[5]

This chapter seeks to chart a middle course between these two dominant responses by joining constitutionalism and pluralism into an alternative to the purported choice between the local and the global. The basic idea is to understand the competing claims of local and global authority as fundamentally unresolved and – at a general level – unresolvable. The only solutions that emerge are specific solutions derived

Non-Self-Execution', 55 *Stanford Law Review* (2003) 1557; Ku, Julian G., 'The Delegation of Federal Power to International Organizations: New Problems with Old Solutions', 85 *Minnesota Law Review* (2000) 71; Swaine, Edward T., 'The Constitutionality of International Delegations', 104 *Columbia Law Review* (2004) 1492; Young, Ernest A., 'Dual Federalism, Concurrent Jurisdiction, and the Foreign Affairs Exception', 69 *The George Washington Law Review* (2001) 139. For a discussion of this approach, see Spiro, 'The New Sovereigntists' (2000), at 9–15; Hathaway, Oona A. and Ariel N. Lavinbuk, 'Rationalism and Revisionism in International Law', 119 *Harvard Law Review* (2006) 1404 (reviewing Posner and Golsmith). Cf. Section 4.2.1.

[3] See, e.g., Habermas, Jürgen, *The Divided West*, trans. Ciaran Cronin (Cambridge: Polity Press, 2006); Held, David, *Democracy and the Global Order: From the Modern State to Cosmopolitan Governance* (Cambridge: Polity Press, 1995), at 17; Petersmann, Ernst-Ulrich, 'The WTO Constitution and Human Rights', 3 *Journal of International Economic Law* 1 (2000) 19–25; Tomuschat, Christian, 'International Law: Ensuring the Survival of Mankind on the Eve of A New Century. General Course on Public International Law', 281 *Recueil des Cours* (1999) 9–438; Fassbender, Bardo, 'The United Nations Charter as Constitution of the International Community', 36 *Columbia Journal of Transnational Law* (1998) 529–619. Cf. Section 4.3.2 at 170.

[4] A more moderate version of this second response seeks to avoid the register of constitutionalism altogether by speaking about good governance in global administrative law. This chapter does not specifically address the distinctions between constitutional pluralism and global administrative law. Suffice it to say, however, that global administrative law increasingly seems unable to elide the difficulties of constitutionalism in that administrative law, too, depends on an understanding of who is to be served and to what end by global agencies of administrative law. See, e.g., Krish, Nico, 'The Pluralism of Global Adminstrative Law', 17 *European Journal of International Law* (2006) 247–278.

[5] See Section 4.2.2.

from specific interactions among specific actors. To be sure, broad habits of reliable mutual accommodation emerge that provide a good deal of consistency and daily predictability across issues and over time. But in the absence of universal settlement these habits are ever open to revision by the participating actors.

Pluralism in this sense rejects hierarchy and foundation. But it does not operate in a legal or normative vacuum. The kind of pluralism of actors, systems, sources and norms described here is based not only on mutual autonomy and lack of hierarchy, but also on mutually embedded openness of the various participants to the authority of the other or to some form of collective governance.[6] Pluralism, then, is different from plurality. Pluralism is not the inevitable product of multiplicity but only a contingent possibility in the light of certain preconditions.

The idea of constitutionalism as limited collective self-governance can serve as a kind of grammar of legitimacy to which the various participants appeal in their mutual conflict and accommodation surrounding their competing claims of authority.[7] This, too, is not an inevitable fact, but a potential that arises out of the nature of the participating systems and their mutually embedded commitment to some kind of shared governance. Hierarchy in all this remains unsettled; contest, conflict and accommodation remain decentralized. The result is not troublesome fragmentation but beneficial multiplicity that fosters a collective yet piecemeal process of shaping and reshaping the practice of constitutionalism to suit our present needs.

The European Union figures strongly in this debate, as Union governance is perhaps the most advanced institutional embodiment of taking constitutionalism beyond the state.[8] The European Union itself is a response to the failure of local constitutionalism within Europe. And yet, the European Union is an attempt to forge a larger project of shared governance that can co-exist sympathetically with the continuation of

---

[6] Cf. Section 4.3.1.   [7] Cf. Section 4.3.2.

[8] For the sake of simplicity, the terms 'European Union', 'European Community', 'Union' and 'Community' will generally be used interchangeably – and the term 'European Economic Community' will be avoided entirely – despite the fact that doing so may at times lead to minor technical inaccuracies or anachronistic turns of phrases.

national constitutional traditions. As a result, the Union seems especially well suited to the project of constitutional pluralism.[9]

As the European Union matures, however, the question becomes whether it will follow a path of self-absorption and seclusion or whether it will reproduce the constitutional openness of its component states in its own dealings with the world beyond its borders. Put another way, will Europe retreat into a regional brand of local constitutionalism or will it take more innovative strides to serve as beacon for the possibilities of global governance? After discussing the dilemma of modern constitutionalism and the pluralist approach, this chapter analyses the European question, with a specific focus on the litigation over the implementation of the United Nations Security Council's targeted economic sanctions within Europe.[10]

This chapter will proceed in four parts. Section 4.2 will discuss local constitutionalism, global constitutionalism and the challenge of pluralism. Section 4.3 will take a brief step back and unpack the ideas of pluralism and constitutionalism into their component parts. Section 4.4 will then analyse the various judicial pronouncements in the *Kadi* case through the lens of local constitutionalism, global constitutionalism and plural constitutionalism. The last part is the conclusion.

4.2 From sovereignty to pluralism in global governance

In recent decades, we have witnessed the proliferation of global governance regimes as well as the expansion (and expanded assertion) of powers of both old and new actors in the international arena. Organizations such as the United Nations (UN), the World Trade Organization (WTO), the World Health Organization (WHO), the International Labor Organization (ILO), the Organization of American States (OAS), the African Union (AU) and the European Union (EU), to name only a few, have, to varying degrees, taken on governance functions previously performed by states. International

---

[9] MacCormick, Neil, *Questioning Sovereignty: Law, State and Nation in the European Commonwealth* (Oxford University Press, 1999); Walker, Neil, 'The EU and the WTO: Constitutionalism in a New Key', in G. de Búrca and J. Scott, eds., *The EU and the WTO: Legal and Constitutional Issues* (Oxford: Hart Publishing, 2001) 31–57.

[10] Cf. Section 4.4 at 175.

(and supranational) organizations have become 'law-makers'.[11] They have interpreted and applied laws, often through the creation of judicial bodies.[12] And, with the helping hand of participating states, they have increasingly taken effective enforcement action as well.

The broadening and deepening of European integration over the years has catapulted the EU into a league of its own, but even more traditional international organizations have significantly expanded their powers. The United Nations and its Security Council, for example, have become more active than ever before on several fronts. Since the end of the (first) Cold War, the number of Security Council Resolutions is on the rise, the number of peacekeeping missions is at an all-time high and the United Nations is increasingly taking on governance tasks in administering the territories of failed states.[13] With the creation of the criminal tribunals for Rwanda and Yugoslavia, as well as the UN-related International Criminal Court, the United Nations has begun to tighten its grasp on administering justice directly to individuals. And with UN Sanctions Committees ordering coercive action not only against states, but also against named individuals suspected of funding international terrorism, the UN is expanding its reach with regard to individuals here, too.

The WTO has been at the forefront of global governance as well. The 'judicialization' of the General Agreement on Tariffs and Trade (GATT)

---

[11] See Alvarez, José, 'International Organizations: Then and Now', 100 *American Journal of International Law* (2006) 324 at 333; Alvarez, José, *International Organizations as Law-makers* (Oxford University Press, 2005).

[12] Shany, Yuval, 'No Longer a Weak Department of Power? Reflections on the Emergence of a New International Judiciary', 20 *European Journal of International Law* (2009) 73.

[13] See Fry, James, 'Dionysian Disarmament: Security Council WMD Coercive Disarmament Measures and their Legal Implications', 29 *Michigan Journal of International Law* (2008) 197 (observing an increase in Security Council resolutions regarding disarmament after the Cold War); Ratner, Steven, 'Foreign Occupation and Territorial Administration: The Challenges of Convergence', 16 *European Journal of International Law* (2005) 695; United Nations Peacekeeping Operations, available at <www.un.org/Depts/dpko/dpko/bnote.htm> (last accessed 21 April 2009) (depicting the eighteen current peacekeeping missions out of the sixty-three peacekeeping missions in the United Nations history); UN Security Council Resolutions, available at <www.un.org/Docs/sc/unsc_resolutions. html> (last accessed 21 April 2009) (recording that the Security Council adopted 1,144 resolutions from 1992 until present and 725 resolutions from 1946 to 1991).

in the 1970s and 1980s,[14] culminating in the creation of the WTO and its stringent Dispute Resolution Understanding in 1995, has established a practice by which domestic governance decisions affecting international trade are increasingly subject to a kind of global judicial review.[15] The creation of the WTO strengthened the legal effect of such review, expanded the importance of adjudication to the authoritative interpretation of the GATT/WTO and broadened the potential scope of questions (such as environmental policies) that might be drawn into the WTO's purview in the context of settling disputes.[16]

A vast array of scholarship has cropped up to help make sense of this proliferation and intensification of global governance activity. For present purposes, we can distinguish between three principle strands that have approached this phenomenon in the language of constitutionalism. The first seeks to ground international governance exclusively in local constitutions and the consent of states. The second, by contrast, seeks to reimagine states at the service of a cosmopolitan constitutional order. The third approach leaves the question of hierarchy among various sites of governance unsettled, and embraces the resulting multiplicity of authority in the spirit of pluralism. This section discusses each of these in turn.

4.2.1 Local constitutionalism and the new sovereigntists

One group of scholars, sometimes referred to as 'new sovereigntists', resists the very idea of 'global governance' (in the sense of shifting

---

[14] E.g., Shapiro, M. and A. Stone Sweet, *On Law, Politics and Judicialization* (Oxford University Press, 2003), at 72–75.

[15] See, e.g., Jackson, J., 'The WTO Dispute Settlement Understanding – Misunderstandings on the Nature of Legal Obligations', 91 *American Journal of International Law* (1997) 60. It would be mistaken, however, to view this kind of judicial review as being on a par with the role of courts in domestic legal systems. See, e.g., Howse, Robert and Kalypso Nicolaidis, 'Democracy without Sovereignty: The Global Vocation of Political Ethics', in T. Broude and Y. Shany, eds., *The Shifting Allocation of Authority in International Law* (Oxford, Portland: Hart Publishing, 2008), 163 ('The regulation of trade at the global level has not yet established the kind of dialogue and division of labour between the judicial and political sphere that has characterized governance both in the domestic and the European contexts.').

[16] See, e.g., Trebilcock, M. and R. Howse, *The Regulation of International Trade* (London: Routledge, 2005), at 507–556 (discussing the role of environmental disputes in WTO law).

authority beyond the state).[17] Building on the 'realist' approach to international relations[18] and traditional notions of state sovereignty, these scholars place international law strictly in the service of states. These scholars often go well beyond the traditional 'dualist' claim that international and domestic legal obligations are distinct.[19] They claim that domestic actors adhere to their international legal obligations only in so far as autonomously determined domestic legal norms or policy considerations induce them to do so.[20] Indeed, sovereigntists make an even stronger claim that goes to the very heart of what international law is. International law, these scholars suggest, is '*endogenous* to state interests'.[21] This means that 'international law is not a check on state self-interest' but merely 'a product of state self-interest'.[22] The descriptive and the normative run together here: on the sovereigntists' view, authority (whether legal, moral, democratic or epistemic) ultimately resides in domestic constitutional arrangements.[23]

From a purely domestic perspective, sovereigntists have thus restored order to the raging proliferation among international regimes. Any claim of normative pull from beyond the state is presented as illegitimate.[24] Conflicts among the various international regimes as well as between any given regime and the domestic legal order should therefore not arise – at least not in any troublesome manner. Although various rules of international law may point in different directions or may suggest a certain path of state behaviour, the various obligations will be (and should be)

---

[17] See, e.g., Posner and Goldsmith, *Limits* (2005); Yoo, *Powers of War and Peace* (2005); Bradley, 'International Delegations' (2003); Ku, 'Delegation' (2000); Swaine, 'Constitutionality' (2004); Young, 'Dual Federalism' (2001). For a discussion of this approach, see Spiro, 'The New Sovereigntists' (2000), at 9–15; Hathaway and Lavinbuk, 'Rationalism and Revisionism' (2006) (reviewing Posner and Goldsmith).

[18] E.g. Donnelly, Jack, *Realism and International Relations* (Cambridge University Press, 2000).

[19] For a critical review of this distinction see, e.g., Walker, Neil, 'Beyond Boundary Disputes and Basic Grids: Mapping the Global Disorder of Normative Orders', 6 *International Journal of Constitutional Law* 3–4 (2008) 373–396 at 378.

[20] Posner and Goldsmith, *Limits* (2005), at 39, 100–106.

[21] Ibid., at 13 (italicization as original).

[22] Ibid.

[23] See Rabkin, Jeremy, *Why Sovereignty Matters* (Washington, DC: American Enterprise Institute Press, 1998).

[24] See, e.g., Kagan, Robert, 'America's Crisis of Legitimacy', 83 *Foreign Affairs* (March/April 2004) 65, at 65.

conclusively mediated by the rational self-interest of states. States, on this view, do not (and need not) observe international law that does not serve their autonomously defined rational self-interest.[25]

The new sovereigntists thus defend a rather traditional vision of hierarchy. On their view, international law is fully subordinated to the ultimate (and exclusively legitimate) authority of the state and its domestic legal process. To be sure, conflicts among the various regimes of global governance or among the (purported) norms of any of these regimes and state behaviour will emerge. For new sovereigntists, however, such conflicts are not the result of any novel proliferation of global governance regimes that represent multiple sites of public authority, but simply a reflection of the age-old conflict among nations based on power and interest.[26]

4.2.2 Global constitutionalism and the cosmopolitan ideal

At the opposite end of the scholarly spectrum a different school of thought seeks to promote order in the arena of global governance and its interaction with the domestic sphere from a distinctly universal perspective. These authors strive to impose a cosmopolitan order based on the collective exploration of the common good, shared values or the common acceptance of a minimum set of rights.[27]

A frequent starting point for cosmopolitan approaches are basic Kantian ideas that the individual is the ultimate unit of concern, that all individuals can lay claim to this status, and that this status has global force.[28] Beginning from these premises, Thomas Pogge, for example, advocates 'institutional cosmopolitanism', which demands that each of

---

[25] Posner and Goldsmith, *Limits* (2005), at 202 ('[I]nternational law can be binding and robust, but only when it is rational for states to comply with it.').

[26] Kagan, 'America's Crisis' (2004).

[27] See Pogge, Thomas, *World Poverty and Human Rights* (Cambridge: Polity Press, 2002); Backer, Larry, 'From Constitution to Constitutionalism: A Global Framework for Legitimate Public Power Systems', 113 *Penn State Law Review* (2009) 671; Besson, Samantha, 'Human Rights, Institutional Duties and Cosmopolitan Responsibilities', 23 *Oxford Journal of Legal Studies* (2003) 507; Feldman, Noah, 'Cosmopolitan Law?', 116 *Yale Law Journal* (2007) 1022; Pogge, Thomas, 'Cosmopolitanism and Sovereignty', 103 *Ethics* 1 (1992) 48–75. For a critical description of cosmopolitanism, see Goldsmith, Jack, 'Liberal Democracy and Cosmopolitan Duty', 55 *Stanford Law Review* (2003) 1667.

[28] Pogge, *World Poverty* (2002).

us take responsibility for the global effects on individuals of the national and global governance regimes we help establish. He makes out a moral argument for the dispersal of sovereignty into vertically nested regimes that are better suited to ensuring the satisfaction of a minimal set of universal social and economic human rights. David Held's conception of 'cosmopolitan democratic law', by contrast, focuses principally on the inability of national democracies to live up to the idea of self-government even with regard to their own populations in our modern interconnected world.[29] For this reason alone, 'national democracies require an international cosmopolitan democracy if they are to be sustained and developed in the contemporary era'.[30] And so, too, Held supports 'the subordination of regional, national and local "sovereignties" to an overarching legal framework'.[31]

A distinctly German school of scholarship presents a legal variant of these ideas under the rubric of global constitutionalism.[32] Christian Tomuschat, for instance, has prominently argued for turning the traditional sovereigntists' argument on its head.[33] In Tomuschat's view, international law does not serve the interests of states. Instead, states serve the function defined by the 'international community' and international law, such as fulfilling their obligation each 'to perform specific services for the benefit of its citizens'.[34] Tomuschat insists that the idea of an 'international community' is not 'simply *une façon de parler*', but that it 'constitutes indeed an entity which may be identified as a legal actor'.[35] For Tomuschat, the international community 'is not a homogenous organizational unit, but can be defined as an ensemble of rules, procedures and mechanisms designed to protect collective interests of

---

[29] Held, *Democracy and the Global Order* (1995).
[30] Ibid., at 23.   [31] Ibid., at 234.
[32] Bogdandy, Armin von, 'Constitutionalism in International Law: Comment on a Proposal from Germany', 47 *Harvard Journal of International Law* (2006) 223–242 at 223–224. The roots of this tradition go back to Mosler and Kelsen. See, e.g., Kelsen, Hans, *Reine Rechtslehre* (2nd reprint of first edition, Leipzig und Wien; Aalen: Scientia Verlag, 1994 [1934]); Mosler, Hermann, 'The International Society as a Legal Community', 140 *Receuil des Cours* (1974) 1–320 at 11.
[33] Tomuschat, 'International Law' (1999).   [34] Ibid., at 95.   [35] Ibid., at 72–73.

humankind, based on a perception of commonly shared values'.[36] Tomuschat thus even speaks of a 'constitution of humankind' that comprises this normative framework at the international level.[37] The upshot is a global hierarchy built on the foundation of shared rights, according to which '[s]tates are no more than instruments whose inherent function it is to serve the interests of their citizens as legally expressed in human rights'.[38]

Building on revised Kantian premises, Jürgen Habermas similarly urges a 'constitutional' understanding of the United Nations as a 'framework for a [...] politically constituted world society'.[39] Like Tomuschat, Habermas hedges somewhat on the success of this enterprise,[40] and he recognizes the continued centrality of states as repositories of law and the legitimate use of power.[41] And yet, he, too, argues for the 'constitutionalization of international law'.[42] Habermas's vision focuses specifically on the UN Charter, on protecting human rights and on controlling the use of force.[43] But he nonetheless warns against underestimating the 'expanding horizon of a world society that is increasingly self-programming, even at the cultural level'.[44] Habermas thus promotes a vision of states, transnational and regional organizations operating within the overarching global order of the United Nations to address issues from the more basic preservation of fundamental rights and peace among nations to environmental regulation and social fairness.[45]

---

[36] Ibid., at 88. Grand in aspiration as this is, Tomuschat injects a certain realism of expectations. See page 80 (noting that the international community can come about only in so far as it receives the 'backing from societal and historical realities to become a driving force in international relations'). As one illustration that this is not pure utopia, however, Tomuschat cites the system of criminal prosecution at the international level.

[37] Ibid., at 90.   [38] Ibid., at 162.   [39] Habermas, *Divided West* (2006).

[40] Ibid.   [41] Ibid., at 176.   [42] Ibid., at 143, 177.

[43] Ibid., at 165. Habermas emphasizes the common recognition of rights, the inclusion of individuals as immediate subjects of international law, effective control of the (non-legitimate) use of violence at the UN level and the 'hierarchization' of international law in Article 103 of the UN Charter and *ius cogens*. See generally pages 160–175.

[44] Ibid., at 176.

[45] Many others – too numerous to discuss in any detail here – write in this tradition. Suffice it to say that alongside generalists, such as Habermas, Tomuschat, Mosler and Kelsen, there are also regime-specific advocates in this tradition. In this latter vein, for example, Bardo Fassbender builds on Alfred

Putting aside the many differences among the various contributions in this tradition, global constitutionalists share several important intellectual commitments that are diametrically opposed to those of the local constitutionalists: first, an understanding (both descriptive and normative) of the arena of global governance as not grounded merely in the consent of states but as a legitimate site for the independent production of politics and norms; second, a desire to increase the normative strength of international law in terms of legal and moral obligation, as well as domestic internalization, application and enforcement; and third, an aspiration to subsume the multiplicity of global governance sites, along with states, under a single hierarchically ordered system of multilevel global governance.

Local and global constitutionalists, however, have one thing in common. Both perspectives impose a settled normative hierarchy on the arena of global governance. Whereas local constitutionalists anchor their vision in the supremacy of the rational self-interest of states, global constitutionalists privilege a cosmopolitan idea of community. One way or another, legal conflicts do not endure, but can be authoritatively resolved. Under either vision, the fragmentation of global governance is ultimately tamed.

4.2.3 The pluralist challenge

In contrast to both local and global constitutionalists, a third group of scholars embraces fragmentation in the name of 'pluralism'. What began as a theory about the distribution of constitutional authority within Europe is increasingly being presented as an attractive vision of global governance writ large.

Within Europe, the so-called 'pluralist movement' blossomed in reaction to the German *Bundesverfassungsgericht*'s Maastricht decision.[46] In that case, Germany's constitutional court tolerated the

---

Verdross and Bruno Simma's work to argue for an understanding of the UN Charter as a constitutional framework governing the international community (Fassbender, 'The United Nations Charter' (1998)), whereas Ernst-Ulrich Petersman argues for a constitutional vision of the WTO as a regime to bring order to the realm of global governance; see, e.g., Petersmann, 'WTO Constitution' (2000).

[46] See Baquero Cruz, Julio, 'The Legacy of the Maastricht-Urteil and the Pluralist Movement', 14 *European Law Journal* (2008) 389–420 at 412–418.

Union's expansion of powers (including the assertion of supremacy and direct effect within Germany) while formally retaining the national court's ultimate control over German constitutional space.[47] Neil MacCormick originally described this as the idea of 'constitutional pluralism,' which he defined as follows:

> Where there is a plurality of institutional normative orders, each with a functioning constitution (at least in the sense of a body of higher-order norms establishing and conditioning relevant governmental powers), it is possible that each acknowledge the legitimacy of every other within its own sphere, while none asserts or acknowledges constitutional superiority over another.[48]

To be sure, as a matter of formal rhetoric, both the Court of Justice of the European Union,[49] on the one hand, and national constitutional courts (such as the German *Bundesverfassungsgericht*), on the other, have each laid claim to the ultimate supremacy of (its own interpretation of) its own legal order. But the judicial practice has, in fact, been one of principled mutual accommodation.

The kind of mutual respect and accommodation within Europe thus represents a genuine third way between the particularism of the local constitutionalists (which subjects the global realm to national interests) and the cosmopolitanism of the global constitutionalists (which incorporates the national and the global into a single unity of interest). As a broader social ethos, Europe's pluralism reflects what Joseph Weiler has called the principle of 'constitutional tolerance'.[50] The pressing question, however, is the extent to which (if at all) these principles can find application beyond the special case of Europe's internal system of governance.

---

[47] *Manfred Brunner et al. v. European Union Treaty*, 89 BVerfGE 155 (1993), English translation at [1994] 1 C.M.L.R. 57.

[48] MacCormick, *Questioning Sovereignty* (1999), at 104.

[49] In the following, for the sake of simplicity, the terms 'Court of Justice of the European Union', 'European Court of Justice' and 'Court of Justice', as well as the abbreviations 'CJEU' and 'ECJ', will at times be used interchangeably despite the fact that doing so may create technical inaccuracies or anachronistic turns of phrases.

[50] Weiler, J. H. H., 'Federalism without Constitutionalism: Europe's Sonderweg', in Kalypso Nicolaidis and Robert Howse, eds., *The Federal Vision: Legitimacy and Levels of Governance in the US and the EU* (Oxford University Press, 2001), 54, at 62–70.

Addressing this question, Neil Walker has suggested that just as we can relax the statist assumptions of constitutionalism within Europe, so, too, we can view constitutionalism (and hence constitutional pluralism) as applying to various sites of global governance. After disaggregating constitutionalism into seven indices,[51] Walker agrees that the European Union is in the vanguard of non-state entities exhibiting constitutional features.[52] But he argues that it would be mistaken to dismiss the 'modes[t]' constitutional elements present in other entities as well.[53]

Responding to this argument in the context of the WTO, scholars such as Robert Howse and Kalypso Nicolaidis resist constitutionaliza-tion on normative grounds.[54] Whether the goal is to protect certain economic rights by placing their enforcement above politics or to draw on the WTO system for an authoritative balancing of an ever-broadening scope of interests from human rights to labour to environ-mental concerns, Howse and Nicolaidis are wary.[55] This kind of constitutionalization does not help to alleviate the 'legitimacy conun-drum' of global governance.[56] Nor does it lead to an adequate consid-eration of the multiple sites of norm production at the national as well as global level of governance:

Instead of presupposing that that the treaty text is animated by a constitu-tional *telos* of freer trade, or looking primarily *within* the WTO for the relevant structural principles, we emphasize the importance of non-WTO

---

[51] See Walker, 'The EU and the WTO' (2001). Walker indices are a self-conscious constitutional discourse, foundational (i.e. non-derivative) legal authority, 'multi-functionality' (in the sense of jurisdiction beyond the pursuit of a single regulatory goal or policy), interpretive autonomy, institutional structures of governance, specification of membership or citizenship (of individuals and non-state actors), and mechanisms for representing the members in the decision-making process of the organization or system.

[52] Ibid., at 36 (referring to the EU as currently the 'most mature non-state polity').

[53] Ibid., at 50.

[54] Howse and Nicolaidis oppose the general move towards allowing individuals to invoke WTO law as 'rights' in WTO review bodies and in domestic courts, making WTO law and the WTO *acquis* supreme and difficult to change, and unifying the 'complex, messily negotiated bargain of diverse rule, principles, and norms' of the WTO into a 'single structure'; see Howse, Robert and Kalypso Nicolaidis, 'Legitimacy through "Higher Law"? Why Constitutionalizing the WTO Is a Step Too Far', in T. Cottier, P. Mavroidis and P. Blatter, eds., *The Role of the Judge in International Trade Regulation: Experience and Lessons for the WTO* (Ann Arbor: University of Michigan Press, 2003), 307 at 308.

[55] Ibid., at 309–310.   [56] Ibid., at 310.

institutions and norms in treaty interpretation, which represent values other than free or freer trade. The WTO dispute settlement organs must display considerable deference to substantive domestic regulatory choices as well as draw on and defer to other international regimes whose rules, policies, and institutions represent and articulate such values, whether in respect of health, labor standards, environment, or human rights.[57]

Properly understood, then, this critique of constitutionalization responds less to a vision of plural constitutionalism than to a kind of global constitutionalism in which any one site is privileged over all others. Indeed, Howse and Nicolaidis make a plea for a kind of pluralism that, in principle, should be compatible with constitutionalism at least in the expansive use of that term. Even absent the kind of coherent polity creation that Walker ultimately seems to focus on, global governance sites and institutions may stand in a pluralist relation to one another as well as to state actors, and they may draw on the principles of constitutionalism to mediate conflict and contestation among these various sites of authority.

4.3 Unpacking pluralism and constitutionalism

Two principal ingredients are necessary for pluralism to obtain: first, a plurality of partially autonomous sites or institutions of public governance with mutually conflicting claims of authority; and second, mutually embedded openness within these sites or institutions with regard to each other's claims of authority. This is often true for the relation between states and the realm of international law in which organizations of global governance operate, as well as in the relation among the various sites of public governance within the global arena. Furthermore, this is also often true for the co-existence of multiple systems or regimes as well as for the co-existence of multiple interpretative institutions within a single regime.

The claim here is not that every single regime and system – whether domestic, international, transnational or global – displays the same openness to every other system. Nor that every interpretive institution recognizes the claims of its rivals to an equal extent. Instead, the claim is that whenever we find a deeply embedded mutual openness among semi-

---

[57] Ibid., at 311.

autonomous systems or regimes, the stage for pluralism is set. Whenever such openness is embedded in the law of one system or regime with respect to that of another, conflicts of authority may be negotiated by resort to conflict and accommodation based in principle not power.

This leads us to the final ingredient of the plural constellation discussed here: constitutionalism. To the extent that the idea of limited collective self-governance frames the understanding of the competing sites and institutions, and to the extent that the competing sites and institutions are structurally open to each other, constitutionalism can serve as a common grammar for making claims of authority acceptable. Constitutionalism can be further unpacked into the primary elements of legitimacy of modern governance. These can be combined with one another in various ways to make out a specific claim to public authority. Constitutionalism itself is thus not unitary, becoming plural instead.

4.3.1 The pluralist constellation in global governance

The first kind of pluralism we see is a pluralism of legal systems, that is, the basic hierarchy of authority between international law and domestic law remains fundamentally unresolved. The rather unhelpful theoretical debate between 'monism' and 'dualism' ended long ago in a draw with each position effectively calling the other 'illogical'.[58] Indeed, as Kelsen showed, even 'monism' itself can be turned on its head by arguing for 'monism' grounded in international law and 'monism' grounded in national law.[59] If we by-pass this debate and simply look to the content of both municipal and international law, the fundamental tension between multiple claims of authority is readily apparent. On the one hand, the general rules of international law bind state actors (and sometimes non-state actors and individuals as well) regardless of whether these actors are legally or constitutionally unwilling or unable to comply.[60] On the other hand, as far as domestic actors are concerned, domestic   constitutions   ultimately   control   the   penetration   of

---

[58] Bogdandy, Armin von, 'Pluralism, Direct Effect, and the Ultimate Say: On the Relationship between International and Domestic Constitutional Law', 6 *International Journal of Constitutional Law* (2008) 397 at 400.

[59] Kelsen, Hans, 'Die Einheit von Völkerrecht und staatlichem Recht', 19 *ZaöRV* (1958) 234.

[60] The Vienna Convention on Treaties, Article 27, 23 May 1969, 1155 U.N.T.S. 331.

international norms into the domestic legal sphere regardless of whether international law makes room for this choice.[61]

Furthermore, at the international, transnational or global level of governance, which might be thought of as generally organized under public international law, different actors, systems, sources and norms often stand in a similar relation of unsettled hierarchy to one another. As the International Law Commission's report on fragmentation suggests, for example, established principles of public international law, such as Article 103 of the UN Treaty, the lexical priority of *ius cogens*, or the Vienna Convention on the Law of Treaties, do not generally resolve the conflicts among different norms and regimes at the global level of governance.[62] There is no universally mandated rule that would authoritatively and conclusively mediate among all the rivalling claims of jurisdiction. Moreover, each of these systems or regimes – from the WTO to the UN to regional environmental or human rights conventions – comes with its own rules as well as 'its own principles, its own form of expertise and its own "ethos", not necessarily identical to the ethos of neighboring specialization".[63] The advanced state of institutionalization of such bodies, as in the case of the UN or the WTO, further enhances these features. In short, at the global level of governance, we find a multiplicity of governance sites that are semi-autonomous from one another with overlapping (and rivalling) claims of legal authority.

Despite their separateness, however, these various levels and regimes are not entirely unconnected but often display a deeply embedded mutual openness to one another. For instance, many domestic legal systems in one form or another are fundamentally committed to recognizing the authority of international legal norms. At one end of the spectrum, there are provisions as simple as the United States Constitution's recognition that treaties to which the United States is a

---

[61] Even in the Netherlands, the (selective) incorporation of international law as directly operative domestic law is the result of a domestic constitutional choice embedded in the state's own founding constitution, not of an inexorable international command. See de Wet, Erika, 'The Reception Process in the Netherlands and Belgium', in H. Keller and A. Stone Sweet, eds., *A Europe of Rights: The Impact of the ECHR on National Legal Systems* (Oxford University Press, 2008), 229 at 235–242.

[62] See International Law Commission, Fragmentation of International Law: Difficulties Arising from the Diversification and Expansion of International Law, U.N. Doc. A/CN.4/L.682 (13 April 2006) (finalized by Martii Koskenniemi).

[63] Ibid., at para 15.

party become an integral part of the 'law of the land'.[64] At the other, we find deeper commitments such as the German Constitution's elevation of general principles of general international law above ordinary federal law as well as an authorization of the transfer of sovereign powers to international organizations.[65] Each in their own way, many domestic systems are constitutionally committed to the general project of law and governance beyond the state.[66] Even countries that strictly separate domestic from international legal orders, such as the United Kingdom, have at times adopted quasi-constitutional commitments to governance beyond the state by adopting special laws that broadly shape the interpretation and application of ordinary domestic laws so as to conform the latter to the needs of transnational norms.[67]

Conversely, the global level of governance is both normatively and institutionally deeply dependent on states. From customary law that grows out of state practice and the state-based system of international conventions to the general reliance on state judges to interpret global legal norms and on state resources for the effective enforcement of global legal norms, global governance deeply demands state support.[68]

---

[64] US Constitution Article 6.   [65] Grundgesetz Articles 24, 25.

[66] See, e.g., Keller, H. and A. Stone Sweet, eds., *A Europe of Rights: The Impact of the ECHR on National Legal Systems* (Oxford University Press, 2008); Conforti, B. and F. Francioni, eds., *Enforcing International Human Rights in Domestic Courts* (The Hague: Martinus Nijhoff, 1997); Franck, T. and G. Fox, eds., *International Law Decisions in National Courts* (Irvington-on-Hudson, NY: Transnational Publishers, 1996); Jacobs F. G. and S. Roberts, eds., *The Effect of Treaties in Domestic Law* (London: Sweet & Maxwell, 1987); Slyz, G., 'International Law in National Courts', 28 *NYU Journal of International Law and Politics* (1996) 65 (discussing incorporation of international law in the United States, Germany and Canada); Walters, M., 'Creeping Monism: The Judicial Trend Towards Interpretative Incorporation of Human Rights Treaties', 107 *Columbia Law Review* (2007) 628 (discussing the incorporation of human rights treaties in common law courts).

[67] See European Communities Act of 1972, c. 68; *Thoburn v. Sunderland* [2002] EWHC 195 (Admin), paras 60–67 (classifying the European Communities Act of 1972 as a constitutional statute).

[68] See, e.g., Picker, Colin, 'International Law's Mixed Heritage: A Common/Civil Law Jurisdiction', 41 *Vanderbilt Journal of Transnational Law* (2008) 1083 at 1090–1094; Charney, Jonathan, 'Universal International Law', 87 *American Journal of International Law* (1993) 529 at 534–543 (discussing the role of states in the formation of public international law). For an examination of self-enforcement and its alternatives in international law, see, e.g., Scott, Robert E. and Paul B. Stephan, 'Self-Enforcing International Agreements and the Limits of Coercion', *Wisconsin Law Review* (2004) 551.

Even those global regimes that are most advanced in terms of institutional development, such as the WTO, still depend critically on the participation of states in the creation, interpretation and application of norms.[69] This kind of structural embrace of states not only as subjects but as essential partners in governance is not a temporary defect of the international legal system but a core characteristic of global governance.

Mutual openness of the various regimes to one another also extends to the relationship among the various regimes at the level of global governance. At a basic level, international and transnational regimes are built on the common foundations of public international law. This suggests a presumptive respect of a common set of rules ranging from customary international law (including human rights law and the law of responsibility for states and international institutions) to general rules governing the creation, modification and interpretation of treaties.[70] Next, as different global regimes are often created by an overlapping set of signatory states, here, too, we find an embedded interconnectedness in that, for example, later regimes cannot legally undermine the functioning of earlier ones absent the consent of all parties to that earlier convention.[71] At the most detailed level, many regimes of global governance contain specific provisions that suggest openness to other global regimes, as in the UN Charter's apparent incorporation of international human rights law[72] or the European Union's apparent accommodation of treaties (including the UN Treaty) that precede the Treaty of Rome.[73]

---

[69] See Agreement Establishing the World Trade Organization, Article IX(2), 15 April, 1994; Bhuiyan, Sharif, *National Law in WTO Law* (Cambridge University Press, 2007); Cheyne, I., 'Gateways to the Precautionary Principle in International Law', 19 *Journal of Environmental Law* (2007) 155 at 171 (observing that state practice influences the interpretation of WTO law); Shell, G., 'Trade Legalism and International Relations Theory: An Analysis of the World Trade Organization', 44 *Duke Law Journal* (1995) 829 at 897–98 (observing that WTO rules require a trade adjudicator to apply the customary rules of interpretation of public international law).

[70] See Alvarez, José, 'Governing the World: International Organizations as Lawmakers', 31 *Suffolk Transnational Law Review* (2008) 591 at 592 (noting the traditional view that international organizations are structured around the basic sources of international law: treaties, custom and general principles).

[71] See, e.g., The Vienna Convention on Treaties, Article 30, 23 May 1969, 1155 U.N.T.S. 331.; Fox, Gregory, 'International Organizations: Conflicts in International Law', 95 *American Society of International Law Proceedings* (2001) 183 at 184.

[72] UN Charter, Articles 1, 55.   [73] Treaty on European Community, Article 307.

Moreover, in addition to this pluralism of legal systems ('systems pluralism'), we also find a pluralism of interpretive institutions ('institutional pluralism' or 'interpretive pluralism').[74] Put another way, alongside the combination of mutual openness and autonomy of legal systems and regimes, we find a similar combination of mutual openness and autonomy among different institutions that seek to access the norms of a common regime. The idea is rather simple. Individual interpretive institutions will often be situated within a particular national, supranational or international legal system. And yet, despite their structural separation, these various interpreters share a common purpose, such as interpreting a shared legal system or norm. Whenever this shared legal system does not definitively designate a final arbiter of meaning for the shared system as a whole, the stage for pluralism is set yet again.

We see this unsettled hierarchy of interpretive authority in the relation between international and domestic courts as well as in the relation among different institutions at the global level. As for the former, the United States Supreme Court, for example, recently asserted its authority to interpret international conventions to which the United States is a party according to its own best lights, as opposed to following the judgment of the International Court of Justice. As the US Supreme Court held in Sanchez-Llamas, '[n]othing in the structure or purpose of the [International Court of Justice] suggests that its interpretations were intended to be conclusive on our courts'.[75] In a subsequent iteration of the dispute, the Supreme Court rejected being bound by an ICJ determination that the United States had violated the rights of named individuals under the Vienna Convention on Consular Relations.[76] The Israeli Supreme Court has come to a similar conclusion about the significance of ICJ opinions for the Supreme Court's own interpretation of international law.[77] In another example, the United States, the United Kingdom and France disagreed with the UN Human Rights

---

[74] Halberstam, Daniel, 'Constitutional Heterarchy: The Centrality of Conflict in the European Union and the United States', in Jeffrey L. Dunoff and Joel P. Trachtman, eds., *Constitutionalism, International Law and Global Government* (Cambridge University Press, 2009), 326–355, available at <http://ssrn.com/abstract=1147769>.

[75] *Sanchez-Llamas* v. *Oregon*, 548 U.S. 331, 354 (2006).

[76] *Medellin* v. *Texas*, 552 U.S. 491, 128 S. Ct. 1346 (2008).

[77] HCJ 7957/04 Mara'abe v. Prime Minister of Israel, para 56., available at <http://elyon1.court.gov.il/eng/home/index.html>.

Committee's assertion of authority to determine whether a state reservation is inconsistent with the object and purpose of the International Convention on Civil and Political Rights (ICCPR).[78] And the United States disagreed with the Human Rights Committee's assertion of authority to interpret the ICCPR as containing an implicit obligation of *non-refoulement*.[79] These national assertions of interpretive authority are not deemed universally valid, but instead reflect particular, national views.

Among global institutions the question of hierarchy is frequently unsettled as well. Consider only the decision of the International Criminal Tribunal for the former Yugoslavia (ICTY) disagreeing with the previous judgment of the ICJ about attributing to a state only such actions of third parties over which the state had 'effective control'.[80] Although the ICJ has reiterated its original position in a subsequent case, there is no authoritative resolution of this conflict. Similarly, there have been prominent disagreements between the European Court of Human Rights and the Court of Justice of the European Union on the interpretation of certain provisions of the European Convention on Human Rights.[81] The WTO Appellate Body, International Court of Justice and the International Tribunal for the Law of the Sea (ITLOS)

---

[78] See U.N. Human Rights Comm., General Comment 24, U.N. Doc. CCPR/C/21/ Rev.1/Add.6 (11 April 1994); Report of the Human Rights Committee, U.N. Doc. A/51/40 117–19 (16 September 1996) (objections by France); Report of the Human Rights Committee, Vol. 1, U.N. Doc. A/50/40[Vol.1](Supp) 126–34 (4 February 1996) (objections by the USA and the UK); Guzman, A., 'International Tribunals: A Rational Choice Analysis', 157 *University of Pennsylvania Law Review* (2008) 171 at 232 and note 168.

[79] See U.N. Human Rights Comm., *Comments by the Government of the United States of America on the Concluding Observations of the Human Rights Committee*, at 8–11, U.N. Doc. CCPR/C/USA/CO/3/ Rev.1/Add.1 (12 February 2008).

[80] Cf. *Nicaragua* v. *United States of America*, Judgment, I. C. J. Reports 1986, p. 14 (announcing an effective control standard); Case No. IT-94-1-A, *Prosecutor* v. *Tadic*, Judgment of 15 July 1999, paras 115–145 (ICTY Appeals Chamber) (rejecting an effective control standard); *Case Concerning the Application of the Convention on the Prevention and Punishment of the Crime of Genocide (Bosnia Herzegovina* v. *Serbia & Montenegro)*, I.C.J. Reports 2007, paras 396–407 (reasserting an effective control standard).

[81] See Defeis, Elizabeth, 'Human Rights and the European Union: Who Decides? Possible Conflicts Between the European Court of Justice and the European Court of Human Rights', 19 *Dickinson Journal of International Law* (2001) 301 (discussing disagreements between the ECJ and ECHR). Such conflicts may lessen with the impending accession of the Union to the ECHR.

have differed on the role of the precautionary principle in international environmental disputes.[82] And the ITLOS and an arbitral tribunal have rendered conflicting interpretations on the applicability of the UNCLOS (United Nations Convention on the Law of the Sea) dispute settlement provisions.[83]

4.3.2 A grammar of legitimacy: pluralism and constitutionalism rejoined

Pluralism need not spell anarchy or chaos. As the English political pluralist Harold Laski observed, the 'facts before us are anarchical', but we 'reduce them ourselves to order by being able to convince men [and women] that some unity we make means added richness to their lives'.[84] Contrary to what some scholars have suggested,[85] however, order, on this view, does not depend on subsuming the multiple claims of authority under an external hierarchy of institutions or of thick substantive norms. Instead, order may be created from the bottom up by accommodating claims of authority when they are warranted and resisting them when they are not. In this way, as Laski again put it, institutions 'only secure obedience in terms of the values that obedience creates'.[86] Pluralism is therefore 'consistently experimentalist in temper'.[87] It involves a contest for legitimacy among various institutions, each of which necessarily represents only a partial view of the balance of

---

[82] See *Southern Bluefin Tuna (New Zealand v. Japan; Australia v. Japan)*, Order of 27 August 1999, paras 77–80 (ITLOS); *EC Measures Concerning Meat and Meat Products*, Report of the Appellate Body, WTO Doc. WT/DS26/AB/R, WT/DS48/AB/R, sec. VI (1998); *Gabcikovo-Nagymaros (Hungary/Slovakia)* 1997 I.C.J. 3, 42–45. Cf. Shany, Yuval, *The Competing Jurisdictions of International Courts and Tribunals* (Oxford University Press, 2003), at 112–113.

[83] See *Southern Bluefin Tuna (Australia & New Zealand v. Japan)*, Award of 4 August 2000, 39 I.L.M. 1359 (2000); *Southern Bluefin Tuna (New Zealand v. Japan; Australia v. Japan)*, Order of 27 August 1999, paras 77–80 (ITLOS); cf. Shany, *Competing Jurisdictions* (2003).

[84] Laski, Harold J., 'Law and the State', in Paul Q. Hirst, ed., *A Pluralist Theory of the State* (London: Routledge, 1989), 197–227 at 226.

[85] See, e.g., MacCormick, *Questioning Sovereignty* (1999), at 121. MacCormick, for example, rejects radical pluralism in favour of pluralism organized under the hierarchical umbrella of public international law.

[86] Laski, 'Law and the State' (1989).

[87] Laski, Harold J., 'The Pluralistic State', in Paul Q. Hirst, ed., *A Pluralist Theory of the State* (London: Routledge, 1989), 188.

relevant interests to be struck. Pluralism might even be seen as a new form of legal process that brings together the New Haven School's vision of international (or, better, global) legal process[88] and ideas of 'jurisdictional redundancy'[89] to help us overcome the necessary limitations of any individual site of governance taken alone.[90]

If all this is true, pluralism must mean more than plurality. Pluralism is not the mere multiplication of mutually exclusive claims of authority across many domains (i.e. a kind of dualism among more than two systems). Instead, pluralism is a synthesis of monism and dualism in that it stands for conversation, contest and conflict among the different claims of authority by common reference to the values that obedience to one or the other of these actors, systems, sources or norms would promote.

This is where constitutionalism joins pluralism. Constitutionalism, simply put, is the idea of limited collective self-governance. Constitutionalism is a particular theory of public authority that grows out of the modern liberal enlightenment tradition. It is embodied most prominently in the modern constitutional movement with national constitutions as its dominant expression. But constitutionalism, as an idea and a theory of public power, is broader and more varied than its various instantiations in national constitutions might suggest. As a theory of the legitimacy of public power, the idea of constitutionalism provides an answer to the question of why we have constitutions. It tells us what constitutions are for. And in so doing, it ultimately provides a point of access for claims regarding the legitimacy of public power even from beyond the particular tradition of national constitutions from which the idea of constitutionalism first emerged.

The constitutional idea of limited collective self-governance can be broken down into three primary values – call them 'voice', 'rights' and 'expertise'. Let us define the first of these as asking which actor has the superior claim of representing the relevant political will; the second as asking which actor has the superior claim of vindicating individual rights; and the third as asking which actor has the superior claim of instrumental capacity (understood broadly as encompassing claims to

---

[88] See, e.g., Koh, Harold, 'Is there a "New" New Haven School of International Law?', 32 *Yale Journal of International Law* (2007) 559.

[89] See Cover, Robert M., 'The Uses of Jurisdictional Redundancy', 22 *William & Mary Law Review* (1980–81) 639.

[90] See Schiff Berman, Paul, 'A Pluralist Approach to International Law', 32 *Yale Journal of International Law* (2007) 301.

knowledge-based resources as well as bureaucratic capacity). These primary values are not set with any accepted particularity or richness, nor are they measured on a universally shared metric. Instead, these values frame the debate. They form a kind of grammar of legitimacy employed by the various competing actors as they make their respective claims of authority.

Simply and boldly put, voice, rights and expertise provide the basis for legitimacy of public power in modern liberal governance. The first two are informed by the ideas of positive and negative liberty, respectively – albeit with some notable modification. Positive liberty, as elaborated by Benjamin Constant and later popularized by Isaiah Berlin, is, of course, as old as democratic theory itself.[91] It grounds the legitimacy of public power in the individual's right to participate in the process of governance. Calling this 'voice' is meant to abstract from any actual process of collective self-governance by complicating the question of whose political will is relevant and who represents that will best. As applied to a national constitutional system like the United States, the idea of voice thus highlights such problems as legislative capture and other shortcomings of the ordinary political process as presently constituted.[92] As applied to the European Union, the idea of voice highlights such problems as the thin nature of the European polity, on the one hand, as well as the shortcomings of national political processes in representing all the relevant political wills within and throughout the nation states of Europe, on the other.[93] As applied to global governance, voice highlights such problems as, for example, various forms of capture within domestic and

---

[91] See, generally, Holmes, Stephen, *Benjamin Constant and the Making of Modern Liberalism* (New Haven: Yale University Press, 1984); and Berlin, Isaiah, *Four Essays on Liberty* (Oxford University Press, 1969) (discussing positive liberty).

[92] Cf. Farber, D. and P. Frickey, *Law and Public Choice: A Critical Introduction* (University of Chicago Press, 1991) at 12–62; Friedman, Barry, 'Dialogue and Judicial Review', 91 *Michigan Law Review* (1993) 577 at 629–44. This idea is also implicit in Bruce Ackerman's reconceptualization of the counter-majoritarian difficulty as an inter-temporal difficulty with democratic claims on the side of the judiciary; see Ackerman, Bruce, *We the People: Foundations* (Cambridge, Mass.: Harvard University Press, 1993).

[93] For a discussion, see Halberstam, 'Constitutional Heterarchy' (2009); Kumm, Mattias, 'Why Europeans Will Not Embrace Constitutional Patriotism', 6 *International Journal of Constitutional Law* (2008) 117; Grimm, Dieter, 'Integration by Constitution', 3 *International Journal of Constitutional Law* (2005) 193–208 at 197; Haltern, U., 'Pathos and Patina: The Failure and Promise of Constitutionalism in the European Imagination', 9 *European Law Journal* 1

international legal institutions as well as the debate about the representation of interests of affected individuals and groups around the globe in the absence of a global demos.[94]

The idea of rights, as employed here, draws on the foundational insight of negative liberty as constitutive of legitimacy, albeit once again with some modification. Notoriously absent from Constant's and Berlin's formulations are modern rights to government assistance, such as education, housing or welfare.[95] Indeed, even more traditional anti-discrimination norms that sound in simple prohibition, may require considerable positive government action.[96] Benjamin Constant's felicitous phrase of the 'liberty of the moderns' seems open to this development (although imputing an understanding of affirmative rights to Constant himself would be anachronistic). In any event, the idea of rights as used here is not necessarily limited to negative rights, but may encompass rights to certain kinds of positive government action as well.

Expertise (in the expansive sense of instrumental rationality in which I use the term here) provides the third legitimating ingredient of public power in modern governance. At its core, the idea of 'expertise' stands for two connected concepts of instrumental rationality: knowledge and effectiveness. With its origins in Enlightenment thought and the rational production of knowledge, safeguarding the production and deployment of knowledge as a means of effective governance has become a central ingredient of the legitimacy of modern liberal authority.

Since the rise of Weberian bureaucracy in the nineteenth century,[97] and the explosive growth of the 'administrative state' in the twentieth,[98]

(2003) 14–44; Nicolaidis, Kalypso, 'The New Constitution as European Demoi-cracy?', *Federal Trust Online Working Paper No. 38/03* (2003), available at <http://ssrn.com/abstract=517423>; Maduro, Miguel, 'Europe and the Constitution: What If This Is As Good As It Gets?', in J. H. H. Weiler and M. Wind, eds., *European Constitutionalism Beyond the State* (Cambridge University Press, 2003), 74–102; Weiler, J. H. H., 'European Constitutionalism and its Discontents', 17 *Northwestern Journal of International Law and Business* (1996–97) 354.

[94] See Howse and Nicolaidis, 'Legitimacy through "Higher Law"?' (2003).

[95] See Holmes, *Benjamin Constant* (1984); and Berlin, *Four Essays* (1969), at 122–131 (discussing negative liberty).

[96] Sunstein, Cass, 'Judicial Relief and Public Tort Law' (book review), 92 *Yale Law Journal* (1983) 749.

[97] See, generally, Weber, Max, *Economy and Society*, trans. Max Rheinstein and Edward Shils (Cambridge, Mass.: Harvard University Press, 1954).

[98] See, e.g., Rabin, Robert, 'Federal Regulation in Historical Perspective', 38 *Stanford Law Review* (1986) 1189.

expertise in governance has been a key component of the legitimacy of liberal government. To be sure, there may be times when procedures for collective action are everything and the process of inclusive decision-making is more important than the accuracy of the outcome.[99] At the same time, however, the legitimacy of modern liberal governance also depends on getting certain jobs done and on getting them done right. This corresponds to what Fritz Scharpf has termed 'output legitimacy',[100] and which has figured strongly especially in the early arguments supporting the legitimacy of EU governance. A similar idea has at times been prominent in the United States, animating for instance the original enthusiasm for administrative agencies in the early part of the twentieth century.[101] Here the thought was to take certain decisions away from politics and lodge them in expert agencies in order to ensure effective knowledge-based governance that produced beneficial results. In the global war on terror or climate change, we are witnessing renewed arguments for global collaboration as the only practically feasible way to solve a given problem.

Note that, as defined here, the three foundational principles of legitimacy – voice, rights and expertise – are mutually constitutive. For example, a claim to represent the relevant political will invariably includes implicit claims about rights and expertise, as in the participatory rights of those represented or the minimal knowledge base of those expressing their political will. A claim to the vindication of rights also invariably depends on epistemic and representational claims to establish the basis for the particular right asserted. And finally, a claim to legitimacy based on knowledge and effectiveness invariably depends on certain conceptions of voice – as in understanding the impact of a given policy on the relevant interests or in understanding 'knowledge' and 'effectiveness' as inter-subjectively shared among the relevant parties. Despite (and perhaps even because of) their mutually constitutive

---

[99] Shapiro, S., 'Authority', in J. Coleman and S. Shapiro, eds., *The Oxford Handbook of Jurisprudence and Philosophy of Law* (Oxford University Press, 2002), 382 at 437–438; Gutmann, A. and D. Thompson, *Democracy and Disagreement* (Cambridge, Mass., London: Belknap Press 1996) at 18; Hershovitz, S., 'Legitimacy, Democracy, and Razian Authority', 9 *Legal Theory* (2003) 201 at 216–19.

[100] Scharpf, Fritz, *Governing in Europe: Effective and Democratic?* (Oxford University Press, 1999) at 6.

[101] See Frug, G., 'Ideology of Bureaucracy in American Law', 97 *Harvard Law Review* (1984) 1276.

nature, voice, rights and expertise can be usefully teased out as the primacy elements of the legitimacy of public authority.

The point of pluralism is not to settle any of these claims reliably in favour of one or another institution or system of governance. Instead, the pluralist practice is one of conflict and accommodation among semi-autonomous institutions or systems of governance in the absence of hierarchy. Accommodation is a bottom-up practice. It is decentralized and spontaneous but not arbitrary happenstance. Pluralism thus depends on an embedded openness of the various actors, systems, sources and norms to one another and a certain common ground for principled contest. The idea of constitutionalism, with all its problems and vagueness, so the argument here goes, can provide that common ground. On this vision, demands for deference draw not simply on claims of relative power or formal legality but on the foundations of legitimacy of public authority understood as limited collective self-governance. The specific terms will be contested, but the more general aspiration is, in an important sense, shared. Put another way, the choice among multiple claims of formal legality is managed by conversation, contest, conflict and, ultimately, mutual accommodation within this common grammar of legitimacy. And resort to this grammar on the part of the actors involved transforms what would otherwise be a clash of raw power into the more principled contest of authority that is pluralism.

4.4 Taking pluralism seriously? The Court of Justice and the *Kadi* case

Pluralism opens up new possibilities in the stale and largely unfruitful debates between monism and dualism in international law. Unlike its binary counterparts, the idea of pluralism approaches the plurality of actors, systems, sources and norms in the arena of global governance as a source of strength, not weakness. On the pluralist view, fragmentation is not a problem to be 'solved' by institutional or normative hierarchies. Instead, the multiplicity of jurisdictional claims represents an element of unsettledness that can serve to strengthen the legitimacy of governance.

The possibility of pluralism as a kind of synthesis of monism and dualism presented itself in the recent *Kadi* case concerning the implementation of UN sanctions against individuals within the European Union. After discussing the background to the conflict, this section examines the various judicial responses in that litigation through the lens of global, local and plural constitutionalism. As we shall see, the Court of First Instance (CFI)[102] in that case sought to resolve the multiplicity of systems by placing the European legal order strictly under the global hierarchy of the legal order of the United Nations. At the same time, however, the CFI sought to preserve interpretive pluralism by asserting its own authority to judge the common legal framework of international law in which the United Nations Security Council operates.

The Court of Justice sitting in its Grand Chamber formation took a more local approach. The judgment of the ECJ (European Court of Justice) sought to resolve both the multiplicity of systems as well as the multiplicity of interpretive institutions in favour of the Union. The ECJ focused not on pluralism but on vindicating the constitutional primacy of the European legal order. Although the Court of Justice was somewhat sympathetic to the preservation of the UN's legal authority, it appears to have rejected any pluralist claim of a coordinate status on the part of the United Nations vis-à-vis the European Union.

Only the Advocate General seems to have pushed for pluralism. His opinion suggests recognizing not only the autonomy of the European legal order but also its deep openness to international law. The Advocate General thus aimed for neither the constitutional submission of the CFI nor the constitutional resistance of the ECJ, but for a coexistence of the legal orders of the United Nations and the European Union in the spirit of pluralism.

Taking pluralism seriously, however, would have required something more than even the Advocate General suggested. As we shall see, by focusing on systems pluralism, each of the judicial pronouncements ultimately seems to have lost sight of the question of pluralism in the interpretation of international law itself.

4.4.1 The United Nations sanctions regime in Europe

In 1999, as part of the collective battle against terrorism, the United Nations Security Council began to issue a series of Resolutions calling for sanctions against the Taliban and Osama bin Laden, as well as Al-Qaeda and its supporters. Beginning with Resolution 1267 (1999), the

---

[102] The Lisbon Treaty rebranded this court as the 'General Court'. The following discussion will, however, use the designation that was effective at the time the *Kadi* case was decided.

Security Council demanded that all states freeze the assets and ban the travel of groups and individuals with connections to Al-Qaeda.[103] The Security Council established a Sanctions Committee, composed of members of the Security Council, to promulgate and to periodically review a list of named individuals subject to these measures.[104] Individuals at first had no access to the Sanctions Committee directly but had to petition the government of their citizenship or residence to intervene and demand information from the designating government. In the absence of disagreement between the two governments, the matter would come before the Sanctions Committee (which acts by consensus) and ultimately before the Security Council itself.[105]

In response to criticism about the lack of individual access, the UN Security Council modified its procedure in December 2006.[106] The Secretary General established a 'focal point' within the Secretariat to receive de-listing petitions directly from individuals. Even under the modified procedures, however, individuals are unable to participate directly – either in person or via a representative – in the deliberations surrounding a de-listing request. Nor are individuals entitled to any additional information about their case other than the status of the consideration of their request. The collective evaluation of an individual de-listing petition remains, at bottom, a diplomatic matter for resolution among the governments represented in the Security Council.[107]

---

[103] S.C. Res. 1267, U.N. Doc. S/RES/1267 (1999) (15 October 1999).

[104] Ibid., at para. 6.

[105] As an exception to the freezing of assets, a state can release funds for basic expenses and fees, including legal fees, but must give advance notification to the Sanctions Committee, which may object to such exceptions within forty-eight hours; see S.C. Res. 1452, U.N. Doc. S/RES/1452 (2002) (20 December 2002).

[106] See S.C. Res. 1730, U.N. Doc. S/RES/1730 (19 December 2006).

[107] In addition to the Resolution 1267 Sanctions Regime, in which the UN promulgates a specific list of individuals connected with the Taliban and Al-Qaeda, the Security Council issued a broader anti-terrorist Resolution 1373 (2001); see S.C. Res. 1373, U.N. Doc. S/RES/1373 (28 September 2001). This second resolution creates less immediate friction with domestic legal systems in that it leaves the determination of individual blacklisting targets up to the states. Although the matter of individual blacklisting has led to considerable litigation here as well, the states' (and the EU's) autonomous decision to target certain individuals has therefore not conjured up the same multiplicity of claims to legal authority that arose in the implementation of the anti-Taliban resolution. Fifteen law suits were filed in the national courts in Belgium, the UK, Germany Italy, Switzerland, the Netherlands, Pakistan, Turkey and the United States, all with

In an effort to implement the Resolution 1267 Sanctions Regime, the Council of the European Union, acting under the Common Foreign and Security Policy (CFSP) provisions of the Treaty on European Union,[108] adopted a series of common positions calling for EC (European Community) measures to freeze the assets of individuals named by the UN Sanctions Committee as supporters of the Taliban and Al-Qaeda.[109] Responding, in turn, to these CFSP common positions, the Council, this time acting on the basis of Articles 60, 301 and later also 308 EC passed a series of EC regulations.[110] In particular, Community Regulations 467/2001/EC and 881/2002/EC (and subsequent amendments) ordered the freezing of assets of the UN-named individuals and groups throughout the territory of the European Union. Among these were Yassin Abdullah Kadi, a Saudi national residing in Saudi Arabia, and Al Barakaat, a Swedish organization connected to a Somali financial network.

Mr Kadi and Al Barakaat sued the Council and Commission before the European Court of First Instance in an effort to annul the EC Regulation that applied to them.[111] After the CFI upheld the contested regulation, the plaintiffs appealed to the Court of Justice. Following the Advocate General's recommendation in part, the Court of Justice set aside the CFI's judgment and granted the requested relief.

the exception of Belgium, without success. See Third Report of the Analytical Support and Sanctions Monitoring Team, Annex II, U.N. Doc. S/2005/572 (9 September 2005), pp. 48–49 (hereinafter Third Report) and Fourth Report of the Analytical Support and Sanctions Monitoring Team, Annex, U.N. Doc. S/2006/154 (10 March 2006), pp. 45–47. On implementation of Security Council Sanctions in Sweden, see Andersson, T., I. Cameron and K. Nordback, 'EU Blacklisting: The Renaissance of Imperial Power but on a Global Scale', 14 *European Business Law Review* (2003) 111–141 at 119.

[108] The relevant actions discussed here all predated the passage of the Lisbon Treaty. Accordingly, the discussion will reference the treaty provisions only as they stood at the time of the dispute.

[109] Council Common Position of 5 November 2001, 2001 O.J. (L 89) 36; Council Common Position 2001/154/CFSP, 2001 O.J. (L 57) 1; Council Common Position 1999/727/CFSP, 1999 O.J. (L 294) 1.

[110] Cf. note 108 above. Council Regulation (EC) No. 561/2003, 2003 O.J. (L 82) 1; Council Regulation (EC) No. 881/2002, 2002 O.J. (L 139) 9; Council Regulation (EC) No. 467/2001, 2001 O.J. (L 67) 1; Council Regulation (EC) No. 337/2000, 2000 O.J. (L 43) 1.

[111] Case T-315/01, *Kadi* v. *Council of European Union*, 2005 ECR II-3649 (21 September 2005) (hereinafter *Kadi* (CFI)).

4.4.2 *The Court of First Instance: global constitutionalism with a pluralist twist*

The Court of First Instance took two significant steps with regard to this controversy. First, the Court of First Instance approached the relationship between the European Union and the United Nations from the perspective of global constitutionalism. By reading the provisions of the United Nations Charter alongside the foundational provisions of the European Union against the background of basic principles of public international law, the CFI privileged the operation of the UN system over that of the European Union. The CFI thus overcame the potential multiplicity of authoritative legal systems by subsuming the European Union – and possibly even the Member States as well – under the single global hierarchy of public international law. Second, within this unified hierarchy of systems, however, the CFI preserved a measure of institutional pluralism by claiming for itself the power to interpret international law alongside the UN Security Council. This latter step was bold in principle but turned out to be modest in application. The CFI limited its interpretation of public international law to the norms of *ius cogens*. The result, as we shall see, was untenable. It would have denuded the European Union of two of its principal claims of legitimacy – voice and rights – vis-à-vis the Member States.

Considering the Member States' obligations under customary international law (as codified by the Vienna Convention on the Law of Treaties), the CFI noted that Member States cannot invoke provisions of internal law to justify their failure to live up to their obligations under an international treaty such as the UN Charter.[112] The CFI pointed further to the fact that Article 103 of the UN Charter obligation expressly elevates a Member States' Charter obligations over those contained in any other international agreement.[113] From all this, the CFI concluded that Member States' UN obligations supersede those imposed by the EU/EC treaties.[114]

---

[112] Ibid., at para 182.

[113] Ibid., at para 181; see UN Charter, Article 103 ('In the event of a conflict between the obligations of the Members of the United Nations under the present Charter and their obligations under any other international agreement, their obligations under the present Charter shall prevail.').

[114] Ibid., at para 190.

The CFI further noted that the primacy of a Member State's obligations under the UN Charter over its obligations under the EC Treaty is confirmed by the EC Treaty itself. Here, the CFI pointed to Article 307 EC (now 351 TFEU (Treaty on the Functioning of the EU)), which expressly privileges pre-existing international legal obligations over EC treaty obligations,[115] And the CFI pointed to Article 297 EC (now 347 TFEU),[116] which seems to recognize implicitly that Member States will take actions otherwise incompatible with their Community (now Union) obligations in an effort to comply with international legal obligations aimed at maintaining international peace and security.[117] Based on these provisions, the CFI concluded that, as a matter of international law as well as Community law, the Member States must 'leave unapplied any provision of Community law, whether a provision of primary law or a general principle of that law' whenever such law 'raises any impediment to their proper performance of their obligations under the Charter of the United Nations'.[118]

Having subsumed Member States' various legal obligations into a single hierarchy ordered under public international law with the United Nations at the apex, the CFI turned to the Union's own obligations. According to the CFI, the EU, too, must abide by Security Council Resolutions. To be sure, the CFI recognized that the Union is not bound directly by the UN mandate. The Union is neither a member nor a successor of a member of the United Nations.[119] Nor, in the CFI's

---

[115] See ibid., at paras 185–186; EC Treaty, Article 307 (now Article 351 TFEU) ('The rights and obligations arising from agreements concluded before 1 January 1958 or, for acceding States, before the date of their accession, between one or more Member States on the one hand, and one or more third countries on the other, shall not be affected by the provisions of this Treaty. To the extent that such agreements are not compatible with this Treaty, the Member State or States concerned shall take all appropriate steps to eliminate the incompatibilities established. Member States shall, where necessary, assist each other to this end and shall, where appropriate, adopt a common attitude.').

[116] EC Treaty, Article 237 (now Article 347 TFEU) ('Member States shall consult each other with a view to taking together the steps needed to prevent the functioning of the common [now "internal"] market being affected by measures which a Member State may be called upon to take in the event of serious internal disturbances affecting the maintenance of law and order, in the event of war, serious international tension constituting a threat of war, or in order to carry out obligations it has accepted for the purpose of maintaining peace and international security.').

[117] See ibid., at paras 185–186.   [118] Ibid., at para 190.   [119] Ibid., at para 192.

view, was the Union an addressee of the Security Council Resolution in question.[120] Nonetheless, several factors led the CFI to conclude that the Union is bound to implement the Security Council Resolution. The CFI noted once again that the Member States cannot circumvent their international legal obligations by creating the Union, and that this preservation of international legal obligations is expressly recognized in the Treaty itself.[121] Second, the CFI suggested that the Community (as it then was) had functionally succeeded the Member States in the area of economic sanctions, which the CFI took to mean that the international legal obligations of the Member States in this area had transferred to the Community.[122] Finally, the CFI pointed to Article 301 EC (the provision authorizing the Community at the time to pass economic sanctions)[123] as confirming the conclusion that the EC was bound to implement UN Security Council's sanctions Resolutions.[124]

Putting aside for purposes of this discussion the soundness of the CFI's doctrinal reasoning,[125] the CFI's judgment is significant for having opted for global constitutionalism. The CFI absolutely rejected the idea of systems pluralism, that is, of multiple conflicting claims of coordinate authority among different legal systems. Instead, it subsumed the various legal spaces of the Member States, the European Union and the United Nations under a single nested hierarchy in which the UN system reigns supreme. As a result, the CFI rejected the

---

[120] Ibid.　　[121] Ibid., at paras 195–196.　　[122] Ibid., at para 198.

[123] EC Treaty, Article 301 ('Where it is provided, in a common position or in a joint action adopted according to the provisions of the Treaty on European Union relating to the common foreign and security policy, for an action by the Community to interrupt or to reduce, in part or completely, economic relations with one or more third countries, the Council shall take the necessary urgent measures. The Council shall act by a qualified majority on a proposal from the Commission.'). Article 301 has been replaced by Article 215 TFEU.

[124] Ibid., at para 202.

[125] For a discussion, see de Wet, Erika, 'Holding the United Nations Security Council Accountable for Human Rights Violations through Domestic and Regional Courts: A Case of Beware What You Ask For?, in J. Farrall and K. Rubenstein, eds., *Sanctions Accountability and Governance in a Globalised World* (Cambridge University Press, 2009); Halberstam, D. and E. Stein, 'The United Nations, the European Union, and the King of Sweden: Economic Sanctions and Individual Rights in a Plural World Order', 46 *The Common Market Law Review* (2009) 13; Tridimas, Takis, 'EU Law, International Law, and Economic Sanctions Against Terrorism: The Judiciary in Distress', 32 *Fordham International Law Journal* (2009) 660.

possibility of reviewing the contested regulation for compatibility with the EU's internal fundamental rights norms. Such review, on the CFI's reasoning, would only pit the EU's legal order against that of the United Nations and thereby run contrary to the systemic unity and hierarchy that privileges the United Nations.

Having rejected the idea of *systems* pluralism, however, the CFI introduced a certain measure of *interpretive* pluralism within the public international legal system. The CFI held that UN Security Council commands are authoritative as a matter of public international law only in so far as Security Council Resolutions preserve the rights embodied in the norms of *ius cogens*.[126] Implicit in this judgment was the CFI's claim of authority to determine that public international law demands the observance of rights on the part of the United Nations. And implicit further in considering the substance of *ius cogens* was the CFI's claim of authority to interpret the actual rights that make up this *ius cogens* limitation on UN authority. The CFI thereby asserted the power to review the legality of UN actions – even though conducting such review only indirectly in judging the Union's implementation measures, and even though such review was limited to compliance with the norms of *ius cogens*.

The CFI's bold assertion of interpretive authority with regard to the UN system, however, was ultimately muted by the decision's substantive approach on the applicable law. The CFI gave *ius cogens* broad scope but little depth. The CFI held that *ius cogens* contains rights to property and due process, but found that neither was breached in this case.[127] As for the right to property, the exemptions for basic expenses from the asset-freeze regime, coupled with the important (and hence non-arbitrary) interest served in preventing the funding of terrorism, and the periodic review of the asset-freeze orders, sufficed to protect this right.[128] The CFI was satisfied by the individual's ability to approach the UN Security Council through his or her state, again especially in the light of the important interest in preventing the funding of terrorism and the temporary nature of the deprivation.[129]

---

[126] Case T-315/01, *Kadi* v. *Council of European Union*, 2005 ECR II-3649 (21 September 2005) at paras 226, 230.
[127] Ibid., at paras 233–292.
[128] Ibid., at paras 239, 245, 251.   [129] Ibid., at paras 249–250.

Putting aside, once again, the soundness of the CFI's doctrinal interpretation of *ius cogens*,[130] the radical significance of subordinating the EU's legal order to that of the United Nations is not substantially muted by the CFI's assertion of review of the UN Security Council Resolutions for compliance with *ius cogens*. Taken as a whole, the CFI's approach, if followed by the Court of Justice, would have had profound implications for the legitimacy of the European legal order. In one fell swoop, the CFI would have effectively eliminated two core elements of constitutional authority – namely voice and rights – from the European Union's arsenal of legitimacy.

Take rights first. The CFI would have imposed upon the Member States an obligation to respect an EC Regulation in the absence of any protection of fundamental rights at the Union level of governance. To be sure, the CFI may well have read *ius cogens* rather generously to include protection of property and due process despite the fact that both are likely beyond the generally recognized non-derogable floor of international human rights. And yet, by restricting its rights review to *ius cogens* and by giving the rights so recognized rather limited effect in application, the CFI substantively eliminated fundamental rights as a significant restraint on the EU's implementation of economic sanctions.

In so doing, the CFI would have led the Member States to reconsider their own deference to the European Union within the constellation of pluralism that reigns inside the Union itself. Here, Member State and EU claims of authority have clashed, in that each system has claimed primacy over the other. As is well known, the Member States have only accommodated the primacy and direct effect of Union law because the latter incorporated a meaningful protection of fundamental rights. This has been the governing accommodation of constitutional pluralism within Europe on the dimension of rights. Now, however, the CFI would have effectively abandoned that arrangement by eliminating meaningful human rights review of individually targeted economic

---

[130] The CFI's decision raises significant questions, as, for example, whether *ius cogens* encompasses the right to property or, indeed, any interest that is subject to be overridden for non-arbitrary reasons. For a critical discussion, see, e.g., Halberstam and Stein, 'The United Nations' (2009); Tridimas, 'EU Law', (2009); Defeis, Elizabeth, 'Targeted Sanctions, Human Rights, and the Court of First Instance of the European Community', 30 *Fordham Journal of International Law* (2007) 1449.

sanctions. In response, national courts would have been justified in abandoning their accommodation of the Union's claim of authority under the *Solange* compromise.[131] Member States could have rightly reasserted their review of the Union's own compliance with fundamental rights – at least within this particular area of Union law from which the Union courts would have effectively withdrawn.

Second, by integrating the European Union into a constitutional hierarchy of legal systems in which UN decisions are binding and supreme, the CFI would have eliminated the Union's political processes as a separate locus of voice. Put another way, the CFI's judgment denied the creation of any authoritative political will at the Union level of governance. Under the CFI's reasoning, the European legal order would become a mere instrument in Member State compliance with international law.

Indeed, the consequences of this approach would have been even more extreme. The CFI would have set up the Union as a bootstrap to the Member States' implementation of their own international legal obligations. First, on the CFI's reading, both international law and EU law require the EU to implement Security Council sanctions. Next, EU law generally demands that Member States heed EC/EU Regulations. As a result, the CFI would have circumvented not only the voice of the European Union level of governance, but effectively that of the Member States, too. Enforcement of the Member States' international legal obligations, on this view, would be an inexorable product of the operation of EU law.

This view from nowhere could hardly have been sustained. The CFI's proposed path of decision would have eliminated two core elements of the EU's constitutional legitimacy: voice and rights. By thus eliminating any relevance of the Union's independent creation of political will as well as any meaningful control for fundamental rights, the CFI would have undermined the autonomy and legitimacy of the European legal order.

4.4.3 *The Court of Justice: consolidating local constitutionalism*

The Court of Justice was well aware of the damage that the CFI's global constitutionalism could have done to the authority of the European

---

[131] See Frowein, J., '*Solange II*', 25 *Common Market Law Review* (1988) 201.

legal order. Under the CFI's vision, the Union's authority would be wholly derivative of that of the Member States and organized under the overarching system of public international law with the United Nations at its peak. This would have rendered the Union ineffectual as a separate site of governance, thereby undermining its legitimacy in the eyes of the Member States.

The ECJ's response was to reject the CFI's approach by taking a more local path of dualism, that is, protecting the constitutional autonomy of the European legal order itself. The ECJ saw the Union's implementation of the UN sanctions regime as a matter of European voice, i.e. the product of a European political choice not of an inexorable international command. And the ECJ chose to protect a conception of rights that was distinctly European, not international. And despite some sympathy for complying with the international rule of law, the Court of Justice focused on one task above all else: laying down the final constitutional building block to consolidate the autonomous European legal order that the Court had been promising since *Van Gend*.

Prior to the *Kadi* case, the gaze of European 'constitutionalism' had mostly been focused inward. The evolution of an autonomous legal order with supremacy and direct effect throughout the Union – all too well known to bear repetition here – was all about setting the European legal order off from, while at the same time integrating it with, the legal orders of the Member States.[132] The primary theme of this story was the relationship between the European Union and its Member States. Even external relations decisions (in so far as they were part of the constitutional canon) concerned, for the most part, distinctly internal aspects of Union governance, i.e. the division of powers and the elements of cooperation among the European and national levels of governance in foreign affairs.[133] Call this relationship between the European Union

---

[132] See Mancini, F., *Democracy and Constitutionalism in Europe* (Oxford: Hart Publishing, 2000) at 1–30, 51–66, 243–258; Weiler, J. H. H., 'The Transformation of Europe', in J. H. H. Weiler, ed., *The Constitution of Europe: 'Do the New Clothes Have an Emperor?' and Other Essays on European Integration* (Cambridge University Press, 1999), 10–101; Stein, Eric, 'Lawyers, Judges, and the Making of a Transnational Constitution', 75 *American Journal of International Law* (1981) 1.

[133] See, e.g., Opinion 1/03 of 7 February 2006, 2006 E.C.R. I-1145 (upholding the Community's exclusive competence to conclude the Lugano convention); Case C-233/02, *France* v. *Commission*, Judgment of the Court of 23 March 2004, 2004 E.C.R. 2759 (upholding the Community's competence to negotiate an

and the Member States' legal orders the 'internal dimension' of European constitutionalism.

The internal dimension of European constitutionalism, however, is only half the promise of an autonomous legal order. The internal dimension speaks only to the relationship between the Union's legal order and that of the Member States. This aspect of constitutionalism does not immediately address the relationship between the Union's legal order and that of international law. To be complete, however, the claim of constitutional autonomy of the European legal order must ultimately address this latter dimension as well. Understanding the Union as an extension of Member State legal orders would render the Union a mere tool in the hands of Member State governments. So, too, understanding the Union as thoroughly grounded in, and controlled by, international law would render the European enterprise an empty vessel for international governance writ large. Properly understood, the Union is neither.

To complete the promise of an autonomous legal order, then, the Union must assert a measure of independence from international law as well. Call this the 'external dimension' of European constitutionalism. This has old roots, too. Only one year after having coined the idea of a 'new legal order of international law' in *Van Gend*, the Court quietly restated the existence of that 'new legal order' without reference to the realm of 'international law'.[134] And so it has been ever since.[135] As Europe's 'new legal order' asserted supremacy and direct effect within Member State legal orders, it implicitly challenged its connection to

agreement with the United States); Opinion 2/00 of 6 December 2001, 2001 E.C.R. 9713 (addressing the legal basis for entering an agreement with a non-Member State); Opinion 1/94 of 15 November 1994, 1994 E.C.R. I-5267; Case 22–70, *Commission* v. *Council (European Agreement on Road Transport)*, Judgment of the Court of 31 March 1971, 1971 E.C.R. 263. See, generally, Stein, Eric, 'External Relations of the European Community', 1 *Collected Courses of the Academy of European Law* (1991) 115–132; Tridimas, Takis and P. Eeckhout, 'The External Competence of the Community and the Case-Law of the Court of Justice: Principle versus Pragmatism', 14 *Yearbook of European Law* (1994) 143; Kapteyn, P. J. G. and P. Verloren Van Themaat, *Introduction to the Law of the European Communities*, trans. C. Dikshoorn (The Hague: Kluwer, 1973) at 348–370; Steinberger, E., 'The WTO Treaty as a Mixed Agreement: Problems with the EC's and the EC Member States' Membership of the WTO', 17 *European Journal of International Law* (2006) 837 (discussing difficulties arising from the breach of a mixed agreement).

[134] Cases 90/63 and 91/63, *Commission* v. *Luxembourg and Belgium*, 1964 E.C.R. 625.

[135] E.g. Opinion 1/91 of 14 December 1991, 1991 E.C.R. I-6079.

the *Grundnorm* of international law. Now, in the *Kadi* opinion, the Court of Justice finally made whole on its promise of an autonomous legal order by clarifying the external dimension of European constitutionalism.

The ECJ firmly anchored European public power in the European legal order itself, rejecting the claim that the European Union was bound to act due to any political determination made beyond its borders. Instead, it was Europe's political voice that mattered. Nor was the Union to compromise on the protection of rights as they were specifically conceived of within the Union. (In a related case about the Union's own system of identifying individual targets, the ECJ further questioned the UK Home Secretary's decision to designate a particular target of individual sanctions. This raised concerns about the instrumental rationality of the diplomatic process by which targets are identified at the UN level as well.[136] The *Kadi* case, however, most prominently focused on voice and rights, not expertise.)

On the matter of voice, the ECJ asserted the independence of the European Union's political will from the international legal order by rejecting the CFI's notion that either the Community or the Union as a whole was somehow bound to give effect to UN sanctions within its own legal order. To be sure, the ECJ judgment gives a highly sympathetic treatment of international law. The ECJ suggested that Community action would indeed need to conform to international legal obligations and that the Community would have to heed its international legal obligations more generally.[137] And yet, the ECJ insisted that 'an international agreement cannot affect [...] the autonomy of the Community legal system'.[138] The decision makes clear that the Union's implementation of the Security Council Resolution was ultimately grounded not in an international decision

---

[136] Case T-228/02, *Organisation des Modjahedines du peuple d'Iran* v. *Council*, 2006 ECR II-4665.

[137] See Joined Cases C-402/05 P and C-415/05 P, *Kadi* v. *Council of European Union*, Judgment of the Court of 3 September 2008, paras 6, 291, 293–294 (hereinafter '*Kadi* (Judgment)').

[138] Ibid., at para 282. See also at para 281 ('[N]either the Member States nor its institutions can void review of the conformity of their acts with the basic constitutional charter, the EC Treaty, which establishes a complete system of legal remedies and procedures designed to enable the Court of Justice to review the legality of acts of the institutions.').

of the UN Security Council but in a political decision on the part of the European Council acting under the CFSP provisions.[139]

Never before was the assertion of a European voice and the protection of European constitutional integrity from intrusion by the international legal order as emphatic as in this judgment.[140] No international agreement (not even one entered into by the Member States prior to the existence of the Union) could affect the fundamental principles of the Union's legal order, so the Court held. Although it may be possible to read these statements as compatible with a softer, more hospitable attitude towards public international law, in this case the final emphasis was on the autonomy of the Union, not on the latter's openness towards international law.

On the matter of rights, the Court of Justice judgment begins by striking a conciliatory tone with regard to international law and ends with an assertion of the autonomy and supremacy of European rights. The ECJ suggests an interpretation of the UN Security Council regulation that would allow for just the kind of fundamental rights review at the Union level that the Union itself demands. In the Court's charitable interpretation of the UN Security Council Resolution, the latter only calls for implementation of sanctions in conformity with whatever procedures govern within the domestic legal system that effectuates the implementation.[141] According to the ECJ, then, there is ultimately no incompatibility between UN command and ECJ review in this case. Nevertheless, the ECJ strongly suggests that if there were any incompatibility between fundamental principles of EU law and an international command, the Court would be obligated to vindicate the EU's conception of rights above all else.

The Court further rejects the idea of any deference to other institutions, such as the UN Security Council, in reviewing the lawfulness of the sanctions even under a common standard of rights. Even a system of

---

[139] Ibid., at para 295.

[140] There was some precedent for protecting principles of European law from being eroded by international legal compliance. See Joined Cases C-317/04 and C-318/04, *Parliament* v. *Council and Commission*, 2006 E.C.R. I-4721; Opinion 2/94, 1996 E.C.R. I-1759 (barring the Community's accession to the ECHR via Article 308 EC); Case C-122/95, *Germany* v. *Council*, 1988 E.C.R. I-973. Cf. *Kadi* (AG), Joined Cases C-402//05 P and C-415/05 P , *Kadi* v. *Council of Europe*, Opinion of the Advocate General on January 23 2008, para 23.

[141] See Joined Cases C-402//05 P and C-415/05 P, *Kadi* v. *Council of Europe*, Opinion of the Advocate General on 23 January 2008 at paras 298–299.

human rights protection at the UN level would not seem to obviate the need for the ECJ to conduct its own review with regard to the protection of the EU's own version of these rights. Ruling out any '*Solange*' compromise such as that governing the EU's relationship with the legal order of its Member States, the Court holds:

[T]he existence, within th[e] United Nations system, of the re-examination procedure before the Sanctions Committee, even having regard to the amendments recently made to it, cannot give rise to generalised immunity from jurisdiction within the internal legal order of the Community.[142]

Although this passage (along with much of the judgment) is open to several interpretations, the choice of words and the location of the passage within the opinion suggests that the ECJ does not merely reject deference under the particular circumstances of this case. Instead, the ECJ seems to rule out categorically even the possibility of dialogue or deference between the UN and the EU on the question of rights.

Finally, the Court of Justice makes plain that in no case would the Court's review or the EU's rejection of an international command implicate the legality of the Security Council Resolution under international law:

[T]he review of lawfulness thus to be ensured by the Community judicature applies to the Community act intended to give effect to the international agreement at issue, and not to the latter as such [. . .] [A]ny judgment given by the Community judicature deciding that a Community measure intended to give effect to such a resolution is contrary to higher rule of law in the Community legal order would not entail any challenge to the primacy of that resolution in international law.[143]

This, then, is nothing short of the formal separation of legal orders – a kind of dualism – albeit a sympathetic version in which an autonomous EU legal order aims to fulfil whatever international legal obligations it may have. The control of voice and rights are consolidated exclusively within the constitutional confines of the European legal order itself.

In conceiving of the relationship between the European Union and the international legal order, the ECJ thus seems to have rejected both global and plural constitutionalism. The ECJ judgment in *Kadi* separates the international legal order from that of the European Union and

---

[142] Ibid., at para 321. Caveat about interpretation here. [143] Ibid., at para. 4.

then asserts the simple supremacy of the latter over the former. As such, the external dimension of European constitutionalism rejects the more fluid nature of authority that has been the hallmark of the Union's relation to the Member States. And it shifts away from an earlier jurisprudence that suggested the possibility of a similar kind of openness to the realm of international law.[144] The approach we seem to see now is one of dualism and of insistence on the supremacy of the local constitutional legal order of the European Union alone.

4.4.4 *The Advocate General: a path to pluralism?*

Advocate General Miguel Maduro's opinion, by contrast, had urged the Court to move beyond constitutional resistance and towards more open engagement and dialogue with the United Nations. To be sure, the Advocate General's opinion, too, emphasizes the foundational nature of the European constitutional order and the centrality of the Court of Justice as its 'constitutional court'.[145] At the same time, however, the Advocate General's opinion recognizes the potential multiplicity of claims of authority that lie beyond. Maduro's opinion thus entails significant strides towards taking pluralism seriously.

The Advocate General begins by emphasizing the constitutional credentials of the EU's legal order, and of the Court of Justice in particular. Using the international law term hitherto reserved for the domestic legal orders of states, the Advocate General for the first time in the history of published decisions of the Court refers to the European 'municipal' legal order,[146] albeit one of 'transnational dimensions, of which [the Treaty] forms the "basic constitutional charter"'.[147] Much as the ECJ's final decision does, the Advocate General thus separates the Union's legal order from that of international law and anchors the relationship between the two orders firmly in the constitutional law of the European Union.[148] Recognizing the constitutional nature of the Treaty, the

---

[144] The court's earlier jurisprudence seemed more open to this idea. See Schuetze, R., 'On "Middle Ground": The European Community and Public International Law', *European University Institute Working Paper LAW No. 2007/13* 2007), available at <http://www.ssrn.com/abstract=995780>; Gráinne de Búrca, Chapter 3 in this volume.

[145] Joined Cases C-402//05 P and C-415/05 P , *Kadi* v. *Council of Europe*, Opinion of the Advocate General on 23 January 2008, para 37 (hereinafter '*Kadi* (AG)').

[146] Ibid., at para. 21.   [147] Ibid.   [148] See ibid., at para 24.

Advocate General's opinion suggests that '[t]he duty of the Court of Justice is to act as the constitutional court of the municipal legal order that is the Community'.[149] In that capacity, the Court must 'determine the effect of international obligations within the Community legal order by reference to conditions set by Community law'.[150] So far there is not too much difference between the Advocate General and the Court of Justice. Nor need there be any great departure on this basic point of the constitutional foundation of the Union for the idea of pluralism to flourish. Pluralism, after all, demands a solid claim of authority not only on the part of international law, but on the part of European Union law as well.

The Advocate General's opinion also rejects the idea of the EU's compliance with the EU's (or the Member States') international legal obligations as a matter of inexorable (international, EU or Member State law) command. In so doing, the Advocate General rejects the CFI's move to subsume the European Union under the voice of the United Nations. Instead, compliance with international law is based on an expression of the EU's political will. As the Advocate General puts it, there is a '*presumption* that the Community *wants* to honor its international commitments'.[151] This statement both suggests the existence of an independent political voice on the part of the Union and, at the same time, recognizes a structural openness to international legal compliance that runs deeper than whatever the latest vote in the Council may be on a given regulation. Although the presumption can, of course, ultimately be overcome, it nonetheless significantly 'guide[s]' the 'application and interpretation of Community law'.[152] As the Advocate General explains:

[T]he Community's municipal legal order and the international legal order [do not] pass by each other like ships in the night [. . .] [T]he Community has traditionally played an active and constructive part on the international stage [. . .] The Community Courts therefore carefully examine the obligations by which the Community is bound on the international stage and take judicial notice of those obligations.[153]

When it comes to the protection of rights and to the recognition of the expertise of the United Nations, the Advocate General similarly shifts ever so slightly off the course charted by the ECJ. To be sure, the

---

[149] Ibid., at para 37.   [150] Ibid., at para 23.
[151] Ibid., at para 22 (emphasis supplied).   [152] Ibid.   [153] Ibid.

Advocate General is equally keen on protecting rights that form part of
the constitutional framework of the European Union. In the Advocate
General's view, as in the ECJ's, no implementation of international legal
obligations within the Union can override the protection of fundamental
rights. And yet, in contrast to the ECJ's judgment, the Advocate
General's opinion admits of the possibility that the EU might defer to
the institutions of another legal system that might be better equipped to
balance the fundamental interests at stake in a particular case:

> In an increasingly interdependent world, different legal orders will have to
> endeavour to accommodate each other's jurisdictional claims. As a result, the
> Court cannot always assert a monopoly on determining how certain funda-
> mental interests ought to be reconciled. It must, where possible, recognize the
> authority of institutions, such as the Security Council, that are established
> under a different legal order than its own and that are sometimes better placed
> to weigh those fundamental interests.[154]

Such deference, however, is not automatic. Nor can it rest on presumed
subject matter expertise alone. Instead, 'respect for other institutions is
meaningful only if it can be built on a shared understanding of these
values and on a mutual commitment to protect them'.[155]

The Advocate General thereby leads the way towards a pluralist
stance with regard to the relationship between the European Union
and the realm of global governance. This entails the recognition that
the EU legal order is not the sole source of authoritative guidance on
realizing the appropriate balance between collective security and individual liberty. To be sure, as an EU actor, the Advocate General locates
(as he must) the ultimate regulation of the relationship between the EU's
legal order and international law within the foundational treaties of the
Union. And yet, this admits of a structural openness of the EU to the
various systems as well as institutions (interpretive and otherwise) in the
realm of global governance. These systems and institutions beyond the
borders of the European Union may, on this vision, at times lay a
superior institutional claim to vindicating the constitutional values
that underlie the European Union itself. This, then, is the essence of
pluralism. In contrast with the unilateral approach of the ECJ, the
Advocate General suggests a dialogue.

---

[154] Ibid., at para 44.   [155] Ibid.

Whereas the ECJ's path of local constitutional resistance seeks to protect the particularistic conception of EU rights, the Advocate General implicitly invokes the pluralism paradigm of *Solange*:

Had there been a genuine and effective mechanism of judicial control by an independent tribunal at the level of the United Nations, then this might have released the Community from the obligation to provide for judicial control of implementing measures that apply within the Community legal order. However, no such mechanism currently exists.[156]

The Advocate General would accordingly not insist on the ECJ's own application of the Union's particular conception of rights in every case. Instead, the Advocate General acknowledges the possibility, in principle, of an accommodation of both systems pluralism and some measure of interpretive pluralism.

In contrast with the Court of Justice, the Advocate General thus draws on the model of pluralism that governs the internal dimension of European constitutionalism to approach the external dimension of constitutionalism as well. Whatever multiplicity of authority might exist in the Union's relation with the Member States, the ECJ's judgment recognizes no such multiplicity in the Union's relation with international law. For the Advocate General, by contrast, certain elements of pluralism may transfer from the internal to the external dimension of European constitutionalism. Although the specific calculus of accommodation will differ (especially in the fact that claims to voice will become more problematic at the international level than they are even at the European Union level), pluralism in the external dimension of European constitutionalism nonetheless suggests an openness to the authority of the other here as well.

4.4.5 *Taking pluralism seriously: the curious case of international law*

In taking up the suggestion of pluralism in the *Kadi* case, however, one important link still seems to be missing: the interpretation of international law. With the exception of *ius cogens*, customary international law was conspicuously absent from all three judicial pronouncements in *Kadi*. And the law of the United Nations was similarly pushed off stage, except in the

---

[156] Ibid., at para 54.

ECJ's interpretation of the Security Council Resolution as allowing ample room for the implementation of sanctions subject to local procedural dictates. A more systematic or comprehensive consideration of customary international law or the law of the United Nations was nowhere to be found.

With regard to the Court of Justice this neglect is understandable. The focus of the final judgment was, after all, on consolidating local constitutionalism against outside intrusion. With regard to the CFI, however, the absence of a more searching review of international law is somewhat puzzling. To be sure, the CFI opted for a global hierarchy of systems. But the CFI nonetheless asserted its own authority within that global system of systems to interpret the principles of *ius cogens* as governing the exercise of UN authority. Finally, Advocate General Maduro's opinion, which most openly acknowledges the idea of pluralism, seems to have focused on the pluralism of systems as well as the lack of multiple institutions committed to rights protection at the international level, while neglecting the potential pluralism of institutions with regard to the interpretation of the UN system and of public international law more generally.

As a doctrinal matter, fundamental principles of both UN law and public international law could have played into the legality of the contested regulation in three basic ways. First, such principles might serve as a limitation on the UN Security Council's powers and thus figure into a determination of the scope and legality of the underlying international legal obligation to which the European Union measure responded.[157] Second, public international law (such as customary international human rights law) may figure into the international legal responsibility that the EU would incur by implementing a smart sanctions regime.[158] And third, principles of public international law might

---

[157] The United Nations, along with the UN Security Council and all states implementing a UN mandate, may be bound by international human rights norms by virtue of the provisions of the UN Charter itself. Moreover, the United Nations, as a legal person under international law, may be bound directly by customary international law. Finally, UN law may have begun to incorporate certain principles of rights that go beyond what customary international law or general principles currently demand. See, generally, Halberstam and Stein, 'The United Nations' (2009).

[158] Cf. e.g. Orakhelashvili, A., 'The Idea of European International Law', 17 *European Journal of International Law* (2006) 315–347 at 345–346 and note 151 ('That the European institutions operate within the field of international law is also affirmed by the fact that they are bound by customary international law in the same way as any legal entity is', citing Lowe, Vaughan, 'Can the European Community Bind the Member States on Questions of Customary International

determine the domestic scope or legality of the EU's own decisions and implementation measures.[159] Without presuming to bind the UN Security Council with its judicial pronouncements, the Court of Justice had ample doctrinal means to consider the international dimension of the alleged infringement on individual rights.[160] The ECJ could have drawn on fundamental principles of customary international law, as well as the UN Charter and the UN Security Council Resolution itself, in reviewing the scope and legality of an EC/EU regulation implementing that Resolution.

The mere fact that the UN Security Council may have implicitly judged the international legality of its own Resolution should not

Law?', in Koskenniemi, Martti, ed., *International Law Aspects of the European Union* (The Hague, London: Kluwer Law International, 1998) 149–196).

[159] See Case C-308–06, *The Queen* v. *The Secretary of State for Transport*, Judgment of 3 June 2008, 2008 E.C.R. I-4057, paras 42–45 ('[T]he validity of a measure of secondary Community legislation may be affected by the fact that it is incompatible with such rules of international law [, referring to an international agreement concluded by the Community.]); Case C-162/96, *A. Racke GmbH & Co.* v. *Hauptzollamt Mainz.*, Judgment of the Court of 16 June 1988, 1988 E.C.R. I-3655, paras 45–46 ('[T]he European Community must respect international law in the exercise of its powers. It is therefore required to comply with the rules of customary international law when adopting a regulation suspending the trade concessions granted by, or by virtue of, an agreement which it has concluded with a non-member country.'); Koutrakos, P., *EU International Relations Law* (Oxford: Hart Publishing, 2006) (discussing the ECJ's incorporation of customary international law as an interpretational method for the EC Treaty).

[160] A nuanced doctrinal case can be made that puts together the principles of implementation and indirect effect to allow for jurisdiction over customary international law here. See Case C-69/89, *Nakajima All Precision Co.* v. *Council*, Judgment of the Court of 7 May 1991, 1991 E.C.R. I-2069 (upholding an anti-dumping regulation that did not go against the spirit of GATT); Case 70/87, *Fediol* v. *Commission*, Judgment of the Court of 22 June 1989, 1989 E.C.R. 1781 (allowing a party to rely upon GATT to define an illicit commercial practice); Case 188/85, *EEC Seed Crushers' and Oil Processors' Federation (Fediol)* v. *Commission*, Judgment of the Court of 14 July 1988, 1988 E.C.R. 4193 (upholding the Commission's definition of subsidy while noting that the definition was not incompatible with GATT); Case C-162/96, *A. Racke GmbH & Co.* v. *Hauptzollamt Mainz.*, Judgment of the Court of 16 June 1988, 1988 E.C.R. I-3655. Fitting these precedents together carefully would allow the ECJ to interpret fundamental principles of public international law (even those that do not themselves have direct effect) when interpreting a Community directive that implements a CFSP Common Position, which, in turn, is intended to implement a UN Security Council Resolution. For an elaboration on this doctrinal argument, see Halberstam and Stein, 'The United Nations' (2009), at 37–39, 43–46, 51–53.

present an impediment to the ECJ's consideration of the same. Interpretive pluralism comes alive by just this sort of lack of settled hierarchy among the various institutions laying claim to interpret the same norms. On this point, too, there is some precedent. The Court of Justice has in the past resisted being legally bound even by the decisions of international judicial tribunals.[161] The Court will give varying degrees of deference to these other actors in their interpretation of the relevant international treaty norm without being legally bound by their decisions.[162]

Although the idea of interpretive pluralism was not entirely lost in *Kadi*, the various opinions seemed to avoid considering customary international human rights law or the law of the United Nations out of a sense of deliberate avoidance. This concern was palpable as the CFI cautiously approached its limited review of *ius cogens*.[163] And it undoubtedly explains the painstaking disclaimer on the part of the ECJ as well as the Advocate General that the judgment would not in any way implicate the legality of the United Nation's actions under

---

[161] To be sure, the Court has acknowledged, in principle, the possibility of being bound by the decisions of international tribunals on the interpretation of international treaties. See, e.g., Opinion 1/91 of 14 December 1991, 1991 E.C.R. I-6079, at para 39. And yet, time and again, it has refused to find that the conditions obtain under any particular treaty to so bind the Court. For instance, the Court has found itself to be not legally bound by the EFTA (European Free Trade Association) Court, the European Court of Human Rights or WTO dispute resolution panels. The reasons differ from case to case, but the practical result is the same. For example, the EFTA treaty does not make the decisions of the EFTA court binding on the ECJ, see Agreement on the European Economic Area, Article 6, 1994 O.J. (L 1) 3 and The Surveillance and Court Agreement, Article 3, 1994 O.J. (L 344) 3; the EC/EU is not (yet) a member of the European Convention on Human Rights, cf. Opinion 2/94, Opinion of the Court of 28 March 1996, 1996 E.C.R. I-1759; and the Court has held that WTO decisions do not have direct effect. See, e.g., C-377/02, *Van Parys* v. *BIRB*, Judgment of the Court of 1 March 2005, 2005 E.C.R. I-1465; C-351/04, *Ikea Wholesale Ltd.* v. *Commissioners of Customs & Excise*, Judgment of the Court 27 September 2007, 2007 E.C.R. I-7723.

[162] See generally, Bronckers, Marco, 'The Relationship of the EC Courts with Other International Tribunals: Non-Committal, Respectful or Submissive?', 44 *Common Market Law Review* (2007) 601.

[163] See Case T-315/01, *Kadi* v. *Council of European Union*, 2005 ECR II-3649 (21 September 2005), at paras 234–292; Shelton, Dinah, 'Normative Hierarchy in International Law', 100 *American Journal of International Law* 2 (2006) 291–323 at 312 (describing *jus cogens* review in *Kadi* as '[winning] a battle only to lose the war').

principles of international law. Indeed, for the ECJ to declare that the Union's implementing measures themselves infringed customary international human rights or the law of the United Nations would have placed the conflict of norms squarely within the realm from which the UN Security Council draws its legitimacy. And finally, even declaring only that the EU's implementing measures were illegal under EU law because the Court believes they violate principles of customary international human rights law or the law of the United Nations might also have bled into questioning the international legality of UN action itself.

And yet, taking interpretive pluralism seriously suggests that EU courts can and should draw on, and interpret, international legal norms where such norms legally apply to cases before them. This is especially true where no alternative institution with a superior claim of authority has considered these issues. In the decentralized system of international governance, a host of courts (including domestic and supranational courts) take on the function of authoritative interpreters of international law. In recognizing this, we need not commit to Georges Scelle's theory of '*dédoublement fonctionnel*',[164] with its overly optimistic view of particularly situated courts' universal perspective.[165] Putting aside any unwarranted idealism about the predilections of particularly situated courts (such as national courts or EU courts), these institutions form an important part of the institutional framework for the creation and interpretation of international law.

Even where domestic institutions' structural commitment to the universal is less than complete, the interpretation of international law is still ultimately a collective endeavour, i.e. a shared enterprise among the various judicial and other participants around the world who can lay claim to interpret these common legal norms. Domestic courts must accordingly not give a purely partial interpretation that considers only their particularistic point of view; they must consider the international norm – whether it be treaty, custom or general – as a norm shared by all

---

[164] See Scelle, Georges, *Le Phénomène juridique du dédoublement fonctionnel*, in W. Schätzel, ed., *Rechtsfragen der internationalen Organisation – Festschrift für Hans Wehberg su seinem 70* (Frankfurt-am-Main: Vittorio Klostermann, 1956), 324, e.g. at 331.

[165] Cf. e.g. Cassese, Antonio, 'Remarks on Scelle's Theory of "Role Splitting" (dédoublement fonctionnel) in International Law', 1 *European Journal of International Law* (1990) 210 at 213.

participants.[166] All this means, of course, that in the absence of a designated international institution with a superior and exclusive claim of interpretive authority with regard to international law, domestic courts do not overstep their jurisdictional bounds by participating in the interpretation, and hence development, of international law. Accordingly, the Court of Justice (even as it conceives of itself as being situated in a 'municipal' legal order) can and should interpret international law and even the law of the United Nations to the extent that such law is a component of a dispute about EU law over which the Court has jurisdiction and there is no other tribunal or institution with a superior claim to interpretive authority.

This recognition of interpretive pluralism would have allowed the Court to consider in this case whether the EU's implementation measures violated international law, as well as the far more delicate question of whether individual rights norms legally bind the UN Security Council itself. No other presently constituted institution has been formally granted superior interpretive authority in this case. And no forum can lay a superior claim of interpretive authority in this case relative to the Court of Justice to examine even the most delicate question whether the UN Security Council had overstepped its bounds by neglecting individual rights.

There was no other institution with a greater claim in either political will, functional expertise or a promise of protecting rights to which the Court of Justice should have deferred on these questions. To be sure, a case between two states might conceivably arise or a request for an advisory opinion could be made before the International Court of Justice raising the validity of the UN Security Council measure. But the ICJ has not yet reliably conceived of itself as able to question the validity of UN Security Council actions.[167] What is more, by enlisting states and regional organizations to impose economic sanctions on individuals, the Security Council has reached out to burden individuals directly without

---

[166] See Maduro, Miguel, 'Contrapunctual Law: Europe's Constitutional Pluralism in Action', in Neil Walker, ed., *Sovereignty in Transition* (Oxford University Press, 2003), 501–538; Van Alstine, M., 'Dynamic Treaty Interpretation', 146 *University of Pennsylvania Law Review* (1998) 687.

[167] Alvarez, José, 'The New Dispute Settlers: (Half) Truths and Consequences', 38 *Texas International Law Journal* (2003) 405 at 418–419, 431. Cf. Case IT-94-1-T, *Prosecutor* v. *Tadic*, Decision of 2 October 1995 on the Defence Motion for Interlocutory Appeal on Jurisdiction, paras 4, 15–19 (distinguishing a tribunal from a subsidiary organ entirely within the control of the UN Security Council and supplementing the Statute of the International Tribunal).

providing them with a corresponding forum in which to contest the action. In the absence of any such forum at the international level, the United Nations should be open to challenges based on individual rights as well as the accuracy of the underlying substantive decisions. In short, the Security Council's actions on this score should not be insulated from indirect judicial review at the level of domestic courts.

The Court of Justice is uniquely situated to engage in a dialogue with the United Nations on the international rule of law. As a court charged with considering the Member States' underlying international legal obligations, the ECJ would have the same warrant to engage with international law and the law of the United Nations as would any domestic high court, despite the fact that the European Union is not a member of the UN. The Court of Justice is furthermore in a unique position with regard to international law by virtue of the Union's historical grounding in international law,[168] its normative commitment to international law,[169] and the continued structural significance of international law to its internal operations.[170]

The Court of Justice sits at the intersection between domestic and international law like no other court in the world. By relying solely on domestic constitutional rights as a backstop, the Court of Justice seemed to have ignored its special standing on this score. By taking pluralism seriously and relying on the law of the United Nations and public international law as well, the ECJ could have led the way for a broader conversation about the public international law constraints that help ensure the legitimacy of United Nations action for all.

4.5 Conclusion

Globalization challenges constitutionalism. As interactions across diverse jurisdictions multiply and deepen, the idea of limited collective

---

[168] Kapteyn and Verloren Van Themaat, *Introduction* (1973), at 1–19; Nuttall, S., *European Political Cooperation* (Oxford: Clarendon Press 1992); Koutrakos, *EU International Relations Law* (2006), at 244–249 (discussing the ECJ's incorporation of customary international law as binding on the Community and as an interpretational method for the EC Treaty).

[169] See, e.g., Treaty on European Union, Article 11 (listing as an objective of the Common Foreign and Security Policy 'to promote international cooperation').

[170] See Koutrakos, *EU International Relations Law* (2006), at 137–182, 184–185, 217–249.

self-governance seems increasingly unattainable. The interconnectedness of modern life around the world has challenged the ability of the
modern state to meet the security and policy demands of their local
constituencies and has raised questions of distributive justice writ large.
Regimes of global governance have sprung up to provide a kind of
global public order, but these seem to strain the conventional demand
for legitimacy in the exercise of public power. Although states still stand
generally as intermediaries between the global and the local, governance
beyond the state increasingly takes on a life of its own, shaping – if not
coercively determining – local choices.[171]

Whereas some would retreat into local constitutions as the exclusive
site of legitimate public power, others have urged what has been critically called a 'constitutional *fuite en avant*' in the arena of global
governance.[172] Where local constitutionalists seek to deny the power
and influence of transnational regimes, global constitutionalists seek to
augment the authority of global governance often by turning some of
these regimes into sites of super-supranational governance. On the
global constitutionalist view, the United Nations, or the WTO, as the
preferred case may be, would sit at the apex of a comprehensive regime
of globally constituted governance.

Instead of viewing constitutionalism in binary terms – as either local
or global – this chapter has explored a third alternative, that of plural
constitutionalism. This view cautiously builds on the European experience of pluralism within its borders. Without suggesting a wholesale
transplant of the idea to the global arena, this approach nonetheless
suggests certain parallels: first the partial autonomy of the various sites
of governance at national, supranational and global levels of governance; second, the mutually embedded openness of certain sites to one
another; and third, the resort to the disaggregated values of constitutionalism as a common grammar of legitimacy in the conflict and
accommodation of competing claims of authority. The argument is
not that plural constitutionalism is the inevitable product of a plurality

---

[171] See, e.g., Bogdandy, Armin von, Phillipp Dann and Matthias Goldmann,
'Developing the Publicness of Public International Law: Towards a Legal
Framework for Global Governance Activities', 9 *German Law Journal* (2008)
1371 at 1381–1382.

[172] Cf. Howse and Nicolaidis, 'Democracy without Sovereignty (2008), at 177
(criticizing the 'constitutional *fuite en avant*' in the trade arena).

of authority. Instead, it is a contingent possibility whenever the three elements of plural constitutionalism obtain.

Plural constitutionalism embraces the lack of settlement and hierarchy as generating productive decentralized engagement for a piecemeal approach to limited collective self-governance. On the pluralist vision, the state is only one site among many for fulfilling the aspiration of self-governance. Pluralists do not simply reverse the logic of legitimacy in favour of the global over the local as global constitutionalists do. Neither the global nor the local is necessarily privileged over the other. And even at the global level itself, no single site of governance takes general precedence over the others.

Whereas internationally minded critics complain about an inconvenient, inefficient or even dangerous fragmentation,[173] pluralists see the lament of fragmentation as misplaced nostalgia for a time that never was. Indeed, at its worst, the critique of fragmentation displays a self-interested dismay on the part of champions of a particular organization about the inability to consolidate power and authority in their own institution.[174] Pluralists add to this a normative claim: that the multiplicity of pluralism is all the more beneficial as there are no worldwide democratic institutions that could hope to consolidate governance meaningfully and legitimately into a single settled structure – even a nested one based on federal principles.

The Court of Justice of the European Union recently engaged with these questions in the *Kadi* litigation surrounding the implementation of UN sanctions against individuals in Europe. In the various judicial pronouncements all three positions in one way or another came to the fore. Whereas the Court of First Instance opted for a global constitutionalism, the Court of Justice seems to have kept constitutionalism local – at least with regard to Europe; at least for now. Only the

---

[173] Critics charge that fragmentation undermines the coherence and credibility of international law and allows for particular interests to evade considerations of global justice through forum shopping. See, e.g., Koskenniemi, Martti and Päivi Leino, 'Fragmentation of International Law? Postmodern Anxieties', 15 *Leiden Journal of International Law* (2002) 553–579 (discussing complaints on the part of ICJ members); Shany, Yuval, 'The First MOX Plant Award: The Need to Harmonize Competing Environmental Regimes and Dispute Settlement Procedures', 17 *Leiden Journal of International Law* (2004) 815 (describing some of these concerns in cases of jurisdictional competition without mutual comity).

[174] See Koskenniemi and Leino, 'Fragmentation' (2002).

Advocate General clearly opted for the path of pluralism, by suggesting a greater openness to governance beyond Europe.

In the context of Europe's relation with the world, one might venture to describe the pluralist vision as one of the *primacy, not supremacy* of EU law. Although a difference between these two terms is frequently not drawn out – and at other times is drawn in a fashion that simply wreaks havoc[175] – one might nonetheless cautiously fashion the following useful distinction. Whereas the idea of supremacy denotes hierarchical superiority to the exclusion of all other claims of authority, the idea of primacy suggests a more tentative claim of *primus inter pares* – a kind of precedence in the horizontal accommodation among equals.

When Europe meets the world, the constitutional law of the Union is necessarily privileged for actors within that system. Supremacy would therefore reject any competing claim of authority. Primacy, by contrast, invites actors within the Union nonetheless to engage in a practice of conflict and accommodation with claims of authority from beyond the Union. The choice between local and global constitutionalism, then, is a false one. But to see our way out of the fly bottle, pluralism dares us to rethink constitutionalism itself.

---

[175] See Re EU Constitutional Treaty and the Spanish Constitution (Spanish Constitutional Court) [2005] 1 CMLR 981, at paras 52–54.

5 | The case for pluralism in postnational law

NICO KRISCH [*]

5.1 Introduction

Times of transition are often more exciting than those of routine and continuity, but they are typically also disorderly and confusing. Old paradigms fade, but new ones only emerge slowly, and their multiplicity leads to protracted phases of co-existence, competition and conflict. The current 'disorder of orders'[1] in the conceptualization of postnational law is a signal of such a transition and an indication of its depth. The 'Westphalian' system, with its clear separation between domestic and international levels of law and only relatively thin forms of coordination and cooperation in the latter, has broken down under the weight of Europeanization and globalization, but its successor has not been appointed yet. Several candidates are in the race,[2] and one main dividing line – the one this chapter focuses on – is between constitutionalist and pluralist approaches to postnational order. Both of these come in many guises, but they typically differ in their understanding of central structural traits of the legal and political order. While constitutionalists, drawing on domestic inspirations, generally strive for a common frame to define both the substantive principles of the overall order and the relations between its different parts, pluralists prefer to see the postnational realm as characterized by heterarchy, by an interaction of different

---

[*] Hertie School of Governance, Berlin. I am grateful to Nicolas Lamp, Richard Stewart, Chandran Kukathas and the participants in a workshop at NYU Law School, a colloquium at the LSE Law Department and a conference at Oxford University for comments and discussion on an earlier draft. The present chapter draws in part on my *Beyond Constitutionalism: The Pluralist Structure of Postnational Law* (Oxford University Press, 2010), Chapters 2 and 3.
[1] Walker, Neil, 'Beyond Boundary Disputes and Basic Grids: Mapping the Global Disorder of Normative Orders', 6 *International Journal of Constitutional Law* 3–4 (2008) 373–396.
[2] See the survey ibid.

suborders that is not subject to common legal rules but takes a more open, political form.

This contrast may seem overdrawn; perhaps one should steer a less conflictive path and work towards reconciling these two visions in some form of 'constitutional pluralism'.[3] But such a conciliatory move would conceal, rather than bring into relief, the theoretical and practical differences that exist between constitutionalist, unity-oriented and pluralist, heterarchical conceptions. Even if in the current debate some of the positions may be relatively close, highlighting the contrast between the two strands will be useful to probe more deeply into their respective foundations and into the choices we face in the conceptualization and construction of the postnational legal order.

The contest between constitutionalism and pluralism has so far largely lacked a common basis – pluralists have typically made their case on analytical grounds, while constitutionalists have mostly turned to the normative sphere. So whereas pluralism seems to provide a strong (though contested) interpretation of the current, disorderly state of postnational law, constitutionalism – if not yet realized today – appears as the more attractive vision for the future.[4] As I will try to show in this chapter, however, this picture does not quite capture the normative appeal of the pluralist approach. In a postnational society characterized by diversity and rapid change, constitutionalist models face serious difficulties and their appeal risks being diluted by the (necessary) accommodation of the divergent interests and values of different parts of the polity. Pluralism, on the other hand, has significant strengths in providing adaptability, space for contestation and a possibility of steering between conflicting supremacy claims of different polity levels. This does not imply that a pluralist approach would be free from difficulties, or that it would be necessarily superior to constitutionalism on all counts. But it would likely resonate better with the divided allegiances and preferences in postnational society which, more than substantive evaluations, should guide any design of the institutional order in and beyond the state.

---

[3] See, e.g., Walker, Neil, 'The Idea of Constitutional Pluralism', 65 *Modern Law Review* (2002) 317–359.

[4] See, e.g., Baquero Cruz, Julio, 'The Legacy of the Maastricht-Urteil and the Pluralist Movement', 14 *European Law Journal* (2008) 389–420 at 417–418.

This chapter develops this argument in five steps. In Section 5.2, I begin by analysing the normative claims of postnational constitutionalism by reconstructing constitutionalism's appeal as a model for domestic order and by inquiring into the extent to which this appeal carries over into the very different postnational environment. The focus here is on constitutionalism's engagement with divided societies – the institutional forms it has developed to respond to deep diversity and the problems it continues to face in this respect. This focus should help in assessing constitutionalism's prospect in a society such as the postnational which, more than anything, is diverse; and it should help to avoid the idealizations implicit in analogies with more benign domestic circumstances. Section 5.3 of the chapter will then lay the conceptual ground for an analysis of a pluralist order as an alternative to a constitutionalist one, by identifying more clearly different understandings of pluralism and their implications. On this basis, Section 5.4 begins to inquire into the normative appeal of pluralism by developing further the three main arguments suggested so far in the literature – greater adaptability, the provision of contestatory space and the equidistance to conflicting claims to ultimate authority. Despite their merits, though, such substantive benefits alone will be insufficient to ground our structural choices; they have to be integrated into an account that gives much greater weight to procedures in the determination of a polity's structural framework. In Section 5.5, I outline such a more procedural, participatory account and how it would frame the contest between constitutionalism and pluralism. It is on this basis that pluralist proposals are likely to gain their real strength, which lies in their greater resonance with current, divided social practices towards the sites of political authority. Even so, a pluralist order faces fundamental problems, and Section 5.6 begins to address some of them, including those related to power, stability and democracy. In all these respects, pluralism may not emerge as flawless, but the constitutionalist alternative rarely fares much better and is often likely to fare worse. In the postnational order, ideal solutions are scarce – yet among the non-ideal ones, pluralism may be the least problematic.

5.2 Postnational constitutionalism and its limits

Constitutionalism has become attractive as a vision for ordering the postnational space mainly because of the close link it provides with central categories of domestic political order. As domestic, European and global politics have become ever more intertwined and much public power has moved beyond the state, it seems only natural to extend domestic concepts of legitimacy and democracy into the new, broader spaces. If there was a justification for a different – and thinner – notion of legitimacy in the international sphere before, it is now severely weakened, not least because the main tool to legitimate international law-making – inter-state consent – has lost much of its force in an era of delegated law-making, soft law and, more broadly, global governance.[5] Having recourse to domestic concepts for structuring and limiting government then seems to be an obvious move, and constitutionalism a prime candidate.

5.2.1 Constitutionalism's appeal

Unsurprisingly, then, both in the EU context and in the broader global realm, constitutionalist discourse has grown exponentially in the last decade, reflecting and building on the importance of constitutionalism in the national context. Over the last two centuries, in the wake of the American and French revolutions, constitutionalism has become key to ensuring the legitimacy of domestic governments, and it has come to be regarded as a unique institutional reflection of central tenets of modern political theory.[6] The form of the constitution, as a higher law that frames, organizes and limits the public power exercised in a polity, is seen to promote the joint realization of the rule of law and of democracy, marrying the rule of men with the rule of laws and thus appealing to liberals and republicans alike.[7] All government in the constitutional state has to act within the limits the constitution sets, but because the constitution supposedly derives from 'the people', these limits appear as expressions rather than limitations on democratic action. It is precisely through the constitution that a people can come together and, in a form

---

[5] See, e.g., Weiler, J. H. H., 'The Geology of International Law – Governance, Democracy, Legitimacy', 64 *Zeitschrift für ausländisches öffentliches Recht und Völkerrecht* (2004) 547–562.

[6] See Grimm, Dieter, *Die Zukunft der Verfassung* (Frankfurt am Main: Suhrkamp, 1991), Chapter 2.

[7] On the complementarity of, and tension between, the two concepts in American constitutionalism, see, e.g., Michelman, Frank, 'Law's Republic', 97 *Yale Law Journal* (1988), 1493–1537 at 1499–1500.

of 'higher politics', set the terms of their association and representation, thereby vindicating their power to frame the daily politics conducted by their representatives at a distance.[8]

Yet the appeal of constitutionalism goes further than this. It also encapsulates the very modern, Enlightenment idea of agency: it provides a form by which a polity can wrestle its affairs back from the forces of chance, history and power and remake, indeed refound, its institutions in a comprehensive way. Ideally, at the moment of constitution-making all traditional sites of public power come under scrutiny and are examined in the light of reason, and none of them can survive outside the constitutional framework.[9] Yet constitutionalism does not draw its appeal exclusively from questioning tradition; in part, it is also seen as a tool to strengthen it. Constitutions may entrench universal values, but they typically also give expression to particularist ones, thus restating the distinct foundations of the polity and sometimes allowing for a deepening of the national community through attachment to common values and institutions. This provides the link to that other central element of modern political theory, the idea of the nation, and helps integrate the polity over time, leading to greater stability of its institutions.[10] In more liberal terms, this stabilizing and integrating function is captured in diagnoses of an emerging 'constitutional patriotism'.[11]

This may be an ideal characterization of what constitutions and constitutionalism may embody, but it is easy to see why it has given them sufficient appeal to become such central elements of modern politics and political theory. And it is clear why it would be a crucial resource for thinking about, and constructing, institutions beyond the nation-state. After all, the institutional structure at the global level today often appears just as accidental, as 'monstrous'[12] as that of

---

[8] Ackerman, Bruce, *We the People: Foundations* (Cambridge, Mass.: Harvard University Press, 1993).

[9] Klein, Claude, 'Pourquoi écrit-on une constitution?', in Troper, M. and L. Jaume, eds., *1789 et l'invention de la constitution* (Brussels, Paris: Bruylant, 1994), 89–99 at 94–96.

[10] See, e.g., Grimm, Dieter, 'Integration by Constitution', 3 *International Journal of Constitutional Law* (2005) 193–208.

[11] See Mueller, Jan-Werner, *Constitutional Patriotism* (Princeton University Press, 2007).

[12] Severinus de Monzambano (Samuel von Pufendorf), *De Statu Imperii Germanici*. Nach dem ersten Druck mit Berücksichtigung der Ausgabe letzter Hand hrsg. von Fritz Salomon (Weimar: H. Böhlaus Nachfolger, 1910 [1667]) Chapter VI, §9.

early modernity which modern, revolutionary constitutionalism sought to overcome. Substituting reason and agency for historical force and material power in the design of global institutions must then appear just as urgent, and using constitutionalism to that end becomes an obvious choice. A global constitution could safeguard individual rights, hedge global governance in, and help popular sovereignty to catch up with, the expansion of the political space beyond state boundaries. And finally, it could crystallize the values of, and give shape to, an international community that so far has remained largely abstract.

In varying constellations, these themes dominate the burgeoning debate on postnational constitutionalism.[13] Many of the proposed constitutionalisms, both for the European and the global contexts, focus on one particular theme, often that of legalization, the limitation of powers and the entrenchment of individual rights.[14] Others emphasize the community-building, integrative function of constitutionalization, the commonality of values expressed in norms of a particular, elevated status in international law.[15] And yet others see the very fact of emerging hierarchies in the international legal order as a reflection of a move towards a constitution, towards a 'higher' law that frames and limits global politics.[16] Such visions, however, connect only partly to the domestic tradition of constitutionalism described above. They connect to a particular tradition, that of 'power-limiting' constitutionalism that has been strong in England and in nineteenth-century Germany, but in influence and appeal has since given way to the more comprehensive, foundational type of constitutionalism the American and French Revolutions have made prominent and that has found almost universal acceptance as a yardstick for governmental legitimacy.[17] By

---

[13] For a survey, see Walker, Neil, 'Taking Constitutionalism Beyond the State', 56 *Political Studies* (2008) 519–543.

[14] See the overview of such approaches in Klabbers, Jan, 'Constitutionalism Lite', 1 *International Organizations Law Review* (2004) 31–58 at 32–36.

[15] See, e.g., de Wet, Erika, 'The Emergence of International and Regional Value Systems as a Manifestation of an International Constitutional Order', 19 *Leiden Journal of International Law* (2006) 611–632.

[16] See, e.g., Peters, Anne, 'Compensatory Constitutionalism: The Function and Potential of Fundamental International Norms and Structures', 19 *Leiden Journal of International Law* 3 (2006) 579–610.

[17] On the two types, see Möllers, Christoph, 'Verfassunggebende Gewalt – Verfassung – Konstitutionalisierung', in Armin von Bogdandy, ed., *Europäisches Verfassungsrecht* (Berlin, Heidelberg: Springer, 2003), 1–57 at 3–18.

insisting on a constitution as the comprehensive foundation of public power – not only a partial limitation – this foundational type combines the various dimensions of appeal in the domestic context, and it is this tradition that should therefore guide us in any effort at translating 'constitutionalism' into the postnational sphere.[18]

This foundational variant of constitutionalism will be my focus in this chapter, and it has also proved increasingly attractive in the practice and theory of postnational politics. The most tangible result has been the European Constitutional Treaty, which was seen as an opportunity to place the European Union on a new foundation and open up stronger legitimacy resources; among theorists, Jürgen Habermas, for example, explicitly defends a vision of foundational constitutionalism for Europe.[19] On the global level, the United Nations Charter has been reinterpreted by some as a constitutional document, towering above and framing other regimes of global governance as well as individual states.[20] More broadly, though, such a tendency is visible in a multiplicity of approaches that seek to give the current, largely unstructured, historically accidental and power-driven order of global governance a rational, justifiable shape in which the powers of institutions and their relationships with one another are clearly delimited.

Such approaches are widespread among political theorists and legal scholars alike. A good example is David Held's quasi-federal vision of the global order.[21] Held envisions a political structure in which all those affected by a particular issue have a right to participate in decisions on it; combined with a principle of subsidiarity, this results in a layered setup of institutions with a distribution of powers among the different levels that resembles federal states. He acknowledges that this distribution of powers will – as in many national contexts – often be contested and complex to resolve, but in his view, a resolution in a public setting based on an overarching principle is preferable to leaving them 'to

---

[18] For a more detailed argument to this effect, see Krisch, Nico, *Beyond Constitutionalism: The Pluralist Structure of Postnational Law* (Oxford University Press, 2010), Chapter 2.

[19] Habermas, Jürgen, *The Postnational Constellation*, trans. M. Pensky (Cambridge, Mass.: MIT Press, 2001), Chapter 4.

[20] Fassbender, Bardo, 'The United Nations Charter as Constitution of the International Community', 36 *Columbia Journal of Transnational Law* (1998) 529–619.

[21] Held, David, *Democracy and the Global Order: From the Modern State to Cosmopolitan Governance* (Cambridge: Polity Press, 1995).

powerful geopolitical interests (dominant states) or market based organizations to resolve them alone'.[22] In good constitutionalist fashion, a principled construction of the global institutional order is thus presented as an antidote to power, history and chance.[23]

5.2.2 Constitutionalism and postnational society

Such grand designs are appealing for their readiness to disregard the vagaries of the current, path-dependent, often accidental shape of global governance and their attempt to realize human agency in the construction of common institutions. In that sense, they do indeed recapture the spirit of the early constitutionalists of the American and French Revolutions, so neatly reflected in Hegel's dictum that never before 'had it been perceived that man's existence centres in his head, *i.e.* in Thought, inspired by which he builds up the world of reality'.[24] Postnational constitutionalism seems to be the tool to institutionalize precepts of transboundary, global justice and thus enrich the common values of international society and further its integration into a common polity of mankind.

Yet it is this integrationist, universalizing tendency that also provokes concerns for its potential disconnect with social realities. For Habermas, for example, the preconditions for the collective exercise of public autonomy, a central element of foundational constitutionalism, are simply lacking in the current, diverse international society, forcing us to limit our aspirations.[25] And for Iris Young, the idea of common political institutions to tackle problems of global justice, as attractive as it might be in the abstract, stands in tension with the allegiances of

---

[22] Held, David, 'Democratic Accountability and Effectiveness from a Cosmopolitan Perspective', 39 *Government & Opposition* (2004) 365–391 at 382.

[23] For similar proposals see, e.g., Young, Iris Marion, *Inclusion and Democracy* (Oxford University Press, 2000), Chapter 7; and among legal scholars, Kumm, Mattias, 'The Legitimacy of International Law: A Constitutionalist Framework of Analysis', 15 *European Journal of International Law* (2004) 907–931.

[24] Hegel, G. W. F., *The Philosophy of History*, trans. J. Sibree (Buffalo: Prometheus Books, 1991), at 447 (Part IV, Section III, Chapter III).

[25] Habermas, Jürgen, *Der gespaltene Westen* (Frankfurt am Main: Suhrkamp, 2004), Chapter 8. Habermas only sees potential for 'power-limiting', rather than foundational, constitutionalism at the global scale; see page 138.

individuals to their particular, mostly national, communities and their ensuing claims for self-determination.[26]

It is indeed the divided character of the global polity that poses the greatest challenge to the globalization of constitutionalism. After all, international society is characterized by a high degree of diversity and contestation, and even the small signs of increasing convergence that we can observe are by no means unambiguous. Diversity may today not be as radical as it was in the 1970s, when Hedley Bull's vision of an anarchical society within a pluralist international order appeared as highly plausible, given the deep-seated frictions between West and East and North and South.[27] Today, we can find indications of a stronger solidaristic, perhaps even cosmopolitan turn in greater agreement on fundamental principles, such as basic human rights, and in a much higher degree of institutionalization of policy- and law-making beyond the state.[28] Whether this warrants the diagnosis of an emerging 'international community', however, is still questionable,[29] and it certainly is if we think of such a community as one that its members rank supreme in the sense that they accept global solutions to problems as trumping those of other communities (regional, national, subnational). Allegiance to national communities may have been complemented by those of a local, religious, ideological nature, some of them with a clear transnational, perhaps even cosmopolitan, tinge, and this may have led to a world of multiple rather than exclusive loyalties, and to a variety of foundational discourses competing for dominance.[30] But cultural, ideological, religious and political diversity remains strong and is often coupled with an insistence on ultimate authority on the national level – reflecting a vision of the international order as one of intergovernmental negotiation and exchange rather than an expression of

---

[26] Young, *Inclusion* (2000). Young seeks to respond through a federal-style model that is 'jurisdictionally open'; I will return to this theme below.

[27] Bull, Hedley, *The Anarchical Society* (London: Macmillan, 1977).

[28] See Hurrell, Andrew, *On Global Order* (Oxford University Press, 2007), Chapters 3 and 4.

[29] See Paulus, Andreas, *Die internationale Gemeinschaft im Völkerrecht* (München: C. H. Beck, 2001).

[30] Sandel, Michael, *Democracy's Discontent* (Cambridge, Mass., Harvard University Press, 1996), at 338–351; Dryzek, John, *Deliberative Global Politics* (Cambridge: Polity Press, 2006), Chapter 1; see also Bohman, James, *Democracy across Borders* (Cambridge, Mass.: MIT Press, 2007), at 28–36.

a deeper common project.[31] Even in the European Union, where diversity is clearly weaker than in a global context, allegiance to national communities still trumps that to Europe by a large margin.[32] And identities seem to become more rather than less fragmented as European integration proceeds. As Peter Katzenstein and Jeffrey Checkel note:

The number of unambiguously committed Europeans (10–15% of the total population) is simply too small for the emergence of a strong cultural European sense of belonging. The number of committed nationalists (40–50% of the total) is also too small for a hegemonic reassertion of nationalist sentiments. The remaining part of the population (35–40% of the total) holds to primarily national identifications that also permit an element of European identification.[33]

All this may not be fatal to the postnational constitutionalist project; after all, just as attempts have been undertaken to move from democracy to 'demoicracy',[34] we might come to imagine a constitutionalism on a plurinational basis.[35] But such an undertaking faces serious challenges based on critiques that have for long highlighted the difficulties modern constitutionalism has had in diverse societies. James Tully's is one of the most prominent among them. For Tully, modern constitutionalism as it has emerged with the American and French Revolutions – and has framed much of political thought ever since – cannot cope with serious social and cultural diversity because of its strong link to ideas of impartiality and uniformity.[36] Given its roots in the Enlightenment, it seeks to erect a regular, well-structured framework of government

---

[31] See Hurrell, *On Global Order* (2007), Chapter 5.

[32] See Fligstein, Neil, *Euroclash: The EU, European Identity, and the Future of Europe* (Oxford University Press, 2008), Chapter 5; Caporaso, James A. and Min-Hyung Kim, 'The Dual Nature of European Identity: Subjective Awareness and Coherence', 16 *Journal of European Public Policy* (2009) 19–42 at 23–30.

[33] Katzenstein, Peter J. and Jeffrey T. Checkel, 'Conclusion – European Identity in Context', in J. T. Checkel and P. J. Katzenstein, eds., *European Identity* (Cambridge University Press, 2009), 213–27 at 215–16. For a very similar assessment see Fligstein, *Euroclash* (2008), at 250.

[34] E.g. Bohman, *Democracy* (2007); Nicolaidis, Kalypso, 'We, the Peoples of Europe . . .', 83 *Foreign Affairs* 6 (November/December 2004) 97–110.

[35] E.g. Tierney, Stephen, *Constitutional Law and National Pluralism* (Oxford University Press, 2004).

[36] Tully, James, *Strange Multiplicity: Constitutionalism in an Age of Diversity*, (Cambridge University Press, 1995), Chapters 2 and 3.

based on reason and distinct from the irregular, historically grown structures that characterized previous eras. In this uniformity, however, it fails to reflect the different customs and culturally grounded ideas of particular groups in society; and this even more so if these groups do not subscribe to the liberal vision of a 'modern', free individual, able and willing to transcend her history and culture and ready to engage with all others in an unconditional deliberation over the course of the common polity. The impartiality sought through such mechanisms as Rawls's veil of ignorance or Habermas's adoption of the interlocutor's perspective only makes sense if individuals are ready to leave particular allegiances behind; for all others, it means exclusion from the supposedly neutral frame.[37]

For Tully then, the integrationist, universalizing tendencies of foundational constitutionalism sit uneasily with the diverse identities of individuals in divided societies; the emphasis on common values and self-government by a shared, overarching collective stands in tension with their diverging allegiances. Historically, the tension may have been resolved by policies of nation-building which, over time, succeeded in overcoming linguistic and cultural divides but involved measures of forced assimilation that today would be regarded as grave violations of human rights. Such forcible integration would in any event be hardly conceivable in international society. For constitutionalism to remain attractive as a model for the global polity, it would thus have to find other ways to cope with that polity's deep diversity.

5.2.3 *The constitutionalist accommodation of diversity*

Tully accuses modern constitutionalism of creating an 'empire of uniformity', but in this he fails to appreciate the many ways in which it has come to respond to the challenges of divided societies. It may have started out as a quest for a reasoned, uniform order, and as we have seen, much of its appeal derives from this aspiration. Also today, many constitutional states pursue integrationist aims, build common institutions and seek to 'privatize' diversity, relying on individual rights to

---

[37] For related critiques, see, e.g., Sandel, Michael J., 'The Procedural Republic and the Unencumbered Self', 12 *Political Theory* (1984) 81–96; Taylor, Charles, 'The Politics of Recognition', in *Philosophical Arguments* (Cambridge, Mass., Harvard University Press, 1995), 225–256.

accommodate differences in ways of life.[38] But while this is often seen as
a suitable solution in societies that are characterized by cross-cutting
cleavages, it is more problematic where the divides are stable and fairly
unidimensional and thus lead to structural minorities with little hope
for sharing power in common institutions. Responses to such situations
typically eschew strong integrationist ideals and seek instead to deal
with diversity through accommodation, mainly in the form of consociationalism and/or devolution.[39] It is such responses to diversity that a
postnational constitutionalism might be able to draw on for inspiration.

5.2.3.1 Consociationalism and federalism

Consociationalism is characterized by an insistence on common
decision-making: prominent in a number of smaller European countries
especially in the post-war period and later adopted in several other
settings, consociationalism seeks to manage deep disagreement through
executive power sharing and the creation of veto positions for minority
groups.[40] These force all actors to reach common ground rather than
impose their views on the others; none of the constituencies enjoys
formal primacy. The precise institutional arrangements may vary, as
do the mechanisms to determine the relevant groups, but central to
consociationalism is the assumption that societal groups should not
only be granted autonomy rights as regards their own cultural and
linguistic affairs but should also enjoy a particular, protected position
in the central decision-making structure of the state. Otherwise, con-
sociationalists believe, those groups will be at a permanent disadvan-
tage in the struggle over common policies, and ever greater antagonism
and conflict are likely to ensue.[41]

---

[38] For a theoretical defence, see Barry, Brian, *Culture and Equality: An Egalitarian Critique of Multiculturalism* (Cambridge, Mass.: Harvard University Press, 2002).

[39] See the survey of the debate in McGarry, J., B. O'Leary and R. Simeon, 'Integration or Accommodation? The Enduring Debate in Conflict Regulation', in Sujit Choudhry, ed., *Constitutional Design for Divided Societies: Integration or Accommodation?* (Oxford University Press, 2008), 41–88; see also Tierney, *Constitutional Law* (2004).

[40] See Lijphart, Arend, *Democracy in Plural Societies* (New Haven: Yale University Press, 1978); *Thinking About Democracy: Power Sharing and Majority Rule in Theory and Practice* (London: Routledge, 2008).

[41] But see also the critiques, e.g. Horowitz, Donald, 'Constitutional Design: Proposals Versus Processes', in A. Reynolds, ed., *The Architecture of Democracy:*

Federalist responses, on the other hand, focus less on central, common decision-making and emphasize instead the need to devolve as many state functions as possible to the groups that make up society. This can occur in the form of territorial pluralism, in which those functions are exercised by federal units that largely follow the lines of inter-group boundaries.[42] Such an approach can be combined with consociationalist, co-decision arrangements at the federal level, but it is feasible only if the relevant groups are territorially concentrated. Moreover, it does not require fully federal states but can instead involve asymmetrical arrangements, granting minority groups particular powers beyond those of majority groups because the latter find sufficient representation in central decision-making processes. However, when groups are territorially dispersed, devolution has to follow personal rather than territorial lines and is accordingly more limited in its extent; it typically focuses on group rights to govern cultural and educational affairs.

On the postnational level, as most divides follow territorial lines, both consociationalism and territorial federalism, or a combination of both, may provide resources for the accommodation of diversity. This may alleviate some of the concerns raised by Tully, as uniformity would be less at the centre of the constitutionalist project than in its classical variety. However, it might also dilute the appeal of the project that, as we have seen, has originally drawn precisely on the virtues of reason, order and collective decision-making. The accommodationist response to diversity, though perhaps inevitable, may thus involve serious trade-offs.

5.2.3.2 Trade-offs

The most obvious such trade-off concerns the integrative force of constitutionalism and the stability that is seen to flow from it. Foundational constitutionalism is typically regarded as a potent tool to integrate society, by creating a common framework as an expression of both common values and collective decision-making processes. The need to

Constitutional Design, Conflict Management, and Democracy (Oxford University Press, 2002), 15–36; Barry, Brian, 'Political Accommodation and Consociational Democracy', 5 *British Journal of Political Science* (1975) 477–505.

[42] See, e.g., the discussion in McGarry, O'Leary and Simeon, 'Integration or Accommodation?', 2008), at 63–67.

find common solutions does indeed seem to lead typically to an attenu-
ation of diversity, while accommodationist approaches may help
entrench the boundaries between different groups and are often seen
as widening, rather than closing the gaps in society, thus creating
greater instability and potentially leading to secession or break-up.[43]
Yet in deeply divided societies, the option of integrationist policies
rarely exists; minority groups are typically not ready to agree to them
for fear of losing out to the majority. And if integration is pursued
despite such opposition, it will typically lead to greater friction, resistance
and instability of the overall constitutional structure. Accommodation
may not come with the full stabilizing promise of the original, more
unitary strain of foundational constitutionalism, but there is little alternative to it when divisions run deep.[44]

The second trade-off concerns the effectiveness of collective decision-
making. As I have sketched above, constitutionalism draws much of its
appeal from the realization of public autonomy over collective affairs in
the face of forces of history and chance. But by many, especially majority groups, accommodation may be seen precisely as a surrender to such
forces. Even if normatively justified,[45] it often comes to be seen as a
respect for difference that is based on historically grown, passion-based
allegiances quite in contrast with detached, reasoned construction. And
accommodationist approaches may dilute the promise of public
autonomy on yet another level. Because consociationalism emphasizes
the commonality of decision-making and, as a result, veto rights of
minority groups, it runs the risk of institutionalizing blockade: it
might lead to a 'joint-decision trap'[46] and thus limit collective decision-
making capacity significantly. For the greater the number of groups in
society (and in postnational society the number is bound to be high), the

---

[43] See, e.g., Pildes, Richard H., 'Ethnic Identity and Democratic Institutions: A
Dynamic Perspective', in Sujit Choudhry, ed., *Constitutional Design for Divided
Societies: Integration or Accommodation?* (Oxford University Press, 2008),
173–201.

[44] McGarry, O'Leary and Simeon, 'Integration or Accommodation?', 2008), at
85–87.

[45] For normative defences of group rights, see Kymlicka, Will, *Multicultural
Citizenship* (Oxford: Clarendon Press, 1995); Torbisco Casals, Neus, *Group
Rights as Human Rights* (Dordrecht: Springer, 2006).

[46] Scharpf, Fritz, 'Die Politikverflechtungsfalle: Europäische Integration und
deutscher Föderalismus im Vergleich', 26 *Politische Vierteljahresschrift* (1985)
323–356 at 346–350.

greater the risk that collective negotiations collapse.[47] And if unanimity has to be achieved, policies will have to be pareto-optimal – they have to benefit each and every group – but this severely reduces the range of possible options and limits prospects of, for example, distributive justice.[48]

Another challenge that consociationalism poses to the ideal of public autonomy lies in the extent of individual participation in government.[49] One of the central elements of consociationalism is its reliance on the cooperation of *elites*: because on many issues genuine consensus among the different groups will be elusive, problem-solving requires bargaining, package-deals, log-rolling. This, however, can only be achieved by elites that stand in constant contact with each other and are socialized into cooperation. Stronger participation of the general public in the various groups renders this cooperation difficult because it is usually focused only on a particular decision, not the whole of the deal struck. Accordingly, as Lijphart stresses, '[i]t is [. . .] helpful if [leaders] possess considerable independent power and a secure position of leadership'.[50] Even though this is not incompatible with public participation in general, it considerably limits its scope.[51] And the introduction of further accountability mechanisms into the already difficult framework of negotiations on the postnational level would only aggravate the risk of a complete blockade of decision-making.

5.2.3.3 Remaining tensions

Yet even with such tools, and despite these trade-offs, the accommodation of diversity in foundational constitutionalism has limits. After all, if it wants to retain its central promise – to create a comprehensive framework for all public power in a given polity under the rule of law – constitutionalism has to ultimately resolve the tension between the sovereignty claims of both the federal and the group level, if only by defining rules for constitutional amendment. Visions of a federalism

---

[47] Accordingly, also for Lijphart consociational orders ideally operate with no more than four main groups; see Lijphart, *Democracy in Plural Societies* (1978), at 56.

[48] On such problems in the EU context, see, e.g., Scharpf, Fritz, 'The Joint-Decision Trap Revisited', 44 *Journal of Common Market Studies* (2006) 845–864 at 851.

[49] See, e.g., Dryzek, *Deliberative Global Politics* (2006), at 50–51.

[50] Lijphart, *Democracy in Plural Societies* (1978), at 50.

[51] For a nuanced account, see McGarry, O'Leary and Simeon, 'Integration or Accommodation?' (2008), at 82–84.

with 'suspended' ultimate authority, which were influential until the late nineteenth century, stand in conflict with this comprehensive ambition and find little reflection in contemporary federal orders.[52] This leaves foundational constitutionalism with two options: it either resolves the sovereignty question in favour of the groups, and their interaction remains a non-constitutionalist affair; it is that of a federation under international law. Or it resolves it in favour of the federal level (for example, by denying group vetos in amendment processes); it can then realize the constitutionalist promise to some extent, but this realization might remain formal as long as some groups actively contest the solution. One may only think of the Canadian constitutional crisis, provoked by Québec's insistence on a unilateral right to secede, throughout the 1980s and 1990s. The federal claim to define the rules for constitutional amendment (including the framework for secession) and thus to regulate the relationship with its constituent units, remained fragile in the face of resistance by a powerful minority – in fact, it antagonized this minority only further.[53] Unless the constitutionalist ambition to create a comprehensive framework meets matching societal conditions, such fragility is bound to continue, and the hope to create a constitutional framework *for* politics keeps being called into question by its dependence *on* politics.

Constitutionalism thus finds itself in a dilemma when faced with divided societies. It can retain its purity, pursue the integration of society and seek to level difference, but this is typically not only normatively problematic but also practically impossible; it may enflame tensions rather than calm them. However, the alternative – accommodation – also comes at a high cost: as we have seen, it diminishes the constitutionalist promise in so far as it reduces the potential for long-term social stability, for public autonomy and often enough also for the rule of law. After all, in order to remain true to its core, constitutionalism has to maintain the idea of a comprehensive framework that assigns different

---

[52] See Schütze, Robert, 'Federalism as Constitutional Pluralism: Sovereignty Suspended', unpublished manuscript (on file with Krisch) (2009); Oeter, Stefan, 'Föderalismus', in Armin von Bogdandy, ed., *Europäisches Verfassungsrecht* (Berlin, Heidelberg: Springer, 2003), 59–119 at 76–92.

[53] Choudhry, Sujit, 'Does the world need more Canada? The Politics of the Canadian Model in Constitutional Politics and Political Theory', in Choudhry, ed., *Constitutional Design for Divided Societies: Integration or Accommodation?* (Oxford University Press, 2008), 141–172 at 159–171.

organs and groups their places. And this requires hierarchies that all too often might stand in tension with the (diverging) claims of different parts of society.

This element of hierarchy brings me back to Tully's critique I have mentioned above. After what we have seen in this section, this critique seems overdrawn in its attack on constitutionalism's 'empire of uniformity' – constitutionalist thought and practice certainly know more ways of accommodating difference than Tully gives credit for. But he is right in pointing to the fact that the supposed commonality of the constitutional project requires members of the 'nation' to recognize it as the *primary* political framework, taking precedence over whatever other structures might exist in sub-groups. It presupposes the acceptance of a priority of the common over the particular (typically within limits of human rights) – an acceptance we might not find among distinct cultural groups within states, and certainly not among states vis-à-vis the 'common' European or global realm. This emphasis on the collective, the common framework, poses not only normative problems from the perspective of minority groups, but it may also aggravate the tensions within society and thus create less rather than more stability. Sovereign authority is simply too precious, and the quest for it typically attracts pernicious contest and drives competing groups further apart.[54] But such a dynamic may be difficult to avoid in the binary, hierarchical structure of constitutionalism. We may thus have to consider eschewing principled, constitutional frameworks in such circumstances and instead work around societal divides in a more pragmatic fashion. As John Dryzek puts it, in some circumstances '[t]he peace is disturbed only by philosophers who believe a constitutional solution is required'.[55] If this is true in domestic societies with high degrees of diversity, it will be even more so in the postnational context.

5.3 The pluralist alternative

The challenge of societal diversity thus leaves constitutionalism in a quandary. The more it seeks to accommodate diversity, the more it loses its original appeal, and still, if it wants to maintain some of its promise, it has to uphold the ambition of forming a comprehensive framework, thus

---

[54] Dryzek, *Deliberative Global Politics* (2006), Chapter 3.
[55] Ibid., at 64.

creating tension with claims for ultimate authority from different sides. This creates a significant problem in our quest for a structuring model for the postnational space. As I suggested in Section 5.1, the classical model – the idea of an inter-national order in which ultimate authority lies with states – is unable to cope with the increasing enmeshment of levels of governance in today's globalized world. Constitutionalism, given its domestic pedigree and appeal, would have seemed the obvious candidate for succeeding it, but our discussion above indicates that it conflicts with the persistent diversity of the postnational polity. Yet how else could we conceive of the global legal and political order?

In this chapter, I want to examine (and eventually defend) an alternative model: pluralism. 'Pluralism' suggests a particular responsiveness to issues of diversity, and it might also sound appealing as a more positive approach to phenomena of fragmentation that, in the international law literature at least, have provoked considerable anxiety.[56] Yet pluralism has many meanings, and it can serve as a description of the shape and diversity of society, of substantive commitments in matters of rights or institutions, or of the structure of a polity's institutions. It is this last meaning that interests me most, as it operates on the same (structural) level as constitutionalism and may therefore provide a true alternative. Yet even here, the usage of pluralism varies widely. The differences could be seen as a matter of degree – as between 'soft' and 'hard' or 'moderate' and 'radical' pluralism. Analytically, though, they are better captured as differences in kind, as between what may be termed 'institutional' and 'systemic' pluralism.

To illustrate this distinction, and to work out more clearly what could be an alternative model to the constitutionalist one, it is worth taking a closer look at Neil MacCormick's work, which has inspired much recent pluralist thinking.[57] MacCormick sought to theorize the impact of the conflicting supremacy claims of the national and Union levels in the European Union and came to regard the resulting legal structure as one in which both levels, as systemic units, had internally plausible claims to ultimate authority; their conflict was due to the fact that they did not

---

[56] See the analysis in Koskenniemi, Martti and Päivi Leino, 'Fragmentation of International Law? Postmodern Anxieties', 15 *Leiden Journal of International Law* (2002) 553–579.

[57] MacCormick, Neil, 'Beyond the Sovereign State', 56 *Modern Law Review* (1993) 1–18; 'The Maastricht-Urteil: Sovereignty Now', 1 *European Law Journal* (1995) 259–266.

agree on the ultimate point of reference from which they were arguing. For the national level, national constitutions remained the ultimate source of authority, and all exercises of public power (including by the EU) had to be traced back to them; for the EU, the EU treaty was seen as independent from, and superior to, national law including national constitutions. In MacCormick's view, there was thus no common legal framework that could have decided the conflict – the two views were (on a fundamental level) irreconcilably opposed; the two levels of law ran in parallel without subordination or external coordination. This description borrowed some of its ideas from sociological and anthropological accounts of legal pluralism that had become influential since the 1970s[58], but took the idea beyond the relationship of official and non-official law (or norms) that those studies were interested in and applied it to the co-existence of different official systems of law, all with their own *Grundnormen* or rules of recognition. In this sense, MacCormick's approach was one of 'systemic' (or in his words, 'radical') pluralism.[59]

Whether consciously or not, this approach had ancestors not only in medieval thought,[60] but also in the early theory and practice of federalism.[61] Especially the situation in the United States after the Constitution of 1787 had created an awareness that the classical categories – unitary state or federal union under international law – did not adequately reflect the character of federal polities. In the USA, the Constitution was described as 'neither a national nor a federal Constitution, but a composition of both',[62] and it certainly sought to balance the powers of the federal government and those of the states. More importantly perhaps, it left unsettled rival claims to ultimate authority: throughout the first half of the nineteenth century, such authority was claimed for both the

[58] See Moore, Sally F., 'Law and Social Change: The Semi-Autonomous Social Field as an Appropriate Subject of Study', 7 *Law and Society Review* (1973) 719–746; Griffiths, John, 'What is Legal Pluralism?', 24 *Journal of Legal Pluralism* (1986) 1–55; Merry, Sally Engle, 'Legal Pluralism', 22 *Law and Society Review* (1988) 869–896.

[59] See MacCormick, Neil, 'Risking Constitutional Collision in Europe?', 18 *Oxford Journal of Legal Studies* (1998) 517–532 at 528–532.

[60] Berman, Harold J., *Law and Revolution: The Formation of the Western Legal Tradition* (Cambridge, Mass.: Harvard University Press, 1983), 115–119.

[61] Schütze, 'Federalism' (2009); see also Beaud, Olivier, *Théorie de la Fédération* (Paris: Presses Universitaires de France, 2007).

[62] Madison, James, *Federalist* no. 39 in Hamilton, A., J. Madison and J. Jay, *The Federalist Papers*, ed. L. Goldman (Oxford University Press, 2008), 192 .

federal and the state levels, and the contest was eventually decided only through the civil war.[63] In Europe, parallel conceptions existed (and were influential until the late nineteenth century[64]), and it was Carl Schmitt who later captured them most cogently in his theory of federal union by placing the undecided, 'suspended' character of ultimate authority at its centre.[65]

If Neil MacCormick initially envisioned the EU in a similar way, he softened his account considerably in his later work. Mindful of the risk of friction and collision inherent in an unregulated parallelism of different orders, he came to see a greater potential for coordination in the overarching framework of international law. 'Pluralism under international law', as he terms it, is in fact a monist conception, but one that assigns EU law and domestic constitutional law equal positions and does not subordinate one to the other as a matter of principle.[66] This has been criticized for taking the edge out of the approach, and analytically it is indeed categorically distinct from the systemic pluralism MacCormick had initially diagnosed. It accepts pluralism not on the systemic level, but only in the institutional structure – different parts of one order operate on a basis of coordination, in the framework of common rules but without a clearly defined hierarchy, in a form of what I would call 'institutional pluralism'. The tamed nature of this variant can be glanced when considering other articulations of it, for example Daniel Halberstam's account of 'interpretive pluralism' under the US Constitution. Pluralism, in this view, denotes the fact that the authority to interpret the United States Constitution is ultimately undefined, and that in the extreme case three organs compete for it – Congress, the President, and the Supreme Court.[67] This may indeed lead at times

---

[63] See Amar, Akil R., 'Of Sovereignty and Federalism', 96 *Yale Law Journal* (1987) 1425–1520 at 1429–1466.

[64] See, e.g., Oeter, Stefan, 'Souveränität und Demokratie als Probleme in der "Verfassungsentwicklung" der Europäischen Union', 55 *Zeitschrift für ausländisches öffentliches Recht und Völkerrecht* (1995), 659–707 at 664–670; Stolleis, Michael, *Geschichte des öffentlichen Rechts in Deutschland*, vol. 2 (München: Verlag C. H. Beck, 1992), at 365–368.

[65] Schmitt, Carl, *Verfassungslehre* (9th edn, Berlin: Duncker & Humblot, 1993 [1928]), at 371–375.

[66] MacCormick, 'Risking Constitutional Collision' (1998).

[67] Halberstam, Daniel, 'Constitutional Heterarchy: The Centrality of Conflict in the European Union and the United States', in Jeffrey L. Dunoff and Joel P. Trachtman, eds., *Constitutionalism, International Law and Global Government* (Cambridge University Press, 2009), 326–355.

to similar political dynamics as in instances of systemic pluralism such as the EU where *Grundnormen* themselves diverge. In particular, as Halberstam points out, the actors in both cases may have recourse to comparable sources of political authority to bolster their claims.[68] But such similarities should not conceal the crucial difference that lies in the fact that interpretive pluralism operates with respect to a common point of reference – constitutional norms that form a background framework and lay the ground for arguments about authority – while in systemic pluralism such a common point of reference *within* the legal or institutional structure is lacking. In Halberstam's example, conflict might not be fully regulated but it occurs in a bounded legal and political universe that contains (some) resources for its solution. Practically, the extent of this difference will depend on how thick the common framework is – in this respect, institutional and systemic pluralism may differ only gradually. If foundational constitutionalism and systemic pluralism mark the extremes of a continuum, institutional pluralism may occupy some place in the middle. Analytically, however, the difference between institutional and systemic pluralism is one in kind, defined by the presence *vel* absence of a common frame of reference.

Other pluralist approaches to postnational law follow a similarly institutionalist route. Mattias Kumm's 'cosmopolitan constitutionalism', for example, presents itself as pluralist as it does not seek to construct firm hierarchies between different levels of law.[69] But this pluralism is embedded in a thick set of overarching norms, such as subsidiarity, due process or democracy, that are meant to direct the solution of conflicts. There may be no one institution to settle disputes, and thus such disputes may, as a matter of fact, remain undecided for a long time. This, however, is typical enough for all kinds of constitutional structures – after all, law or constitutions can never determine the outcome of conflicts, but only offer certain (institutional, normative) resources for their solution. Kumm's proposal may indeed be institutionally pluralist, but structurally it retains (as its self-description as

---

[68] Ibid.

[69] See Kumm, Mattias, 'The Cosmopolitan Turn in Constitutionalism: On the Relationship between Constitutionalism in and beyond the State', in Jeffrey L. Dunoff and Joel P. Trachtman, eds., *Constitutionalism, International Law and Global Government* (Cambridge University Press, 2009), 258–324; see also Kumm, 'Legitimacy' (2004).

cosmopolitan *constitutionalism* suggests) a constitutionalist character: in his vision, it is rules of 'hard law' – constitutional rules – that guide and contain conflict resolution. To use another example, Paul Schiff Berman situates his own approach clearly on the pluralist rather than the constitutionalist side[70] and his account of the hybrid and contested nature of the global legal order is close to the systemic pluralism we see in the earlier work of MacCormick. Yet his discussion of the forms that may allow managing the resulting conflicts recalls the instruments by which constitutionalist models seek to accommodate diversity: limited autonomy regimes or subsidiarity principles reflect devolutionist ideas, while hybrid-participation regimes are close to models of consociation-alism as set out in Section 5.2.[71] Just as the later MacCormick, Schiff Berman seems to become afraid of the 'messy' picture he describes and clings to some degree of institutionalized harmony.

Harmony is also a prominent aim in another, more ambiguous take on postnational pluralism, that of Miguel Poiares Maduro.[72] Maduro seeks to contain the risk of friction that results from the conflicting claims of national and EU law by introducing, as part of his idea of a 'counterpunctual law', a requirement for both levels to strive for coher-ence and integrity in the overall order. The formal status of this obliga-tion remains open, and so does the nature of the resulting, common European order: the emphasis on commonality might suggest a tamed, 'institutional' pluralism, but the character of the coherence requirement can also be interpreted in a more radical fashion, as merely a moral requirement for the different actors to show respect to each other, to display an orientation towards cooperation rather than conflict. In this reading, it could be seen as a conflict-of-laws approach, much closer to systemic pluralism.

Conflict-of-laws ideas are sometimes used to infuse an ethos of rec-ognition and respect into the rules that define the relationships of differ-ent levels of law in the postnational order. Christian Joerges takes this

---

[70] Schiff Berman, Paul, 'Global Legal Pluralism', 80 *Southern California Law Review* (2007) 1155–1237.

[71] Ibid., at 1196–1235.

[72] Maduro, Miguel, 'Europe and the Constitution: What If This Is As Good As It Gets?', in J. H. H. Weiler and M. Wind, eds., *European Constitutionalism Beyond the State* (Cambridge University Press, 2003), 74–102; 'Contrapunctual Law: Europe's Constitutional Pluralism in Action', in Neil Walker, ed., *Sovereignty in Transition* (Oxford University Press, 2003), 501–538.

path, but it largely remains within a constitutional mindset, as it defines merely the substantive content of a framework that remains shared.[73] Yet a conflict-of-laws model can also be seen as an architectural inspiration: as an inspiration to manage conflicts between different legal suborders not through overarching rules but through reliance on the capacity of those suborders to define adequate rules for mutual engagement. As in traditional conflict-of-laws, certain issues could then be subject to more than one set of rules, and the different legal subsystems would seek to define for themselves when to claim authority or cede it to another level. This forms the basis of the approach of Andreas Fischer-Lescano and Gunther Teubner: for them, the global legal order is irredeemably pluralist as the functional differentiation of society is reproduced (though not directly reflected) in a differentiation of legal subsystems, all with their own particular rationalities.[74] Interactions occur in network fashion, through interfaces defined by each subsystem in reaction to its environment, but without the hope for an overarching framework that would structure their relationships; too divergent are their own inner logics. Fischer-Lescano and Teubner's is a systemic pluralism without compromise or melancholical remnants of a constitutional structure, but it is also one in which the inevitability of social forces reigns and emancipatory ideas find little, if any, institutional home. If Martti Koskenniemi's critique that 'pluralism ceases to pose demands on the world'[75] fits anywhere, then here.

One does not have to be a follower of systems theory, though, to interpret the postnational legal order as systemically pluralist; in fact, many such accounts are driven by sociological observation based on actors and agency. Thus, Francis Snyder's analysis of global legal pluralism is based on the emergence and development of a plurality of 'sites of governance' through the strategic action of economic players across boundaries.[76] And Boaventura de Sousa Santos's approach starts

---

[73] Joerges, Christian, 'Rethinking the Supremacy of European Law', *European University Institute Working Paper LAW No. 2005/12* (2005); 'Conflict of Laws as Constitutional Form: Reflections on International Trade Law and the *Biotech* Panel Report', *RECON Online Working Paper 2007/3* (2007).

[74] Fischer-Lescano, Andreas and Guenther Teubner, *Regime-Kollisionen: Zur Fragmentierung des globalen Rechts* (Frankfurt am Main: Suhrkamp, 2006).

[75] Koskenniemi, Martti, 'The Fate of International Law: Between Technique and Politics', 70 *Modern Law Review* (2007) 1–30 at 23.

[76] Snyder, Francis, 'Governing Economic Globalisation: Global Legal Pluralism and European Law', 5 *European Law Journal* (1999) 334–374.

from the uses of law by actors, including social movements, in the interstices between normative orders where different sets of norms conflict and can be played out against each other.[77]

Here is not the place to enter into a discussion of the relative value of these analytical approaches; the aim of this section was merely to gain greater conceptual clarity about the options at our disposal when thinking about alternatives to constitutionalism. And as we have seen, the 'institutionalist' variant of pluralism represents less an alternative to than a continuation of constitutionalist themes: even though its different expressions in the literature all focus on diversity and contestation, they see this contestation as contained in a common, constitutional framework. In that, they resemble closely the accommodationist variants of constitutionalism discussed in Section 5.2, and they are likely to share the latter's problems.

In contrast, systemic pluralism has emerged as a distinct alternative that eschews a common framework in favour of a decentred management of diversity. This differs from constitutionalism, but also from the classical dualist approach that has dominated debates about the relationship between national and international law for long. For dualism was built on the idea that those two legal orders were clearly separate – the domestic order applied inside the state whereas the international order regulated states in their mutual interactions. Pluralism instead responds to the increasing enmeshment of different layers of law and acknowledges that a relationship may be governed by competing rules from a number of them. In this vision, domestic and international law also do not exhaust the range of competing layers – other regionally, personally or functionally defined layers may complement them. Thus while dualism focuses on two separate spheres and their relationship, pluralism deals with interactions among multiple, enmeshed orders.

---

[77] de Sousa Santos, Boaventura, *Toward a New Legal Common Sense* (2nd edn, London: Butterworths, 2002); 'Beyond Neoliberal Governance: The World Social Forum as Subaltern Cosmopolitan Politics and Legality', in B. de Sousa Santos and C. A. Rodríguez-Garavito, eds., *Law and Globalization from Below* (Cambridge University Press, 2005), 29–63. See also Rajagopal, Balakrishnan, 'Limits of Law in Counter-hegemonic Globalization: The Indian Supreme Court and the Narmada Valley Struggle', in B. de Sousa Santos and C. A. Rodríguez-Garavito, eds., *Law and Globalization from Below* (Cambridge University Press, 2005), 183–217.

Pluralism may thus be a distinct concept, but whether it is also normatively appealing is another matter. Most accounts of pluralism in postnational law are of an analytical kind, and even those who highlight its
normative virtues typically emphasize the risk of friction it entails.[78] And
from the perspective of most modern political theory, the irregularity of
pluralist structures must appear as diametrically opposed to a reasoned,
justifiable structure of government.[79] The risk that pluralism represents
no more than a transitional, perhaps (for the time being) inevitable
digression from a good order is therefore real. But as I will try to show
in the remainder of the chapter, seeing systemic pluralism in these terms
would downplay the features that make it attractive in a postnational
space that, after all, looks very different from the world of the nation-
state constitutionalism has so effectively come to inhabit.

5.4 Pluralist virtues

Most of the interest in pluralism in postnational law has, as I have just
mentioned, focused on the analytical aspect rather than the normative
case, and much of it has been accompanied by that systems-theoretical
sense of inevitability that sees pluralism largely as an unavoidable
consequence of the dynamics of society.[80] Yet once beyond that sentiment, the literature offers three main strands of normative arguments
for pluralism (or intimations thereof). One highlights the capacity for
adaptation, the second the space for contestation pluralism provides,
the third its usefulness for building checks and balances into the postnational order. All three strands capture important aspects of pluralism's
appeal, but as will become clear, they are ultimately insufficient to
ground a pluralist order in and of themselves.

5.4.1 Adaptation

As any order based on law, constitutionalism is in a constant tension
with changing social circumstances. Whatever view one holds on the

---

[78] E.g. Maduro, 'Europe and the Constitution' (2003).
[79] Allott, Philip, 'Epilogue: Europe and the dream of reason', in J. H. H. Weiler and
M. Wind, eds., *European Constitutionalism Beyond the State* (Cambridge
University Press, 2003), 202–225.
[80] See Fischer-Lescano and Teubner, *Regime-Kollisionen* (2006).

methods of constitutional interpretation, written text, judicial precedent or previous constitutional moments will always play an important,
sometimes the decisive, role.[81] Whether in a stronger or weaker form, a
constitution always ties a polity to its past and thus creates tensions in
the present.

Pluralism promises to relax such ties, to allow for adaptation to new
circumstances in a more rapid and less formalised way: by leaving the
relationships between legal suborders undetermined, it keeps them open
to political redefinition over time. Whether or not this is advisable in
domestic politics, it certainly has some appeal in the postnational space.
Here, social and political relations are much more in flux, ideas about
political justice are constantly shifting and our imagination of what
governance arrangements may be feasible keeps changing. This means
on the one hand that rules we might formulate today may soon look
outdated because of a change of our normative sentiments or an
expanded horizon of institutional options. On the other hand, such
rules may soon seem anachronistic because of a change in the structure
of society. All constitutions are as much expressions of abstract normative values as they are reflections of a particular social structure, and
they tend to stabilize and immunize that structure. For example, in the
elaboration of a postnational constitution we would currently operate
under the constraint that beyond the state social cohesion and communicative structures are such that we have to ground democracy in something other than the classical idea of a relatively unitary postnational
'people' and that we would have to give significant weight to national
democratic deliberations in order to legitimize postnational decision-
making. This constraint, however, may ease over time, particularly in
contexts of strong integration like the European Union,[82] and if this
happened it would open up manifold new procedural and institutional
possibilities. Exploiting these possibilities would be much easier in an
order in which the old structure is not inscribed in institutional settings
that defy informal change. Think only of the equality of US states in the
Senate: whereas in the late eighteenth century, population differences

---

[81] This is obvious in originalist approaches, but even for a theory that places as
much emphasis on moral theory as Ronald Dworkin's, the dimension of 'fit' with
history continues to provide a central anchor; see Dworkin, R., *Law's Empire*
(Cambridge, Mass.: Harvard University Press, 1986).

[82] For one vision of such a trajectory, see Habermas, *Postnational Constellation*,
(2001).

among states were small enough to make such a solution allowable, they have now grown to proportions that place the institutional structure under significant strain. Because of the high hurdles for adaptation, though, change is most unlikely to happen.[83]

All constitutional settings, including domestic ones, face this challenge of adaptation, but it is particularly pronounced in the postnational context where, to measure by today's standards, the speed and magnitude of social and institutional change are much greater than in most domestic settings. Freezing particular solutions in constitutional form then risks rendering them soon obsolete or even positively harmful; keeping institutional settings flexible in a pluralist structure may be the better option.

Such an argument may gain particular force because of the divided character of postnational society. As we have seen above, most constitutionalist responses to this fact involve institutional structures that accommodate but thereby also stabilize societal divides. This is most pronounced in consociationalist settings where rights that attach to particular groups are likely to reinforce existing group divides and maintain them even if individuals' identities change.[84] As Richard Pildes has recently emphasized, in divided societies adaptability and dynamism are primary virtues of institutional settlements as they allow for a reflection of changing social circumstances – more than particular institutional provisions at the outset, revisability may help reflect and further social integration over time.[85] And though he focuses on the (limited) options for adaptation that exist *within* a constitutional framework, choosing a pluralist setting instead might be a further-reaching step towards that aim.

Another virtue deriving from adaptability may be a greater capacity for learning. Charles Sabel has repeatedly argued that heterarchical networks and revisable rather than rigid norms facilitate processes of experimentation and mutual learning better than hierarchies with rigid norms.[86] Because they rely on the engagement and experiences of all

---

[83] Pildes, 'Ethnic Identity' (2008), at 174.

[84] For a survey of such claims, see McGarry, O'Leary and Simeon, 'Integration or Accommodation?' (2008), at 71–78.

[85] Pildes, 'Ethnic Identity' (2008), at 184–201.

[86] See, e.g., Sabel, Charles F. and Jonathan Zeitlin, 'Learning from Difference: The New Architecture of Experimentalist Governance in the EU', 14 *European Law Journal* (2008) 271–327.

actors, they are able to generate sounder insights than hierarchical organizations, and because of the easier revisability they are better able to respond to changes in both circumstances and knowledge. This holds especially when the regulatory landscape is characterized by great diversity and the issues at stake involve significant uncertainty and change at a quick pace. In postnational governance, the former is generally true and the latter in most areas, so pluralist, heterarchical structures may be particularly adequate here.

However, adaptability, transformative capacity and openness to learning have a downside: greater flexibility comes with the risk of a surrender to social forces.[87] It may be highly beneficial in benign circumstances, when the relevant actors show the required disposition for responding to argument and exchanging experiences and knowledge. Adaptability in the institutional structure may also be desirable when social change goes in the right direction (whichever that may be): then flexible structures will also change for the better rather than hold progress back. But none of this can be taken for granted; when shifts take an adverse direction and actors show less goodwill, more rigid forms may prove preferable. Pluralism's greater adaptability may thus be a virtue only in certain, potentially quite limited conditions.

5.4.2 Contestation

If the argument from adaptation is based on an optimistic view of the social environment and its trajectory, that from contestation starts from a more pessimistic one. It assumes that constitutional frameworks are typically elite products, expressions of power and social hegemony, and that the element of disruption and openness in a pluralist order may provide greater contestatory space for weaker actors.[88]

This argument can take a weak or a strong form. In its weak form, it is based on an appreciation of the *current* political constraints that attempts at postnational constitutionalization would face. After all, international politics remains dominated by intergovernmental bargaining in which the pursuit of states' self-interest on the basis of material power plays at least a prominent, perhaps the dominant

---

[87] See, e.g., the critique by Koskenniemi, 'Fate' (2007).
[88] Thus the emphasis on subaltern, alternative legalities in de Sousa Santos, *Toward a New Legal Common Sense* (2002), Chapters 3 and 9.

role.[89] As a result, current structures follow an unjust distribution of power to an inordinate extent, and efforts at reconceiving them in a constitutional fashion are bound to stabilize and reinforce the inequalities behind them – the rereading of the United Nations Charter as a constitution is a good example here.[90] But the current distribution of power also limits the options we could imagine to form part of a fresh constitutional settlement, and it certainly limits what we could hope to achieve in such a settlement – it may largely end up in an institutionalization of the preferences of the dominant actors of the day, as many large-scale attempts at institutionalization have before.[91] Even in the European Union, where the intergovernmental mode of operation may have been complemented by broader, transnational and civil-society-oriented politics to a greater extent than elsewhere, large-scale institutional change so far appears to have followed an intergovernmental logic, based on self-interest and power.[92] An explicit attempt at constitution-making may trigger a shift here, as it has with the establishment of the convention process leading up to the 2004 draft constitutional treaty. But even this convention seems to have operated largely in the shadow of what dominant players could be expected to agree to and thus may not have seriously challenged the intergovernmental mode.[93] For truly different (and fairer) processes, one might have to wait for a more radical transformation of European and global politics. Assuming that alternative forms of power (ideational, communicative) are likely to play a stronger rather than weaker role in the future, seeking a

---

[89] See, e.g., Keohane, Robert O., 'Governance in a Partially Globalized World', 95 *American Political Science Review* (2001) 1–13.

[90] Fassbender, 'United Nations Charter' (1998), highlights the critical potential of the constitutional idea, especially as regards the issue of veto powers, but the greater legitimation the unequal structure of the UN would gain from such a move is on balance far weightier.

[91] Ikenberry, John, *After Victory: Institutions, Strategic Restraint, and the Rebuilding of Order After Major Wars* (Princeton University Press, 2001).

[92] Moravcsik, Andrew, *The Choice for Europe: Social Purpose and State Power from Messina to Maastricht* (University College London Press, 1998).

[93] Magnette, Paul and Kalypso Nicolaïdis, 'The European Convention: Bargaining in the Shadow of Rhetoric', 27 *West European Politics* (2004) 381–404; but see also the different emphasis in the appraisals by Fossum, John Eric and Augustin Menendez, 'The Constitution's Gift? A Deliberative Democratic Analysis of Constitution Making in the European Union', 11 *European Law Journal* (2005) 380–410; Karlsson, Christer, 'Deliberation at the European Convention: The Final Verdict', 14 *European Law Journal* (2008) 604–619.

constitution now would only benefit those holding the greatest material power today: it would allow them to 'lock in' their dominant position.

This argument for pluralism, based on the fluidity of the postnational order and the role of material power in it, is powerful, but it is also transitional. Pluralism seems to emerge as an attractive option for times of change when better alternatives cannot be realized. But it continues to lack appeal as a long-term vision of what the global order should look like – it seems constitutionalism still provides the better alternative once postnational politics has become more settled and 'domesticated'.

The strong version of the argument from contestation, however, is of a less transitional nature. In this variant, the contestatory space pluralism opens up will be crucial to any postnational order, not just the current one. This depends on a much more pessimistic appraisal of the prospects of reform in the official institutional setting: it typically starts from the view that tools for counter-hegemonic action are necessary in any polity, and that a pluralist legal order would facilitate their exercise. In the argument put forward for example by Boaventura de Sousa Santos, alternative legalities can become central tools for the articulation of subaltern politics against the mainstream forms of global governance sustained by dominant economic and military power.[94]

What distinguishes this approach from the weak version of the argument is the lack of hope to eventually institutionalize a just or legitimate order in a constitutionalist form, and in this it connects with some of the critiques of modern constitutionalism I have sketched above. As we have seen, for James Tully constitutions in multicultural societies are typically expressions of dominant cultures, and he therefore seeks to destabilize processes of constitutionalization in the modern, foundational way.[95] This analysis resonates with broader critiques. Constitutionalism's aspiration to establish an impartial framework is questioned also by those who, like Chantal Mouffe, are sceptical about the chances for attaining a neutral consensus in diverse societies more generally.[96] This does not have to go as far as to deny the possibility of reasoned deliberation and consensus between worldviews altogether, as some postmodernists do.

---

[94] de Sousa Santos, *Toward a New Legal Common Sense* (2002), Chapter 9; 'Beyond Neoliberal Governance' (2005).

[95] See Section 5.2.2.

[96] Mouffe, Chantal, *The Democratic Paradox* (London: Verso Books, 2000), Chapter 4.

Mouffe's scepticism is grounded in the observation that in practice forms of consensus are typically expressions not of an inclusive process leading to an impartial result, but instead of social mechanisms that favour powerful actors whose dominance is then concealed by the supposed neutrality of broad agreement. And those conditions which political theorists defend to ground impartial consensus favour a particular rationality and abstract so much from the circumstances of the individual (in social relations, language, culture) that they can hardly count as truly inclusive.[97] Mouffe's viewpoint is mirrored, for example, in Ran Hirschl's much more empirically minded, comparative study of the political origins of recent constitutionalization and the concomitant emergence of judicial review.[98] Hirschl interprets these developments, despite their apparent claim to inclusiveness and impartiality, as attempts by political elites to lock in their privileged position and defend it from challenge; constitutions then come to appear as hegemonic tools. If this is true, one would indeed want to deny them full legitimation and provide space for continuous contestation on a fundamental level – something a pluralist, heterarchical order may indeed be able to do.

The argument from contestation usefully draws attention to the fact that law – including constitutions – is not the product of abstract ideas but that of real, and normally problematic, social and political processes. Whether or not one accepts the argument then comes to depend on one's general views about the degree to which such processes can be transformed. Caution is warranted here: already in domestic politics we will hardly ever find the ideal communicative structures that would render a truly fair consensus possible; constitutions, as a result, typically display some of the features of power politics Hirschl's study identifies. If this holds true in the relatively well-integrated, homogeneous contexts of nation-states, we can expect it to be even more pronounced in the far more divided postnational space in which organized material power (through states) is generally seen to play an even more dominant role. Even if constructivists have rightly pointed to the continued (and perhaps increased) impact of ideas and values and the concomitant influence of arguments in international politics, this need not imply a weakening of power in this context; after all, material power is often enough reflected in,

---

[97] Ibid., at 92–96.
[98] Hirschl, Ran, *Towards Juristocracy: The Origins and Consequences of the New Constitutionalism* (Cambridge, Mass.: Harvard University Press, 2004).

and furthered through, ideas and values.[99] There is little hope for transcending the predominance of power in the postnational space – neither in the near future nor in the long term, especially if we take the limited success of such attempts in the more benign domestic context as a guide.

In these circumstances, an attempt at constitution-making can appear as simply another hegemonic move.[100] But it may also give the communicative power of weaker actors a greater role: the powerful may be willing to make concessions in order to gain stronger legitimacy for an order that is overall beneficial to them, and this may help change the political logic of the postnational space to some extent. It may also provide tools that can be mobilized later for a transformation of the structure quite at odds with that intended at the inception; powerful actors may well be trapped in their own argumentative and legal strategies.[101] This only reflects the always Janus-faced character of law as both a tool of the powerful and an instrument of resistance;[102] which of them gains the upper hand depends on the environment and the success of mobilization on either side. Balakrishnan Rajagopal has recently pursued this ambiguity with a focus on legal pluralism, tracing the ways in which the multiplicity of applicable legal orders granted social activists in India space, but also meant that successes in one order did not necessarily translate into the others.[103] Thus a pluralist structure does not, in and of itself, allow for more effective contestation than a constitutionalist one.[104] Whether it does will depend on the context: the greater the power differential behind a potential constitution, and the more that constitution is likely to reflect it, the greater is the likelihood that a pluralist order will provide more effective tools of contestation and delegitimation than the concessions that might be extracted in a constitutional settlement. On the global level at least, this likelihood would appear to be relatively high.

---

[99] On links between realist/rationalist and constructivist approaches in world politics, see Hurd, Ian, *After Anarchy: Legitimacy and Power in the United Nations Security Council* (Princeton University Press, 2007); also Risse, T., '"Let's Argue!" Communicative Action in World Politics', 54 *International Organization* (2000), 1–39.

[100] See Koskenniemi, 'Fate' (2007), at 19.

[101] See Risse, 'Let's Argue!' (2000), at 32–33, on such 'self-entrapment'.

[102] In the context of international law, see Krisch, Nico, 'International Law in Times of Hegemony: Unequal Power and the Shaping of the International Legal Order', 16 *European Journal of International Law* (2005) 369–408.

[103] Rajagopal, 'Limits of Law' (2005).

[104] Cf. de Sousa Santos, *Toward a New Legal Common Sense* (2002), at 98, 495.

5.4.3 Checks and balances

The most common argument for a pluralist order stems from an analogy with checks and balances in domestic constitutions. The most obvious grounding for such an analogy lies in the difficulty of justifying the supremacy of any level of postnational governance over the others: if no level can claim superiority, a constitutionalist order that implies ultimate authority (if only that of the constitution, the common framework) will appear problematic.[105] In order to respect the competing claims of the different levels, we might instead choose a path that aims not so much at integration but at dissociation: one that keeps an equal distance from the ideals of all of them, that refrains from according full control over decisions – through veto rights or otherwise – to either of the competing collectives. If all constituencies are to have decision-making powers beyond merely being listened to, but shall not be able to dictate or veto a particular decision, then no decision can fully bind them all, and each level has to retain the right to challenge it. The resulting picture of postnational governance would then be one of a constant potential for mutual challenge: of decisions with limited authority that may be contested through diverse channels until some (perhaps provisional) closure might be achieved. It would be a picture of checks and balances that result in a form of systemic pluralism.

The first step in this argument is indeed plausible if we consider the normative grounding of the competing polities. Different collectives – subnational, national, regional or global – have a strong initial case, based on culture, nationalism, cosmopolitanism, etc., but they all come with serious deficits as well. Subnational and national constituencies are limited in that they cannot fully respond to the needs and interests of those outsiders who are affected by their decisions or have a claim to be considered, for example for reasons of transboundary justice.[106] The global polity is not capable of instituting structures of democratic participation nearly as thick and effective as those possible on the national level. It is too far removed from individuals, and intergovernmental negotiations will never come with the deliberative structures necessary for effective public involvement; moreover, as mentioned above, we face serious

---

[105] See Maduro, 'Europe and the Constitution' (2003); Schiff Berman, 'Global Legal Pluralism' (2007), at 1179–196; Halberstam, 'Constitutional Heterarchy' (2009).

[106] See, e.g., Young, *Inclusion* (2000), at 246–251.

limits of communication across cultural, linguistic and political boundaries.[107] Regional levels typically combine the advantages, but also the
problems of the lower and higher levels – they are not fully inclusive and
their democratic structures are not sufficiently deep.[108]

It might be tempting to see these tensions simply as a reflection of
competing approaches in political and democratic theory. For example,
a cosmopolitan model would delimit the relevant collectives according
to the scope of individuals who are significantly affected by particular
issues or decisions; as a result, it would locate the relevant collective on a
relatively high level.[109] Liberal nationalists, however, would emphasize
the importance of social ties for the realization of requirements of justice,
and would therefore keep decisions on a lower, largely national level.[110]
More republican-minded theories would seek to balance communal ties
with concerns about the effectiveness and inclusiveness of self-government
regarding issues of broader reach.[111] Those theories that regard some
form of historical or cultural demos as central to democracy will hardly
accept decisions taken beyond the national level.[112] Others that are primarily concerned about the discursive conditions for democratic decision-
making may accept regional but perhaps not global institutions.[113]

This list could easily be extended further, but the details of the various
approaches matter less than the broader point that the difficulties in the
determination of the right level of governance may boil down to a need
to choose between theoretical frameworks. Once this choice is made,
one could then proceed to assign particular issues to levels of decision-
making and would arrive either at a federal-style model such as David
Held's, at an intergovernmental one that retains the nation-state as the
main anchor of the overall edifice, or at some other coherent structure

---

[107] See, e.g., Habermas, *Der gespaltene Westen* (2004), at 137–142.
[108] In a similar vein, Halberstam, 'Constitutional Heterarchy' (2009), reconstructs
the competing views as deriving from the three values of 'voice, expertise and
rights' that create competing authority claims.
[109] E.g. Held, *Democracy and the Global Order* (1995); 'Democratic
Accountability' (2004).
[110] E.g. Miller, David, *National Responsibility and Global Justice* (Oxford
University Press, 2007).
[111] E.g. Benhabib, Seyla, *The Rights of Others* (Cambridge University Press, 2004),
at 217–221.
[112] E.g. Kirchhof, Paul, 'Der deutsche Staat im Prozeß der europäischen
Integration', in J. Isensee, and P. Kirchhof, eds., *Handbuch des Staatsrechts*, VII
(Heidelberg: CF Müller, 1993), 855–886.
[113] E.g. Habermas, *Der gespaltene Westen* (2004).

depending on the particular substantive principle at work. The tensions that seemed to suggest a pluralist order would then appear merely as a result of theoretical indecision.

Yet the solution may not be so easy. I already mentioned Iris Young's view that abstract principles, such as inclusion of all those affected by a decision, are in tension with the actual allegiances of individuals and that any institutional structure has to reflect those countervailing concerns.[114] This can be redescribed as a tension in the liberal project between two directions of autonomy: one insisting on the individual's right to co-determine whatever decision has an effect on her, the other emphasizing the importance for autonomy of the individual's (cultural, social) particularity that should be reflected in the decision-making framework. Here lurks a deeper conflict that in the domestic context long remained inconsequential and only came to the surface once traditional models of politics were called into question; it is, in James Bohman's words, 'the fundamental tension between universality and particularity that is built into the constitutions of modern states'.[115] The modern state was built onto a relative congruence not only between decision-makers and decision-takers, but also on that between a particular social community and the scope of those affected by political decisions. However much this community may have been imagined or (forcibly) constructed,[116] the resulting congruence allowed democratic participation to be constructed in a coherent, unitary way. Tensions between community allegiances and political structures only became apparent where subnational groups retained or developed a stronger collective consciousness that made them claim self-determination on their own. Federal, sometimes asymmetrical, arrangements were the typical, though not always stable, institutional response to such claims.[117]

If the tension between the scope of communities and that of affected individuals could be largely contained in the context of the nation-state,

---

[114] Young, *Inclusion* (2000).
[115] Bohman, *Democracy* (2007), at 29; see also Benhabib, Seyla, 'Reclaiming Universalism: Negotiating Republican Self-Determination and Cosmopolitan Norms', 25 *The Tanner Lectures on Human Values* (2005) 113–166 at 132. ('The tension between universal human rights claims and particularistic cultural and national identities is constitutive of democratic legitimacy.')
[116] Anderson, Benedict, *Imagined Communities: Reflections on the Origin and Spread of Nationalism* (London: Verso, 1983); Connor, Walker, 'Nation-Building or Nation-Destroying?', 24 *World Politics* (1972) 319–355.
[117] See Tierney, *Constitutional Law* (2004); and the discussion Section 5.2.3.

in the postnational context the gap is too big for a similar containment to work. The conflicting principles may be formulated differently depending on the theoretical framework one operates in, but however the precise conceptualization, the tension between them is likely to condition the institutional structure to a significant extent. For many issue areas, it will prevent singling out one collective as determinative; instead, several levels will have claims with similar degrees of justification, and the structural framework should grant them equal importance. Doing so in forms of co-decision (as in consociationalism) would risk serious blockade in a context such as the postnational where the number of players is high.[118] The best solution might then be a pluralist one: one that withholds full legitimacy from all of the different levels, does not grant any of them ultimate decision-making capacity and instead establishes equidistance to all of them.

Functionally, such an approach may indeed be close to domestic constitutional checks and balances – in both cases, no single site enjoys ultimate decision-making powers but has to face checks by others that, in some respects, may have equally strong claims to authority.[119] However, as I have pointed out in the conceptual discussion above, domestic checks and balances are typically part of a structured constitutional framework and operate in a common frame of reference – in our context, they would instead operate between such frameworks, not within one of them. In this way, the checks-and-balances idea is radicalized and taken to the systemic level; it has to be if the equal deficits of the different polities are to be reflected.

5.5 Pluralism and public autonomy

Checks and balances sound immediately attractive, almost uncontroversial on a background of modern constitutional theory, but the above account leaves open a crucial question: Who should be entitled to check whom, and why? To some extent, the response may seem too obvious in the context from which the idea originates, the European Union. Here both the national and the European levels have a strong basis both in abstract normative terms and in social practices as they have developed over the last decades. In this case, it might seem clear that checks and

---

[118] See Section 5.2.3.
[119] Halberstam, 'Constitutional Heterarchy' (2009).

balances between those two polity levels are appropriate, and it might also make the proposition attractive that they should grant each other some 'constitutional tolerance' – that they should refrain from demanding obedience from one another but rather operate on a basis of mutual invitations to cooperate.[120] A pluralist order might be much more suited to such a vision than a constitutionalist one that comes with hierarchies and obligations to comply with the other's orders.

However, the situation is less clear-cut once we move beyond the European to the global realm. Here too, as I have sketched above, there are good arguments for different levels of decision-making on issues of transboundary concerns, yet what this implies in practice is far less obvious. A multiplicity of different regimes are vying for authority, and their relationship with one another and with regional or state organs is far from settled. Should the UN (United Nations), the WTO (World Trade Organization) or the Financial Action Task Force (FATF) be equally entitled to 'tolerance' from states? Are regimes such as those of the SPS (Sanitary and Phytosanitary) Agreement and the Biosafety Protocol on an equal footing and related to one another only as a matter of tolerance, or are there hierarchies at play? And can states or regional entities only expect tolerance from global bodies or claim more, perhaps an ultimate right to decide? The determination of the relevant collectives and of their link to particular institutions, seemingly easy in the European context, proves to be highly problematic on the global level.

The most obvious solution here would be to go back to the normative arguments discussed in Section 5.4 and probe further into how they would apply to those multiple regimes. The conflicting arguments for keeping decision-making at lower or higher levels might play out differently for the different regimes, and in some cases mutual tolerance might be called for, in others not. We might think, for example, that if decision-making on the global level is primarily justified by greater inclusion of those affected, a body such as the FATF, with a very limited membership but far-reaching effects on outsiders, hardly deserves deference or respect.[121] On the other hand, the Kyoto Protocol's climate change

---

[120] Weiler, J. H. H., 'In Defence of the Status Quo: Europe's Constitutional *Sonderweg*', in J. H. H. Weiler and M. Wind, eds., *European Constitutionalism Beyond the State* (Cambridge University Press, 2003), 7–23.

[121] On the legitimacy problems of the FATF, see Hülsse, Rainer, 'Even Clubs Can't Do without Legitimacy: Why the Anti-money Laundering Blacklist was Suspended', 2 *Regulation & Governance* 4 (2008) 459–479.

regime could be seen to respond to the need for non-exclusive, global solutions for transboundary environmental problems and thus to warrant a high degree of tolerance (and perhaps compliance) from states.

5.5.1 Pluralisms of choice

This approach seems fairly straightforward but it is only superficially so. For the method we have used so far, relying as it does on a substantive evaluation of the claims of different regimes or collectives, contrasts starkly with pluralist approaches developed by political theorists for the domestic level, which typically start from some form of choice of the individuals involved. In order to gain a clearer view of the difference, it is worth analysing these domestic theories briefly before we return to the postnational level.

Pluralist theories of the state have typically been grounded in the freedom of association. An early influential strand of this kind was English political pluralism, associated especially with Frederick William Maitland, G. D. H. Cole, John Neville Figgis and Harold Laski.[122] For them, a political order based on voluntary associations appeared superior to a state-centred one because it promised individuals greater control of their own affairs. Because they originated in individual choice, such associations were also independent from the state in their basis of legitimacy and possessed non-derived powers. Laski, in some of his works, took this so far as to assert that the state was in effect just another association, with no *a priori* claim to supremacy and dependent on acceptance by other associations and individuals whenever it sought to act on them.[123] Yet despite their general emphasis on the importance of associations, most English pluralists, including Laski in his most influential writings, accepted a superior role of the state as a guardian of the

---

[122] See Hirst, Paul Q., ed., *A Pluralist Theory of the State* (London: Routledge, 1989), 1–47; Nicholls, David, *The Pluralist State: The Political Ideas of J. N. Figgis and his Contemporaries* (2nd edn, Basingstoke: Macmillan, 1994); also Runciman, D., *Pluralism and the Personality of the State* (Cambridge University Press, 1997).

[123] See Laski, Harold J., 'Law and the State', in Paul Q. Hirst, ed., *A Pluralist Theory of the State* (London: Routledge, 1989), 197–227 at 214; also Hirst, Paul Q., 'Introduction', in *A Pluralist Theory of the State* (London: Routledge, 1989), 1–45 at 28.

system: as a guarantor of the freedom of association, as an enforcer of common norms and as an arbiter between associations.[124]

These theories thus defend forms of institutional, not systemic, pluralism, but here this fact interests me less than their foundation. As we have seen, protagonists of postnational pluralism have typically determined the relevant collectives on an objective basis, starting from substantive theories of where decision-making power should lie. In contrast, the English pluralists used as a foundation individuals' choices of the associations they want to form part of. Even if these choices might not settle the question entirely (as we have seen, a framework of common norms was still seen as necessary), such an approach is nevertheless of a distinctly more participatory, proceduralist character than its postnational analogues. Contemporary theorists of pluralism in the domestic context, such as Paul Hirst and William Galston, follow this participatory path.[125]

The distinctive character of such an approach is demonstrated in Chandran Kukathas's recent work, which develops the idea of freedom of association further and radicalizes its institutional implications.[126] In Kukathas's vision, society is an 'archipelago' of (partly overlapping) associations that co-exist both next to each other and on different levels, but not in hierarchical relationships: all depend on negotiations and compromises with the others; none can command; and the basic operational principle is toleration. In this order, the state occupies an elevated place but is confined to an even more minimal role than in the approaches mentioned above. It is supposed to ensure order as an 'umpire' between associations, but questions of justice are out of its reach since they are contested among different associations and no neutral ground can be found to adjudicate between them. What is just and right must therefore remain undecided; competing views will seek to broaden their support

---

[124] See Hirst, 'Introduction' (1989), at 28–30; Nicholls, *Pluralist State* (1994), Chapter 5; Laski, Harold J., 'The Problem of Administrative Areas', in Paul Q. Hirst, ed., *A Pluralist Theory of the State* (1989), 131–163 at 155.

[125] See Hirst, Paul Q., *Associative Democracy* (Cambridge: Polity Press, 1994); Galston, William A., *Liberal Pluralism* (Cambridge University Press, 2002), Chapter 9.

[126] Kukathas, Chandran, *The Liberal Archipelago* (Oxford University Press, 2003). Kukathas bases freedom of association not on autonomy but on freedom of conscience (pp. 36–37); but this difference is of little importance in the present context.

but cannot be enforced against associations that are unwilling to share them.[127]

In Kukathas's vision, thus, toleration operates between the polities founded upon individuals' allegiances, not between collectives delineated in the abstract. What is more, an abstract delineation would be groundless: there are no overarching principles of justice that would transcend those produced within the different islands of the archipelago. Those islands owe each other respect merely because they are forms of individual association, not for any further-reaching qualities. If associational choices diverge, therefore, the structure will necessarily be pluralist; if they do not, it will not. Here the participatory, association-based logic gains its clearest form; and its implications are not limited to the diverse domestic societies that form the primary focus of Kukathas's work but extend well into the international, postnational spheres.[128]

5.5.2 Public autonomy and the scope of the polity

One does not have to share all of Kukathas's conclusions, or his libertarian outlook, to see the force of this kind of approach. By insisting on the centrality of individuals' allegiances and choices for the determination of the polity, it resonates much more closely than an abstract, objective approach with the emphasis on procedure in most contemporary political theory.

This emphasis has always been characteristic of civic republican approaches that have placed popular sovereignty at the centre of their concern; for them, the (political) 'liberties of the ancients' had to trump, or at least parallel the (private) 'liberties of the moderns'. But also for neo-republicans who reject the 'populist' character of such a recourse to the 'ancients',[129] the primary good – non-domination – depends crucially on participatory opportunities for individuals, be they expressed as possibilities for contestation[130] or the capacity for individuals 'as free and equal citizens to form and change the terms of their common life

---

[127] Ibid., Chapter 6, and especially page 252 ('The state should not be concerned about anything except order or peace.').

[128] Ibid., at 27–29.

[129] See Pettit, Philip, *Republicanism: A Theory of Freedom and Government* (Oxford University Press, 1997), at 7–8.

[130] Ibid., at 183–205.

together'.[131] Perhaps less naturally, most contemporary liberals share in the emphasis on participation. Thus David Held regards as crucial to liberal democracy the ability for individuals 'to choose freely the conditions of their own association',[132] and Jeremy Waldron sees participation as 'the right of rights' that allows for the creation of political structures in the face of substantive disagreement – for Waldron, it is indeed participation all the way down.[133] And John Rawls, responding to Habermas's charge that his views emphasized abstract rights over the exercise of popular sovereignty, insists that the people's constituent power has long been a cornerstone of liberal constitutional and political (as opposed to merely moral) theories.[134] Thus, it is mainly for those who remain committed to natural law theories to demote participatory procedures to a secondary role.

If participation and the public autonomy of citizens are such pervasive elements of a political theory, their reach has to extend to all elements of the framework of a polity. In constitutional settings, this is realized through the idea of a 'dualist' democracy: a comprehensive role for popular sovereignty in the making of a constitution, where it defines all terms of the constitutional settlement, and a more attenuated role in the operation of daily politics within the constitutional frame.[135] However, if participation is thought to extend to all questions of a constitutional character, it also has to apply to the scope of the polity itself. If individuals are 'to choose freely the conditions of their own association',[136] they have to be able to determine with whom to associate. As James Bohman puts it, 'to the extent that borders and jurisdictions set the terms of democratic arrangements, they must be open to democratic deliberation'[137] – and, we can add, revision.

Yet applying democracy to itself seems to lead into an infinite regress – in order to determine the scope of the polity, we must already know that scope, for otherwise a democratic determination could not take place.

---

[131] Bohman, *Democracy* (2007), at 45.
[132] Held, *Democracy and the Global Order* (1995), at 145.
[133] Waldron, Jeremy, *Law and Disagreement* (Oxford University Press, 1996), Chapters 11, 13.
[134] Rawls, John, 'Political Liberalism: Reply to Habermas', 92 *Journal of Philosophy* (1995) 132–180 at 165.
[135] See Ackerman, *We the People* (1993), Chapter 1; see also Rawls, John, *Political Liberalism* (New York: Columbia University Press, 1993), at 233.
[136] Held, *Democracy and the Global Order* (1995), at 145.
[137] Bohman, *Democracy* (2007), at 17.

This chicken-and-egg problem[138] did not pose grave difficulties during the era of the nation-state: the determination of the polity seemed self-evident and fixed – democratic politics took place in the national realm, providing the ground for views such as Robert Dahl's that '[t]he criteria of the democratic process presupposes [sic] the rightfulness of the unit itself'.[139] The scope of the polity seemed only conceivable as exogenous to the democratic process, as settled prior to its operation, usually through historical events, sometimes a constitution.

This corresponds with the observation that the collective behind democratic self-determination is ever only reflectively constituted, i.e. through the attribution of a later act as a representation of the supposed entity.[140] Normatively, though, this remains unsatisfactory as it excludes public autonomy from one of the most consequential areas of our political framework, and it can also hardly be presented as necessary to cope with an entirely exceptional problem. For democracy's beginnings are *typically* marred with similar paradoxes: if we want the rules of democracy to be subject to democratic determination, we end up in an infinite regress.[141] Yet there are ways out of this problem. Take only the most prominent problem, that of democracy's relationship with rights, such as free speech or equality of the vote. Like the scope of the polity, these are both a precondition for, and in need of definition by, the democratic process. If popular sovereignty is no longer conceived as the mere exercise of will by a given collective and therefore depends on qualitative attributes such as rights to count as such, and if rights are no longer just given but require procedural elaboration through democratic action, the two are mutually dependent, but in a circular way. None can be thought of independently of the other, both

---

[138] See Shapiro, Ian and Cassiano Hacker-Cordón, 'Outer Edges and Inner Edges', in *Democracy's Edges*. (Cambridge University Press, 1999), 1–16 at 1.

[139] Dahl, Robert A., 'Federalism and the Democratic Process', in J. R. Pennock and J. W. Chapman, eds., *NOMOS XXV: Liberal Democracy* (New York University Press, 1983), 95–108 at 103 (emphasis omitted).

[140] See Lindahl, Hans, 'Constituent Power and Reflexive Identity: Towards an Ontology of Collective Selfhood', in Martin Loughlin and Neil Walker, eds., *The Paradox of Constitutionalism: Constituent Power and Constitutional Form* (Oxford University Press, 2007), 9–26.

[141] Richardson, Henry S., *Democratic Autonomy* (Oxford University Press, 2002), at 67.

require the other to even come into existence.[142] This relationship is captured in Habermas's diagnosis of a 'co-originality' of private and public autonomy where neither can be thought of as prior to the other. But this holds only in so far as we are concerned with their *positive* dimension – in order to become positive law, to become institutionalized, the two have to complement each other. In the *moral* dimension, however, we can theorize the rights individuals have to grant each other and introduce them as presuppositions of an institutionalization through public autonomy – aware of their imperfection, their need to be reinterpreted in the very processes by which such public autonomy constitutes itself.[143]

Democracy's relationship with its preconditions is thus complex, even circular, and this complexity is not limited to the question of the scope of the polity but reaches much farther. There is thus no reason to abandon normative theorizing about these preconditions – otherwise, democratic theory would surrender precisely at the point where it is confronted with its most serious challenges. It certainly has refused to do so thus far, and important strands of contemporary political theory have in fact sought to tackle precisely the question of the relevant polity, albeit under a different heading and in the domestic, not the postnational framework. For the interest in the rights of minority groups is, at least in part, about the multiplication and contestation of polities within the state setting. We have already seen some of the implications in Chandran Kukathas's work, but also those theories operating on more classical liberal ground are ultimately concerned with the scope of the polity. Will Kymlicka's influential vision of group rights, for example, does not only focus on the classical individual or collective rights to protect cultural spaces from state intervention, but also takes into view the political rights necessary for the realization of individual autonomy.[144] Self-government rights – through distinct group institutions as well as through participation in central decision-making structures of the state – are crucial to this approach. But this is only another way to express the idea that within the state different polities compete.

[142] Habermas, Jürgen, *Between Facts and Norms* (Cambridge, Mass.: MIT Press, 1996), at 121–122.

[143] Ibid., Chapter 3, especially page 128; in a similar vein, Rawls, 'Political Liberalism' (1995), at 163–170.

[144] Kymlicka, *Multicultural Citizenship* (1995).

And this idea is taken further by those who call for the recognition of difference beyond the realm of classical minorities – difference on the basis of culture, gender, belief, etc. What had classically merely engendered calls for negative individual rights, has now often turned into arguments for political rights – for the acceptance of a multiplicity of publics that need to be related to formal institutions in novel, often still uncharted ways.[145]

5.5.3 From public autonomy to pluralism in postnational law

We have now established a basis for thinking about the structure of the postnational order, one in which the public autonomy of citizens, not abstract moral considerations, carries the central burden. This emphasis may, as Waldron has noted in a similar context, lead to 'a dissonance between what one takes to be the right choice and what one takes to be the authoritative choice in political decision-making',[146] but, as he points out, this is an unavoidable dissonance in any theory of political authority operating in circumstances of disagreement.[147] Thus we might think that a state-based, a global constitutionalist or indeed a pluralist order would be most justified in the light of abstract precepts of morality and political theory, but it is only by observing the practices of public autonomy that we can determine which type of order deserves acceptance. As we will see below, a pluralist order does indeed seem to resonate well with such practices at the present time.

5.5.3.1 Social practices

Identifying practices of public autonomy in the postnational context is not an easy task. In the absence of structured public discourses on what the postnational order should look like (instances one might liken to those of 'constitution-making'), indications of how citizens relate to diverging visions of that order remain vague. And what we know about them is likely to engender some pessimism about the possibility of transnational polities. As mentioned earlier, even in the (politically closely integrated and socially relatively homogeneous) EU context, people still identify to a much larger extent with their national polity

---

[145] See, e.g., Young, *Inclusion* (2000), Chapters 3, 5.
[146] Waldron, *Law and Disagreement* (1996), at 246.
[147] Ibid.

than with a European one.[148] One might thus share Alexander Wendt's scepticism as to the possibility of transcending national allegiances – and thus socially grounding deeper postnational integration, perhaps a 'world state' – in the foreseeable future.[149] This certainly casts doubts on visions of global constitutionalism that situate ultimate authority in a (however much imagined) global constitution – for this would imply a primacy of the polity framework determined in a global polity which does not correspond, even remotely, with the preferences expressed by citizens.

Yet does this imply a return to the primacy of national polities? It probably would if we were faced with a binary choice: if individuals had to choose between being part of a transnational (global or European) and a national polity, we can safely assume that they would opt for the latter. In the European context, when asked to rank their different identifications, citizens rank that with their Member State consistently, and by a large margin, higher than that with Europe. However, more than half see themselves not solely as 'nationals' but also as 'Europeans'.[150] This suggests a multiplication of feelings of belonging among relatively large parts of the population, certainly beyond the elites that are typically thought to be more cosmopolitan-minded.[151] How deep this runs, and to what degree it might extend beyond Europe, is unclear; comprehensive data on such questions on a worldwide scale is simply lacking. However, anecdotal evidence shows that citizens might be readier to grant global institutions extensive powers than is often assumed. For example, in the USA, a 2009 poll found that more than a quarter of respondents supported 'a leading role [for the United Nations] where all countries are required to follow U.N. policies'.[152] In a 2004 poll, 68% of respondents supported majority decision-making in international economic

---

[148] See text at note 32 above.
[149] Wendt, Alexander, 'A Comment on Held's Cosmopolitanism', in Ian Shapiro and Cassiano Hacker-Cordón, eds., *Democracy's Edges* (Cambridge University Press, 1999), 127–133.
[150] See Fligstein, *Euroclash* (2008); Caporaso and Kim, 'Dual Nature' (2009). See also the Eurobarometer of Autumn 2003, 27–28, available at <http://www.ec.europa.eu/public_opinion/archives/eb/eb60/eb60_en.htm>, at 27: 54% of respondents regarded themselves as Europeans and citizens of their own country (though 47% as citizens of their own country firstly).
[151] For such a focus on elites, see Wendt, 'Comment' (1999), at 128–129.
[152] Gallup, 'Americans Remain Critical of the United Nations', 13 March 2009, available at <www.gallup.com/poll/116812/Americans-Remain-Critical-United-Nations.aspx>.

organizations while only 29% insisted on a veto power for the USA;[153] other polls suggest that at least one-third, and possibly as many as two-thirds, of Americans want the USA to comply with WTO dispute settlement decisions even when they conflict with domestic policies.[154] And a 1999 poll found that 73% of respondents regarded themselves as 'citizens of the world' as well as as citizens of the United States.[155] Relatively broad acceptance of global decision-making can also be found in worldwide polls. In 2007, between 26% and 78% of respondents in sixteen countries (and pluralities or majorities in ten of them) agreed that their country 'should be more willing to make decisions within the United Nations even if this means that [their country] will sometimes have to go along with a policy that is not its first choice'.[156]

We should not read too much into these data,[157] but they do suggest that the nation-state is no longer the sole focus of political loyalties. Instead, they reflect a multiplicity of overlapping, sometimes conflicting, identities and loyalties, of varying acceptances of different political structures depending on the issue and the situation at hand.[158] This is closely linked to the diagnosis of a multiplication of 'publics', of structures of communication and identification, both in domestic and transnational relations.[159] If we think that such facts matter as part of the practices by which individuals determine the shape and size of their polities, we might indeed regard as most adequate a framework in which ultimate authority is diffused. As Michael Sandel suggests:

---

[153] Chicago Council on Foreign Relations, 'Global Views 2004: American Public Opinion and Foreign Policy', 42, available at <www.ccfr.org/UserFiles/File/POS_Topline%20Reports/POS%202004/US%20Public%20Opinion%20Global_Views_2004_US.pdf>.

[154] See the conflicting evidence in Chicago Council, ibid., and that reported in Americans and the World, 'International Trade', available at <www.americans-world.org/digest/global_issues/intertrade/wto.cfm>.

[155] See the report, Americans and the World, 'Globalization', available at <www.americans-world.org/digest/global_issues/globalization/values.cfm>.

[156] WorldPublicOpinion.org, 'World Publics Favor New Powers for the UN', 9 May 2007, available at <www.worldpublicopinion.org/pipa/articles/btunitednationsra/355.php?lb=btun&pnt=355&nid=&id=>.

[157] On problems with the European data, based on Eurobarometer polls, see Caporaso and Kim, 'Dual Nature' (2009), at 23.

[158] For a similar description, see, e.g., Sandel, *Democracy's Discontent* (1996), at 350.

[159] Dryzek, *Deliberative Global Politics* (2006); see also Bohman, *Democracy* (2007).

[o]nly a regime that disperses sovereignty both upward and downward can combine the power required to rival global market forces with the differentiation required of a public life that hopes to inspire the reflective allegiance of citizens.[160]

In this vein, a pluralist postnational order may well be the best reflection of contemporary social practices – or at least a better reflection of them than either nationalist or global constitutionalist visions.

5.5.3.2 Public autonomy

Social practices alone, however, will be insufficient to ground a normatively satisfactory conception of the postnational order. Throughout the previous sections, and in contrast to the more abstract moral approaches that have so far dominated the debate, I have emphasized participation and public autonomy as crucial elements of such a conception. But 'public autonomy' is not exhausted by a mere expression of attitudes or will by citizens. If we think of public autonomy as an expression of a right to 'self-legislation', the element of will has to be complemented by a specification of the conditions under which it can coincide with everybody else's self-legislation: for it is only conceivable as a consequence of the equal autonomy of all. In a Habermasian interpretation, social practices deserve the attribute 'public autonomy' when they concretize the discursive requirements that allow all to be the authors of the rules they are subject to. As we have seen above in the example of rights, this leads to a circular relationship between social practices and the conditions under which they acquire normative, democratic significance: for the practices have to both satisfy and specify such conditions. Popular sovereignty in this reading

is no longer embodied in a visibly identifiable gathering of autonomous citizens. It pulls back into the, as it were, 'subjectless' forms of communication circulating through forums and legislative bodies.[161]

In the constitution-making acts of a legally binding interpretation of the system of rights, citizens make an originary use of a civic autonomy that thereby constitutes itself in a self-referential manner.[162]

---

[160] Sandel, *Democracy's Discontent* (1996), at 345.
[161] Habermas, *Between Facts and Norms* (1996), at 136.
[162] Ibid., at 128.

Social practices therefore constitute exercises of public autonomy when they can be understood as a specification of the idea of 'self-legislation'. For Habermas, public autonomy is typically exercised within an existing polity frame; in fact, the discursive conditions of democracy 'explain the performative meaning of the practice of self-determination on the part of legal consociates who recognize one another as free and equal members of an association they have joined voluntarily'.[163] Yet constructively, there is no need to limit this approach to the discourse *within* a pre-established association – if, as I have argued above, democracy has to apply to the determination of the polity itself, the reach of public autonomy has to extend to the processes by which an association, or multiple associations, are formed.[164] Processes pertaining to the scope of a polity would then count as an exercise of public autonomy when they represent a plausible interpretation of what it means, for self-legislating individuals, to order the global political space.

It is at this point that more substantive considerations about the right scope of the polity re-enter the debate. As we have seen in the discussion in Section 5.4, various theoretical frameworks compete here – cosmopolitan, republican, nationalist, etc. Yet one defining trait of the debate, certainly from a broadly liberal perspective, is the tension between universality and particularity: the tension between an emphasis on inclusiveness of all those affected on the one hand, and an insistence on self-determination by groups with particular commonalities and common goals on the other. There is little ground for prioritizing one of these aspects over the other, and, as I have shown, this difficulty, and the more general problem of countervailing principles, has led commentators to argue for a pluralist order as a means to accommodate the different claims.[165]

As we now return to the issue from a more procedural vantage point, this competition of plausible approaches suggests that individuals have multiple options when it comes to defining what it would mean, for self-legislating individuals, to order the global political space. Yet any

---

[163] Ibid., at 110.
[164] If one sees discursive requirements, as Habermas does, as the necessary *implications* of communicative practices, a restriction to the national polity seems hardly warranted: even within the nation-state, communication with most others only takes place in a mediated way, so the difference with the postnational realm is largely a gradual one.
[165] See Section 5.4.3.

determination of the relevant polity through the social practices of some will always have to give an account of how it takes seriously, on the one hand, the claims of outsiders to be included, and on the other, the claims of groups of insiders to pursue their particular goals through their own structures. If it cannot give an account of how to strike that balance, it will hardly count as an exercise of public autonomy.

5.5.3.3 Plural polities

What kind of order does this suggest after all? As we have seen, social practices pertaining to the structure of the postnational order, reflecting as they do a multiplicity of identities and loyalties, would certainly allow for, and probably favour, an order that disperses ultimate authority, that leaves contests for ultimate authority open – a pluralist order. Such an order would not stand in tension with the idea of self-legislation whose implications for public autonomy I have just sketched. As the discussion in Section 5.4 had suggested, a pluralist order might indeed be a way to avoid singling out one level of decision-making over others: it might steer clear from the absolute (and problematic) claims of all polities and bring them into a relationship of checks and balances.[166] For alternative accounts, a justification in terms of public autonomy is more difficult. This is clearest for global constitutionalist models which, as I have already mentioned, do not resonate well with current social practices. And nationalist models, which are closer to such practices, have problems showing a sufficient orientation towards inclusiveness. They may rightly claim that decision-making in a national framework allows for denser democratic deliberation and thicker forms of solidarity,[167] but this is an argument based on benefits to insiders, and it does not seem to give much weight to the right of outsiders to be self-legislating. This problem should at least caution us not to interpret social practices too easily in nationalist terms.

All this may not be entirely conclusive when it comes to structuring the postnational space – too unstructured, undeliberative, uninclusive are current social practices to live up to the full promise of public autonomy and thus provide for authoritative solutions. Yet I would contend that thinking about the problem in a public autonomy framework is the best available approach, and what I have begun to outline here is one way in which such a framework can be developed in a

---

[166] See Section 5.4.3.
[167] See Miller, *National Responsibility* (2007).

non-ideal context[168] – and one way in which it might support an argument in favour of a pluralist structure of postnational law.

This framework should also be able to guide us when it comes to the more concrete shape of such a pluralist order. As I mentioned above, conceptualizations of pluralism in the European Union typically do not (and need not) problematize the question as to what polities (and what institutions) deserve respect – too obviously are these the national and European polities and their respective institutions. Beyond the EU, though, the candidates are many and their credentials often unclear; moreover, the link between polities and institutions will often be tenuous.

Which polities deserve respect and tolerance will then depend, again, on the degree to which they are based on practices of public autonomy: on social practices that concretize the idea of self-legislation. The weight of a collective's claim will follow from the strength of its social grounding, of the participatory practices that support it as well as the plausibility of its attempt to balance inclusiveness and particularity. And whether an *institution* deserves respect will result from the links it has with a given polity. An international institution may, for example, derive its powers from national polities and thus benefit from their standing if it is sufficiently controlled by them. Or it may claim to represent a broader, transnational (and necessarily less graspable) polity; whether this claim succeeds will then depend on whether there is actual social support for such a polity and its institutional expression.

In all cases, such support will have to be scrutinized as to its public autonomy credentials: as to its deliberative pedigree as well as to its inclusiveness or the strength of its argument for furthering particular goals. Thus, polities and institutions will not deserve respect if they are based on exclusion, leaving out substantial parts of those affected by its decisions, without providing a compelling justification. Cases such as the Organisaton for Economic Cooperation and Development (OECD) negotiating foreign investment rules mainly targeted at outsiders, the Basel Committee drawing up financial regulation for the rest of the world, or the FATF enforcing money-laundering standards against

---

[168] The context is non-ideal because, in the postnational space, public autonomy does not (and probably cannot) find a fully adequate expression. But this does not suggest that the national space, in contrast, provides an ideal context: because of the multiplication of identities and the enmeshment of institutions, it can no longer be disentangled from the postnational – public autonomy can no longer be thought of as simply national.

recalcitrant third parties would be the most obvious examples.[169] Likewise, private regulation may easily fail to satisfy public autonomy demands – it typically represents rule-making efforts by corporate actors without broader civil society input or a link to domestic political processes. For example, the *lex mercatoria* – so celebrated by Teubner[170] – will have to be scrutinized for its links to public processes beyond the reciprocal commitments of global traders. Some forms of private regulation may be able to make more plausible claims: the Forest Stewardship Council, for example, has established a complex institutional structure by which it integrates civil society and business groups as well as state representatives in its decision-making.[171]

More broadly, where a polity shows a strong mobilization of deliberative resources or puts forward an effective claim to respect for particular values, it might gain standing vis-à-vis others, and it might endow institutions that represent it with a strong position in the global institutional interplay. For example, in the US–EU dispute over trade with genetically modified organisms (GMO) products, WTO law can base its claim to regulatory power on delegation from and broader inclusiveness than national or regional settings, but the latter point suffers from its refusal to take account of the widely supported Biosafety Protocol.[172] On the other hand, the European, national and local insistence on ultimate decision-making power puts forward a claim deeply rooted in popular sentiment and democratic practices, thus counterbalancing its lack of inclusiveness to a certain extent. None of these sites of governance can assert a full realization of public autonomy, which is in any event elusive in postnational governance. But

[169] On those processes, see, e.g. Salzman, James, 'Labor Rights, Globalization and Institutions: The Role and Influence of the Organization for Economic Cooperation and Development', 21 *Michigan Journal of International Law* (2000) 769–848 at 805–31; Barr, Michael S. and Geoffrey P. Miller, 'Global Administrative Law: The View from Basel', 17 *European Journal of International Law* (2006) 15–46; Hülsse, 'Even Clubs Can't Do without Legitimacy' (2008).

[170] See, e.g. Teubner, Günther, 'Global Bukowina: Legal Pluralism in the World Society', in Teubner, ed., *Global Law Without a State* (Aldershot: Dartmouth, 1997), 3–28.

[171] See Meidinger, Errol, 'The Administrative Law of Global Public–Private Regulation: The Case of Forestry', 17 *European Journal of International Law* (2006) 47–87.

[172] See Krisch, Nico, 'Pluralism in Postnational Risk Regulation: The Dispute over GMOs and Trade', 1 *Transnational Legal Theory* (2010) 1–29.

the picture is one of gradual differences – some sites' claims have a stronger justification than others.

In practice, a claim's effectiveness will hinge on its persuasiveness to other collectives and institutions. For if we take seriously the multiplication of polities and their pluralist, heterarchical character, we will not conceive of any overarching, unifying polity, institution or framework of rules. We will instead lean towards the conflict-of-laws model I have sketched earlier as an example of systemic pluralism:[173] a model that requires each polity, in an exercise of public autonomy through its institutions, to define the terms on which it interacts with others. Different polities may then come to conflicting terms: as the idea of public autonomy leaves concretization to social practice, such conflicts are only to be expected. Yet this does not imply an all-out *laissez-faire*; as we have seen, to gain the attribute of 'public autonomy', social practices have to meet substantial conditions.[174]

The resulting structure of the postnational order is likely to be complex and fluid, constantly subject to readjustment and challenge. Different polities compete for recognition, and different institutions seek to link with them (though not necessarily in exclusive ways) to ground their standing. This pluralist structure might resemble an 'archipelago'[175] and will be hard to navigate, but this difficulty is only a reflection of the undecided, diverse character of postnational society in which a recognition of the need to cooperate coincides with the insistence on local, particular allegiances and values. We have to respect this if we are to take seriously the idea of individuals as self-legislating equals in the definition of the political framework. Pursuing unity and coherence through clear-cut hierarchies or constitutionalization would be an imposition on them, however well-meaning or advisable in the abstract.

5.6 Pluralism's challenges

A pluralist order, with all its complexity and institutional openness, may reflect the fragmented shape of today's societies, but it also creates anxieties. It lacks the clarity and coherence we expect from a

[173] See Section 5.3.
[174] I specify these conditions further in *Beyond Constitutionalism* (2010), Chapter 8.
[175] Kukathas, *Liberal Archipelago* (2003).

constitutionalist framework, and it seems to surrender the modern hope of ensuring, through an institutional structure, key values of political order: the rule of law, democracy, social stability and the containment of material power. In this section, I will briefly discuss the particular challenge these present for a pluralist vision. In the space of this chapter I cannot discuss them conclusively: this would require not only deeper theoretical explorations, but also empirical investigations into the ways in which pluralist orders function. Here I can only outline ways of approaching these challenges, mainly by sketching a suitable framework of comparison.[176] As we will see, if this framework is constructed realistically, pluralism is unlikely to fare badly at all.

In order to clarify this, let me return to the challenge of *power* that I have already touched upon in the discussion of pluralism's capacity to create space for contestation.[177] Pluralism certainly does not erect an institutional framework that could serve as a bulwark against the exercise of material power in the way constitutionalism, in its ideal form, aspires to. But in order to adequately assess comparative advantages, we should leave idealizations behind and turn to what we can realistically expect from constitutionalist and pluralist models under the circumstances of postnational politics and society, with all their divisions and enormous power differentials between actors. If pluralism cannot save us from the exercise of material power, constitutionalism is also entangled with it: a constitutional order has to be close enough to societal conditions to maintain its relevance, and this often requires painful compromises. Moreover, the more divided and unequal a society is, the greater is the temptation for powerful groups to use legal processes to entrench their position – a constitution may then become an instrument of, rather than a bulwark against, hegemony. In turn, the greater space a pluralist order provides may appear less as an inroad for unrestrained power than as an opportunity for resistance.

A non-idealized vision of constitutionalism also helps us to relativize the challenge for pluralism that stems from concerns about *stability and integration*. An order as institutionally undefined as a pluralist one obviously can hardly guarantee stability in the same way as a settled, institutionally fixed order sometimes can. Stanley Hoffmann thought

---

[176] I develop the argument further in *Beyond Constitutionalism* (2010), Chapters 7 and 8.

[177] See the discussion in Section 5.4.2.

that, in any event, '[b]etween the cooperation of existing nations and the breaking of a new one there is no stable middle ground',[178] and Carl Schmitt held that the stability of (pluralist) federal unions depended on a high degree of homogeneity.[179] Now, homogeneity is in short supply in postnational society, but it is also doubtful whether, in conditions of divided societies, constitutionalism offers a more promising alternative. For we have seen in the discussion of strategies to accommodate diversity, constitutional rules are unlikely to succeed if they are not based on sufficient social acceptance of the institutional solutions they entrench.[180] Thus, in deeply divided societies, stability and integration may not be guaranteed by constitutionalist approaches to any greater extent than by pluralist ones. Even the contrary may be true: for as we have also seen above, pluralism's capacity for adaptation may actually facilitate integration over time better than might be possible in a relatively rigid constitutional framework.[181] As I have sought to show in an article on the European human rights regime, the stability of a postnational order, with its initially often fragile institutions, can actually benefit from the openness of fundamental questions that pluralism implies. For this openness can reduce the antagonism between crucial actors and pave the way for more pragmatic settlements and incremental change, both of which are key to creating a stable institutional structure over time.[182]

The assessment is more complex when it comes to ensuring the *rule of law*. Pluralism's openness of legal relationships may be seen to allow for greater arbitrariness and create a lack of legal certainty; the multiplicity of applicable rules may subject the individual to different regulatory regimes, or grant it different sets of rights, and leave undecided which one will ultimately be decisive.[183] The result might appear close to the 'checkerboard laws' Ronald Dworkin regards as violating the principle

---

[178] Hoffmann, Stanley, 'Obstinate or Obsolete? The Fate of the Nation State and the Case of Western Europe', 95 *Daedalus* (1966) 862–915 at 910.

[179] Schmitt, *Verfassungslehre* (1993 [1928]), at 375–379.

[180] See the discussion in Section 5.2.3.

[181] See the discussion in Section 5.4.1.

[182] Krisch, Nico, 'The Open Architecture of European Human Rights Law', 71 *Modern Law Review* (2008) 183–216.

[183] Baquero Cruz, 'Legacy' (2008) at 414.

of integrity.[184] Yet integrity is only one value that a legal, institutional order should aspire to, and it may sometimes conflict with others.[185] Democratic procedures, for example, may lead to incoherent rules; in our case, the multiplicity of competing polities is likely to render this all the more likely. Ideally, decision-making processes would respect integrity, but when they do not (as is bound to happen in real life), the value of integrity should not simply trump that of legitimate authority. Moreover, integrity and legal certainty are often enough elusive even in domestic constitutional settings: whenever the law is unsettled, the individual has little ability to know how a dispute will eventually be resolved. The decisions of highest courts on contested matters of principle are, after all, rarely predictable on legal grounds. Certainty is then produced less through the rules themselves than through established practices of key institutions – which is no different in a pluralist order in which routine interactions often follow predictable lines.[186] Moreover, a multiplicity of rules may also benefit the individual. The *Kadi* case in the EU courts, around the fundamental rights protection against UN sanctions, is a case in point: in a constitutionalist reading, as favoured by the European Court of First Instance, individual rights enjoy only limited protection as the supposed interests of international institutions and global politics take precedence. Yet in the more pluralist interpretation of the European Court of Justice, which rejects the superiority of the UN Charter, this precedence vanishes and fundamental rights, as enshrined in EU law, take centre stage.[187] Thus, even from an individual's perspective, the legal certainty of a unified, constitutionalist order may not always be the most desirable state of affairs. Predictability of decisions is, after all, only one factor among others in the assessment of an institutional structure.

---

[184] Eleftheriadis, Pavlos, 'Pluralism and Integrity', 23 *Ratio Juris* (2010) 365–389. For the general argument on integrity, see Dworkin, *Law's Empire* (1986), Chapters 6 and 7.

[185] This is conceded by Dworkin himself; ibid., at 217–219.

[186] For an example, see Krisch, Nico, 'The Pluralism of Global Adminstrative Law', 17 *European Journal of International Law* (2006) 247–278 at 256–263.

[187] European Court of First Instance, Judgment of 21 September 2005, T-315/01; European Court of Justice, Judgment of 3 September 2008, C, 402/05 and 415/05. For a reading in terms of constitutionalism and pluralism, see de Búrca, Gráinne, 'The EU, the European Court of Justice and the International Legal Order after Kadi', 51 *Harvard International Law Journal* (2010) 1–49.

Another fundamental challenge to pluralism arises from ideals of *democracy*. While constitutionalism ensures the centrality of 'the people' by granting it authorship of the constitution all public power derives from, in a pluralist order no such clear links exist. Popular influence on politics is not structurally secured, and, what is more, participation in the decentred, multiple of sites of governance is likely to be thin and diffused. But then again, it is of little help to compare pluralism with an ideal version of constitutionalism that has scarce hopes of realization in the postnational, or at least the global, context. For the link between a supposed constitution and 'the people' is bound to be extremely tenuous as participatory procedures are nearly impossible to establish: elections are incompatible with the size of the global polity, and deliberative processes lack the communicative preconditions which alone could make them effective. Yet withdrawing into the comfortable, traditional home of national constitutionalism is not an option either – unless interdependence between countries is radically reduced, domestic democracy's ability to influence processes of governance beyond the state is simply too limited. Moreover, as I have discussed at length in this chapter, classical forms of democracy are in tension with the contestated character of the polity. If this causes problems in divided national settings, it is bound to cause even greater ones in the postnational context: there is no longer one 'people' that one could place at the centre of an institutional construction.[188] As a result, national models of democracy face serious difficulties in the postnational sphere, and it is no surprise that much democratic theory today is engaged in developing alternatives.

In this chapter, I have begun to delineate some of the implications of public autonomy in a world of multiple, decentred polities, and I have tried to suggest that such public autonomy may best be realized in a pluralist order that does not establish rigid hierarchies but retains fluidity in the constant readjustment of the relations of different polities. Here is not the place to explore this issue further; suffice it to point to the proximity of this approach to two main themes in contemporary democratic theory. The first is the attempt, especially by proponents of deliberative democracy such as Iris Young, John Dryzek or James Bohman, to respond to the multiplication of publics both within and

---

[188] But see Benhabib, *Rights of Others* (2004), who upholds the idea of a territorially bounded, central 'demos', even if reinterpreted in a process of iteration.

beyond the state framework;[189] I have mentioned this before. The second is the emphasis, among theorists as diverse as Philip Pettit and Pierre Rosanvallon, on contestation as a centerpiece of democracy.[190] Here the focus shifts from participation prior to decision-making – through electoral and deliberative processes – to later acts of questioning, holding to account and, more broadly, to greater reversibility and reflexivity of decision-making processes.

I cannot here discuss the promise and problems of those approaches or inquire further into how their foundations relate to the largely Habermasian vision of public autonomy I have used as a starting point.[191] Yet it is worth stressing that common to all those visions is an awareness of the need to look to models of democracy that are quite different from those we have become used to – not necessarily because our ideals have changed, but because they have to find a different expression in the changed context of (especially postnational) society. Measuring the democratic prospects of a pluralist order against traditional, nation-state democracy (which probably has always been idealized itself) would thus distort the picture, and it would blind us to the aspects of pluralism that resonate with democratic ideals – challenge, contestation and a responsiveness to the multiple 'demoi' that characterize postnational society.

5.7 Conclusion

In the search for paradigms for the emerging postnational order, pluralism has long been seen as, at best, a fitting description. Normatively, it has been regarded as inferior to constitutionalist models that promise a principled, reasoned framework for a structure of global governance which today appears as accidental, haphazard and driven by material power rather than good argument. In this chapter, I have tried to show that this view seriously underestimates pluralism's normative appeal. For not only does a pluralist order have considerable strengths in terms

---

[189] Young, *Inclusion* (2000); Dryzek, *Deliberative Global Politics* (2006); Bohman, *Democracy* (2007).

[190] Pettit, *Republicanism* (1997); Rosanvallon, Pierre, *Counter-Democracy: Politics in an Age of Distrust*, trans. A. Goldhammer (Cambridge University Press, 2008).

[191] See Krisch, *Beyond Constitutionalism* (2010), Chapter 8, for further elaboration.

of its adaptability, of the space for contestation it opens up, and of the checks and balances between different polities that it creates by leaving the relationships between legal systems undefined. Pluralism is also closer to foundational ideals of political order – namely public autonomy – than rival approaches: the plural, divided identities, loyalties and allegiances that characterize society today are better reflected in a multiplicity of orders than in an overarching framework that implies ultimate authority.

Connected to the ideal of public autonomy, pluralism is also not the *laissez-faire* approach it is sometimes thought to be. Instead, polities and institutions gain respect from others only if they reflect a vision of how self-legislating equals might order the postnational political space – if they are grounded in social practices with deliberative pedigree and can make a claim to bring inclusiveness and attention to particularity into a plausible balance. This kind of pluralism does 'pose demands on reality',[192] yet the demands are not institutionalized in an overarching legal framework, and such an institutional openness naturally creates anxiety regarding stability, the rule of law and the influence of power. But pluralism does not necessarily fare worse in these respects than a constitutionalism realistically constructed. For in the circumstances of postnational society, we should not expect to attain constitutionalism in its ideal form: as in divided domestic societies, the necessary accommodation of diversity is likely to weaken its promise of a reasoned, principled order to a significant extent. After all, constitutionalism, just as pluralism, is heavily conditioned by the society it operates in.

This suggests that in the conceptualization and construction of the postnational order we should proceed with significant caution. Caution, first, as regards the deficits of the competing visions: for in the non-ideal circumstances of postnational society, all attempts at constructing order will have serious weaknesses, and it is of little use to compare them to domestic political orders which often operate in far more benign conditions. Caution, second, as regards the transferability of domestic models: for we cannot expect those models to achieve the same goals and further the same values in the postnational as in the domestic context; we have observed here the problems in terms of stability, democracy and the rule of law for a constitutionalism that

---

[192] *Pace* Koskenniemi, 'Fate' (2007).

seriously seeks to accommodate diversity. And caution, third, as regards the prospects of institutionalization: most modern political theory is closely linked to the idea that institutions and law, if rightly designed, are crucial to furthering political justice. In the postnational realm, this is less certain: here, as in other highly unequal settings, institutions may instead largely serve to reflect and entrench the interests and values of particular actors, of particular parts of society.

In this light, pluralism's openness comes to appear as a chance more than as a menace: as a chance to contest, destabilize, deligitimize entrenched power positions – and to pursue progressive causes by other means than constitutional settlements. This chance comes with a greater burden for everyday political action: if the realization of key values is not left to institutional structures, it depends on continuous engagement and struggle. This implies greater fluidity and also risk: but as we have seen, the hope of eliminating this risk in postnational society is in any case slim and fraught with high costs. In the divided, highly contested space of the postnational, ideal solutions are elusive – and pluralism may be the best option we have.

Dialogical epilogue

J. H. H. WEILER

Chapter 1: Joseph H. H. Weiler and Bruno de Witte

JW: I would like to query the revision clause analysis which seems the apex of Section 1.3 of your chapter dealing with the relevance of the practice of the Member States in resolving the issue – international, yes or no.

At its heart the argument seems to flow as follows. In general international treaty law, revision is flexible and subject to a normal default rule of amendment by unanimity of the contracting parties. In concluding a treaty, parties may, however, specify a different revision procedure which, as is often the case, may provide for flexibility such as amendment by majority rather than unanimity. In the EU, by contrast, the revision provisions agreed by the parties are rigidified: not only is unanimity required, but further restrictions apply, such as the involvement of the EU institutions and ratification by each state according to its own constitutional requirements. Further, you correctly point out that, whereas under general international treaty law, the High Contracting Parties of a treaty can effectively amend it by a new treaty, riding roughshod not only over the provisions for conclusion under which the original treaty came into force, but even riding roughshod over the revision provisions in the original treaty. States, as you point out, are Masters of the Treaties they make, both as to form and as to substance. By contrast, you point out, under the EU, the Member States do not have this freedom of form. They must follow the procedural rules in the EU treaties in order to revise them. At least procedurally, they seem to lose something of their 'mastery of the treaty'.

It is your conclusion – that 'European Union treaty revisions are thus firmly situated within the scope of the international law of treaties' – which is somewhat puzzling. After all, you pointed out a remarkable difference where the doctrine, jurisprudence and practice of EU revision depart from general international law in its procedural rigidity. And yet you conclude that it is situated firmly within such law. I speculate that the reason is the following: frequently in the literature there is a claim or an assumption that unanimous treaty revision is a hallmark of international law, and that, by contrast, revision by majority is a hallmark of constitutional federal arrangements. Although, as you point out, actually international law allows states to provide for revision by majority and other flexible arrangements, the EU does not only stick firmly to the default unanimity rule of the VCLT (Vienna Convention on the Law of Treaties) but is even more rigid in conditioning revision on the consent of further actors such as the institutions of the EU, insisting as a matter of EU law on state ratification according to constitutional provisions of the state and it excludes the technique of amendment through new treaty. All this suggests a legal regime that is 'holier than the Pope' – even more international than international law requires.

I think this is an optical illusion, and your very own characteristically refined and subtle differentiation leads to the opposite conclusion.

Let me explain: general international law is not only flexible in relation to revision procedures, but, as you yourself point out, lax when it comes to the conclusion of new treaties, including treaties the purpose and effect of which is to amend a prior treaty and to avoid its revision procedures. It is not simply that the new 'revising treaty' need not follow the same procedures as the original one. Certain organs of the state, almost invariably from the executive branch, such as, say, the foreign minister, are presumed to act with the authority to bind their state to such a new treaty, and that presumption can be overturned only subject to the rather stringent conditions of Article 46 VCLT. I am unaware of a modern successful invocation of Article 46. International law massively empowers the executive branch – which is why at least in some states there are valiant attempts to reign in that branch in the international arena by various devices, more or less successful.

One of the things that happen in the move from the 'international' to the 'constitutional' is an important political shift: the bonds of the states which unite in a federal state are not only among such states, but among their citizens, jointly and severally. It is not only that the duties and rights created by such agreements (and I advisedly avoid here using the words 'treaty' or 'constitution') are owed not only to and among the states but also to and among citizens. I have endlessly argued (I argue everything endlessly ...) that even an agreement among slave owners can bestow rights and duties on the slaves. But citizens are recognized in such constitutional order as being the ultimate 'masters of the agreement', whereas in international treaty law, 'states' are typically but a proxy for the executive branch. Constituting a federal state is politically, in this respect, significantly different from concluding even a complex agreement among states such as, say, the NAFTA (North American Free Trade Agreement).

Curiously, though you pointed out the singularity of the EU which departs from classical international practice by joining the other institutions such as the Commission and the Parliament as required actors in the revision, by insisting at the 'international' level on constitutional ratification in the states and most importantly by forcing procedural revision rigidity and not allowing amendment by new treaty, you did not enquire either as to the reason or significance of this singularity. May I suggest that the reason, or at least the significance, is political? It underscores that in the EU the states might be as you argue Masters of the Treaty, but the state must be understood in a very different way: not as a proxy for the executive branch alone. The Commission and Parliament, the constitutional ratification process, the rigidity of the revision which would militate against various 'drawer plans' to circumvent the Irish Veto, are all devices which are in place to empower voices other than the executive branch; to give citizens not only rights and duties (bestowed by their Masters) but an attempt at *power* to shape what will be the rights and duties. In other words, when we contextualize politically the revision procedures which you bring, they point away from international law and practice and towards different forms of political organization. I think your focus on the formal legal structure, rather than its purpose and/or significance, obscures what is really important about the very examples you bring.

BdW: I am in complete agreement with your analysis of the reasons why the EU treaty revision procedure was made and kept so rigid. My only additional comment is that I am not sure how much this feature distinguishes the EU treaties from other international treaties concluded by the EU Member States. The reference to the constitutional requirements, in Article 48 TEU (Treaty on European Union), is of course tautological: it is quite obvious that states must ratify international treaties in accordance with their own constitutional requirements, and there was no need to repeat this in the text of Article 48, except as a political reminder of the fact that these are treaties which should not be left within the discretion and free disposal of the executive branch but require, at the very least, the approval by the national parliaments. The contemporary practice of European states, with the marked exception of the UK, shows that parliaments must approve all international agreements of any importance before the executive is allowed to ratify them. In that sense, foreign relations have been slowly democratized ever since 1945, and more visibly so in the last few decades, and whereas it is true, as you write, that 'international law massively empowers the executive branch', that empowerment has been reduced by national constitutional norms and practices – not just in respect of the European Union treaties.

JW: I would like now to query your methodology in three related ways. Here, too, in my view, there is a very formal analysis of legal structure which leads to the same blind spot.

My first methodological challenge relates to the way the chapter purports to refute most of the claims about a difference 'in kind' between the EU legal order and the international legal order. It seems to me that whilst the chapter makes valid points on the genealogy of the European legal order, it avoids the more important issue of an objective and conceptual classification. Let me explain what I mean and why I think this is important.

The important discussion on state responsibility is indicative. You point out that the rules of state responsibility in the EU are very different from the way state responsibility is typically thought of in international law. The difference is most visible in relation to the regime of sanctions and counter-measures, i.e. the practice of consequences of breach. But one could also mention that beyond that very visible point, the deeper strata of the jurisprudence and the doctrine are conspicuous in the absence of the vocabulary or analytical concepts of state responsibility. Even the words 'state responsibility' feature very infrequently in cases and the literature. Scarce issues of attribution, no distinction between primary and secondary responsibility. No mention at all of the duty to discharge state responsibility only the failure of which gives rise to a regime of sanctions. State responsibility is from Mars, the EU regime of violation and breach from Venus. The reply to all of this is simply to classify the EU system as 'a specific system of state responsibility'. It is in line with a more general approach in the chapter which seems to say at the same time two things: there is nothing to stop states from agreeing among themselves that they will not have the normal rules of state responsibility, or have a specific system which, nonetheless, since states agreed on it, must be regarded as being part of international law. I could add myself that the Articles on state responsibility contemplate departure from the general rules by special agreement. But here, as in the discussion about revision, what is absent is any discussion of the significance of this very radical departure from the default position of international law. The significance, in a nutshell, since here I want to make a methodological rather than a substantive point, could again be related to the fact that, as in federal states, the fact that one constituent unit (state, province, land) might violate a norm vis-à-vis another such state, province or land, does not give the right to counter-measures (indeed the world of counter-measures which is at the root of state responsibility is alien to it) because the commitments which may have been violated involve other actors and principals such as individuals. In the EU, even when states defined the European Court of Justice (as in 'Sheep Meat') no other Member State claimed the right to adopt counter-measures. Methodologically, the mode of reasoning seems to be that if formally a legal structure or process or institution may have originated in an agreement among sovereign states operating within an international law 'operating system',[1] that genealogical fact will (forever?) mark it as 'international'. It is 'international' because it was decided within an international law framework. What is often lacking is a discussion not of the form or origin of the decision but of the content of the 'experiment' and its substantive meaning for the legal order. Here is an analogy. Humans, Homo sapiens, evolved from apes. Your formal reasoning seems to run as something like this: there were apes. Then there were apes with a lot less hair – but they are still apes with a lot less hair. Then they stood up straight. These are apes which stand up straight. Then they developed a power of reasoning greater than the primitive power of reasoning of even so-called 'intelligent apes' – these are simply apes with superior power of reasoning. Genealogically, all this is correct. It is possible to describe humans as 'advanced apes', as

---

[1] Sorry to use an à la mode term. When I used it for the first time in 1997 – 'The Reformation of European Constitutionalism', 35 *Journal of Common Market Studies* (1997) 97 – it was less à la mode then . . . .

'experimental apes', but at a certain point, genealogy notwithstanding, it begins to make sense and there seems to be a substantive and substantial (rather than lexical) pay-off to speak of 'humans' rather than 'apes' – for example if we want to introduce the notion of, say, moral agency and moral responsibility.

But it is not merely genealogy – I do not think that anywhere in the chapter you explicitly state what would have to happen for you to accept the EU as a constitutional order. But implicitly, especially in your discussion on the different judicial systems, one gets the impression that (maybe unintentionally) you equate constitutionalism with statism, because your conceptual 'proof' so to speak is to show how the EU is different from federal *states*. If I am right in this, but even if I am not, it is a good juncture to clarify one point that maybe does not emerge so well in your presentation: all those you cite as using the term 'constitutional' to describe the EU legal order (and one should add the European Court itself(!), which in more than one case has referred to the treaties as the 'Constitutional Charter' of the legal order) never intend to say that it is a state, indeed, would not wish it to be a state. So in the very claim of a constitutional legal order there is a claim that also a 'non-state' – i.e. a polity which in some respects continues to reside within the international legal order – can have a 'constitutional operating system'. It appears that for you it is an either–or proposition. This is a respectable position, but it is not the premise of most Euro-constitutionalists. Long before that other à la mode neologism 'multilevel governance' became current, I argued that the Community could be simultaneously international, supranational and infranational. Here a physics metaphor may be in order rather than one borrowed from the cyberworld. When the Union is Newtonian, large objects moving at a slow speed, as in the Treaty(!) revision process, it has very distinct international legal features – though even there, as I argued before, these have a distinct constitutional colour. When it is in legislative mode it operates in a supranational–constitutional mode. When it is in administrative mode, etc., I find it difficult to accept the Hegelian approach, also shared, for example, by our mutual friend and distinguished colleague, Armin von Bogdandy, that there has to be an overarching conceptualization that would encompass the Union in all its modes of operation.

BdW: These are very important comments, addressing the role and functions of academic lawyers which (among other things of course!)

*include offering an 'objective and conceptual classification' (your words)
of chaotic reality. To start from your last comments above, I would
sympathize with Armin von Bogdandy and others as to the usefulness
of offering an overarching conceptualization of the Union in all its modes
of operation. For me, this attitude does not reflect a psychological com-
pulsion to conceptualize, but it reflects the reality as perceived by all the
actors of the European integration process, both inside and outside the
EU institutions: they see the European Union as an overarching framework of cooperation and integration with some general characteristics.
Beyond the bewildering variety of its modes of operation, there is a
widespread feeling that there is an 'EU label' which fits on some legal
and political activities or bodies, and not on others. Therefore, it makes
sense, for me, to try to understand and describe the overall nature of the
European Union. In fact, my entire chapter is based on the premise that it
is useful, indeed, to try to do that. But perhaps I am too much of a legal
modernist here, and not sufficiently post-modernist.*

*Given that premise, what my chapter argues is something very simple
really. The European Communities and European Union have been
created by means of international treaties, and the revision of the
Union's central rules of operation continues to happen in the same
way. Therefore, the overall nature of the European Union is prima
facie that of an international organization and I then look for convincing reasons why this prima facie characterization is no longer appropriate. Using your illuminating biological metaphor, I do not deny that
there can be a point where it does not make much sense to talk of
'advanced apes' and where it is better to invent the new term 'humans'.
I am just not convinced that the European Union is so different from the
other 'apes' that it ceases to be just that, namely an 'advanced ape'.
What has happened in the last few years, in particular in the context of
the elaboration and ratification of the Lisbon Treaty, seems to me a
sobering confirmation of the fact that the EU is still seen by the states as
their creature under international law. (I should add, to dispel what
could be the wrong impression, that I do not defend this view for
ideological reasons – I am, politically speaking, one of those now rare
European federalists – but as a scholar, I feel bound to admit that the
reality does not lead in the direction I would have preferred.)*

JW: I agree with your analysis as regards the difference between the
method of enforcing its (alleged) constitutionalism and that practised in

federal states. I would still claim that in the discipline the Union demands from its constituent Member States it is 'indistinguishable' from that demanded by federal states, but would readily admit that it is not a federal state and would readily admit that it achieves that discipline through different means. But I do not agree, or perhaps do not understand, why the fact that this discipline is achieved by national courts and through national constitutional provisions makes the Union more 'international' and less 'constitutional'? For me it is the opposite – it is the key to achieving a discipline that is even stronger than federal states, more Kantian (since it depends on internalization by the national legal orders), more federal since less centralized, and at the core of the spiritual advantage the Union has over classical federal states, for within that very difference you so precisely point out resides the virtue of constitutional tolerance – accepting, voluntarily the discipline of a constitutional order, despite the absence of a constitutional demos. It is the special brand of European Constitutionalism. Its *Sonderweg*.

BdW: I have avoided using the term 'constitutional' in my chapter, and I don't think that I have anywhere contrasted 'constitutional' and 'international'. I agree with you and many others that constitutional terminology should not be reserved to states, but can also usefully be employed to describe the actual or desirable features of the European Union legal order and, possibly, of other international organizations as well. What I would argue is that the existence of constitutional features in the EU legal order (in particular, a rather strict and judicially enforceable distinction between primary and secondary law) is not a good reason for concluding that it is therefore no longer an international organization.

JW: My final question in this first round of our exchange relates to the 'ends'. For you, to mask the international character of the Union comes with a price – it cannot serve as a model and inspiration for others. This has been a theme since your celebrated article on *Costa* v. *ENEL*. It is an important and shining point, but it too has a dark side. One advantage, internally, of reverting to a constitutional vocabulary is that it alerts the interpretative communities to the need to back up the constitutional disciplines demanded of Member States and individuals, with the appropriate political institutions and processes which are needed to legitimate such a deep legal reach and legal loyalty. The 'constitutional' has to be accompanied by a different political and social matrix – which the Community and Union have had and which they still strive to perfect. Externally, it warns others that one cannot try and emulate certain central features of the European system – its 'constitutional' devices, without that accompanying political and social matrices. When it has been tried, as in the Andean Pact or ASEAN (Association of Southeast Asian Nations), the results may be laughable or worse.

BdW: Again, I am not convinced that this is an either/or situation. Since it is possible to argue that the European Union is a subsystem of international law with many constitutional features, its observation can both serve as a model and inspiration for international cooperation elsewhere, and encourage institutional and judicial practice inside the EU which is inspired by the traditions of national constitutional law. So, the advantages of using the international and the constitutional vocabulary when describing the Union can be combined.

Chapter 2: Joseph Weiler and Neil Walker

JW: I find the tripartite division – collective identity, generative resources and political ontology – fecund as a means to ask consequential, indeed profound, questions about the EU as a polity or would-be polity. As a side issue, I am little persuaded that they constitute some hallmark of modernity. In relation to the first, it is true that popular sovereignty is a hallmark of modernity. But in the literature, and regularly in your chapter, there is a most common slippage from the idea of popular sovereignty to the very notion of the nation-state, as if the latter refracts modernity. That, though endlessly reiterated, simply cannot be true. In the West, the nation and nation-state are both the most common and most fundamental political unit. Likewise, the realm of the 'international' (perceptively and convincingly articulated by you as derivative from, even parasitic on, the state, predates the modern. The questions of political agency, and collectivity, which you ask could be pertinently asked in relation to the nation and nation-state from antiquity onwards. Identifying this slippage might seem a quibble – but it actually has significant opportunity costs in understanding the EU under the terms of your very project. First, and less importantly, there is, it seems to me, an arbitrary decision, that it will be the modern state and the modern 'international' which will be the referent against which the EU must be understood. Other models like the Austro-Hungarian Empire (which by different definitions of the modern straddles the modern and pre-modern) or even the Holy Roman Empire, to give two examples, are taken out of the picture. That arbitrary decision is based on another – that modernity and its conflicts encompass what is relevant in a contemporary understanding of the human condition and political organization. But that, too, cannot be true else we would stop reading *The Republic* and its like. You exclude interpretative keys which may yield richer pickings by the attachment to modernity and to this particular definition of modernity. Even if there is some truth to my statement about the arbitrariness of insisting on the modern as defined by you as the principal referent, you may still insist that I illustrate the opportunity cost. Here goes. If one were rigorously to stick to popular sovereignty of the nation-state as a hallmark of modernity, and not slip to the nation-state as such, the enquiry would focus on the significance of the *change* from a nation-state in which sovereignty was not understood as flowing from the people but from a sovereign legitimated otherwise. One significance of the change is the real jolt which popular sovereignty signifies, which is the responsibilizing of the people for their fate. Indeed, for many, the most significant hallmark of modernity is the shift from a worldview of fate to a worldview of choice. The shift is accompanied by huge anxiety – somewhat reminiscent of the anxiety of adulthood. (The sociologist Peter Berger and the social psychologist Erich Fromm write perceptively on this hallmark and its consequences.) This worldview shift reaches deep into the human condition as such from Adam and Eve onwards – the oscillation between autonomous and heteronymous authority. The fear of, and escape from, true responsibility, Kantian autonomy, is a constant but modernity accentuates it dramatically. For this one must simply read T. S. Elliot as the *grand maître*. The attachment to state symbols (like monarchy, state churches, conservatism in general) is in part a manifestation of that anxiety. Rethinking somewhat, as I suggest here, the first of your criteria, that of collective agency, takes away nothing from the brilliance of the tripartite refraction lens you propose, but does not put it in the straightjacket of modernity, and allows different sets of answers to both the issues of regenerative resources (EU as, for example, a modern form of Fromm's *Escape from Freedom* – a more disquieting but no less real option to the dichotomy you suggest) and even to political ontology – by applying your framework to, say, the Austro-Hungarian Empire, one may gain insight into the EU. (Not the silliness that the EU is 'like' the Empire, but that the Empire exemplifies alternatives to the strict state-international which in some ways is the holy grail you are after. I have focused on the first refracting lens, because the second and third, by your own analysis, are not really tied to modernity at all and can and should be asked about any polity.

NW: I agree that my threefold scheme for understanding modernity – collective agency, generative resources and political ontology – could also be employed as an analytical frame for making sense of other phases in human history, although clearly it would yield different conclusions for these other periods. I nevertheless chose to concentrate on the state and the international in the age of modernity because the EU – the entity with which I am ultimately concerned – is itself a product of modernity. I take your point that we may gain additional insights into the EU by looking at pre-modern or only incipiently modern forms such as the Austro-Hungarian Empire, but I think we gain more by concentrating on the adjacent forms of the modern. The EU inhabits the same geopolitical space, the same global economy, the same peculiar dynamic of cultural convergence and divergence, as these other modern political forms. Not only is the EU constructed in interaction with these forms, but it will also simply be more like them, at least in the sense of drawing from the same raw material, than it will be like predecessor forms. This does not, of course, mean that we should entirely discount the pre-modern. After all, as I tried to show in my chapter at various points, the modern emerges from the pre-modern and retains much of the latter in new modalities. We do not and should not stop reading The Republic *for precisely that reason. Plato and his fellow Greeks introduced us to ideas of public authority, of citizenship, of civic virtue, of political equality and so of the general idea of collective political agency, in the highly specialist and atypical forum of the classical city-state. We understand something about the general adoption of these ideas under the template of the modern state from a consideration of these classical origins, although it is an appreciation that owes as much to contrast as to continuity. Your unease over my preoccupation with modernity also extends to a critique of my invocation of the nation as if it were somehow exclusive to the modern age and interchangeable with the undoubtedly modern idea of popular sovereignty. I agree that the nation as a form of community predates the modern age, but what I am concerned with is not the nation as such but nationalism. Like*

Bernard Yack, whom I cite, I believe that popular sovereignty and nationalism are intimately connected, and indeed that the former contributes greatly to the latter by introducing an image of political community as a collective achievement that tends both to politicize an older tradition of national loyalties and to nationalize an older tradition of political loyalties. This interpenetration of nationalism and political sovereignty, in turn, lies at the heart of my explanation of the propensity of popular sovereignty to tack in a particularizing rather than a universalizing direction. But while I would want to retain nationalism for modernity, I also appreciate your point that something is lost if we do not look carefully at popular sovereignty in its own terms – perhaps more carefully than I did – without the background noise of nationalism. I agree with you that popular sovereignty is not just a political form in which individualism and equality attain an unprecedented prominence, but also one in which we move from a worldview of fate to one of choice and responsibility, that this movement is accompanied by a deep ambivalence towards freedom, and that in their different ways all modern political forms, including the EU, express this ambivalence towards political freedom.

JW: I want to contest a second feature of your use of modernity. Within modernity itself – understood here in the way you do, namely rooted in the shift to popular sovereignty – there seem to me to be two phases. In the first phase – very evident in the post World War I break-up of the Ottoman Empire – and theorized by Herder (to which the Nazis gave a bad name, but, thankfully, Isaiah Berlin redeemed), one saw the emergence of the non-liberal nation-state as an expression of popular sovereignty, in which nations had 'destinies', in which the bonds of the 'nation' were very thick – organic, even ethnic at times – and where the 'pay off' was 'greatness' and a secular form of salvation. The Wild Grapes (Isaiah 5:2) of this was, of course, fascism in its various murderous and less murderous versions. The liberal state understood as a polity which is an open framework for different projects and which entertains a far less organic notion of citizenry and nation becomes ubiquitous only after World War II with the collapse of the first order of modernity. So? It is again, opportunity cost. If one were to accept this depiction, it opens richer veins to understand the Union within your very framework. The EU on this reading is clearly *not* a liberal project. It is not an open framework for realizing different projects. It is rooted in a very distinct project, with a very distinct ideology. It is a Herder-like community of destiny and fate in which the substantive ends are far more important than the (democratic) means for their achievement. This is, *nota bene,* how it was originally designed (with the European Parliament as a mere talking chamber, reminiscent of similar institutions in the illiberal modern state) and this still informs the ethos of its civil service, in which legitimacy of outcome is always considered far more important than legitimacy of process. In other words, by unpacking the modern state to the illiberal and liberal, one arguably gains a sharper tool of analysis for the EU and its current discontents. There is of course a deep irony here. The EU emerges as the antidote to the failings of the international system based on the illiberal nation-state, but at its deepest it assumes the hallmarks of that which it is attempting to replace. Lampedusa will be smiling from his grave: if we want things to stay as they are, things will have to change.

NW: *The liberal state has certainly become more prominent in the postwar years, but just as I may have failed to distinguish sufficiently between different stages of modernity, it is equally important not to overstate the extent of transformation. For the reasons I gave in my previous answer, wherever the claim to popular sovereignty and collective self-rule is made in the context of the state, nationalist sentiment will never be far away – whether liberal or illiberal nationalism. Part of the challenge of the EU today, indeed, as is so vividly portrayed in your own writings, involves not only dealing with the legacy of Europe's illiberal nationalist past, but also, especially on the EU's eastern borders, addressing Europe's illiberal nationalist present. As for the EU as a throwback to the illiberal past – a Herder-like community of destiny – I think that is only part of the story. Alongside its particularism and collectivism, as I have tried to argue, there is also a distinct strand of universalism and individualism in the EU's DNA. There is a liberalism to dilute the collectivism, but it is a (qualified) economic liberalism rather than a political liberalism, even if the public philosophy of many of the states that make up the EU would be one of political liberalism. This compounds the irony that you describe. It is not just that the EU is going back to the future in its attempt to combat the pathologies of illiberalism, but that in so doing it risks turning freedom into its opposite – the right to choose a lifestyle into the imposition of a lifestyle of choice.*

JW: Though I am, I believe, using the very tool of analysis you offer us, and faithfully, I hope, try to answer the very questions which you articulate as critical (and with which I admiringly agree), the direction of my answers is far darker than yours. This, I believe, is due to a strangely uncritical strand in your chapter. It is evident in assigning a priori a 'key' position to the EU: it is important. Is it really, other than giving the likes of you and me gainful employment? Is it really important to the big problems of the world? To matters of war and peace? Economic dislocation? The current crisis? The shabby world ecology? By my lights, the jury is out. It is evident in the absence of any normative critique of the EU and the EU project – you describe failings, but from the position of a neutral social scientist, not a normative political theorist. And it is evident very notably at the end of the chapter where what emerges is indeed 'a vague sense of a dual constituent power', but not the vagueness you intend of the phenomenon but a vagueness in the description and analysis of the phenomenon. The crispness and sharpness which are so typical of your preceding analysis and indeed of your entire corpus suddenly melt down to a touchy-feely miasma. 'The second-order people must instead describe a compound structure, incorporating but also augmenting the aggregate of first-order collective peoples' would need a lot of articulation. It is surely saying more than my own notion, in *Eros and Civilization*, that in understanding one's self as, say, Italian, there would be embedded a European element. Part of what it means to be Italian is to be European. But what exactly more is intended by you? But much more importantly, one may ask: Why does it seem so important to believe that Europe will offer whatever it is that you believe it will and can? This is not simply a question of 'whence the optimism' but what is it about the EU which evidently to any reader makes you so passionately want it 'to deliver'? Answering that question – a serious question – may not only address what I claimed was the strange non-critical strand in the chapter, but also shed light on the generative resources of Europe. Of the kind of patriotism it manages to evoke.

NW: *You pose a number of challenging questions. How can we be sure that the EU really does matter in the global scheme of things? To the extent that it does matter, why does it matter, and why should we assume or conclude that it matters or can be made to matter in a positive rather than a negative way? And what, if anything, does its mattering* have to do with the distinctiveness of its political title – with the special kind of collective agency that it embodies? The short answer to the first question is that none of us can be sure how much it matters. Indeed, perhaps it does not matter how much the EU matters provided it matters somewhat! But that is too easy. As you say, although I do not believe that I am one of the worst sinners in this regard, there is a broad and somewhat complacent assumption within the EU commentariat that the EU stands centre stage on the global theatre. That in itself is an interesting phenomenon. I suspect that we have passed the high point of collective self-confidence in this regard. Some of the discussions about the global role of the EU, such as the 'normative power Europe' debate or the external face of the constitutional debate, betray the anxiety of an entity increasingly unsure of its global standing and relevance. A key question concerns whether the uniqueness of the EU, its non-martial outlook, its supranational law or its highly dispersed system of political power, is the harbinger of an importantly new way of doing things in a world where the political categories of high modernity are of declining significance, or whether it simply implies quaintness – that the EU has become a local curiosity, the diminished form of a fading regional power. Of course, these are stylized responses to a stylized question, but it is certainly true that part of what is of interest in studying the EU today has to do with capturing just that growing sense of existential doubt – that anxiety of influence – which affects the whole enterprise, and which casts its future in such an uncertain light.

My own view is that what is innovative and path-breaking about the EU continues to outweigh what is merely idiosyncratic. In my chapter I said that the EU was a continuation of modernity through other means. More specifically, it offers a very particular answer to the question whether and how we might retain much of what is valuable in state polity in a world in which, due to the globalization of so many registers of influence and all the collective action problems and 'externalities' associated with this, the state can no longer do the job itself. Yet unlike many private or hybrid public/private or functionally specialist forms of transnational governance, the EU still looks somewhat state-like in the alternative it offers; in its range of internal and external authority, in its systemic legal properties and, to my mind perhaps most importantly of all, in the potential amplitude of its political imagination and forms. That is why, finally, I am so interested in the question of the 'second-order people' of Europe, and whether and how this might be more than *the sum of the 'first-order peoples' of the Member States. The EU is unprecedented in the extent to which it seeks to superimpose an autonomous political (and legal) authority upon the original authority of the nation-states. It seeks to inaugurate a genuinely multilevel system of political authority where, unlike the federation or the unitary nation-state, power does not in the last analysis collapse back into a single centre. The question whether and how this can be done – whether and how political authority and responsibility can faithfully track the dispersal of power away from the system of states, is itself a political or meta-political question – witness the constitutional debate. This seems to me a matter of great importance both for Europe itself and as indication of how other post-state politics might track other movements of authority away from the states.*

A sceptic might retort that none of this directly connects to whether and how the EU can be a force for good in the world, or indeed even in Europe itself. For that reason perhaps my analysis misses the point, since the true crisis of Europe, in an age where its original virtues, and the manifest collective goods associated with these virtues, have lost their resonance, is not political but ethical. However, I believe that the two are inextricable. Where I discuss the various types of collective goods in my chapter, I argue that the capacity both to identify and generate new explicit common goods, and to develop the implicit common good of solidarity, mutual respect, etc. which are both necessary to the implementation of the explicit goods and self-standing benefits of collective belonging, depend on a degree of common 'political' commitment to engage in finding a common sense of what is properly and feasibly political at the European level. Indeed, it is the absence of such a common commitment to seek to find a basis for common commitment which has led to Europe becoming a blocked project in terms of political energy and substantive ethical goals alike – a deep problem of which the euro crisis is but the latest manifestation. In turn, it is difficult to imagine how this might be rectified except, in a bootstrapping way, through the reconvening of the kind of forums and regeneration of the kind of political ambience – traditionally called 'constitutional' but labels can hinder more than help – in which we are inclined to have talks about how we want to talk to one another. Of course, I have no magic formula for triggering this process, and no way of guaranteeing that Europe will bear its modernist burden of collective responsibility better if such a process does unfold. But without a reinvestment in a sense of common political space, however prescribed and circumscribed, things can only get worse.

Chapter 3: Joseph Weiler and Gráinne de Búrca

JW: One conceit of this book and its distinguished authors is rooted in at least one of the following two propositions and for some of the contributors in both: (a) that in its engagement with the world, the EU represents a different model of 'the Constitutional' – of constitutionalism; and/or (b) that in the engagement with the way the EU engages with the world, the author represents a different analytical/normative perspective of 'the Constitutional' gleaned from either the practice of the EU (analytical approach) or what should be its practice (normative approach).

If we address (a) first – namely the manner in which the ECJ (European Court of Justice) engages with the world – it would seem that your claim is robust and severe: the ECJ represents a traditional even banal self-understanding of 'the Constitutional' in the international arena which, additionally, is retrograde in terms of its prior supportive role of the international. However, even the CFI (now the General Court), which seems to go in the opposite direction, would, on your view, be part of the same traditional paradigm, simply at its other end. Even more interesting is the implicit critique of the Academy in its treatment of *Kadi*, which may be said to fall into the same self-understanding. Would that be a fair implication?

GdeB: Yes, at the core of my criticism of the ECJ's approach to international law in Kadi *is the fact that that approach seems informed by a particular traditional concept of 'the constitutional'. The ECJ has long been active in the 'constitutionalization' of EU law internally, articulating the relationship between EU and national law, and between the ECJ and national courts, and this judicial activity has generated a large academic literature. In the internal EU realm, the idea of the constitutional promoted by the ECJ has been one that emphasizes above all the autonomous, independent and sovereign nature of EU legal authority, which has primacy over conflicting national law. There have been considerably fewer occasions (other than in the WTO (World Trade Organization) context) on which the ECJ has pronounced on the idea of the constitutional in EU external relations, and there has been correspondingly less academic discussion of the issue.* Kadi *represented an unusually high-profile occasion on which the ECJ made an important statement on the external dimensions and implications of its understanding of the constitutional nature of EU law, and consequently on the nature of the relationship between EU law and international law. And the overriding concern which comes through in the judgment is this same fundamental concern with the autonomy and sovereignty of EU law. Despite various statements by the ECJ in* Kadi *about the need for the EC (European Community) to respect international law and to abide by international commitments undertaken, its most striking statements are those which repeatedly assert the autonomy and primacy of the EU constitutional order and the incapacity of international law, including the UN (United Nations) Charter, to alter or affect those. Consider these four separate statements within a few pages of the judgment: 'an international agreement cannot affect the allocation of powers fixed by the Treaties or, consequently, the autonomy of the Community legal system' (para 282); 'the obligations imposed by an international agreement cannot have the effect of prejudicing the constitutional principles of the EC Treaty' (para 285); judicial review by the ECJ for compliance with fundamental rights is 'a constitutional guarantee stemming from the EC Treaty as an autonomous legal system which is not to be prejudiced by an international agreement' (para 316); and finally 'the question of the Court's jurisdiction arises in the context of the internal and autonomous legal order of the Community' (para 317).*

The vision presented by the ECJ is one of a sovereign EU constitutional order to which international law is external and subordinate (except to the extent, within certain limits, to which the EU chooses to commit itself to international obligations and agreements). The approach of the General Court in simple terms, was the reverse: namely the subordination of the EU legal order to the international legal order, with the latter having primacy over the former. Academic reactions to the Kadi *ruling on the part of EU lawyers have, on the whole, tended to line up behind the ECJ's approach, applauding its boldness in confronting the UN Security Council and its determination in asserting the constitutional autonomy and primacy of EU law within its own sphere, while those whose primary disciplinary orientation is in international law rather than EU law have preferred the approach of the General Court.*

Ultimately, the chapter grew out of my disappointment with the failure of the ECJ (or the CFI), after all these years, to develop a richer conceptualization of, and hence a different and more nuanced language for, addressing the complex and important relationship between the 'novel' EU legal order and the international order.

JW: Within its traditional paradigm, you hint to 'instrumentalism' and pragmatism as the reason for the ECJ's shift from its prior 'supportive' stance. Can you elaborate? I do not think that one can simply say that it had a concern to protect rights – since it could have done that with the So Long As device proposed explicitly by the Advocate General and, after all, in very pragmatic terms, it took an easy path by inviting the Council to remedy the process whilst maintaining the suspension of rights. What, then, might be the deeper roots of the shift? Is it really a contingent position, or could it be a creeping 'European exceptionalism' in a world dominated by an American bloc from which Europe feels now much more free to emphasize its distance, and a China and a large Asia/Muslim bloc from all of which Europe feels a distance. In other words, not instrumentalism but something far more profound?

GdeB: By instrumentalism, what I had in mind was that the ECJ's varying approach to the status and enforceability of international law in the EU legal order in general seemed to depend on its view of the substantive merits of the international law norm or claim at issue in the different cases. Thus some have read the WTO cases as reflecting the Court's awareness of the highly political nature of many WTO disputes and its unwillingness to restrict the room for negotiation on the part of the EU in these disputes. Similarly, the Intertanko *case might be read as reflecting the Court's decision to side with the Council in relation to its preference for the substance of the provisions of an EU Directive over the provisions of the International Law of the Sea Conventions dealing with liability for ship-source marine pollution. And one obvious reading of the ECJ approach in* Kadi *is that, since the Court was fully aware of the heated debate about the absence of due process in the application of smart sanctions by the UN Security Council, it was determined to find a way of (at least temporarily) refusing the application of the sanctions to Kadi and Al Barakaat, and that this is what was driving its more general assertions (however cloaked) about the primacy of EU constitutional law over the UN Charter.*

But I agree with you that any such 'instrumentalism' does not reflect the whole story, nor even the most important part of the story of the ECJ's approach to international law. In other words, while specific strategic considerations may be driving the approach of the ECJ to the status of particular international law provisions in each of these cases, there is an increasingly audible and insistent assertion by the ECJ in external relations cases of the autonomy and primacy of the EU constitutional order, and this increasing assertiveness is coming at a time when the EU is consciously promoting its identity as a significant international actor, finding its voice on the global stage, and seeking to advance itself as an alternative to other dominant world actors such as China and the USA.

JW: Let us turn now to (b) – namely the theory of constitutionalism which you put forward as an alternative to the paradigm within which the Court according to you operates. You call it 'soft constitutionalism'. I think many readers, like myself, will have some difficulty disentangling it from the pluralists. After all, the pluralist theorists, including Krisch, whom you use to illustrate the approach, are not isolationists. They differ from the constitutionalist approach in their rejection of a hierarchical system with clear answers at points of conflict. But their project and projection is based on the benefits of challenges, dialogue and engagement. It is not a vision of 'strangers in the night'. There is another way to pose this question: What justifies in the image you have put forward as soft constitutionalism the use of the word 'constitutionalism' at all? Is not soft constitutionalism simply a form of pluralism? As part of your answer would you be willing to give a clear example of an issue – such as *Kadi* – where you could briefly describe the outcome according to the constitutional, the pluralist and the soft constitutional in a manner which would illustrate that there are some reasonably sharp lines that differentiate the three?

GdeB: You are right in pointing to the lack of a sharp distinction between the categories. I see them more as being ranged along a spectrum, with strong – or isolationist, as you put it – pluralism at one end and strong constitutionalism at the other end, with soft constitutionalism meeting soft pluralism somewhere in the middle.

The essence of the difference between a constitutional approach and a pluralist approach in my view is the insistence, in the constitutional approach, on what Kant has called 'universalizability': the obligation always to take account of the position of the other in reaching decisions which have implications for that other, and to articulate one's own position as far as possible in terms which are cognizable to the other. In other words, the constitutional approach presupposes that it is not for one polity or legal system to determine completely autonomously, and without regard to the other system, what the relationship between its norms and the norms of the other should be, or how the obligations imposed by the other system should affect its own. On a pluralist understanding of the global legal order, by comparison, there are multiple legal and political systems, each of which decides entirely for itself what its relationship to other systems and norms will be. One particular system may choose to be more or less open to other systems, but it is always for each system itself to decide on this – whether to adopt a robustly pluralist stance closer to one end of the spectrum, as the USA has often done, or to adopt a fairly open approach to international law and obligations closer to the other end, as the Netherlands is seen to do. On my understanding of the constitutional approach to the international legal order, that approach, unlike the pluralist approach, has as a fundamental principle that the relationship between legal and constitutional orders is always determined by a process of 'mutual perspective-taking'.

You ask me to exemplify the differences between constitutional and pluralist approaches by reference to the Kadi *context: I would say the Court of First Instance in* Kadi *(and the ECtHR (European Court of Human Rights) in* Behrami) *are examples of a strong constitutionalist approach to the international legal order which stipulates that international law always takes precedence over regional or national law. At least some of the statements of the ECJ in* Kadi *reflect a strong pluralist approach, particularly the assertion that no international agreement can affect the allocation of powers fixed by the Treaties, the constitutional principles established in the Treaties, or the autonomy of the Community legal system. This fixedness, immutability, untouchability by international law of EU constitutional law reflects a strong idea of separateness where only the EU can alter itself, and nothing in the international legal order can influence or affect its constitutional principles. On the other hand I would view at least some versions of the* Solange *approach as a soft constitutionalist approach.*

JW: Taking, as I do, soft constitutionalism very seriously, especially as a mode in which to imagine the international arena, I am having difficulty in seeing how and why this promising concept is dependent on, or derivative from, both the practice and theory of the EU and European integration. That is to say, even if it is very promising, it would seem to be a concept that could and should inform the relationship of all state and state-like actors in the international arena and it seems to be offered as an alternative to the self-understanding of the ECJ and of the field of European integration studies. This is a clarificatory question on intellectual provenance rather than a critical question on substance. Another way of putting the question is: Even if we were to imagine a world with no EU (perish the thought . . .) could and should your concept have been put forward?

GdeB: I agree entirely. The EU may be an unusual, even a unique phenomenon in contemporary international relations, but it is certainly not the case that the idea of soft constitutionalism is inspired only or even primarily by the practice of EU Member States over the years in moderating their sovereignty and accommodating the obligations of membership of a new transnational legal order. On the contrary, the idea of soft constitutionalism, as I suggest in my chapter, has its intellectual roots in Kant's ideas about the possibilities of international cooperation, in particular as reinterpreted by contemporary thinkers like Habermas. Having said that, I think that the experience of the EU Member States, and the trajectory of the EU itself, have been interesting and useful in suggesting different ways of approaching and reconciling statehood, sovereignty and a dense network of international obligations. It is hard to imagine circumstances in which it would be appropriate or possible simply to transpose solutions found within the EU to the wider international sphere, given the specificity of circumstances, but the EU in various ways affords an interesting example – e.g. in the way in which national constitutional courts have reconciled their fidelity to the domestic constitution with the evolving legal obligations of EU membership – of how an idea like soft constitutionalism can take root in practice.

JW: Following on the previous question – it is not simply that the EU provenance of the concept is not clear, it would seem to run against the ethos, at least of the ECJ, in its intra-community relations where historically it has put forward a very rigid constitutional approach. Why, then, would soft constitutionalism not be appropriate for intra-Union relationships, at least some of them – yet by its silence your chapter seems to exclude that possibility?

GdeB: I agree entirely that the idea of soft constitutionalism is fully appropriate for intra-EU relationships, and that the traditional idea of constitutionalism promoted by the ECJ – which is focused, as I suggested above, primarily on sovereignty, autonomy and primacy – has become increasingly ill-suited to the complex transnational polity represented by the EU. The silence of the chapter on the subject was certainly not intended to imply that this approach is only for the external relations of the EU.

Chapter 4: Joseph Weiler and Daniel Halberstam

JW: One of the overarching themes in my dialogue with all contributors to this volume is a sceptical even jaundiced view on the use of 'constitutionalism' in one of its variants to describe, conceptualize, evaluate or set up as an ideal type the legal/political reality which exists beyond the state and the European Union. In the literature, as if in some academic reality show, it has spawned an entire set of competing appellations – with international constitutionalism, cosmopolitan constitutionalism, counter-punctual constitutionalism and others vying for the title of constitutional idol. In some of the contributions to this volume the constitutional is contrasted with the plural, but in yours, plural constitutionalism is contrasted with local and global (international) variants. My first two questions are, perhaps, two sides of the same coin – the coin which tries to satisfy myself and the reader that employing the vocabulary of constitutionalism (plural or otherwise) to describe the important phenomena you address results in illumination and theoretical gain.

For the purpose of this first question one could readily accept the factual premises that animate your chapter: the first is that in the age of global governance, classical constitutionalism rooted around the state (and nation) cannot serve its traditional legitimating function. Too much exercise of public power occurs outside the realm of classical statal constitutionalism. The second is that there now exist a multiplicity of legal orders making competing sovereignty and supremacy claims.

I want to challenge your use of 'constitutionalism'. Why does it help here? Pluralism may help, but why is it necessary to stipulate that the international is constitutional (thus presuming features which by your own definition it might not have)? Why make your suggestions inapplicable to an international order in which many states do not correspond to your (thin) definition of constitutionalism but which might profit and even accept the sensibleness of your 'grammar'?

It is a very American view that 'constitutionalism' has dominated the imagination. Certainly constitutionalism has dominated the American legal imagination – and celebratedly so – but to equate liberalism with constitutionalism is to reduce constitutionalism in an unhelpful way, since it is equated with liberalism, rather than a particular arrangement.

My own view is that you make an important contribution to the problem of competing 'sovereignties' or 'supremacies' or legal orders ever more present in the age of increasing global governance. You make a contribution to the discussion of pluralism. But this contribution is not helped, indeed it is obfuscated and even diminished, by employing the vocabulary and conceptual world of constitutionalism.

There are two sleights of hand at the very premise of your chapter. The first concerns the dichotomy you set up between, on the one hand, local constitutionalism for which a very American, exceptionalist and rather radical instantiation is given and, on the other hand, global constitutionalism for which a no less radical idealist and exceptional instantiation is provided. This enables you to situate yourself as mediating two extremes with your version of pluralist constitutionalism. In particular, your version of pluralism seems to provide a way of thinking and a toolkit to address (for want of a better term) the problem of legal orders claiming mutually excluding supremacies. This, after all, was one of the core issues which the unforgettable Neil McCormick addressed and on which the current 'reality show' seeks to improve. In this way you are able, like the great discoverers of yore, to plant a flag and stake a claim to a territory hitherto unoccupied. But, it seems to me, that you end up, like those great discoverers of America or Australia, planting your flag in a territory already comfortably occupied and thinking that by giving it a new name, Constitutionalia, the indigenous conceptual population may at best be enlightened, at worst, dispossessed.

The first sleight of hand is to make believe that the problem of competing sovereignties, or supremacies, or legal orders – the problem to which pluralism seeks to give answers – exists because of competing constitutionalisms or that it is somehow better understood and resolved by using the vocabulary of pluralist 'constitutionalism'. As a matter of argumentation this is just assumed in your piece and never demonstrated. In particular, what is not explained is why the extant vocabulary which differentiates between the constitutional (primarily states) and the international profits from the new lexical grafting of the 'constitutional'. Where you plant your flag of constitutional pluralism is a territory already occupied by the mainstream of both constitutional law and international law as reflected in most textbooks, most law classes and, indeed, in the practice and self-understanding of what are still the principal actors in both realms: states. In this centrist place it is understood that there are distinct legal orders, both domestic and international; that for the most part their functional division of tasks allows them to work harmoniously in parallel even when their 'jurisdictions' overlap; that, as you remarkably explain in your own chapter, they not only interpenetrate one another but are interdependent on one another. To give but one example, even a statist view of international legal authority has long understood that one cannot seek the authority and legitimacy of international norms in the explicit consent of states – one could not otherwise explain the general acceptance of customary law (as an empirical proposition) by all states, including the United States.

Typically, as in federalism, when there are conflicts of norms one has a set of legal jurisdictional rules to resolve them. Again, it has been long understood that the correct expression of the principle of supremacy as the ultimate tie-breaker (in both non-unitary systems such as federal states and in the international sphere) is that each order is supreme within its jurisdiction. It is also understood that with the material expansion of international law and international legal regimes there will be conflicts of norms, vertical (with state orders) or horizontal (among international regimes), where this classical tie-breaker does not work because jurisdictions overlap. The insight of McCormick was to stipulate that in those cases none can claim 'sovereignty'. Beyond this, there are various attempts to describe what actually happens in these 'hard cases', or what should happen. An important dimension is also to note that, though not negligible, the problems are more grave in the classroom or the learned journals than in the reality of international law. Be that as it may, some just 'muddle through', others seek principled approaches. Nobody has found a silver bullet. I think this would be the standard account for at least the last ten to fifteen years, if not more, and your account is comfortably within this mainstream. Your contribution is important and valid in offering ways to diffuse this problem and find principled ways for decision-makers, whether political or judicial, to approach it. Not much is gained by 'constitutionalizing' all the legal orders which create the pluralist challenge, and important things are lost. Because your pluralist sensibility would be useful also in situations where the legal orders or actors involved really cannot in any meaningful ways be called 'constitutional' (such as non-democratic states) but who, experience teaches, would not be averse to the pluralist sensibility you propose. What, then, is the gain in this act of 'constitutional imperialism'?

DH: Thank you for these incisive comments and questions. There is much serious business packed into your opening salvo, so I will tease out the principal comments and objections and respond to them in turn.

Beyond MacCormick

You say I mark out two extremist positions that are essentially occupied by irrelevant nobodies and that I plant my constitutional flag in a spurious 'middle' which is, in truth, 'a territory already comfortably occupied' by Neil MacCormick and all other reasonable people in this world. You then concede that my contribution is nonetheless 'important and valid' in offering ways to diffuse' the problem of jurisdictional conflict in 'principled' ways. But you wonder what is gained by talking about this in terms of constitutionalism, i.e. by what you refer to as my act of 'constitutional imperialism'.

Let me begin the other way around. I have much less at stake in using constitutional language than you might think. Indeed, I have far less at stake in insisting on the language of constitutionalism than you seem to have in insisting on its irrelevance. I am after neither the imperialism of a term nor winning a debater's point on some show. If you take my argument absent the language of constitutionalism, that's fine with me.

I have never claimed originality of language when it comes to using constitutional terminology. Building on MacCormick, my claims have been to distinguish 'systems pluralism' from 'institutional pluralism' (for reasons we need not go into here); to show through careful comparative analysis that pluralism can be a core presence even in rather traditional constitutional law; and to show that there is a coherent plural third way between the two preferred options of privileging either the global or the local.

This is not tilting at windmills. I do not set up a false dichotomy among irrelevant extremists. The scholars I cite on both sides of this issue are important (especially considering the influence of some in government). Moreover, even the less 'extreme' versions of the two rival positions I have laid out tend to privilege massively either the local or the global. The effects of this binary thinking are not the stuff of academic fringe writing either. The effects are real, as you can see in the Kadi case. The CFI went global and the Court went local. Only Miguel Maduro offered the plural as an option in between.

Why might this be? Well, as you know, even MacCormick flinched. He rejected what he termed the idea of 'radical pluralism' in favour of pluralism organized under international law. That is, in an oddly Kelsenian move (which he acknowledged as such), even MacCormick opted for international law as the ultimate tie-breaker. MacCormick rejected radical pluralism because he feared that in such cases nothing more could be said about who should be doing what to resolve the pluralist stand-off. And so, even he who gave us 'constitutional pluralism' sought to resolve the pluralist challenge by going for the primacy of the global over the local.

My contribution tries to address this problem. In this sense it is not imperial but incremental. It addresses MacCormick's puzzle by suggesting a way to understand the practice of pluralism as being radical yet grounded. It is radical in the sense of lacking any overarching hierarchy or tie-breaker. And yet it is grounded in the sense of being a principled practice of contest and accommodation based in the common enterprise of interlocking systems of limited collective self-governance. In my view, this goes beyond MacCormick and the comfortable middle ground occupied by all right-minded people who are just muddling through.

Constitutionalia

I did not conceive of my piece as defending the expansion of any empire of constitutionalism. Nor, as I said, do I have anything deeply at stake in claiming Constitutionalia. My point is far more modest. In my view, the *lens of constitutionalism can be helpful in understanding the pluralist project of interlocking legal systems better. Here's why.*

The pluralist case I am concerned about is not just a set of multiple overlapping legal systems without hierarchy, as you seem to suggest in your question. It's not just like two people competing in a game of musical chairs. Law is important here, and we should attend to its formal, as well as social, significance.

We can give it a try and describe roughly what's going on in pluralism (as I see it) without using the dreaded c-word. But I do need a word for the rules that regulate the rules of a legal system, and not wishing to get into first-order jurisprudence here I shall simply use the phrase 'operating system', which you have used in the past.[2] So here goes:

Each legal system in the pluralist constellation is a separate system with generative legal capacity; neither is hierarchically superior to the other; each is open to the other; this openness is embedded at the level of each system's own 'operating system'; that 'operating system' is what creates each system's claim to legality; each system is not just a random formal legal system but a project of limited collective self-governance; and the project of limited collective self-governance is, in turn, created (dare I say 'constituted'?) by each system's operating system.

As a result, the various actors from the various systems have a legal obligation to consider each other's claim of authority as part of a common project of limited collective self-governance. This legal obligation arises out their very own operating system – the one that establishes their own claim of legal authority in the first place. But there is no overarching hierarchy to resolve the apparent conflict between the claims. And so the actors accommodate each other's claims if, and to the extent that, the claim of the other realizes their common project of governance.

I have no difficulty with this description. More important, though, I am not sure what we gain by avoiding the c-word in this way. The idea of a self-standing operating system with generative legal capacity (i.e. not a system with a purely derivative mission or derivative legality that is controlled entirely by another legal system) is central to this understanding of interlocking systems and can be usefully considered in constitutional terms. The fact that the openness to the rival system is

---

[2] Weiler, J. H. H., ed., *The Constitution of Europe: 'Do the New Clothes Have an Emperor?' and Other Essays on European Integration* (Cambridge University Press, 1999), at 224.

embedded in the very operating system that grounds the actors' own claim of legality can also be understood readily in terms of constitutional frameworks. Moreover, the common purpose of this interlocking collection of legal systems as one of limited collective self-governance corresponds to the grand purpose of constitutionalism.

On the other hand, something important may be lost by not focusing, for example, on the constitutive power of the legal framework. Let me explain. In a twist of reverse imperialism to avoid the c-word, you suggest that federal states and international law are all governed by the same principles when it comes to supremacy. '[I]t has been long understood', you say, 'that the correct expression of the principle of supremacy as the ultimate tie-breaker (in both non-unitary systems such as federal states and in the international sphere) is that each order is supreme within its jurisdiction.' The only problem, you suggest, is that international law has now expanded so much that 'this classical tie-breaker does not work because jurisdictions overlap'.

This way of avoiding the c-word obscures the legal question where the tie-breaker is located. It is one thing for a single tie-breaker to be located in an overarching constitution to which all participants subscribe (as it is in some federal systems). It is quite another for each order to view itself as supreme within whatever jurisdiction it sets out for itself to occupy (as tends to be the case in the relationship between international and domestic law as well as in the European Union). But from your description of what is commonly known and 'long understood' about the right way to understand supremacy, we wouldn't know the difference.

Using constitutional language, by contrast, can help us understand how multiple autonomous legal orders, each with their own tie-breaker, can nonetheless stand in a relationship of mutual legal commitment to one another. It can be important, that is, to focus on the fact that there is no overarching legal framework to contain a tie-breaker and that the overlap is not haphazard but that the mutual openness among the systems is legally embedded in each system's organic framework.

Finally, I do not argue that the WTO should be seen as a separate constitutional order. The WTO may still be just an ordinary part of the system of public international law. Instead, I have argued that to understand an international regime like the WTO in constitutional terms need not entail the kind of rigid hierarchy that global constitutionalists have traditionally envisioned or local constitutionalists have feared. My project has thus been to explore the potential for constitutionalism beyond the two extreme constructs of the local and global, that is, to demonstrate the possibility of joining the constitutional with the plural in a principled legal practice.

JW: The second question follows on the first and is still part of my scepticism towards the vocabulary of constitutionalism as necessary to the pluralist dilemma. Global governance does not just accentuate the problem of competing 'supremacies'. It also, as you explain in the opening paragraphs of your chapter, raises the question of the legitimation of public power beyond the state. This is where your second sleight of hand comes in. Your opening sentence is as follows: 'The idea that constitutionalism is central to the legitimate exercise of public power has dominated the modern liberal imagination since the Enlightenment.' I would say that democracy has dominated the modern liberal imagination since the Enlightenment. Only in America has democracy so forcefully been equated with constitutionalism to justify the claim in your first sentence. Except, that is, if, in your second sleight of hand, you offer such a thin definition of constitutionalism – 'simply put' as 'the idea of limited collective self-governance'.

This definition means that any discourse of limited government as part of the democracy project by definition becomes a constitutional discourse. Like M. Jourdain, all were engaged in constitutionalism even if unknown to themselves. If that is how one defines constitutionalism, this result is predetermined. But this thinness does not only conflict with the self-understanding of polities and theorists, it just tells us too little. It fails to account for the uniqueness of the American experiment, for the constitutional revolution of the twentieth century described in Cappelletti's classic *The Judicial Process*, and in today's discussions of globalization and international governance it renders any discussion about legitimacy and democratization definitionally 'constitutional'. At one level this is a second act of imperialism – the American type – and at another level it is a reductionism so extreme that it actually removes much utility of the very vocabulary of constitutionalism. If that is your definition, even Howse and Nicolaidis would have to concede that the WTO and for that matter any international organization of limited powers – they all are – is constitutional. If you define 'giant' to be any human above the height of 30 cm, even pygmies become giants. Unhelpful. Would it not be far more useful to take your core concepts of voice, rights and expertise and stipulate that they are essential elements in an understanding of legitimacy – without all the constitutional baggage – and should be employed in addressing the pluralist challenge?

DH: I am surprised to hear you reject so forcefully my opening claim that the idea of constitutionalism as central to the legitimate exercise of public power has dominated the modern liberal imagination since the Enlightenment. You counter that 'democracy' has, instead, dominated the modern liberal imagination, and that my claim of the centrality of constitutionalism is uniquely American ('Only in America . . .') and can be maintained elsewhere only by an act of American imperialism or by a 'sleight of hand' that waters down the idea of constitutionalism beyond recognition.

I did not expect my rather generic opening statement to bring on such heated controversy. But all the better. Let me not engage in any grand debate here about whether constitutionalism or democracy is more important in the constellation of liberty. That strikes me as unproductive. Also, I will not perform a close reading of my own text to show that the passage you quote discusses the purpose for which we have constitutions, as opposed to exhaustively defining the legal functions of a constitution. In any event, I am quite happy to defend my opening claim. Even on a strong understanding, constitutionalism has held the position I ascribe to it.

Your colleague Stephen Holmes perhaps put it best. In his excellent book on the theory of liberal democracy, he writes that 'the key concept for understanding the interdependence of liberalism and democracy is constitutionalism'.[3] (The emphasis, by the way, is his.) Holmes carefully shows that the formal limitation of power is not only a restrictive force but a creative one as well, and that these twin aspects of constitutionalism help resolve the apparent paradox between liberalism and democracy. Putting Enlightenment ideas into practice, on Holmes's account (which I largely accept), has therefore focused crucially on the idea of constitutionalism.

Now you might say that this brilliant observation is the typical product of analytical hindsight of an American-based political theorist writing primarily about American constitutional law. But that would be mistaken, too. Constitutionalism was also central to the real-world

---

[3] Holmes, Stephen, *Passions and Constraint* (University of Chicago Press, 1995), at 6.

struggle for liberalism and democracy as it unfolded in Europe. Constitutionalism in one form or another was a key element of the European battles surrounding the legitimate exercise of public power ever since James Whitlocke objected in 1610 to the impositions of James I on the grounds that they were 'against the natural frame and constitution of the policy [i.e. 'polity'] of this kingdom, which is ius publicum regni, *and so subverteth the fundamental law of the realm and induceth a new form of State and government'.*[4] *The struggle in England and, later, on the Continent for liberal self-government quickly came to appreciate the importance of constitutionalism despite the varied forms the latter would take. Whether as the framing of preexisting political power in England and Germany or the radical founding of political power in the United States and France,*[5] *constitutionalism and constitutions took centre stage.*

In particular, the American experience with constitutionalism did not remain of local concern. To the contrary, the idea of a constitution attained 'overarching meaning for the development of European history'.[6] *Dieter Grimm, who is neither American nor subscribes to a watereddown version of constitutionalism, explains: 'The new instrument for solving the old problem of the foundation and limitation of public authority rose to being* the dominant theme of the time. *The controversies about a just social order became controversies about the necessary content of constitutions.'*[7] *(This time, the emphasis is mine.) Grimm goes even one step further. 'European history since 1789', he suggests, 'can be written for a hundred years as a history of constitutional battles.'*[8]

Constitutionalism an American obsession? I think not.

JW: How helpful are your three core concepts. They are, I believe, important articulations of what you call the 'common constitutional

---

[4] Tanner, J. R., *Constitutional Documents of the Reign of James I* (Cambridge University Press, 1961 [1930]), at 260; see also Stourzh, Gerald, *From Vienna to Chicago and Back: Essays on Intellectual History and Political Thought in Europe and America* (University of Chicago Press, 2007), at 90.

[5] See, e.g., Moellers, Christoph, 'Pouvoir Constituant – Constitution – Constitutionalization', in Armin von Bogdandy and J. Bast, eds., *Principles of European Constitutional Law* (Oxford: Hart Publishing, 2005), 183–226.

[6] Grimm, Dieter, *Deutsche Verfassungsgeschichte 1776–1866* (Frankfurt am Main: Suhrkamp, 1988), at 10.

[7] Ibid.   [8] Ibid.

grammar' and what I would have preferred as the common grammar of
political legitimacy. But they are cast at such a level of generality that
they remind me of 'human diginity' in the field of human rights. We can
all agree on the centrality of human dignity, but as Chis McCrudden has
shown convincingly, that agreement does not guarantee even the sem-
blance of uniformity of meaning. Have you not just provided us with a
set of words around which the debates among the competing orders will
simply cast their disagreements? I do not propose to engage with your
analysis of *Kadi* in any depth. But when all is said and done, it would
appear that you split the difference between the CFI and the ECJ in
wanting the ECJ to engage in some international legal interpretation.
I would agree. I belong to the camp which right off the bat deplored the
inward look of the ECJ – its acceptance of international law so long as it
fitted into its constitutional vision. But assume that the ECJ had followed your counsel. Does this in some way not show the limits to
your approach? Imagine further, and I ask you to address directly this
question, that the ICJ had approved the Security Council regime and
only then the matter came before the ECJ. How would your approach
deal with that situation? You depart from McCormick in that he,
ultimately, was willing to fall back onto the tie-breaking principles of
international law. You are not. But does one not pay a price not simply
in making the disagreements once removed, but actually, contrary to
your wishes, entrenching them even deeper since now they will couched
in the vocabulary of deep legitimacy?

*DH: On labels, I say that voice, rights and expertise form a 'common
grammar of legitimacy' not, as you say, a 'common constitutional grammar'. So I am closer to your 'preferred' choice of words than your
question lets on. To be sure, I derive this grammar from the constitutional
tradition in the sense of suggesting that this is what constitutions are for.
But the grammar is broader than the particular tradition of national
constitutions. Voice, rights and expertise provide, I say, 'the basis for
legitimacy of public power in modern liberal governance'.*

*Let me turn, then, to your substantive objection that I have 'just
provided us with a set of words around which the debates among the
competing orders will simply cast their disagreements'.*

*First, if the suggestion is that the competing orders will 'simply cast'
their disagreements in what appear to be principled terms and thereby
mask what are really self-interested and opportunistic power grabs, let's*

recall Jon Elster's all-too-famous 'civilizing force of hypocrisy'. As you know, the path of power can be influenced by terms of debate, that is, by the kinds of claims we can present to a given audience. Just as institutions matter, words matter too. It is not just power all the way down (or, if you think it is, then why are we talking?).

As Elster explained, if claims of authority cannot be presented as merely self-interested power grabs, but must be justified by reference to more principled goals, the claims of authority themselves will often change. This insight suggests that talk of principles will not simply lead to dysfunctional 'entrench[ment]' as you suggest, but to 'civilizing' the claims themselves and moderating them to make them more acceptable. (This does not mean, by the way, that every single 'violation' of international law must be justified in deep foundational terms. Not all international legal obligations are alike. Some, for example, might allow for a kind of efficient breach.) Does talk about principles mean you can sometimes get way with a power grab masquerading as a principled argument? Sure, but what else is new?

Second, as for the terms themselves, they are indeed just that: terms of debate. Contrary to the role that human dignity plays in the discourse Chris McCrudden so excellently purveyed, the terms I set forth do not aspire to settle substantive questions with specificity. They simply provide the grammar within which claims to legitimacy must be made. What specific content an institution or official gives to any one of the three values, how these three primary values are combined, and whether another institution is satisfied by the resulting argument cannot conclusively be specified from a bird's-eye view in advance. The point of the interaction is that these will be matters that are decided on a decentralized basis by the actors themselves. But what it does mean, for example, is that in our concrete case the UN Security Council cannot say that it is not protecting rights in any form and still expect the ECJ to follow its commands.

Now we can say more to flesh out the kinds of legitimacy claims we might expect within the terms of this grammar. But that would take far longer than the short piece I contributed to this volume and certainly longer than we have in this epilogue. But let me add one point about how the grammar may add clarity even to these other 'more specific' claims.

Take subsidiarity, for instance, which is a favourite in both federalism literature and elsewhere to describe why one level should do one thing and another level something else. It is not always clear what subsidiarity means. A shorthand for the dominant view of subsidiarity would be:

Which level of governance can get this particular job done best? This often reflects what I would call an expertise based claim. So why don't I just say voice, rights and subsidiarity? One reason is that subsidiarity is not only about expertise but entails voice- and rights-based claims as well. And it can be useful to break down subsidiarity and tease out what these separate claims are. For example, as I have pointed out elsewhere,[9] the dominant understanding of subsidiarity is instrumental. This ignores the intrinsic (or substantive) aspect of subsidiarity, namely the claim that a given level of governance should have the authority to decide what job should be done in the first place. That claim, in turn, entails mostly claims about voice and rights as opposed to expertise. Now, when levels of governance really clash without an accepted tie-breaker, it behoves us to remember that all of these aspects of subsidiarity are in play.

Another reason why subsidiarity can be misleading in this context is that it does not address the question of horizontal disputes about jurisdiction. Kalypso Nicolaidis and Rob Howse have therefore used the idea of 'horizontal subsidiarity'[10] and I could go along with that, too. So, yes, a thoroughly enlightened view of subsidiarity can indeed play a useful role in this game of conflict and accommodation. But note that even an enlightened idea of horizontal subsidiarity tells you not who should win but simply what the conversation should be about. In that sense, to use your pejorative, subsidiarity, too, is 'just a word'.

There are other examples, but the main point for present purposes is this. We cannot conclusively and universally specify, let alone max-imize, the values of voice, rights and expertise. They provide the basic terms of debate, the grammar within which institutions locked in com-peting legalities make their claims to the legitimate exercise of public power. These institutions come to a mutual accommodation but not necessarily one derived from the overlap of preconceived conceptions. Instead, the interaction and the pressure for mutual accommodation can lead to the modification of an actor's prior understanding of the particular value at stake.

---

[9] Halberstam, Daniel, 'Comparative Federalism and the Role of the Judiciary,' in K. Whittington, D. Kelemen and G. Caldeira, eds., *The Oxford Handbook of Law and Politics* (Oxford University Press, 2008).

[10] Howse, Robert and Kalypso Nicolaidis, 'Enhancing WTO Legitimacy: Constitutionalization or Global Subsidiarity?', 16 *Governance* (2003) 73.

If the ECJ had followed this approach in Kadi, *for instance, it would have neither insisted on judging the rights violations in every instance itself nor demanded the vindication of rights in the precise particularity in which the rights at issue had been conceived of within Europe. Taking its cue from the German* Solange *and* Görgülü *jurisprudence, the ECJ would have suggested a path for future accommodation along both dimensions. First, the ECJ would have held out the possibility of granting the UN the authority to review the protection of certain rights in individual cases (i.e. at the 'retail' level) as long as an acceptable standard of rights was being observed generally (i.e. at the 'wholesale' level). Second, the ECJ would have suggested a willingness to consider whether its own specific (pre)conceptions of the rights involved might be modified in the light of the potentially acceptable alternatives that might be proposed by the UN. The ECJ (at least in my reading of the case) did neither. If I am misreading the case, and the Court in fact did what I say it should have done, so much the better.*

Finally, in answer to your specific sub-question whether it would make a difference if the ICJ had approved the regime, I'd have to know more about what the ICJ said and did. If the ICJ had reviewed Kadi's particular case, granted him certain rights of intervention and satisfied itself by reference to minimally acceptable standards that the charges were accurate and supported by sufficient evidence, the approach outlined above would push in the direction of deference and accommodation on the part of the ECJ. If, by contrast, the ICJ nakedly approved the precise regime as it existed in Kadi *without any further judicial review of the charges and evidence against Kadi or any other vindication of procedural rights, the approach outlined above should not lead to much deference to the ICJ. This is precisely where the grammar of legitimacy enters. What matters at the point of a clash of competing legalities are the respective claims to voice, rights and expertise. A UN regime that disregards Kadi's rights is no more legitimate for having been rubber-stamped by the ICJ.*

JW: There is something very startling in the premise to your discussion of the grammar of legitimacy with the quotes from Laski and the reference to the New Haven School. I have always found the former wishy-washy and the latter so complex and manipulable as to justify any desired result. If the grammar is normatively based on institutions (political and judicial) securing obedience 'in terms of the values that obedience creates', do we not end up preaching to the converted? What chance against the villains? They do exist. Disagreement is not just rooted in misunderstandings and competing identities.

DH: I will neither defend nor add here my own critique of Laski or discussion of the New Haven School. That would take us too far afield. But the short answer to your question about the chance against the villains is: none. The longer answer is: a conversation, perhaps.

Will there be those who want no part in this pluralist conversation because they are not committed to the principles of liberal governance? Yes. As I say in my piece, plural constitutionalism is not a universal phenomenon; it applies only under certain preconditions of minimally shared commitments. But this does not mean that only the faithful can be drawn into the conversation. To quote Dieter Grimm again: 'the universal recognition of constitutionalism as a model for the organization and legitimation of political power is shown by the fact that even rulers who are not inclined to submit themselves to legal norms feel compelled at least to pretend to be exercising their power within the constitutional framework.'[11] We can therefore fall back on Elster here, too, and hope to 'civilize' claims of authority through structured open debate that references the values of legitimacy as a way to make clear to all stakeholders what is at issue.

Once more, the constitutional element of pluralism gives this exchange added bite. After all, where plural constitutionalism obtains, the claim to authority of the various actors derives from a legal framework that itself mandates openness to the claim to authority of the other. Constitutionalism therefore provides the structure of legal authority that gets this conversation going. Moreover, the resulting discourse can then further be made meaningful by tapping into the values that (even if only purportedly) legitimate the various actors, forcing these actors to defend their claims to superior authority in terms of those very same values. Finally, as for the fully converted, i.e. those fully committed to principles of liberal governance, even they may need some help from pluralism to stick to their faith. As we all know, monopolies corrupt, whether in the market-place, politics or law.

---

[11] Grimm, Dieter, 'The Achievement of Constitutionalism and its Prospects in a Changed World', in P. Dobner and M. Loughlin, eds., *The Twilight of Constitutionalism* (Oxford University Press, 2010), 3–23 at 3.

I wonder, then, whether it might not be your question that is either too romantic or too sceptical. Your question about the faithful and the villains could be asked about the rule of law or morality or any other normative system. Pluralism is no panacea. But neither is any other coherent social practice that seeks to take us beyond a Hobbesian state of nature. Yes, any concern for the legitimacy of power is preaching to the (minimally) converted. But what is your alternative? If normative systems really have no pull on practical judgement, then only the sword can bring the villains into the fold. Surely we all know where that leads . . .

JW: I am not so sure whether the European way is a genuine third way between the local and global constitutionalists. But, at least to me, the whole project is hugely harmed, if suddenly, almost ex nihilo, in the text surrounding footnote 48, one discovers that what is presented as a principled approach to pluralism finds its perfect expression in the European Union and this is set up as an ideal type for the rest. With tongue-in-cheek here we are at the third instance of imperialism – Europe as a constitutional model for the world. Europe's constitutional tolerance is enticing – but it is so because of a particular history and particular political choices which are not only inapplicable but also undesirable for others. There is something enticing and even noble in the American experiment with constitutional federalism. It would be a normative calamity if Europe were to follow it. Why imagine then, that Europe's choice would be normatively suitable elsewhere?

DH: *You charge that it 'hugely harms' the whole project when I set up Europe 'almost ex nihilo' as 'an ideal type for the rest' in yet 'a third instance of imperialism'. This seems rather overdrawn. My chapter explains that, as a matter of conceptual history, the idea of constitutional pluralism 'began as a theory about the distribution of constitutional authority within Europe', and then asks about the 'extent to which (if at all) these principles can find application beyond the special case of Europe'. I don't see the imperialism or huge harm in that endeavour.*

We ask all the time about the extent to which the experience of one country or system might be relevant to another. Situated experiences can lead to conceptual innovations or generate understandings and practical approaches that can then be used to understand and develop social practices elsewhere. The American constitutional experience deeply influenced the path of governance abroad despite huge differences between the emancipation of well-to-do colonies from a far-away king, on the one hand, and the task of changing deep political and social structures, on the other. Nonetheless, the United States, and then France, became 'ideal types' that set the stage for battles about the structure of government and modes of legitimation far beyond their particular locations.

I have always insisted on attending to the institutional and contextual differences that might skew comparisons.[12] I remain certain that the European Union is not a United States of Europe and that global governance is not simply Europe writ large. But that should not preclude us from recognizing – here as elsewhere – commonalities of analytic features that governance across very different scenarios may share.[13]

CODA: *Allow me to complement your comments with a coda that goes beyond the intended scope of my chapter but speaks more generally to your opening concern about language.*

I certainly appreciate the scepticism about invoking constitutional terminology when speaking about global governance. At the same time, other terminology has failed to capture this phenomenon properly as well. The shortcomings of 'inter-national' terminology have led scholars for some time now to speak about 'trans-national' law instead. But even talk of 'transnational' law does not pay sufficient heed to certain foundational global claims, such as Article 103 of the UN Charter, human rights law, ius cogens or developing notions such as the 'responsibility to protect'. The language of 'administrative' law is helpful for many reasons as well but it, too, can deflect attention from the generative capacity of the international realm and from serious questions about the principal on whose behalf global 'administrative' agencies (are supposed to) act. Finally, the language of 'pluralism' without more, i.e. speaking of

---

[12] For example, most recently in Halberstam, Daniel, 'The Promise of Comparative Administrative Law: A Constitutional Perspective on Independent Agencies,' in S. Rose-Ackerman and P. Lindseth, eds., *Comparative Administrative Law* (Cheltenham: Edward Elgar, 2010), available at <http://ssrn.com/abstract_id=1589749>, and long ago in Halberstam, Daniel, 'Comparative Federalism and the Issue of Commandeering', in Kalypso Nicolaidis and Robert Howse, eds., *The Federal Vision: Legitimacy and Levels of Governance in the US and the EU* (Oxford University Press, 2001), 213–251.

[13] Cf. Weiler, J. H. H., 'Epilogue: Toward a Common Law of International Trade', in J. H. H. Weiler, ed., *The EU, the WTO, and the NAFTA: Toward a Common Law of International Trade?* (Oxford University Press, 2000).

no more than a multiplicity of legal orders, seems to downplay the principled legal connections embedded in the legal frameworks of the various systems and the purposes that these legal systems serve. Talk of plural constitutionalism (as opposed to a global constitution or other harder invocations of constitutional law at the global level) for all its flaws seeks to provoke by giving a nod to the generative capacity of legality and legal frameworks beyond the state and by challenging the idea of constitutionalism as hierarchy within the state at the same time.

There may be hope. If we can define only that which has no history, as Nietzsche taught us, then our linguistic impasse may only be temporary. Recall in this regard that the American Framers used language in novel ways, too. At the time, 'federal' had a distinctly international connotation, evidenced by frequent juxtapositions back then between the 'national' and 'federal' features of the United States Constitution. And yet, federalism has become today an umbrella term that incorporates both of these features and can be applied to a variety of arrangements. For example, we no longer speak of an American Union that is part federal and part national but simply of American federalism. I will think about coining a neologism that goes beyond constitutionalism (despite the fact that I will surely be taken to task for that in pages such as these). In the meantime, however, history will take its course and constitutionalism might come to be understood as finding some application beyond its traditionally imagined setting as well.

Chapter 5: Joseph Weiler and Nico Krisch

JW: In your impressive and trenchant defence of and advocacy for 'pluralism' as the most promising approach to 'postnational' polities and politics there is a strange disproportion: throughout the chapter there is a detailed and oft persuasive illustration of the manner in which the constitutional approach fails to deliver on many of the desserts it promises. You remind us often, *a titre juste*, to eschew idealizations of the constitutional. The 'case for the prosecution' is strong. Particularly impressive in this regard is the manner in which you argue that institutional pluralists are but constitutionalists in disguise, operating as they do within a bounded set of rules.

All this creates in a reader such as myself, who takes your pluralist claim seriously, a growing expectation to understand the operational image of the pluralist postnational polity and politics: the 'how it works' as a precondition to understanding its myriad alleged virtues – pragmatic and normative. And yet precisely on this point the chapter becomes maddeningly illusive: In a chapter of sixty pages a mere four (under the title 'Plural polities') try to give this depiction. The section begins with the promising words 'What kind of order does this suggest after all?' but rapidly moves into the usual tropes of 'sketching', 'begin to outline', 'framework', etc. and upon reading and rereading the four pages one hardly knows what kind of order all this suggests. Clearly, even in a pluralist order some polities deserve, as you claim, more respect and tolerance than others. This must be determined by public autonomy credentials, of concretization of the idea of self-legislation. By whom? By what method? How will conflicts of evaluation of such be resolved? What does it mean not to give respect or not to tolerate? These are but a small fraction of the questions that these four pages will give rise to among attentive readers. Both the pragmatic/procedural as well as the normative virtues claimed for the systemic pluralist model cannot be reasonably assessed if one does not have a thick description of the pluralist polity. I have the impression that this issue is symptomatic of the pluralist literature: it is acute and perceptive in its critique of hierarchical constitutional designs; it has a meaningful and well-articulated aspirational ideal as an alternative; but it tends to be vague, curt, allusive or illusive and remarkably inarticulate in any attempt at operationalization of the pluralist polity. Could this be a systemic weakness which might suggest that system pluralism should be shelved on the Utopia shelf?

NK: For this chapter, I have indeed chosen a relatively abstract focus. I inquire into the broad comparison of pluralist and constitutionalist structures in the postnational order, not into particular institutional forms or political outcomes. Developing questions of institutional design would have required a clearer view on issues such as those sketched at the very end of the chapter – postnational democracy, the rule of law, the impact of power, etc. Engaging seriously with such questions would have taken me well beyond the space of a single chapter; I try to do so in a recent book.[14]

Yet there is also a more general (and more interesting) hurdle to greater specificity in the structure of the pluralist approach itself. One

---

[14] Krisch, Nico, *Beyond Constitutionalism: The Pluralist Structure of Postnational Law* (Oxford University Press, 2010).

of the reasons why constitutionalism appeals to many people is its ability to provide a clear, graspable, reasonable structure – one that puts institutions into a defined place, one that people can understand, assess, critique directly. It seeks to erect something akin to a modern office building, ideally one as beautiful as the Seagram building or UN headquarters. Pluralism is different – less modern, more medieval if you like. The pluralist edifice resembles more the church begun in Romanesque times, continued in a Gothic style, provisionally finished in the Renaissance, touched again by Baroque hands. Pluralism assumes that the postnational order will – and should – be the product of many minds, the result of the (often diverging) choices of different collectives. Constitutionalism does the opposite – it seeks to erect an aesthetically pleasing structure along the lines of one, coherent, political theory. This is much easier to describe, but as I try to show in the chapter, it misses out on the participatory dimension. It may have an edge in aesthetic terms, but it poses greater problems for realizing self-governance and democracy in the postnational space.

Because of its emphasis on the participatory element, pluralism has greater difficulty depicting the eventual shape of the order it imagines – rather than determining the building, it provides criteria for selecting the architects, and it recognizes that there will be many architects, not one master builder. Who should these architects be? All collectives with a certain autonomy pedigree – all those that can make a plausible claim to realize the private and public autonomy of individuals, especially in terms of inclusiveness and the intensity of self-legislation. But then, you rightly ask, who determines whether they meet this standard? Who selects them? Who solves conflicts? Here lies the particular (and to many, frustrating) characteristic of pluralism: there is no ultimate decision-maker, no umpire to appeal to. These determinations are made decentrally, by the various collectives that raise claims. They decide whether or not to grant respect, to accord authority to the positions of other collectives – authority that may be gradated, persuasive rather than binding, and that may trigger processes of mutual accommodation. Of course, you might say, this all sounds fine, but there is still the possibility that these decentral decisions will follow arbitrary lines. True, I would answer, there is no institutional assurance that they will not. Yet there are political constraints and normative standards, based on public autonomy, that we can hold the different collectives to. In this picture, risks remain, but in the diverse, contested, *non-ideal space of the postnational, constitutionalist approaches run serious risks too: the risk to run roughshod over the governance choices of legitimate groups; the risk to legitimate a structure that caters to the powerful rather than the weak. A postnational constitution would hardly be dreamt up by some theorist, but result from real-world forces rarely guided by reason and justice (whose reason, whose justice should it be anyway?).*

JW: In your powerful critique of the constitutional approach you recommend a non-idealized approach. And yet, ironically, in the advocacy of your alternative, pluralist polities and politics, you seem to rely on the most idealized form of politics in discussion deriving from Habermas's communication theory, the idea of public autonomy and self-legislation. It is most easy to pile up examples of processes within myriad domestic and international settings which do not concretize the idea of self-legislation. But it is extremely difficult to find any meaningful examples of where it actually takes place. I recall some years ago the Bremen school excitedly but laughably suggesting that European Comitology was a locus in which Habermasian discourse (in a slightly different variant) took place. The idea of public autonomy and concretized self-legislation resulting, of course, from a meaningful deliberative process (you would surely agree that it would otherwise be formal and meaningless) reminds me of the Jewish Messiah. A wonderful and noble entity for whom we all fervently await secure in the belief that He will never come. The Messiah that comes is always a false Messiah. If the conditions for respect, legitimacy and tolerance of polities within the plural order would depend on such, would you not say that the imperfect but concrete world of constitutionalism is, under the severe conditions which you pose, better than the more perfect but illusive world of pluralism? And what does one do with self-legislation which is participatory and all, but in its content is simply awful, illiberal, etc.? Do we afford it respect? Is there not, even in your construct of system pluralism, an overarching constitutional framework but an overarching moral framework? And if not, would you really be willing to live up to the implications of your construct of according respect without any substantive limits?

NK: *No doubt Habermasian public autonomy will not govern the postnational space any time soon, not in our lifetime, not in that of a few more generations, perhaps (most probably) never. Domestically, the same is likely to be true. But the point about demanding political ideals is not whether they will ever be realized, but whether they are worth striving for, and whether the world can become a better place in the process. This makes them different from the Messiah – we are not simply bound to wait but can act politically, use theoretical signposts as regulative ideals.*

In my conception of pluralism, public autonomy is not just such a regulative ideal but has yet a further – and structurally more important – dimension. It operates as a yardstick for relative assessments. Authority is granted to different collectives not on the basis of their full realization of the precepts of public autonomy. If this were the case, I agree, there would be little point in the exercise. Instead, the respective autonomy pedigrees of competing positions are used for comparative purposes: to determine who can claim more, who less, authority. Take an example. In the development of money-laundering standards, the OECD's Financial Action Task Force in its original design had a very weak autonomy pedigree – it neither included those states it targeted nor did it provide for any meaningful process of self-legislation. International institutions, such as the IMF, were slightly better on the inclusiveness dimension; national polities may have been better on the self-legislation dimension. For neither the IMF nor for national polities would this suffice to grant absolute authority, but we would expect them to grant each other a certain respect, some degree of deference in the determination of the right standards.

Public autonomy thus becomes the yardstick for the gradated authority different collectives accord each other. This also begins to answer your last question: of course I have a moral framework – I wouldn't know how to construct a normative argument without one. This framework is broadly Habermasian, and it provides an indication as to which collectives deserve more authority, which less. But it is important to highlight that this moral framework has two elements, a procedural and a substantive one. I have a moral view on what would be the right outcome, but this outcome might not be the one that results from the procedure which I believe should determine the outcome authoritatively. This also means that the law will most of the time not follow my substantive moral ideals. This is not an original point: we constantly accept decisions that are wrong from our moral standpoint but result from (roughly) the right processes; and we call them law. This is simply

*a necessary consequence of our recognition that individuals have differ-
ent, yet still legitimate, moral views.*

*Postnational pluralism takes this insight to another level: to the
determination of the polity in which we accept to be governed, and
the meta-institutional structure in which this polity is embedded.
Because of the diversity of (legitimate) views on this point, it suggests
we accept competing authority claims and try to achieve political
accommodation between them, rather than – as constitutionalism
does – institutionalize one vision of what authority claims are justified
and distribute powers accordingly.*

JW: There is a premise of the chapter which is almost axiomatically
assumed, namely that we exist in postnational social reality. Perhaps
some clarification is needed here. The first is simple enough: sometimes
you seem to contrast domestic polities with postnational polities where
really 'domestic' simply seems to be a proxy for national or state or
both. For example, in arguing that in the context of the EU it is not
necessary to problematize which polities deserve respect – the national
and European polities – this dichotomy suggests a coherent national
polity. Elsewhere you challenge the very purchase of the national in
relation to the nation and the state – as in the section on 'Social
practices'. It might be useful to clarify the sense or senses in which you
use 'postnational'.

NK: *Indeed, in this chapter I assume rather than defend the existence of
a postnational constellation. Let me sketch the underlying idea
briefly.*[15] *'Postnational', in my usage, refers to a situation in which the
state (in the most typical form of the nation-state) has lost its position as
ultimate authority, as the principal frame of reference that it used to be
in both the domestic and the international order. This links up with (not
entirely new) diagnoses of political scientists to the effect that '[t]he
nation state is no longer the only site of authority and the normativity
that accompanies it'.*[16]

---

[15] I develop a more detailed argument in Krisch, ibid., Chapter 1.
[16] Zürn, M., 'The State in the Postnational Constellation – Societal
Denationalization and Multi-Level Governance', *ARENA Working Papers*, WP
99/35 (1999), available at <www.arena.uio.no/publications/working-
papers1999/papers/wp99_35.htm>.

This describes a postnational political order; when I talk about post-national society, I refer to the societal structures at the basis of this order. As we see towards the end of the chapter, I also think that this society is postnational in a deeper sense – in the sense that loyalties, feelings of belonging now often extend beyond the framework of the state or the nation, that society is made up (to a significant extent) of 'postnational selves'.[17] *The fact that loyalties just as often pertain to sub-state collectives (of a local, regional, cultural kind) suggests that the centrality of the national (state) framework is challenged in two directions.*

Such political and psychological diagnoses do not necessarily entail that law, too, has become postnational. In this chapter, little hinges on it, but let me mention the two main reasons why I believe that post-nationalism also has legal purchase. In the first place, such a reading better reflects practices – not only in the European Union – in which courts grant authority to rules and decisions from other layers of law. This authority typically does not come in the binary mode of binding/non-binding, but rather in gradated forms. This is not so alien to common law orders with their notion of persuasive authority, but we can also observe it in civil law systems – national courts' respect for European human rights law or their practice of 'weighing' global reg-ulatory decisions are examples here.[18] *Recognizing the postnational character of law not only reflects such practices, it also allows law to connect with questions of legitimacy that arise in postnational politics. In a political order that is ever more closely intertwined, the separation of legal spheres (national/international) prevents us from framing issues of institutional legitimacy properly as legal questions. Regional and global governance is then outside the reach of domestic law, while national governance is outside the (direct) reach of regional and interna-tional law. Law's connection with legitimacy – and as a result, its own legitimacy – are then called into question, and it appears preferable to stress the interlinkages and conceptualize law as more (though not fully) integrated: as 'postnational'.*

[17] See Hedetoft, U. and M. Hjort, eds., *The Postnational Self: Belonging and Identity* (Minneapolis: University of Minnesota Press, 2002).

[18] On the latter point, see, e.g., Kingsbury, B., 'Weighing Global Regulatory Rules and Decisions in National Courts', *Acta Juridica* (2009), 90–119.

JW: When you allude to social practices that are suggestive of postnational sentiments you allude to evidence that suggests that people have
multiple loyalties et cetera. I cannot rid myself from the feeling that your
idea of the national, against which you posit the postnational, is very,
well, national, Schmittian. Is the idea of the nation, even in earlier
periods which one would not describe as postnational, really posited
on a single loyalty? What of Thomas Moore and Becket? What of the
co-existence of family loyalty, religious loyalty and national loyalty –
benign in harmony, potent in conflict but not inimical to most ideas of
the national. One might argue that you miss out on the most powerful
normative claim of constitutionalism, which is not order and stability,
but the education to the spiritual dimension of self-limitation and
tolerance.

NK: *In the social sphere, different forms of loyalty co-exist and have
always co-existed. The modern state has tried to respond by privatizing
them: by assigning family authority to the private sphere, religious authority to the religious, and by protecting both through fundamental rights.
Where competing loyalties were more directly political in nature – as in
multinational, multicultural states – the preferred solution has been federalism: again, the definition of a particular, protected space for the groups
in question. Unlike in the medieval order, the modern, constitutional state
has largely monopolized political authority, and it has based this on its
alleged neutrality vis-à-vis the particular loyalties of its citizens. This
neutrality has also been at the core of the idea you allude to in your
question – namely that one of constitutionalism's key virtues is its institutionalization of (and education towards) the tolerance of different groups.*

    *We know from the experience of very diverse, multicultural, multi-
religious, multinational states that this aspiration to neutrality rests on
shaky grounds.[19] Constitutions have to make crucial choices (from a
common language to decision-making powers) in which any solution
will favour one group over others. They can make such choices if
loyalties to the broader entity outweigh those to particular groups;
otherwise, they risk destabilization. We have observed this in the
Canadian constitutional dispute of the last few decades (and in many*

---

[19] I have been much influenced by Neus Torbisco's thoughts on this issue; see
Torbisco Casals, Neus, *Group Rights as Human Rights* (Dordrecht: Springer,
2006).

*other places). It does not come as a surprise that it is precisely on the
basis of such experiences that modern constitutionalism's connection
with tolerance is called into question – James Tully's work is just one
example.*[20] *A constitution is linked to tolerance only in so far as its
authority to define the terms of tolerance among societal groups is
accepted. Otherwise, it risks becoming just another tool in the struggle
of different groups for political dominance.*

*This suggests that when diversity and contestation are strong, con-
stitutionalism may not be the right institutional form to foster tolerance.
In my chapter in this volume I have tried to show that in such circumstances, a pluralist order may be preferable. This argument is not limited
to the sphere beyond the state; it may also have application within state
settings, which I have not spelled out here. The recent renaissance of
notions of federalism that sees authority lines as parallel and competing,
rather than as hierarchically ordered, indicates such a broader appeal of
pluralist modes of thought.*[21]

---

[20] Tully, James, *Strange Multiplicity: Constitutionalism in an Age of Diversity*,
(Cambridge University Press, 1995).
[21] See, e.g., Beaud, Olivier, *Théorie de la Fédération* (Paris: Presses Universitaires de
France, 2007).

Bibliography

Ackerman, Bruce, *We the People: Foundations* (Cambridge, Mass.: Harvard University Press, 1993).

Aggestam, Lisbeth, 'Introduction', 80 *International Affairs* 1 (2008) 1–11.

Akande, D., 'The ICJ and the Security Council: Is There Room for Judicial Control of the Decisions of the Political Organs of the UN?' 46 *International and Comparative Law Quarterly* (1997) 309–343.

Albi, Anneli, *EU Enlargement and the Constitutions of Central and Eastern Europe* (Cambridge University Press, 2005).

Allott, Philip, 'Epilogue: Europe and the dream of reason', in J. H. H. Weiler and M. Wind, eds., *European Constitutionalism Beyond the State* (Cambridge University Press, 2003), 202–225.

Almquist, J., 'A Human Rights Critique of European Judicial Review: Counter-Terrorism Sanctions', 57 *International and Comparative Law Quarterly* (2008) 303–331.

Al-Nauimi, N. and R. Meese, eds., *International Legal Issues Arising under the United Nations Decade of International Law* (The Hague: Kluwer Law International, 1995).

Alvarez, José, 'Governing the World: International Organizations as Lawmakers', 31 *Suffolk Transnational Law Review* (2008) 591.

International Organizations as Law-makers (Oxford University Press, 2005).

'International Organizations: Then and Now', 100 *American Journal of International Law* (2006) 324.

'Judging the Security Council', 90 *American Journal of International Law* (1996) 1–39.

'The New Dispute Settlers: (Half) Truths and Consequences', 38 *Texas International Law Journal* (2003) 405.

Amar, Akil R., 'Of Sovereignty and Federalism', 96 *Yale Law Journal* (1987) 1425–1520.

Amato, G., H. Bribosia and B. de Witte, eds., *Genesis and Destiny of the European Constitution* (Brussels: Bruylant, 2007).

Anderson, Benedict, *Imagined Communities: Reflections on the Origin and Spread of Nationalism* (London: Verso, 1983).

Andersson, T., I. Cameron and K. Nordback, 'EU Blacklisting: The Renaissance of Imperial Power but on a Global Scale', 14 *European Business Law Review* (2003) 111–141.

Aristotle, *Politics*, Books I and II, trans. with a commentary by Trevor J. Saunders (Oxford University Press, 1995.

Armitage, D., *The Declaration of Independence: A Global History* (Cambridge, Mass.: Harvard University Press, 2007).

D'Aspremont, J. and F. Dopagne, 'Kadi: The ECJ's Reminder of the Elementary Divide between Legal Orders', 5 *International Organizations Law Review* (2008) 365.

Aust, Anthony, *Modern Treaty Law and Practice* (Cambridge University Press, 2000).

Avbelj, M., *Theory of the European Bund* (PhD thesis, European University Institute, 2009).

Avbelj M. and J. Komarek, eds., 'Four Visions of Constitutional Pluralism', *European University Institute Working Paper LAW No.* 2008/21 (2008).

Azoulai, L., 'The Court of Justice and the Social Market Economy: The Emergence of an Ideal and the Conditions for its Realization' 45 *Common Market Law Review* (2008) 1335–1356.

Backer, Larry, 'From Constitution to Constitutionalism: A Global Framework for Legitimate Public Power Systems', 113 *Penn State Law Review* (2009) 671.

Baquero Cruz, Julio, 'The Legacy of the Maastricht-Urteil and the Pluralist Movement', 14 *European Law Journal* (2008) 389–420.

Barents, René, *The Autonomy of Community Law* (The Hague: Kluwer, 2004).

Barr, Michael S. and Geoffrey P. Miller, 'Global Administrative Law: The View from Basel', 17 *European Journal of International Law* (2006) 15–46.

Barry, Brian, *Culture and Equality: An Egalitarian Critique of Multiculturalism* (Cambridge, Mass.: Harvard University Press, 2002).

'Political Accommodation and Consociational Democracy', 5 *British Journal of Political Science* (1975) 477–505.

Beaud, Olivier, *Théorie de la Fédération* (Paris: Presses Universitaires de France, 2007).

Beaumont, P., C. Lyons and N. Walker, eds., *Convergence and Divergence in European Public Law* (Oxford: Hart Publishing, 2002).

Bederman, David J., 'The Souls of International Organizations: Legal Personality and the Lighthouse at Cape Spartel', *Virginia Journal of International Law* 36 (1995–1996) 276–377.

Bellamy, R., 'The Liberty of the Post-Moderns? Market and Civic Freedom in the EU', LSE 'Europe in Question' Discussion Paper Series 01/2009 (2009).

Benhabib, Seyla, *The Rights of Others* (Cambridge University Press, 2004).
'Reclaiming Universalism: Negotiating Republican Self-Determination and Cosmopolitan Norms', 25 *The Tanner Lectures on Human Values* (2005) 113–166.
Berlin, Isaiah, *Four Essays on Liberty* (Oxford University Press, 1969).
Berman, Harold J., *Law and Revolution: The Formation of the Western Legal Tradition* (Cambridge, Mass.: Harvard University Press, 1983).
Berman, Nathaniel, 'But the Alternative is Despair: European Nationalism and the Modernist Renewal of International Law', 106 *Harvard Law Review* (1993) 1792–1903.
Bernitz, Ulf, Joakim Nergelius and Cecelia Gardener, *The General Principles of EC Law in a Process of Development* (2nd edn, The Hague: Kluwer Law International, 2008).
Bernstorff, Jochen von, 'Procedures of Decision-Making and the Role of Law in International Organizations', 9 *German Law Journal* (2008) 1939–1964.
Besson, Samantha, 'Human Rights, Institutional Duties and Cosmopolitan Responsibilities', 23 *Oxford Journal of Legal Studies* (2003) 507.
Bhuiyan, Sharif, *National Law in WTO Law* (Cambridge University Press, 2007).
Bianchi, Andrea, 'Assessing the Effectiveness of the UN Security Council's Anti-Terrorism Measures: The Quest for Legitimacy and Cohesion', 19 *European Journal of International Law* (2008) 881–919.
Bieber, Roland, 'Les limites matérielles et formelles à la révision des traités établissant la Communauté européenne', *Revue du Marché commun et de l'Union européenne* (1993) 343–350.
Bogdandy, Armin von, 'Constitutionalism in International Law: Comment on a Proposal from Germany', 47 *Harvard Journal of International Law* (2006) 223–242.
ed., *Europäisches Verfassungsrecht* (Berlin, Heidelberg: Springer, 2003).
'General Principles of International Public Authority: Sketching a Research Field', 9 *German Law Journal* (2008) 1908–1938.
'Pluralism, Direct Effect, and the Ultimate Say: On the Relationship between International and Domestic Constitutional Law', 6 *International Journal of Constitutional Law* (2008) 397.
Bogdandy, Armin von and J. Bast, eds., *Principles of European Constitutional Law* (Oxford: Hart Publishing, 2005).
Bogdandy, Armin von, Phillipp Dann and Matthias Goldmann, 'Developing the Publicness of Public International Law: Towards a Legal Framework for Global Governance Activities', 9 *German Law Journal* (2008) 1371.
Bohman, James, *Democracy across Borders* (Cambridge, Mass.: MIT Press, 2007).

Bothe, M., 'Security Council's Targeted Sanctions against Presumed Terrorists', 6 *Journal of International Criminal Justice* (2008) 541–555.

Boyle, A. and C. Chinkin, *The Making of International Law* (Oxford University Press, 2007).

Bradley, Curtis, 'International Delegations, the Structural Constitution, and Non-Self-Execution', 55 *Stanford Law Review* (2003) 1557.

Bradley, Curtis, Jack Goldsmith and David Moore, 'Sosa, Customary International Law, and the Continuing Relevance of Erie', 120 *Harvard Law Review* (2007) 869.

Bradley, C. and G. Mitu Gulati, 'Withdrawing from International Custom', 120 *Yale Law Journal* (2010) 202.

Bretherton, Charlotte and John Vogler, *The European Union as a Global Actor* (London: Routledge, 1999).

Bronckers, Marco, 'The Relationship of the EC Courts with Other International Tribunals: Non-Committal, Respectful or Submissive?', 44 *Common Market Law Review* (2007) 601.

Broude, T. and Y. Shany, eds., *The Shifting Allocation of Authority in International Law* (Oxford, Portland: Hart Publishing, 2008).

Bryde, Brun-Otto, 'International Democratic Constitutionalism', in Ronald St. J. Macdonald and Douglas M. Johnston, eds., *Towards World Constitutionalism* (Leiden: Martinus Nijhoff, 2005), 103–125.

Bull, Hedley, *The Anarchical Society* (London: Macmillan, 1977).

de Búrca, Gráinne, 'The EU, the European Court of Justice and the International Legal Order after Kadi', 51 *Harvard International Law Journal* (2010) 1–49.

   'Reflections on the EU's Path from the Constitutional Treaty to the Lisbon Treaty', *Jean Monnet Working Paper* 03/08 (2008).

de Búrca, G. and J. Scott, eds., *The EU and the WTO: Legal and Constitutional Issues* (Oxford: Hart Publishing, 2001).

de Búrca, G. and J. H. H. Weiler, eds., *The European Court of Justice* (Oxford University Press, 2011).

Burgess, Michael, *Federalism and European Union: The Building of Europe, 1950–2000* (London: Routledge, 2000).

Burke-White, William, 'International Legal Pluralism', 25 *Michigan International Law Journal* (2003–2004) 963.

Caflisch, L. , 'Is the International Court Entitled to Review Security Council Resolutions Adopted under Chapter VII of the United Nations Charter?', in N. Al-Nauimi and R. Meese, eds., *International Legal Issues Arising under the United Nations Decade of International Law* (The Hague: Kluwer Law International, 1995), 633–662.

Calhoun, C., *Nations Matter; Culture, History, and the Cosmopolitan Dream* (Minneapolis: University of Minnesota Press, 2007).

Calliess, C., ed., *Verfassungswandel im europäischen Staaten- und Verfassungsverbund* (Mohr Siebeck: Tübingen, 2007).

Cameron, Iain, 'UN Targeted Sanctions, Legal Safeguards and the European Convention on Human Rights', 72 *Nordic Journal of International Law* 2 (2003) 159–214.

Canovan, M., *The People* (Cambridge: Polity Press, 2005).

Caporaso, James and Min-Hyung Kim, 'The Dual Nature of European Identity: Subjective Awareness and Coherence', 16 *Journal of European Public Policy* (2009) 19–42.

Capotorti, Francesco, 'Supranational Organizations', 5 *Encyclopedia of Public International Law* (1983) 262–268.

Capotorti, Francesco et al., *The European Union Treaty: Commentary on the Draft Adopted by the EP on 14 February 1984* (Oxford: Clarendon Press, 1986).

Cappelletti, M., *Il Controllo Giudiziario Di Costituzionalità Delle Leggi Nel Diritto Comparato* (Milan: Dott. A. Giuffrè, 1968, 1972).

The Judicial Process In Comparative Perspective (Oxford University Press, 1989).

Cappelletti, M., M. Seccombe and J. Weiler, eds., *Integration Through Law – Europe and the American Federal Experience*, vol. 1, book 1 (The Hague: de Gruyter, 1986).

Cass, Deborah, *The Constitutionalization of the World Trade Organization* (Oxford University Press, 2005).

Cassese, Antonio, 'Remarks on Scelle's Theory of "Role Splitting" (dédoublement fonctionnel) in International Law', 1 *European Journal of International Law* (1990) 210.

Chalmers, D., 'The Single Market: From Prima Donna to Journeyman' in Jo Shaw and G. More, eds, *New Legal Dynamics of European Union* (Oxford: Clarendon Press, 1996), 55–72.

Charney, Jonathan, 'Universal International Law', 87 *American Journal of International Law* (1993) 529.

Checkel, J. T. & P. J. Katzenstein, eds., *European Identity* (Cambridge University Press, 2009).

Cheyne, I., 'Gateways to the Precautionary Principle in International Law', 19 *Journal of Environmental Law* (2007) 155.

Choudhry, Sujit, ed., *Constitutional Design for Divided Societies: Integration or Accommodation?* (Oxford University Press, 2008).

'Does the world need more Canada? The Politics of the Canadian Model in Constitutional Politics and Political Theory', in Choudhry, ed., *Constitutional Design for Divided Societies: Integration or Accommodation?* (Oxford University Press, 2008), 141–172.

ed., *The Migration of Constitutional Ideas* (Cambridge University Press, 2006).

Cini, M., *European Union Politics* (2nd edn, Oxford University Press, 2007).

Claes, Monica, 'Constitutionalising Europe at its Source: The "European Clauses" in the National Constitutions: Evolution and Typology', 24 *Yearbook of European Law* (2005) 81.

The National Courts' Mandate in the European Constitution (Oxford: Hart Publishing, 2006).

Cohen, Antonin, 'Le Plan Schuman de Paul Reuter: entre communauté nationale et fédération européenne', 48 *Revue française de science politique* (1998) 645–663.

Cohen, Antonin and Mikael Rask Madsen, 'Cold War Law: Legal Entrepreneurs and the Emergence of a European Legal Field (1945–1965)', in V. Gessner and D. Nelken, eds., *European Ways of Law. Towards a European Sociology of Law* (Oxford: Hart Publishing, 2007), 175–201.

Cohen, Jean, 'A Global State of Emergency or the Further Constitutionalization of International Law: A Pluralist Approach', 15 *Constellations* (2008) 456–484.

Coicaud, J. M. and V. Heiskanen, eds., *The Legitimacy of International Organizations* (Tokyo: United Nations University Press, 2001).

Coleman, J. and S. Shapiro, eds., *The Oxford Handbook of Jurisprudence and Philosophy of Law* (Oxford University Press, 2002).

Conforti, B. and F. Francioni, eds., *Enforcing International Human Rights in Domestic Courts* (The Hague: Martinus Nijhoff, 1997).

Connor, Walker, 'Nation-Building or Nation-Destroying?', 24 *World Politics* (1972) 319–355.

Constant, B., 'The Liberty of the Ancients Compared with that of the Moderns', in B. Constant, *Political Writings* (Cambridge University Press, 1988), 307–328.

Political Writings (Cambridge University Press, 1988).

Constantinesco, Vlad, 'Europe fédérale ou fédération d'Etats-nations', in R. Dehousse, ed., *Une constitution pour l'Europe?* (Paris: Presses de Sciences Po, 2002), 115–149.

Constantinesco, V., Y. Gautier and V. Michel, eds., *Le Traité établissant une Constitution pour l'Europe. Analyses et commentaires* (Presses Universitaires de Strasbourg, 2005).

Corbett, Richard, *The European Parliament's Role in Closer EU Integration* (Basingstoke: Palgrave Macmillan, 1998).

Cottier, T., P. Mavroidis and P. Blatter, eds., *The Role of the Judge in International Trade Regulation: Experience and Lessons for the WTO* (Ann Arbor: University of Michigan Press, 2003).

Cover, Robert M., 'The Uses of Jurisdictional Redundancy', 22 *William & Mary Law Review* (1980–81) 639.

Craig, P. and G. de Búrca, eds., *The Evolution of EU Law* (Oxford University Press, 1999).

Craig Barker, J., Paul James Cardwell, Duncan French and Nigel White, 'Kadi and Al Barakaat', 58 *The International and Comparative Law Quarterly* (2009) 241.

Cremona, M., ed., *The Enlargement of the European Union* (Oxford University Press, 2003).

'The European Neighbourhood Policy: Partnership, Security and the Rule of law', in A. Mayhew and N. Copsey, eds., *European Neighbourhood Policy and Ukraine* (Falmer: University of Sussex, Sussex European Institute, 2005), 25–54.

Cremona, M. , F. Francioni and S. Poli, eds., 'Challenging the EU Counter-Terrorism Measures through the Courts', *European University Institute Working Paper LAW No.* 2009/10 (2009).

da Cruz Vilaça, José Luis and Nuno Piçarra, 'Y a-t-il des limites matérielles à la révision des traités instituant les CE?', 29 *Cahiers de droit européen* 1–2 (1993) 3–37.

Curtin, Deirdre and Ige Dekker, 'The EU as a "Layered" International Organization: Institutional Unity in Disguise', in P. Craig and G. de Búrca, eds., *The Evolution of EU Law* (Oxford University Press, 1999), 83–136.

Dahl, Robert A., 'Federalism and the Democratic Process', in J. R. Pennock and J. W. Chapman, eds., *NOMOS XXV: Liberal Democracy* (New York University Press, 1983), 95–108.

Dani, M., 'Remedying European Legal Pluralism: The FIAMM and Fedon Litigation and the Judicial Protection of International Trade Bystanders', 21 *European Journal of International Law* (2010) 303.

Dashwood, Alan, 'States in the European Union', 23 *European Law Review* (1998) 201–216.

Defeis, Elizabeth, 'Human Rights and the European Union: Who Decides? Possible Conflicts Between the European Court of Justice and the European Court of Human Rights', 19 *Dickinson Journal of International Law* (2001) 301.

'Targeted Sanctions, Human Rights, and the Court of First Instance of the European Community', 30 *Fordham Journal of International Law* (2007) 1449.

Dehousse, R., ed., *Une constitution pour l'Europe?* (Paris: Presses de Sciences Po, 2002).

'European Institutional Architecture After Amsterdam: Parliamentary System or Regulatory Structure?', 35 *Common Market Law Review* (1998) 595.

Dehousse, R. and J. Weiler, 'The Legal Dimension', in W. Wallace, ed., *The Dynamics of European Integration* (London: Pinter, 1990), 242–60.

Delahunty, R., 'The Battle of Mars and Venus: Why do American and European Attitudes to International Law Differ?', *St Thomas Law School Working Paper Series No 1744* (2006), available at <http://law.bepress.com/cgi/viewcontent.cgi?article=8181&context=expresso>.

Demaret, P., I. Govaere and D. Hanf, eds., *European Legal Dynamics* (Brussels: Peter Lang, 2007).

Dero, Delphine, *La réciprocité et le droit des Communautés et de l'Union européennes* (Brussels: Bruylant, 2006).

Deudney, D.,'The Philadelphian State System: Sovereignty, Arms Control and Balance of Power in the American State System', 49 *International Organization* (1995) 191–229.

Diehl, Paul F., Charlotte Ku and Daniel Zamora, 'The Dynamics of International Law: The Interaction of Normative and Operating Systems', 57 *International Organization* (2003) 43–75.

Dinan, D., ed., *Origins and Evolution of the European Union* (Oxford University Press, 2006).

Dobner, P. and M. Loughlin, eds., *The Twilight of Constitutionalism* (Oxford University Press, 2010).

Donnelly, Jack, *Realism and International Relations* (Cambridge University Press, 2000).

Douglas-Scott, Sionaidh, *Constitutional Law of the European Union* (London: Longman, 2002).

Doyle, M. W., *Ways of War and Peace* (Princeton University Press, 1997).

Drake, H., *Jacques Delores: Perspectives on a European Leader* (London: Routledge, 2000).

Dryzek, John, *Deliberative Global Politics* (Cambridge: Polity Press, 2006).

Dunne, Tim, 'Good Citizen Europe', 80 *International Affairs* 1 (2008) 13–28.

Dunoff, Jeffrey L., 'Constitutional Conceits: The WTO's "Constitution" and the Discipline of International Law', 17 *European Journal of International Law* (2006) 647–675.

Dunoff, Jeffrey L. and Joel P. Trachtman, eds., *Constitutionalism, International Law and Global Government* (Cambridge University Press, 2009).

Dupuy, Pierre-Marie, 'L'unité de l'ordre juridique international', 297 *Hague Recueil* (2003) 438–450.

Dworkin, R., *Law's Empire* (Cambridge, Mass.: Harvard University Press, 1986).

Eckes, C., 'Judicial Review of European Anti-Terrorism Measures – The Yusuf and Kadi Judgments of the Court of First Instance', 14 *Environmental Law Journal* (2008) 74.

Eeckhout, Piet, 'Community Terrorism Listings, Fundamental Rights, and UN Security Council Resolutions: In Search of the Right Fit', 3 *European Constitutional Law Review* (2007) 183–206.

Eeckhout, P. and W. Wouters, 'Giving Effect to Customary International Law Through EC Law', in J. Prinssen and A. Schrauwen, eds., *Direct Effect: Rethinking a Classic of EC Legal Doctrine* (Groningen: Europa Law Publishing, 2002), 183.

Eleftheriadis, Pavlos, 'Pluralism and Integrity', 23 *Ratio Juris* (2010) 365–389.

Everling, Ulrich, 'The European Union Between Community and National Policies and Legal Orders', in Armin von Bogdandy and J. Bast, eds., *Principles of European Constitutional Law* (Oxford: Hart Publishing, 2005), 677–725.

Fabbrini, S., *Compound Democracies: Why the United States and Europe are Becoming Similar* (Oxford University Press, 2007).

Falk, R., The *Study of Future Worlds* (New York: The Free Press, 1975).

Farber, D. and P. Frickey, *Law and Public Choice: A Critical Introduction* (University of Chicago Press, 1991).

Farrall, J. and K. Rubenstein, eds., *Sanctions Accountability and Governance in a Globalised World* (Cambridge University Press, 2009).

Fassbender, Bardo, 'The Meaning of International Constitutional Law', in Ronald St. J. Macdonald and Douglas M. Johnston, eds., *Towards World Constitutionalism* (Leiden: Martinus Nijhoff, 2005), 837–851.

   'The United Nations Charter as Constitution of the International Community', 36 *Columbia Journal of Transnational Law* (1998) 529–619.

   '"We the Peoples of the United Nations": Constituent Power and Constitutional Form in International Law', in Martin Loughlin and Neil Walker, eds., *The Paradox of Constitutionalism: Constituent Power and Constitutional Form* (Oxford University Press, 2007), 270–290.

Fedtke, J. and B. S. Markesinis, eds., *Patterns of Regionalism and Federalism: Lessons for the UK* (Oxford: Hart Publishing, 2006).

Feldman, Noah, 'Cosmopolitan Law?', 116 *Yale Law Journal* (2007) 1022.

Fischer-Lescano, A. and G. Teubner, *Regime-Kollisionen: Zur Fragmentierung des globalen Rechts* (Frankfurt am Main: Suhrkamp, 2006).

Fligstein, Neil, *Euroclash: The EU, European Identity, and the Future of Europe* (Oxford University Press, 2008).

Follesdal, A. and S. Hix, 'Why there is a Democratic Deficit in the EU: A Reply to Majone and Moravcsik', 44 *Journal of Common Market Studies* (2006) 533–562.

Fossum, John Eric and Augustin Menendez, 'The Constitution's Gift? A Deliberative Democratic Analysis of Constitution Making in the European Union', 11 *European Law Journal* (2005) 380–410.

Fox, Gregory, 'International Organizations: Conflicts in International Law', 95 *American Society of International Law Proceedings* (2001) 183.

Francioni, F. and Conforti, B., eds., *Enforcing International Human Rights in Domestic Courts* (The Hague: Martinus Nijhoff, 1997).

Franck, T. and G. Fox, eds., *International Law Decisions in National Courts* (Irvington-on-Hudson, NY: Transnational Publishers, 1996).

Freeden, M., *Ideologies and Political Theory: A Conceptual Approach* (Oxford: Clarendon Press, 1996).

Friedman, Barry, 'Dialogue and Judicial Review', 91 *Michigan Law Review* (1993) 577.

Friese, H. and P. Wagner, 'Survey Article: The Nascent Political Philosophy of the European Polity', 10 *Journal of Political Philosophy* (2002) 342.

Frowein, J., '*Solange II*', 25 *Common Market Law Review* (1988) 201.

Frug, G., 'Ideology of Bureaucracy in American Law', 97 *Harvard Law Review* (1984) 1276.

Fry, James, 'Dionysian Disarmament: Security Council WMD Coercive Disarmament Measures and their Legal Implications', 29 *Michigan Journal of International Law* (2008) 197.

Fursdon, Edward, *The European Defence Community: A History* (New York: St Martin's Press, 1980).

Galanter, Marc, 'Justice in Many Rooms: Courts, Private Ordering and Indigenous Law', 19 *Journal of Legal Pluralism* 1 (1981) 1–47.

Galston, William A., *Liberal Pluralism* (Cambridge University Press, 2002).

Garton Ash, T., 'Europe's True Stories', *Prospect* 131 (February 2007).

Gessner, V. and D. Nelken, eds., *European Ways of Law. Towards a European Sociology of Law* (Oxford: Hart Publishing, 2007).

Giddens, A., *The Constitution of Society* (Cambridge: Polity, 1984).

Giscard d'Estaing, Valéry, 'The Convention and the Future of Europe: Issues and Goals', 1 *International Journal of Constitutional Law* (2003) 346.

Glencross, A., *What Makes the EU Viable? European Integration in the Light of the US Antebellum Experience* (Basingstoke: Palgrave Macmillan, 2009).

Godhino, J., 'When Worlds Collide: Enforcing United Nations Security Council Asset Freezes in the EU Legal Order', 16 *Environmental Law Journal* (2010) 67.

Goldsmith, Jack, 'Liberal Democracy and Cosmopolitan Duty', 55 *Stanford Law Review* (2003) 1667.

Goldsmith, Jack and Eric Posner, 'Does Europe Believe in International Law?', *Washington Post* (25 November 2008).

The Limits of International Law (Oxford University Press, 2005).

Goldstein, L., *Constituting Federal Sovereignty: The European Union in Comparative Context* (Baltimore, London: Johns Hopkins University Press, 2001).

Gradoni, Lorenzo and Attila Tanzi, 'Diritto comunitario: una *lex specialis* molto speciale', in L. S. Rossi and G. Di Federico, eds., *L'incidenza del*

diritto dell'Unione europea sullo studio delle discipline giuridiche
(Napoli: Editoriale Scientifica, 2008), 37–70.

Green Cowles, M. and M. Smith, eds., *The State of the European Union*, vol.
5 (Oxford University Press, 2000).

Griffiths, John, 'What is Legal Pluralism?', 24 *Journal of Legal Pluralism*
(1986) 1–55.

Griffiths, Richard T., *Europe's First Constitution: The European Political
Community, 1952–1954* (London: The Federal Trust, 2000).

Griller, Stefan, 'International Law, Human Rights and the European
Community's Autonomous Legal Order: Notes on the European Court
of Justice Decision in *Kadi*', 4 *European Constitutional Law Review*
(2008) 528–553.

'Is this a Constitution? Remarks on a Contested Concept', in Stefan Griller
and J. Ziller, eds., *The Lisbon Treaty – EU Constitutionalisation without
a Constitutional Treaty?* (Wien, New York: Springer, 2008), 21–56.

Griller, Stefan and J. Ziller, eds., *The Lisbon Treaty – EU
Constitutionalisation without a Constitutional Treaty?* (Wien, New
York: Springer, 2008).

Grimm, Dieter, 'The Achievement of Constitutionalism and its Prospects in a
Changed World', in P. Dobner and M. Loughlin, eds., *The Twilight of
Constitutionalism* (Oxford University Press, 2010), 3–23.

'The Constitution in the Process of Denationalization', 12 *Constellations*
(2005) 447–463.

Deutsche Verfassungsgeschichte 1776–1866 (Frankfurt am Main:
Suhrkamp, 1988).

'Integration by Constitution', 3 *International Journal of Constitutional
Law* (2005) 193–208.

Die Zukunft der Verfassung (Frankfurt am Main: Suhrkamp, 1991).

Grotius, Hugo, *The Law of War and of Peace [De jure belli ac pacis]*, trans.
Louise R. Loomis, with an introduction by P. E. Corbett (Roslyn, NY: W.
J. Black, 1949 [1625]).

Gustavsson, S. and L. Lewin, eds., *The Future of the Nation State* (Stockholm:
Nerenius & Santérus, 1996).

Gutmann, A. and D. Thompson, *Democracy and Disagreement* (Cambridge,
Mass., London: Belknap Press 1996).

Guzman, A., 'International Tribunals: A Rational Choice Analysis', 157
University of Pennsylvania Law Review (2008) 171.

Habermas, Jürgen, *Between Facts and Norms* (Cambridge, Mass.: MIT Press,
1996).

'Constitutional Democracy: A Paradoxical Union of Contradictory
Principles?', 29 *Political Theory* (2001) 766–81.

The Divided West, trans. Ciaran Cronin (Cambridge: Polity Press, 2006).

'Does the Constitutionalization of International Law Still have a chance?' in Habermas, Jürgen, *The Divided West*, trans. Ciaran Cronin (Cambridge: Polity Press, 2006), 115–193.

Der gespaltene Westen (Frankfurt am Main: Suhrkamp, 2004).

'On Law and Disagreement: Some Comments on 'Interpretative Pluralism', 16 *Ratio Juris* (2003) 187–199.

The Postnational Constellation, trans. M. Pensky (Cambridge, Mass.: MIT Press, 2001).

Halberstam, Daniel, 'Comparative Federalism and the Issue of Commandeering', in Kalypso Nicolaidis and Robert Howse, eds., *The Federal Vision: Legitimacy and Levels of Governance in the US and the EU* (Oxford University Press, 2001), 213–251.

'Comparative Federalism and the Role of the Judiciary', in K. Whittington, D. Kelemen and G. Caldeira, eds., *The Oxford Handbook of Law and Politics* (Oxford University Press, 2008).

'Constitutionalism and Pluralism in Marbury and Van Gend', in M. Maduro and L. Azoulay, *The Past and Future of EU Law* (Oxford: Hart Publishing, 2008).

'Constitutional Heterarchy: The Centrality of Conflict in the European Union and the United States', in J. L. Dunoff and J. P. Trachtman, eds., *Constitutionalism, International Law and Global Government* (Cambridge University Press, 2009), 326–355.

'The Promise of Comparative Administrative Law: A Constitutional Perspective on Independent Agencies', in S. Rose-Ackerman and P. Lindseth, eds., *Comparative Administrative Law* (Cheltenham: Edward Elgar, 2010).

Halberstam, D. and E. Stein, 'The United Nations, the European Union, and the King of Sweden: Economic Sanctions and Individual Rights in a Plural World Order', 46 *The Common Market Law Review* (2009) 13.

Haltern, U., 'Pathos and Patina: The Failure and Promise of Constitutionalism in the European Imagination', 9 *European Law Journal* 1 (2003) 14–44.

Hamilton, A., J. Madison and J. Jay, *The Federalist Papers*, ed. L. Goldman (Oxford University Press, 2008).

Harpaz, G., 'Judicial Review by the European Court of Justice of UN "Smart Sanctions" Against Terror in the *Kadi* Dispute', 14 *European Foreign Affairs Review* (2009) 65.

Hartley, Trevor C., 'International Law and the Law of the European Union – A Reassessment', *British Year Book of International Law* (2001) 1–35.

Hathaway, Oona A. and Ariel N. Lavinbuk, 'Rationalism and Revisionism in International Law', 119 *Harvard Law Review* (2006) 1404.

Hay, Peter, *Federalism and Supranational Organizations: Patterns for New Legal Structures* (University of Illinois Press, 1966).

Hedetoft, U. and M. Hjort, eds., *The Postnational Self: Belonging and Identity* (Minneapolis: University of Minnesota Press, 2002).

Hegel, G. W. F., *The Philosophy of History*, trans. J. Sibree (Buffalo: Prometheus Books, 1991).

Held, David, *Democracy and the Global Order: From the Modern State to Cosmopolitan Governance* (Cambridge: Polity Press, 1995).

'Democratic Accountability and Effectiveness from a Cosmopolitan Perspective', 39 *Government & Opposition* (2004) 365–391.

Helfer, Laurence R. and Karen J. Alter, 'Building Judicial Supranationalism in the Andes: Understanding Preliminary Reference Patterns in the Andean Community', 41 *New York University Journal of International Law and Politics* (2009) 872–928.

Hershovitz, S., 'Legitimacy, Democracy, and Razian Authority', 9 *Legal Theory* (2003) 201.

Hirschl, Ran, *Towards Juristocracy: The Origins and Consequences of the New Constitutionalism* (Cambridge, Mass.: Harvard University Press, 2004).

Hirst, Paul Q., *Associative Democracy* (Cambridge: Polity Press, 1994).

'Introduction', in Paul Q. Hirst, ed., *A Pluralist Theory of the State* (London: Routledge, 1989), 1–45.

ed., *A Pluralist Theory of the State* (London: Routledge, 1989).

Hobsbawm, E., *The Age of Extremes: The Short Twentieth Century, 1914–1991* (London: Michael Joseph, 1994).

Hoffman, Florian and Frédric Mégret, 'The UN as a Human Rights Violator: Some Reflections on The United Nations Changing Human Rights Responsibilities', 25 *Human Rights Quarterly* (2003) 314.

Hoffmann, Stanley, 'Obstinate or Obsolete? The Fate of the Nation State and the Case of Western Europe', 95 *Daedalus* (1966) 862–915.

Holmes, Stephen, *Benjamin Constant and the Making of Modern Liberalism* (New Haven: Yale University Press, 1984).

Passions and Constraint (University of Chicago Press, 1995).

Hooghe, L. and G. Marks, 'A Postfunctionalist Theory of European Integration: From Permissive Consensus to Constraining Dissensus', 39 *British Journal of Political Science* (2008) 1–23.

Horowitz, Donald, 'Constitutional Design: Proposals Versus Processes', in A. Reynolds, ed., *The Architecture of Democracy: Constitutional Design, Conflict Management, and Democracy* (Oxford University Press, 2002), 15–36.

Howse, Robert and Kalypso Nicolaidis, 'Democracy without Sovereignty: The Global Vocation of Political Ethics', in T. Broude and Y. Shany, eds., *The Shifting Allocation of Authority in International Law* (Oxford, Portland: Hart Publishing, 2008), 163.

'Enhancing WTO Legitimacy: Constitutionalization or Global Subsidiarity?', 16 *Governance* (2003) 73.

'Legitimacy and Global Governance: Why Constitutionalizing the WTO is a Step Too Far', in Roger B. Porter, Pierre Sauve, Arvind Subramanian and Americo Beviglia Zampetti, eds., *Efficiency, Equity and Legitimacy: The Multilateral Trading System at The Millennium* (Washington, DC: Brookings Institute Press, 2001).

'Legitimacy through "Higher Law"? Why Constitutionalizing the WTO Is a Step Too Far', in T. Cottier, P. Mavroidis and P. Blatter, eds., *The Role of the Judge in International Trade Regulation: Experience and Lessons for the WTO* (Ann Arbor: University of Michigan Press, 2003), 307.

'This is my EUtopia: Narrative as Power', 40 *Journal of Common Market Studies* (2002) 767–792.

Huber, Ernst R., *Deutsche Verfassungsgeschichte seit 1789*, vol. III (Stuttgart: Kohlhammer, 1981).

Hülsse, Rainer, 'Even Clubs Can't Do without Legitimacy: Why the Anti-money Laundering Blacklist was Suspended', 2 *Regulation & Governance* 4 (2008) 459–479.

Hurd, Ian, *After Anarchy: Legitimacy and Power in the United Nations Security Council* (Princeton University Press, 2007).

Hurrell, Andrew, *On Global Order* (Oxford University Press, 2007).

Ignatieff, Michael, ed., *American Exceptionalism and Human Rights* (Princeton University Press, 2005).

Empire Lite: Nation-Building in Bosnia, Kosovo and Afghanistan (London: Vintage, 2003).

Ikenberry, John, *After Victory: Institutions, Strategic Restraint, and the Rebuilding of Order After Major Wars* (Princeton University Press, 2001).

Imbert, L., 'Le régime juridique actuel du Danube', 58 *Revue générale de droit international public* (1951) 73–76.

Ipsen, H-P., 'Europäische Verfassung – Nationale Verfassung', 22 *Europarecht* (1987) 195–213.

Isensee, J. and P. Kirchhof, eds., *Handbuch des Staatsrechts*, VII (Heidelberg: CF Müller, 1992).

Isiksel, N. T., 'Fundamental Rights in the EU after Kadi and Al Barakaat', 16 *Environmental Law Journal* (2010) 551.

Jackson, J., 'The WTO Dispute Settlement Understanding – Misunderstandings on the Nature of Legal Obligations', 91 *American Journal of International Law* (1997) 60.

Jacobs, Francis and Kenneth Karst, 'The "Federal" Legal Order: The U.S.A. and Europe Compared – A Juridical Perspective', in M. Cappelletti, M. Seccombe and J. Weiler, eds., *Integration Through Law – Europe and the American Federal Experience*, vol. 1, book 1 (The Hague: de Gruyter, 1986), 169–243.

Jacobs F. G. and S. Roberts, eds., *The Effect of Treaties in Domestic Law* (London: Sweet & Maxwell, 1987).

Jacqué, Jean-Paul, 'Le projet de traité établissant une constitution pour l'Europe – Constitutionnalisation ou révision des traités', in P. Demaret, I. Govaere and D. Hanf, eds., *European Legal Dynamics* (Brussels: Peter Lang, 2007), 41–52.

Jaenicke, Günther, 'Der übernationale Charakter der Europäischen Wirtschaftsgemeinschaft', 18 *Zeitschrift für ausländisches öffentliches Recht und Völkerrecht* (1958), 154–196.

Jennings, Robert Y. and Arthur Watts, eds., *Oppenheim's International Law*, vol. I (9th edn, London: Longman, 1992).

Joerges, Christian, 'Conflict of Laws as Constitutional Form: Reflections on International Trade Law and the *Biotech* Panel Report', *RECON Online Working Paper* 2007/3 (2007).

  'Constitutionalism in Postnational Constellations: Contrasting Social Regulation in the EU and the WTO', in Christian Joerges and Ernst-Ulrich Petersmann, *Constitutionalism, Multilevel Trade Governance and Social Regulation* (Oxford: Hart, 2006), 491–527.

  '"Good Governance" in the European Internal Market: An Essay in Honour of Claus-Dieter Ehlermann', European University Institute Working Paper RSC No. 2001/29 (2001).

  'Rethinking the Supremacy of European Law', European University Institute Working Paper LAW No. 2005/12 (2005).

Joerges, Christian and N. S. Ghaleigh, eds., *Darker Legacies of Law in Europe* (Oxford: Hart Publishing, 2003).

Joerges, Christian, Yves Mény and Joseph H. H. Weiler, eds., *What Kind of Constitution for What Kind of Polity? Responses to Joschka Fischer* (Firenze: EUI Robert Schuman Center for Advanced Studies, San Domenico, 2000).

Joerges, Christian and Ernst-Ulrich Petersmann, *Constitutionalism, Multilevel Trade Governance And Social Regulation* (Oxford: Hart, 2006).

Joerges, Christian, I. J. Sand and G. Teubner, eds., *Transnational Governance and Constitutionalism* (Oxford: Hart Publishing, 2004).

Joerges, Christian and E. Vos, eds., *EU Committees: Social Regulation. Law and Politics* (Oxford: Hart Publishing, 1999).

Johansson-Nogues, E., 'The (Non) Normative Power EU and the European Neighbourhood Policy: An Exceptional Policy for an Exceptional Actor', 7 *European Journal of Political Economy* (2007) 181–194.

Johnston, D., 'World Constitutionalism in the Theory of International Law', in Ronald St. J. Macdonald and Douglas M. Johnston, eds., *Towards World Constitutionalism* (Leiden: Martinus Nijhoff, 2005), 3–29.

Joris, T. and J. Vandenberghe, 'The Council of Europe and the European Union: Natural Partners or Uneasy Bedfellows?', 15 *Columbia Journal of European Law* (2008–2009) 1.

Jouannet, E., 'Universalism and Imperialism: The True–False Paradox of International Law?' 18 *European Journal of International Law* (2007) 379–407.

Kaddous, C. and A. Auer, eds., *Les principes fondamentaux de la Constitution européenne* (Helbing & Lichtenhahn: Bruylant, 2006).

Kaeckenbeeck, Georges, *The International Experiment of Upper Silesia* (Oxford University Press, 1942).

Kagan, Robert, 'America's Crisis of Legitimacy', 83 *Foreign Affairs* (March/April 2004) 65.

Of Paradise and Power: America and Europe in the New World Order (New York: Knopf, 2003).

Kahn, P. W., *Putting Liberalism in its Place* (Princeton University Press, 2005).

Kant, Immanuel, 'Idea for a Universal History with a Cosmopolitan Intent', trans. Ted Humphrey, in Immanuel Kant, *Perpetual Peace and Other Essays* (1883).

'Perpetual Peace: A Philosophical Essay', trans. Mary Campbell Smith, in Immanuel Kant, *Perpetual Peace and Other Essays* (1795, 1903).

Toward Perpetual Peace and Other Writings on Politics, Peace, and History, ed. and with an introduction by Pauline Kleingeld, trans. David L. Colclasure, with essays by Jeremy Waldron, Michael W. Doyle and Allen W. Wood (New Haven: Yale University Press, 2006 [1795]).

Kapteyn, P. J. G. and P. Verloren Van Themaat, *Introduction to the Law of the European Communities*, trans. C. Dikshoorn (The Hague: Kluwer, 1973).

Karl, Wolfram, *Vertrag und spätere Praxis im Völkerrecht* (Berlin: Springer Verlag, 1983).

Karlsson, C., 'Deliberation at the European Convention: The Final Verdict', 14 *European Law Journal* (2008) 604–619.

Katzenstein, Peter and Jeffrey T. Checkel, 'Conclusion – European Identity in Context', in J. T. Checkel and P. J. Katzenstein, eds., *European Identity* (Cambridge University Press, 2009), 213–227.

Keller, H. and A. Stone Sweet, eds., *A Europe of Rights: The Impact of the ECHR on National Legal Systems* (Oxford University Press, 2008).

Kelsen, Hans, 'Die Einheit von Völkerrecht und staatlichem Recht', 19 *ZaöRV* (1958) 234.

Reine Rechtslehre (2nd reprint of first edition, Leipzig und Wien; Aalen: Scientia Verlag, 1994 [1934]).

Kennedy, D., 'The Mystery of Global Governance', 34 *Ohio Northern University Law Review* (2008) 827–860.

'One, Two, Three, Many Legal Orders: Legal Pluralism and the Cosmopolitan Dream', 31 *New York University Review of Law and Social Change* (2007) 641.

Keohane, Robert O., 'Governance in a Partially Globalized World', 95 *American Political Science Review* (2001) 1–13.

Kingsbury, B., 'Weighing Global Regulatory Rules and Decisions in National Courts', *Acta Juridica* (2009) 90–119.

Kingsbury, B., N. Krisch and R. Stewart, 'The Emergence of Global Administrative Law', 68 *Law and Contemporary Problems* (2005) 15–61.

Kirchhof, Paul, 'Der deutsche Staat im Prozeß der europäischen Integration', in J. Isensee, and P. Kirchhof, eds., *Handbuch des Staatsrechts*, VII (Heidelberg: CF Müller, 1993), 855–886.

'The Legal Structure of the European Union as a Union of States', in Armin von Bogdandy and J. Bast, eds., *Principles of European Constitutional Law* (Oxford: Hart Publishing, 2005), 765–802.

Klabbers, Jan, 'The Changing Image of International Organizations', in J. M. Coicaud and V. Heiskanen, eds., *The Legitimacy of International Organizations* (Tokyo: United Nations University Press, 2001), 221–255.

'Constitutionalism Lite', 1 *International Organizations Law Review* (2004) 31–58.

An Introduction to International Institutional Law (Cambridge University Press, 2002).

Treaty Conflict and the European Union (Cambridge University Press, 2009).

Klabbers, Jan, A. Peters and G. Ulfstein, *The Constitutionalization of International Law* (Oxford University Press, 2009).

Klein, Claude, 'Pourquoi écrit-on une constitution?', in Troper, M. and L. Jaume, eds., *1789 et l'invention de la constitution* (Brussels, Paris: Bruylant, 1994), 89–99.

Kleinfeld, R. and K. Nicolaidis, 'Can a Post-Colonial Power Export the Rule of Law? Elements of a General Framework', in G. Palombella and N. Walker, eds., *Relocating the Rule of Law* (Oxford: Hart Publishing, 2008), 139–169.

Knoll, Bernhard, *The Legal Status of Territories Subject to Administration by International Organisations* (Cambridge University Press, 2008).

Koh, Harold, 'Is there a "New" New Haven School of International Law', 32 *Yale Journal of International Law* (2007) 559.

'On American Exceptionalism', 55 *Stanford Law Review* (2003) 1479–1529.

Koskenniemi, Martti, 'Constitutionalism as Mindset: Reflections on Kantian Themes About International Law and Globalization,' 8 *Theoretical Inquiries in Law* (2007) 9.

'The Fate of International Law: Between Technique and Politics', 70 *Modern Law Review* (2007) 1–30.

'Global Legal Pluralism: Multiple Legal Regimes and Multiple Modes of Thought' (2005), available at <www.helsinki.fi/eci/Publications/MKPluralism-Harvard-05d%5B1%5D.pdf>.

ed., *International Law Aspects of the European Union* (The Hague, London: Kluwer Law International, 1998).

'International Law in Europe: Between Tradition and Renewal', 16 *European Journal of International Law* (2005) 113–124.

'"The Lady Doth Protest Too Much": Kosovo and the Turn to Ethics in International Law', 65 *Modern Law Review* (2002) 159.

Koskenniemi, Martti and Päivi Leino, 'Fragmentation of International Law? Postmodern Anxieties', 15 *Leiden Journal of International Law* (2002) 553–579.

Koutrakos, P., *EU International Relations Law* (Oxford: Hart Publishing, 2006).

Krajewski, Marcus, 'Democratic Legitimacy and Constitutional Perspectives of WTO Law' *Journal of World Trade* (2001).

Krasner, S., *Sovereignty: Organized Hypocrisy* (Princeton University Press, 1999).

Krastev, Ivan and Mark Leonard, *New World Order: The Balance of Soft Power and the Rise of Herbivorous Powers* (London: European Council on Foreign Relations, 2007).

Krisch, Nico, *Beyond Constitutionalism: The Pluralist Structure of Postnational Law* (Oxford University Press, 2010).

'The Case for Pluralism in Postnational Law', LSE Legal Studies Working Papers 12/2009 (2009), available at http://papers.ssrn.com/sol3/papers.cfm?abstract_id=1418707.

'International Law in Times of Hegemony: Unequal Power and the Shaping of the International Legal Order', 16 *European Journal of International Law* (2005) 369–408.

'The Open Architecture of European Human Rights Law', 71 *Modern Law Review* (2008) 183–216.

'Pluralism in Postnational Risk Regulation: The Dispute over GMOs and Trade', 1 *Transnational Legal Theory* (2010), 1–29.

'The Pluralism of Global Adminstrative Law', 17 *European Journal of International Law* (2006) 247–278.

Kronenberger, V., ed., *The European Union and the International Legal Order: Discord or Harmony?* (The Hague: Martinus Nijhoff, 2001).

Ku, Julian G., 'The Delegation of Federal Power to International Organizations: New Problems with Old Solutions', 85 *Minnesota Law Review* (2000) 71.

Kukathas, Chandran, *The Liberal Archipelago* (Oxford University Press, 2003).

Kumm, Mattias, 'Constitutional Democracy Encounters International Law: Terms of Engagement', *NYU Public Law and Legal Theory Working Papers no. 47* (2006).

'The Cosmopolitan Turn in Constitutionalism: On the Relationship between Constitutionalism in and beyond the State', in J. L. Dunoff and J. P. Trachtman, eds., *Constitutionalism, International Law and Global Government* (Cambridge University Press, 2009), 258–324.

'The Legitimacy of International Law: A Constitutionalist Framework of Analysis', 15 *European Journal of International Law* (2004) 907–931.

'Why Europeans Will Not Embrace Constitutional Patriotism', 6 *International Journal of Constitutional Law* (2008) 117.

Kundera, Milan, *Le rideau* (Paris: Edition Gallimard, 2005).

Kymlicka, Will, *Multicultural Citizenship* (Oxford: Clarendon Press, 1995).

Ladeur, K. H., '"We, the European People . . ." – Relâche?', 14 *European Law Journal* 2 (2008) 147–67.

Laffan, B., *Integration and Co-operation in Europe* (London: Routledge, 1992).

Laski, Harold J., 'Law and the State', in Paul Q. Hirst, ed., *A Pluralist Theory of the State* (London: Routledge, 1989), 197–227.

'The Pluralistic State', in Paul Q. Hirst, ed., *A Pluralist Theory of the State* (London: Routledge, 1989).

'The Problem of Administrative Areas', in Paul Q. Hirst, ed., *A Pluralist Theory of the State* (London: Routledge, 1989), 131–163.

Leben, Charles, 'Fédération d'Etats-nations ou Etat fédéral?', in Christian Joerges, Yves Mény and Joseph H. H. Weiler, eds., *What Kind of Constitution for What Kind of Polity? Responses to Joschka Fischer* (Firenze: EUI Robert Schuman Center for Advanced Studies, San Domenico, 2000), 85–97.

Lenaerts, Koen, 'De Rome à Lisbonne, la Constitution européenne en marche?', 44 *Cahiers de droit européen* 3–4 (2008) 229–253.

Licková, Magdalena, 'European Exceptionalism in International Law', 19 *European Journal of International Law* (2008) 463–490.

Lindahl, Hans, 'Constituent Power and Reflexive Identity: Towards an Ontology of Collective Selfhood', in Martin Loughlin and Neil Walker, eds., *The Paradox of Constitutionalism: Constituent Power and Constitutional Form* (Oxford University Press, 2007), 9–26.

'Sovereignty and the Institutionalization of Normative Order', 21 *Oxford Journal of Legal Studies* (2001) 165–180.

Lijphart, Arend, *Democracy in Plural Societies* (New Haven: Yale University Press, 1978).

Thinking About Democracy: Power Sharing and Majority Rule in Theory and Practice (London: Routledge, 2008).

Loughlin, Martin and Neil Walker, eds., *The Paradox of Constitutionalism: Constituent Power and Constitutional Form* (Oxford University Press, 2007).

Louis, Jean-Victor and Thierry Ronse, *L'ordre juridique de l'Union européenne* (Paris: LGDJ, 2005).

Lowe, Vaughan, 'Can the European Community Bind the Member States on Questions of Customary International Law?', in M. Koskenniemi, ed., *International Law Aspects of the European Union* (The Hague, London: Kluwer Law International, 1998), 149–196.

MacCormick, Neil, 'Beyond the Sovereign State', 56 *Modern Law Review* (1993) 1–18.

'The Maastricht-Urteil: Sovereignty Now', 1 *European Law Journal* (1995) 259–266.

Questioning Sovereignty: Law, State and Nation in the European Commonwealth (Oxford University Press, 1999).

'Risking Constitutional Collision in Europe?', 18 *Oxford Journal of Legal Studies* (1998) 517–532.

Who's Afraid of the European Constitution? (London: Imprint Academic, 1995).

Macdonald, Ronald St. J. and Douglas M. Johnston, eds., *Towards World Constitutionalism* (Leiden: Martinus Nijhoff, 2005).

Maduro, Miguel, 'Contrapunctual Law: Europe's Constitutional Pluralism in Action', in N. Walker, ed., *Sovereignty in Transition* (Oxford University Press, 2003), 501–538.

'Europe and the Constitution: What If This Is As Good As It Gets?', in J. H. H. Weiler and M. Wind, eds., *European Constitutionalism Beyond the State* (Cambridge University Press, 2003), 74–102.

Maduro, M. and L. Azoulay, *The Past and Future of EU Law* (Oxford: Hart Publishing, 2008).

Magnette, Paul and Kalypso Nicolaidis, 'The European Convention: Bargaining in the Shadow of Rhetoric', 27 *West European Politics* (2004) 381–404.

Majone, G., 'The Rise of the Regulatory State in Europe', 17 *West European Politics* 3 (1994) 77–104.

Mancini, F., *Democracy and Constitutionalism in Europe* (Oxford: Hart Publishing, 2000).

'Europe: The Case for Statehood', 4 *European Law Journal* (1998) 29–42.

Mancini, F. and J. H. H. Weiler, 'Europe: The Case for Statehood . . . And the Case Against: An Exchange', *Harvard Jean Monnet Working Paper 6/98*, Cambridge, Mass. (1998).

Manners, Ian, 'Normative Power Europe: A Contradiction in Terms?', 40 *Journal of Common Market Studies* (2002) 235–258.

Manners, Ian and R. Whitman, 'The Difference Engine: Constructing and Representing the International Identity of the European Union', 10 *Journal of European Public* 3 (2003) 380–404.

Marschik, Axel, *Subsysteme im Völkerrecht. Ist die Europäische Union ein 'Self-Contained Regime'?* (Berlin: Duncker & Humblot, 1997).

Mason, A., *Community, Solidarity and Belonging: Levels of Community and Their Normative Significance* (Cambridge University Press, 2000).

Mayhew, A. and N. Copsey, eds., *European Neighbourhood Policy and Ukraine* (Falmer: University of Sussex, Sussex European Institute, 2005).

McCrudden, Christopher, 'Human Dignity and Judicial Interpretation of Human Rights', 19 *European Journal of International Law* (2008) 655–724.

McGarry, J., B. O'Leary and R. Simeon, 'Integration or Accommodation? The Enduring Debate in Conflict Regulation', in Sujit Choudhry, ed., *Constitutional Design for Divided Societies: Integration or Accommodation?* (Oxford University Press, 2008), 41–88.

Meidinger, Errol, 'The Administrative Law of Global Public–Private Regulation: The Case of Forestry', 17 *European Journal of International Law* (2006) 47–87.

Mendez, Mario, *The Legal Effect of Community Agreements: Lessons from the Court* (PhD thesis, European University Institute, 2009).

'The Legal Effect of Community Agreements: Maximalist Treaty Enforcement and Judicial Avoidance Techniques', 21 *European Journal of International Law* (2010) 83.

Menendez, A. J., 'European Union Citizenship after *Martinez Sala* and *Baumbast.* Has European Law Become More Human But Less Social?', *RECON Working Papers 2009/5* (2009).

Merry, Sally Engle, 'Legal Pluralism', 22 *Law and Society Review* (1988) 869–896.

Mestmacker, E.-J., 'On the Legitimacy of European Law', 58 *RabelsZ* (1994) 615.

Meunier, S. and K. McNamara, eds., *Making History. European Integration and Institutional Change at Fifty* (The State of the European Union, Vol. 8) (Oxford University Press, 2007).

Michalski, K., ed., *Religion in the New Europe* (Budapest, New York: CEU Press, 2006).

Michel, Valéri and Aude Bouveresse, 'La notion de constitution', in V. Constantinesco, Y. Gautier and V. Michel, eds., *Le Traité établissant une Constitution pour l'Europe. Analyses et commentaires* (Presses Universitaires de Strasbourg, 2005), 31–60.

Michelman, Frank, *Brennan and Democracy* (Princeton University Press, 2005).

'Law's Republic', 97 *Yale Law Journal* (1988), 1493–1537.

Miller, David, *National Responsibility and Global Justice* (Oxford University Press, 2007).

Moellers, Christoph, 'Pouvoir Constituant – Constitution – Constitutionalization', in Armin von Bogdandy and J. Bast, eds., *Principles of European Constitutional Law* (Oxford: Hart Publishing, 2005), 183–226.

Möllers, Christoph, 'Verfassunggebende Gewalt – Verfassung – Konstitutionalisierung', in Armin von Bogdandy, ed., *Europäisches Verfassungsrecht* (Berlin, Heidelberg: Springer, 2003), 1–57.

Moore, Sally F., 'Law and Social Change: The Semi-Autonomous Social Field as an Appropriate Subject of Study', 7 *Law and Society Review* (1973) 719–746.

Moravcsik, Andrew, *The Choice for Europe: Social Purpose and State Power from Messina to Maastricht* (University College London Press, 1998).

'The European Constitutional Settlement', in S. Meunier and K. McNamara, eds., *Making History. European Integration and Institutional Change at Fifty* (The State of the European Union, Vol. 8) (Oxford University Press, 2007), 23–50.

'What Can We Learn from the Collapse of the European Constitutional Project?', 47 *Politische Vierteljahresschrift* (2006) 2.

Morgan, E. S., *Inventing the People: The Rise of Popular Sovereignty in England and America* (New York: Norton, 1988).

Mosler, Hermann, 'The International Society as a Legal Community', 140 *Receuil des Cours* (1974) 1–320.

Mouffe, Chantal, *The Democratic Paradox* (London: Verso Books, 2000).

Mueller, Jan-Werner, *Constitutional Patriotism* (Princeton University Press, 2007).

'A General Theory of Constitutional Patriotism', 6 *International Journal of Constitutional Law* (2008) 72–95.

Nicholls, David, *The Pluralist State: The Political Ideas of J. N. Figgis and his Contemporaries* (2nd edn, Basingstoke: Macmillan, 1994).

Nicolaidis, Kalypso, 'The New Constitution as European Demoi-cracy?', *Federal Trust Online Working Paper No. 38/03* (2003), available at <http://ssrn.com/abstract=517423>.

'Trusting the Poles? Constructing Europe Through Mutual Recognition', 14 *Journal of European Public Policy* (2007) 682–698.

'We, the Peoples of Europe . . .', 83 *Foreign Affairs* 6 (November/December 2004) 97–110.

Nicolaidis, Kalypso and Robert Howse, eds., *The Federal Vision: Legitimacy and Levels of Governance in the US and the EU* (Oxford University Press, 2001).

Nuttall, S., *European Political Cooperation* (Oxford: Clarendon Press 1992).

Nye, J., *Soft Power, The Means to Success in World Politics* (New York: Public Affairs, 2004).

Oeter, Stefan, 'Föderalismus', in Armin von Bogdandy, ed., *Europäisches Verfassungsrecht* (Berlin, Heidelberg: Springer, 2003), 59–119.

'Souveränität und Demokratie als Probleme in der "Verfassungsentwicklung" der Europäischen Union', 55 *Zeitschrift für ausländisches öffentliches Recht und Völkerrecht* (1995) 659–707.

Olsen, M., *The Logic of Collective Action* (Cambridge, Mass.: Harvard University Press, 1971).

Oosthuizen, Gabriël, 'Playing the Devil's Advocate: The UN Security Council is Unbound by Law', 12 *Leiden Journal of International Law* (1999) 549–563.

Orakhelashvili, A., 'The Idea of European International Law', 17 *European Journal of International Law* (2006) 315–347.

Paasivirta, Esa and Piet Jan Kuijper, 'Does One Size Fit All? The European Community and the Responsibility of International Organizations', 36 *Netherlands Yearbook of International Law* (2005) 169–226.

Paine, Tom, *Rights of Man; Common Sense; and Other Political Writings*, ed. with an introduction by Mark Philp (Oxford University Press, 1995 [1791]).

Palombella, G., and N. Walker, eds., *Relocating the Rule of Law* (Oxford: Hart Publishing, 2008).

Parsons, Craig, 'The Triumph of Community Europe', in D. Dinan, ed., *Origins and Evolution of the European Union* (Oxford University Press, 2006), 107–125.

Paul, T. V., G. J. Ikenberry and J. A. Hall, eds., *The Nation-State in Question* (Princeton University Press, 2003).

Paulus, Andreas, *Die internationale Gemeinschaft im Völkerrecht* (München: C.H. Beck, 2001).

Pellet, Alain, 'Les fondements juridiques internationaux du droit communautaire', in *Collected Courses of the Academy of European Law*, vol. 5, book 2 (The Hague: Kluwer 1994), 193–271.

Pennock, J. R. and J. W. Chapman, eds., *NOMOS XXV: Liberal Democracy* (New York University Press, 1983).

Pernice, Ingolf, 'Multilevel Constitutionalism and the Treaty of Amsterdam: European Constitution-Making Revisited?', 36 *Common Market Law Review* (1999) 703–750.

'Theorie und Praxis des Europäischen Verfassungsverbundes', in C. Calliess, *Verfassungswandel im europäischen Staaten- und Verfassungsverbund* (Mohr Siebeck: Tübingen, 2007), 61–92.

Peters, Anne, 'Compensatory Constitutionalism: The Function and Potential of Fundamental International Norms and Structures', 19 *Leiden Journal of International Law* 3 (2006) 579–610.

'The Constitutionalisation of the European Union – Without the Constitutional Treaty', in S. Puntscher and Riekmann and W. Wessels, eds., *The Making of a European Constitution – Dynamics and Limits of the Convention Experience* (Wiesbaden: Verlag für Sozialwissenschaften, 2006), 35–67.

'The Position of International Law within the European Community Law Legal Order', 40 *German Yearbook of International Law* 9 (1997).

Petersmann, Ernst-Ulrich, 'Constitutionalism and the Regulation of International Markets: How to Define the "Development Objectives" of the World Trading System?', *European University Institute Working Paper LAW No. 2007/23* (2007), available at <http://ssrn.com/abstract=1024105>.

'Justice in International Economic Law? From the "International Law among States" to "International Integration Law" and "Constitutional Law"', *European University Institute Working Paper LAW No. 2006/46* (2006), available at <http://ssrn.com/abstract=964165>.

'State Sovereignty, Popular Sovereignty and Individual Sovereignty: From Constitutional Nationalism to Multilevel Constitutionalism in International Economic Law?', *European University Institute Working Paper LAW No. 2006/45* (2006), available at <http://ssrn.com/abstract=964147>.

'Why Rational Choice Theory Requires a Multilevel Constitutional Approach to International Economic Law – The Case for Reforming the WTO's Enforcement Mechanism', *University of Illinois Law Review* (2008) 359, available at <http://ssrn.com/abstract=1001166>.

'The WTO Constitution and Human Rights', 3 *Journal of International Economic Law* 1 (2000) 19–25.

Pettit, Philip, 'Rawls's Political Ontology', 4 *Politics, Philosophy and Economics* (2005) 157–174.

Republicanism: A Theory of Freedom and Government (Oxford University Press, 1997).

Picker, Colin, 'International Law's Mixed Heritage: A Common/Civil Law Jurisdiction', 41 *Vanderbilt Journal of Transnational Law* (2008) 1083.

Pildes, Richard H., 'Ethnic Identity and Democratic Institutions: A Dynamic Perspective' in Sujit Choudhry, ed., *Constitutional Design for Divided Societies: Integration or Accommodation?* (Oxford University Press, 2008), 173–201.

Piris, Jean-Claude, 'The European Union: Towards a New Form of Federalism?', in J. Fedtke and B. S. Markesinis, eds., *Patterns of Regionalism and Federalism: Lessons for the UK* (Oxford: Hart Publishing, 2006), 69–87.

Pogge, Thomas, 'Cosmopolitanism and Sovereignty', 103 *Ethics* 1 (1992) 48–75.

World Poverty and Human Rights (Cambridge: Polity Press, 2002).

Poli, S. and M. Tzanou, 'The Kadi Rulings: A Survey of the Literature', 28 *Yearbook of European Law* (2009) 533–558.

Porter, Roger B., Pierre Sauve, Arvind Subramanian and Americo Beviglia Zampetti, eds., *Efficiency, Equity and Legitimacy: The Multilateral Trading System at The Millennium* (Washington, DC: Brookings, 2001).

Posner, E. and J. Goldsmith, *The Limits of International Law* (Oxford University Press, 2005).

Prinssen, J. and A. Schrauwen, eds., *Direct Effect: Rethinking a Classic of EC Legal Doctrine* (Groningen: Europa Law Publishing, 2002).

von Pufendorf, Samuel, *Of the Law of Nature and Nations [De Iure Naturae e Gentium]*. [eight books / written in Latin by the Baron Pufendorf; translated into English, from the best edition, with a short introduction] (Oxford: L. Lichfield, 1703 [1672]).

Puntscher Riekmann, S. and W. Wessels, eds., *The Making of a European Constitution – Dynamics and Limits of the Convention Experience* (Wiesbaden: Verlag für Sozialwissenschaften, 2006).

Rabin, Robert, 'Federal Regulation in Historical Perspective', 38 *Stanford Law Review* (1986) 1189.

Rabkin, Jeremy, *Why Sovereignty Matters* (Washington, DC: American Enterprise Institute Press, 1998).

Rajagopal, Balakrishnan, 'Limits of Law in Counter-hegemonic Globalization: The Indian Supreme Court and the Narmada Valley Struggle', in B. de Sousa Santos and C. A. Rodríguez-Garavito, eds., *Law and Globalization from Below* (Cambridge University Press, 2005), 183–217.

Ratner, Steven, 'Foreign Occupation and Territorial Administration: The Challenges of Convergence', 16 *European Journal of International Law* (2005) 695.

Rawls, John, *Political Liberalism* (New York: Columbia University Press, 1993).

'Political Liberalism: Reply to Habermas', 92 *Journal of Philosophy* (1995) 132–180.

Reich, J., 'Due Process and Sanctions Targeted Against Individuals Pursuant to Resolution 1267 (1999)', 33 *Yale Journal of International Law* (2008) 505.

Reinisch, August, 'Developing Human Rights and Humanitarian Law Accountability of the Security Council for the Imposition of Economic Sanctions', 95 *American Journal of International Law* (2001) 851–872.

Reuter, Paul, *La Communauté Européenne du Charbon et de l'Acier* (Paris: Librairie Générale de Droit et de Jurisprudence, 1953).

'Le Plan Schuman – La Communauté Européenne du Charbon et de l'Acier', in *Recueil des Cours de l'Académie de Droit International* (Hague Recueil) 1952–III.

Réveillard, Christophe, *Les premières tentatives de construction d'une Europe fédérale, des projets de la Résistance au Traité de la CED (1940–1954)* (Paris: F-X de Guibert, 2001).

Reynolds, A., ed., *The Architecture of Democracy: Constitutional Design, Conflict Management, and Democracy* (Oxford University Press, 2002).

Richardson, Henry S., *Democratic Autonomy* (Oxford University Press, 2002).

Risse, T., '"Let's Argue!" Communicative Action in World Politics', 54 *International Organization* (2000) 1–39.

Rosanvallon, Pierre, *Counter-Democracy: Politics in an Age of Distrust*, trans. A. Goldhammer (Cambridge University Press, 2008).

Rose-Ackerman, S. and P. Lindseth, eds., *Comparative Administrative Law* (Cheltenham: Edward Elgar, 2010).

van Rossem, J. W., 'Interaction Between EU Law and International Law in the Light of *Intertanko* and *Kadi*', 40 *Netherlands Yearbook of International Law* (2009) 183.

Rossi, L. S. and G. Di Federico, eds., *L'incidenza del diritto dell'Unione europea sullo studio delle discipline giuridiche* (Napoli: Editoriale Scientifica, 2008).

Rousseau, J. J., *The Social Contract*, trans. M. Cranston (Harmondsworth: Penguin, 1968 [1762]).

Rubenfeld, Jed, 'Unilateralism and Constitutionalism', 79 *New York University Law Review* (2004) 1971–2028.

Runciman, D., *Pluralism and the Personality of the State* (Cambridge University Press, 1997).

Sabel, Charles F. and Jonathan Zeitlin, 'Learning from Difference: The New Architecture of Experimentalist Governance in the EU', *European Law Journal* 14 (2008) 271–327.

Sadurski, W., '"Solange, Chapter 3": Constitutional Courts in Central Europe – Democracy – European Union', 14 *Environmental Law Journal* 1 (2008) 1–35.

Safrin, Sabrina, 'The UN-Exceptionalism of US Exceptionalism', 41 *Vanderbilt Journal of Transnational Law* (2008) 1307.

Salzman, James, 'Labor Rights, Globalization and Institutions: The Role and Influence of the Organization for Economic Cooperation and Development', 21 *Michigan Journal of International Law* (2000) 769–848.

Sandel, Michael, *Democracy's Discontent* (Cambridge, Mass., Harvard University Press, 1996).

'The Procedural Republic and the Unencumbered Self', 12 *Political Theory* (1984) 81–96.

Scelle, Georges, 'Le Phénomène juridique du dédoublement fonctionnel', in W. Schätzel, ed., *Rechtsfragen der internationalen Organisation – Festschrift für Hans Wehberg su seinem 70* (Frankfurt-am-Main: Vittorio Klostermann, 1956), 324.

Scharpf, Fritz, *Governing in Europe: Effective and Democratic?* (Oxford University Press, 1999).

'The Joint-Decision Trap Revisited', 44 *Journal of Common Market Studies* (2006) 845–864.

'Legitimacy in the Multilevel European Polity', in P. Dobner and M. Loughlin, eds., *The Twilight of Constitutionalism* (Oxford University Press, 2010).

'Die Politikverflechtungsfalle: Europäische Integration und deutscher Föderalismus im Vergleich', 26 *Politische Vierteljahresschrift* (1985) 323–356.

Schätzel, W., ed., *Rechtsfragen der internationalen Organisation – Festschrift für Hans Wehberg su seinem 70* (Frankfurt-am-Main: Vittorio Klostermann, 1956).

Scheppele, K. L., 'The Migration of Anti-Constitutional Ideas; The Post 9/11 Globalization of Public Law and the International State of Emergency', in Sujit Choudhry, ed., *The Migration of Constitutional Ideas* (Cambridge University Press, 2006), 347–373.

Schermers, Henry and Niels Blokker, *International Institutional Law: Unity within Diversity* (4th edn, The Hague: Martinus Nijhoff, 2003).

Schiff Berman, Paul, 'Global Legal Pluralism', 80 *Southern California Law Review* (2007), 1155–1237.

'A Pluralist Approach to International Law', 32 *Yale Journal of International Law* (2007) 301.

Schilling, T., 'Constitutionalization of General International Law – An Answer to Globalization?: Some Structural Aspects', *Jean Monnet Working Paper No. 6/2005* (2005), available at <www.jeanmonnetpro-gram.org/papers/05/050601.html>.

Schmitt, Carl, *Verfassungslehre* (9th edn, Berlin: Duncker & Humblot, 1993 [1928]).

Schmitter, P., 'If the Nation-State Were to Wither away in Europe, What Might Replace It?', in S. Gustavsson, and L. Lewin, eds., *The Future of the Nation State* (Stockholm: Nerenius & Santérus, 1996).

Schuetze, Robert, 'On "Middle Ground": The European Community and Public International Law', *European University Institute Working Paper LAW No. 2007/13* (2007), available at <http://ssrn.com/abstract=995780>.

Schütze, R., 'Federalism as Constitutional Pluralism: Sovereignty Suspended', unpublished manuscript (on file with Krisch) (2009).

Scott, Robert E. and Paul B. Stephan, 'Self-Enforcing International Agreements and the Limits of Coercion', *Wisconsin Law Review* (2004) 551.

Seidl-Hohenveldern, Ignaz, 'Danube River', in *Encyclopedia of Public International Law*, 1st edn, vol. 12 (Amsterdam: North Holland,1990).

De Sena, P. and M. C. Vitucci, 'The European Courts and the Security Council: Between Dédoublement Fonctionnel and Balancing of Values', 20 *European Journal of International Law* (2009) 193–228.

Severinus de Monzambano (Samuel von Pufendorf), *De Statu Imperii Germanici*. Nach dem ersten Druck mit Berücksichtigung der Ausgabe letzter Hand hrsg. von Fritz Salomon (Weimar: H. Böhlaus Nachfolger, 1910 [1667]).

Sevón, Leif and M. Johansson, 'The Protection of the Rights of Individuals under the EEA Agreement', *European Law Review* 4 (1999) 373–386.

Shany, Yuval, *The Competing Jurisdictions of International Courts and Tribunals* (Oxford University Press, 2003).

'The First MOX Plant Award: The Need to Harmonize Competing Environmental Regimes and Dispute Settlement Procedures', 17 *Leiden Journal of International Law* (2004) 815.

'No Longer a Weak Department of Power? Reflections on the Emergence of a New International Judiciary', 20 *European Journal of International Law* (2009) 73.

Shapiro, Ian and Cassiano Hacker-Cordón, eds., *Democracy's Edges* (Cambridge University Press, 1999).

'Outer Edges and Inner Edges', in Ian Shapiro and Cassiano Hacker-Cordón, eds., *Democracy's Edges* (Cambridge University Press, 1999), 1–16.

Shapiro, M. and A. Stone Sweet, *On Law, Politics and Judicialization* (Oxford University Press, 2003).

Shapiro, S., 'Authority', in J. Coleman and S. Shapiro, eds., *The Oxford Handbook of Jurisprudence and Philosophy of Law* (Oxford University Press, 2002) 382.

Shaw, J., *Law of the European Union* (2nd edn, Basingstoke: Palgrave, 1996).

Shaw, J. and G. More, eds, *New Legal Dynamics of European Union* (Oxford: Clarendon Press, 1996).

Shaw, J. and A. Wiener, 'The Paradox of the "European Polity"', in M. Green Cowles and M. Smith, eds., *The State of the European Union*, vol. 5 (Oxford University Press, 2000) 64–89.

Shell, G., 'Trade Legalism and International Relations Theory: An Analysis of the World Trade Organization', 44 *Duke Law Journal* (1995) 829.

Shelton, Dinah, 'Normative Hierarchy in International Law', 100 *American Journal of International Law* 2 (2006) 291–323.

Simma, Bruno, 'From Bilateralism to Community Interest in International Law', 250 *Hague Academy Course* 6 (1994) 217–384.

'The Contribution of Alfred Verdross to the Theory of International Law', 6 *European Journal of International Law* (1995) 33.

Simma, Bruno and Dirk Pulkowski, 'Of Planets and the Universe: Self-Contained Regimes in International Law', 17 *European Journal of International Law* 3 (2006) 483–529.

Sjursen, H., 'The EU as "Normative" Power: How can this be?', 13 *Journal of European Public Policy* 2 (2006) 235–251.

Slaughter, Anne-Marie, 'International Law in a World of Liberal States', 6 *European Journal of International Law* (1995) 1–39.

Slaughter, Anne-Marie and William Burke-White, 'The Future of International Law is Domestic (or, the European Way of Law)', 47 *Harvard Journal of International Law* (2006) 327–352.

Slaughter, Anne-Marie, Alec Stone Sweet and Joseph H. H. Weiler, eds., *The European Courts and National Courts – Doctrine and Jurisprudence* (Oxford: Hart Publishing, 1998).

Slyz, G., 'International Law in National Courts', 28 *NYU Journal of International Law and Politics* (1996) 65.

Smith, A. H., *National Identity* (Harmondsworth: Penguin, 1991).

Smrkolj, M., 'The Use of the "Disconnection Clause" in International Treaties: What does it tell us about the EC/EU as an Actor in the Sphere of Public International Law?' (2008), available at <http://papers.ssrn.com/sol3/papers.cfm?abstract_id=1133002>.

Snyder, Francis, 'Governing Economic Globalisation: Global Legal Pluralism and European Law', 5 *European Law Journal* (1999), 334–374.

Somek, A., *Individualism: An Essay on the Authority of the European Union* (Oxford University Press, 2008).

de Sousa Santos, Boaventura, 'Beyond Neoliberal Governance: The World Social Forum as Subaltern Cosmopolitan Politics and Legality', in B. de Sousa Santos and C. A. Rodríguez-Garavito, eds., *Law and Globalization from Below* (Cambridge University Press, 2005), 29–63.

Toward a New Legal Common Sense (2nd edn, London: Butterworths, 2002).

de Sousa Santos, B. and C. A. Rodríguez-Garavito, eds., *Law and Globalization from Below* (Cambridge University Press, 2005).

Spiro, Peter J., 'The New Sovereigntists: American Exceptionalism and its False Prophets', 79 *Foreign Affairs* 6 (2000) 9–15.

Stein, Eric, 'External Relations of the European Community', 1 *Collected Courses of the Academy of European Law* (1991) 115–132.

'Lawyers, Judges, and the Making of a Transnational Constitution', 75 *American Journal of International Law* (1981) 1.

Steinberger, E., 'The WTO Treaty as a Mixed Agreement: Problems with the EC's and the EC Member States' Membership of the WTO', 17 *European Journal of International Law* (2006) 837.

Stolleis, Michael, *Geschichte des öffentlichen Rechts in Deutschland*, vol. 2 (München: Verlag C.H. Beck, 1992).

Stourzh, Gerald, *From Vienna to Chicago and Back: Essays on Intellectual History and Political Thought in Europe and America* (University of Chicago Press, 2007).

Sunstein, Cass, 'Judicial Relief and Public Tort Law' (book review), 92 *Yale Law Journal* (1983) 749.

Swaine, Edward T., 'The Constitutionality of International Delegations', 104 *Columbia Law Review* (2004) 1492.

Tamanaha, Brian, 'Understanding Legal Pluralism: Past to Present, Local to Global', 30 *Sydney Law Review* (2008) 375–411.

Tanner, J. R., *Constitutional Documents of the Reign of James I* (Cambridge University Press, 1961 [1930]).

Taylor, Charles, *Modern Social Imaginaries* (Durham, NC: Duke University Press, 2004).

    Philosophical Arguments (Cambridge, Mass., Harvard University Press, 1995).

    'The Politics of Recognition', in *Philosophical Arguments* (Cambridge, Mass., Harvard University Press, 1995), 225–256.

    'Religion and European Integration' in K. Michalski, ed., *Religion in the New Europe* (Budapest, New York: CEU Press, 2006), 1–22.

Teubner, Günther, 'Global Bukowina: Legal Pluralism in the World Society', in G. Teubner, ed., *Global Law Without a State* (Aldershot: Dartmouth, 1997), 3–28.

    ed., *Global Law Without a State* (Aldershot: Dartmouth, 1997).

    'Societal Constitutionalism: Alternatives to State-Centred Constitutional Theory', in Christian Joerges, I. J. Sand and G. Teubner, eds., *Transnational Governance and Constitutionalism* (Oxford: Hart Publishing, 2004), 3–28.

Teubner, G. and A. Fischer-Lescano, 'Regime-Collisions: The Vain Search for Legal Unity in the Fragmentation of Global Law', 25 *Michigan Journal of International Law* (2004) 999.

Tierney, Stephen, *Constitutional Law and National Pluralism* (Oxford University Press, 2004).

Tomuschat, Christian, 'International Law: Ensuring the Survival of Mankind on the Eve of A New Century. General Course on Public International Law', 281 *Recueil des Cours* (1999) 9–438.

    'Note on Kadi', 43 *Common Market Law Review* (2005) 537–551.

    'Obligations Arising for States Without or Against their Will', 241 *Recueil des Cours* IV (1993) 195.

Torbisco Casals, Neus, *Group Rights as Human Rights* (Dordrecht: Springer, 2006).

Trebilcock, M. and R. Howse, *The Regulation of International Trade* (London: Routledge, 2005).

Triantafyllou, Dimitris, 'Les procédures d'adoption et de révision du Traité constitutionnel', in G. Amato, H. Bribosia and B. de Witte, eds., *Genesis and Destiny of the European Constitution* (Brussels: Bruylant, 2007), 223–245.

Tridimas, Takis, 'EU Law, International Law, and Economic Sanctions Against Terrorism: The Judiciary in Distress', 32 *Fordham International Law Journal* (2009) 660.

The General Principles of EC Law (Oxford University Press, 1999).

Tridimas, Takis and P. Eeckhout, 'The External Competence of the Community and the Case-Law of the Court of Justice: Principle versus Pragmatism', 14 *Yearbook of European Law* (1994) 143.

Troper, M. and L. Jaume, eds., *1789 et l'invention de la constitution*, (Brussels, Paris: Bruylant, 1994).

Tully, James, 'The Imperialism of Modern Constitutional Democracy', in Martin Loughlin and Neil Walker, eds., *The Paradox of Constitutionalism: Constituent Power and Constitutional Form* (Oxford University Press, 2007), 315–338.

Strange Multiplicity: Constitutionalism in an Age of Diversity (Cambridge University Press, 1995).

Van Alstine, M., 'Dynamic Treaty Interpretation', 146 *University of Pennsylvania Law Review* (1998) 687.

de Vattel, E., *The Law of Nations, or Principles of the Law of Nature applied to the Conduct and Affairs of Nations and Sovereigns*. [from the French of Monsieur de Vattel; from the new edition by Joseph Chitty; with additional notes and references by Edward D. Ingraham] (Philadelphia: T. & J. W. Johnson, 1883 [1758]).

Vayssière, Bernard, *Vers une Europe fédérale? Les espoirs et les actions fédéralistes au sortir de la Seconde Guerre mondiale* (Bruxelles: Peter Lang, 2006).

Vazquez, Carlos, 'Treaties as the Law of the Land: The Supremacy Clause and Presumption of Self-execution', 121 *Harvard Law Review* (2008) 600–694.

Verdross, A., *Die Verfassung der Völkerrechtsgemeinschaft* (Berlin: Springer, 1926).

Vincent, A., *Nationalism and Particularity* (Cambridge University Press, 2002).

Vlcek, William, 'Hitting the Right Target: EU and Security Council Pursuit of Terrorist Financing' (2007), available at <www.unc.edu/euce/eusa2007/papers/vlcek-w-09h.pdf>.

Waldron, Jeremy, *Law and Disagreement* (Oxford University Press, 1996).

Walker, Neil, 'Beyond Boundary Disputes and Basic Grids: Mapping the Global Disorder of Normative Orders', 6 *International Journal of Constitutional Law* 3–4 (2008) 373–396.

'The EU and the Rule of Law: Necessity's Mixed Virtue', in G. Palombella and N. Walker, eds., *Relocating the Rule of Law* (Oxford: Hart Publishing, 2008), 119–38.

'The EU and the WTO: Constitutionalism in a New Key', in G. de Búrca and J. Scott, eds., *The EU and the WTO: Legal and Constitutional Issues* (Oxford: Hart Publishing, 2001), 31–57.

'Europe at 50: A Midlife Crisis? Democratic Deficit and Sovereignty Surplus', 15 *Irish Journal of European Law* (2008) 23–34.

'Europe's Constitutional Momentum and the Search for Polity Legitimacy' 3 *International Journal of Constitutional Law* (2005) 211–238.

'European Constitutionalism in the State Constitutional Tradition', 59 *Current Legal Problems* (2006) 51–89.

'The Idea of Constitutional Pluralism', 65 *Modern Law Review* (2002) 317–359.

'Late Sovereignty in the European Union', in N. Walker, ed., *Sovereignty in Transition* (Oxford University Press, 2003), 3–32.

'Legal Theory and the European Union: A 25th Anniversary Essay', 25 *Oxford Journal of Legal Studies* (2005) 581–601.

'Making a World of Difference: Habermas, Cosmopolitanism and the Constitutionalization of International Law' *European University Institute Working Paper LAW No. 2005/17* (2005), available at <http://ssrn.com/abstract=891036>.

'Not the European Constitution', 15 *Maastricht Journal of European and Comparative Law* (2008) 135–141.

ed., *Sovereignty in Transition* (Oxford University Press, 2003).

'Taking Constitutionalism Beyond the State', 56 *Political Studies* (2008) 519–543.

Walker, Neil and Gráinne de Burca, 'Reconceiving Law and New Governance', 13 *Columbia Journal of European Law* (2007) 519.

Walker, R. B. J., *Inside/Outside: International Relations as Political Theory* (Cambridge University Press, 1993).

Wallace, W., ed., *The Dynamics of European Integration* (London: Pinter, 1990).

Walters, M., 'Creeping Monism: The Judicial Trend Towards Interpretative Incorporation of Human Rights Treaties', 107 *Columbia Law Review* (2007) 628.

Weber, Max, *Economy and Society*, trans. Max Rheinstein and Edward Shils (Cambridge, Mass.: Harvard University Press, 1954).

Weiler, J.H.H., 'The Community System: The Dual Character of Supranationalism', 1 *Yearbook of European Law* (1981) 267–306.

ed., *The Constitution of Europe: 'Do the New Clothes Have an Emperor?' and Other Essays on European Integration* (Cambridge University Press, 1999).

'Epilogue: Toward a Common Law of International Trade', in J.H.H. Weiler, ed., *The EU, the WTO, and the NAFTA: Toward a Common Law of International Trade?* (Oxford University Press, 2000).

'European Constitutionalism and its Discontents', 17 *Northwestern Journal of International Law and Business* (1996–97) 354.

'Europe – Nous coalisons des Etats, nouse n'unissons pas des hommes', unpublished paper (2009).

'Europe: The Case Against the Case for Statehood', 4 *European Law Journal* (1998) 43.

ed., *The EU, the WTO, and the NAFTA: Toward a Common Law of International Trade?* (Oxford University Press, 2000).

'Federalism and Constitutionalism: Europe's Sonderweg', *Harvard Jean Monnet Working Paper 10/00*, Cambridge, Mass. (2000).

'Federalism without Constitutionalism: Europe's Sonderweg', in Kalypso Nicolaidis and Robert Howse, eds., *The Federal Vision: Legitimacy and Levels of Governance in the US and the EU* (Oxford University Press, 2001), 54.

'The Geology of International Law – Governance, Democracy, Legitimacy', 64 *Zeitschrift für ausländisches öffentliches Recht und Völkerrecht* (2004), 547–562.

'In Defence of the Status Quo: Europe's Constitutional *Sonderweg*', in J.H.H. Weiler and M. Wind, eds., *European Constitutionalism Beyond the State* (Cambridge University Press, 2003), 7–23.

'On the Power of the Word: Europe's Constitutional Iconography', 3 *International Journal of Constitutional Law* (2005) 173–190.

'The Reformation of European Constitutionalism', 35 *Journal of Common Market Studies* (1997) 97.

'The Transformation of Europe', in J.H.H. Weiler, ed., *The Constitution of Europe: 'Do the New Clothes Have an Emperor?' and Other Essays on European Integration* (Cambridge University Press, 1999), 10–101.

'The Transformation of Europe', 100 *Yale Law Journal* (1991) 2403–2484.

'To be a European citizen – Eros and civilization', 4 *Journal of European Public Policy* 4 (1997) 495–519.

Weiler, J.H.H. and Ulrich R. Haltern, 'Constitutional or International? The Foundations of the Community Legal Order and the Question of Judicial Kompetenz-Kompetenz', in Anne-Marie Slaughter, Alec Stone Sweet and Joseph H.H. Weiler, eds., *The European Courts and National*

Courts – Doctrine and Jurisprudence (Oxford: Hart Publishing, 1998), 331–364.

Weiler, J. H. H. and J. Trachtman, 'European Constitutionalism and Its Discontents,' 17 *Northwestern Journal of International Law & Business* (1997) 354.

Weiler, J. H. H., and M. Wind, eds., *European Constitutionalism Beyond the State* (Cambridge University Press, 2003).

Wendt, Alexander, 'A Comment on Held's Cosmopolitanism', in Ian Shapiro and Cassiano Hacker-Cordón, eds., *Democracy's Edges* (Cambridge University Press, 1999), 127–133.

Wessel, R., 'The Kadi Case: Towards a More Substantive Hierarchy in International Law', 5 *International Organizations Law Review* (2008) 323–327.

de Wet, Erika, 'Holding the United Nations Security Council Accountable for Human Rights Violations through Domestic and Regional Courts: A Case of Beware What You Ask For?', in J. Farrall and K. Rubenstein, eds., *Sanctions Accountability and Governance in a Globalised World* (Cambridge University Press, 2009).

'Judicial Review as an Emerging General Principle of Law and Its Implications for the International Court of Justice', 47 *Netherlands International Law Review* (2000) 181–210.

'The Emergence of International and Regional Value Systems as a Manifestation of an International Constitutional Order', 19 *Leiden Journal of International Law* (2006) 611–632.

'The International Constitutional Order', 55 *International and Comparative Law Quarterly* (2006) 51–76.

'The Reception Process in the Netherlands and Belgium', in H. Keller and A. Stone Sweet, eds., *A Europe of Rights: The Impact of the ECHR on National Legal Systems* (Oxford University Press, 2008), 229.

Whittington, K., D. Kelemen and G. Caldeira, eds., *The Oxford Handbook of Law and Politics* (Oxford University Press, 2008).

Wicks, Elizabeth, 'A New Constitution for a New State? The 1707 Union of England and Scotland', 117 *The Law Quarterly Review* (2001) 109–126.

Wind, M., 'The European Union as a Polycentric Polity: Returning to a Neo-medieval Europe?', in J. H. H. Weiler and M. Wind, eds., *European Constitutionalism Beyond the State* (Cambridge University Press, 2003), 103–31.

de Witte, Bruno, 'La procédure de révision: continuité dans le mode de changement', in C. Kaddous and A. Auer, eds., *Les principes fondamentaux de la Constitution européenne* (Helbing & Lichtenhahn: Bruylant, 2006), 147–161.

'Rules of Change in International Law: How Special is the European Community?', 25 *Netherlands Yearbook of International Law* (1994) 299–333.

'The Closest Thing to a Constitutional Conversation in Europe: The Semi-Permanent Treaty Revision Process', in P. Beaumont, C. Lyons and N. Walker, eds., *Convergence and Divergence in European Public Law* (Oxford: Hart Publishing, 2002), 39–57.

'The Emergence of a European System of Public International Law: The EU and its Member States as Strange Subjects', in J. Wouters, A. Nollkaemper and E. de Wet, eds., *The Europeanisation of International Law* (The Hague: TMC Asser Press, 2008), 39–54.

Wouters, W. and P. Eeckhoute, 'Giving Effect to Customary International Law through EC Law', in J. Prinssen and A. Schrauwen, eds., *Direct Effect: Rethinking a Classic of EC Legal Doctrine* (Groningen: Europa Law Publishing, 2002).

Wouters, J., A. Nollkaemper and E. de Wet, eds., *The Europeanisation of International Law* (The Hague: TMC Asser Press, 2008).

Wyatt, Derrick, 'New Legal Order, or Old?', 7 *European Law Review* (1982) 147–166.

Wyatt, D., M. Dougan, B. Rodger, A. Dashwood and E. Spaventa, *Wyatt and Dashwood's European Union Law* (5th edn, London: Sweet & Maxwell, 2006).

Yack, Bernard, 'Nationalism, Popular Sovereignty and the Liberal Democratic State', in T. V. Paul, G. J. Ikenberry and J. A. Hall, eds., *The Nation-State in Question* (Princeton University Press, 2003) 29–50.

Yoo, John, *The Powers of War and Peace: The Constitution and Foreign Affairs After 9/11* (University of Chicago Press, 2005).

Young, Ernest A., 'Dual Federalism, Concurrent Jurisdiction, and the Foreign Affairs Exception', 69 *The George Washington Law Review* (2001) 139.

Young, Iris Marion, *Inclusion and Democracy* (Oxford University Press, 2000).

Zoller, Elizabeth, 'Aspects internationaux du droit constitutionnel. Contribution à la théorie de la fédération d'Etats', 294 *Hague Recueil* (2002) 39–166.

Zonnekeyn, Geert A., *Direct Effect of WTO Law* (London: Cameron May, 2008).

Zurcher, Arnold J., *The Struggle to Unite Europe 1940–1958* (New York University Press, 1958).

Zürn, M., 'The State in the Postnational Constellation – Societal Denationalization and Multi-Level Governance', *ARENA Working Papers*, WP 99/35 (1999), available at <www.arena.uio.no/publications/working-papers1999/papers/wp99_35.htm>.

Index